DEMON SACRED

Vol. 1

By Natsumi Itsuki

HAMBURG // LONDON // LOS ANGELES // TOKYO

Demon Sacred Volume 1
Created by Natsumi Itsuki

Translation - Yuko Fukami
English Adaptation - Ysabet Reinhardt MacFarlane
Copy Editor - Tim Leavey
Retouch and Lettering - Star Print Brokers
Production Artist - Rui Kyo
Graphic Designer - Erika Terriquez

Editor - Cindy Suzuki
Print Production Manager - Lucas Rivera
Managing Editor - Vy Nguyen
Senior Designer - Louis Csontos
Art Director - Al-Insan Lashley
Director of Sales and Manufacturing - Allyson De Simone
Associate Publisher - Marco F. Pavia
President and C.O.O. - John Parker
C.E.O. and Chief Creative Officer - Stu Levy

A  Manga

TOKYOPOP and  are trademarks or registered trademarks of TOKYOPOP Inc.

TOKYOPOP Inc.
5900 Wilshire Blvd. Suite 2000
Los Angeles, CA 90036

E-mail: info@TOKYOPOP.com
Come visit us online at www.TOKYOPOP.com

ISBN: 978-1-4278-1389-3

First TOKYOPOP printing: October 2010
10 9 8 7 6 5 4 3 2 1
Printed in the USA

VOLUME 1
NATSUMI ITSUKI

Contents

Demon Sacred

DEMON

A MALEVOLENT SPIRIT THAT SEEKS TO HARM OR DESTROY HUMANS. FROM THE SANSKRIT WORD DEV (TO BECOME BRIGHT, TO SHINE), THE WORD DEVA SPRINGS FROM THE SAME ETYMOLOGY, BUT IT REFERS TO INCORPOREAL SPIRITS THAT VALUE THE EXISTENCE OF MANKIND.

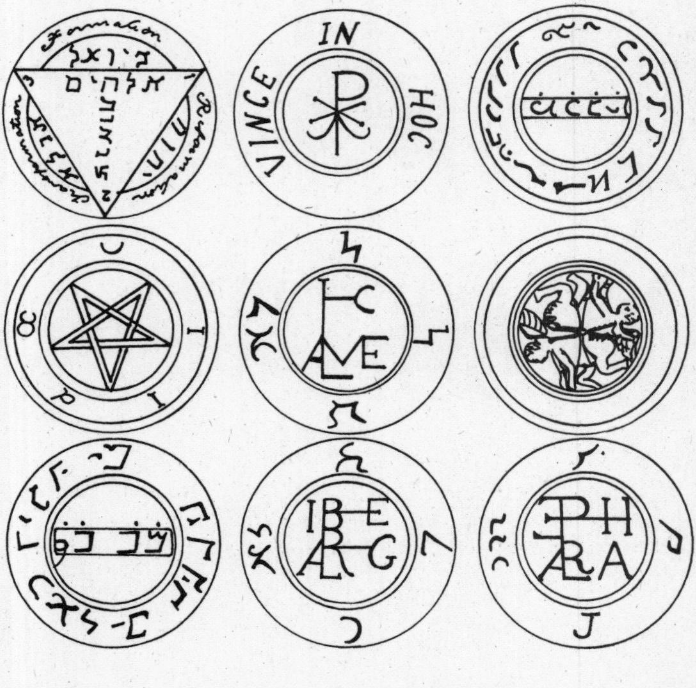
IN
VINCE
HOC

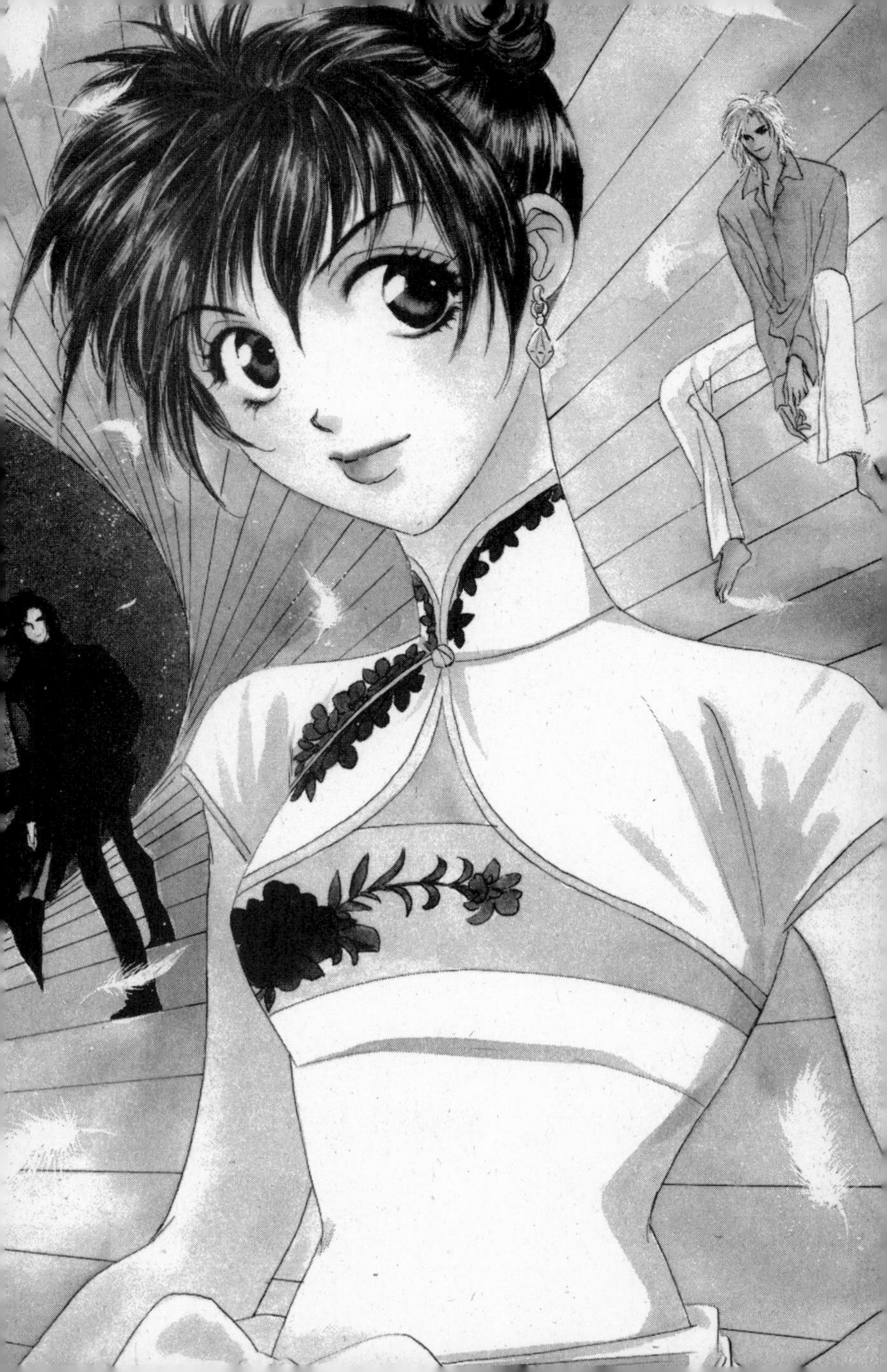

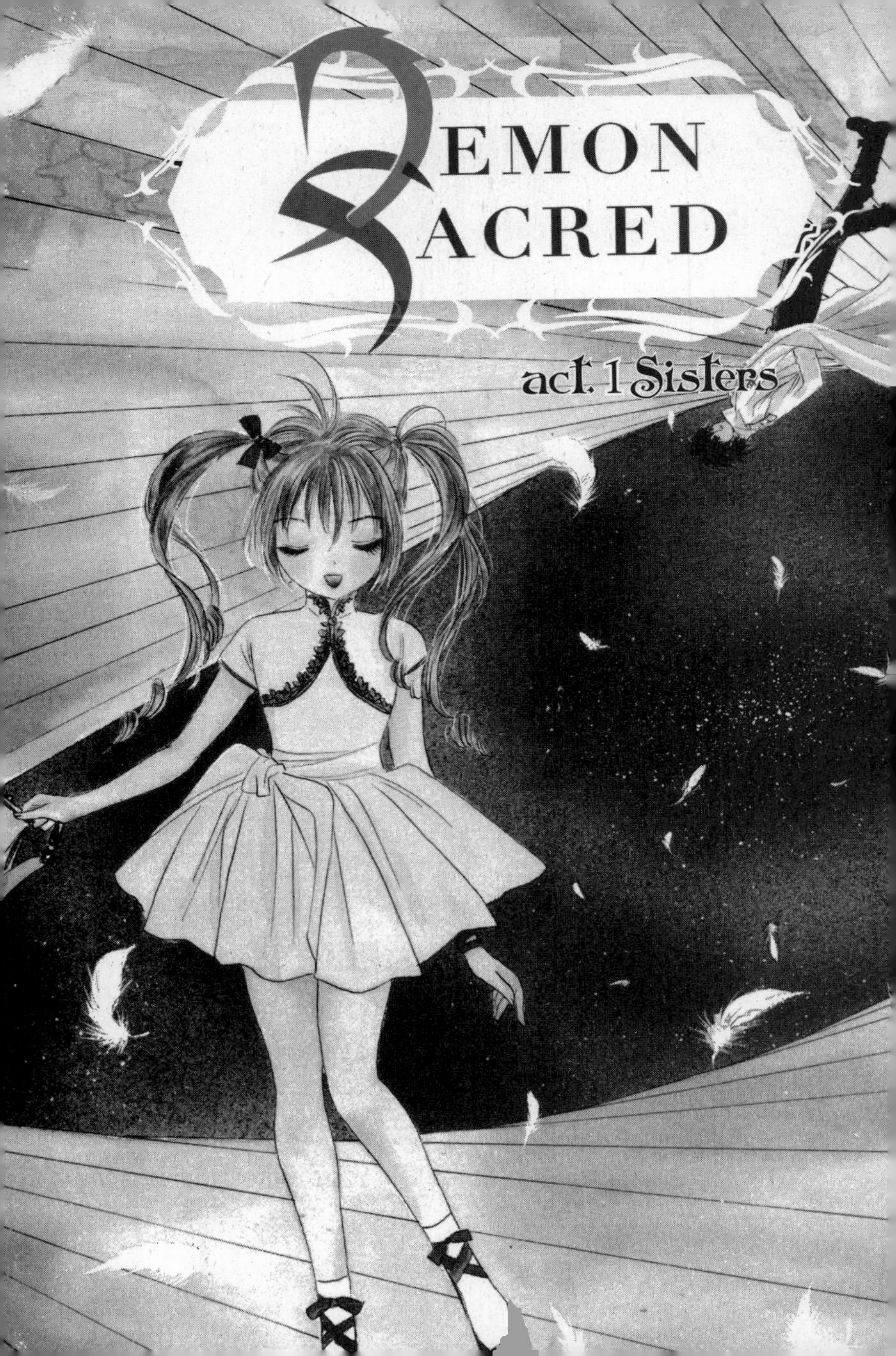
DEMON SACRED
act. 1 Sisters

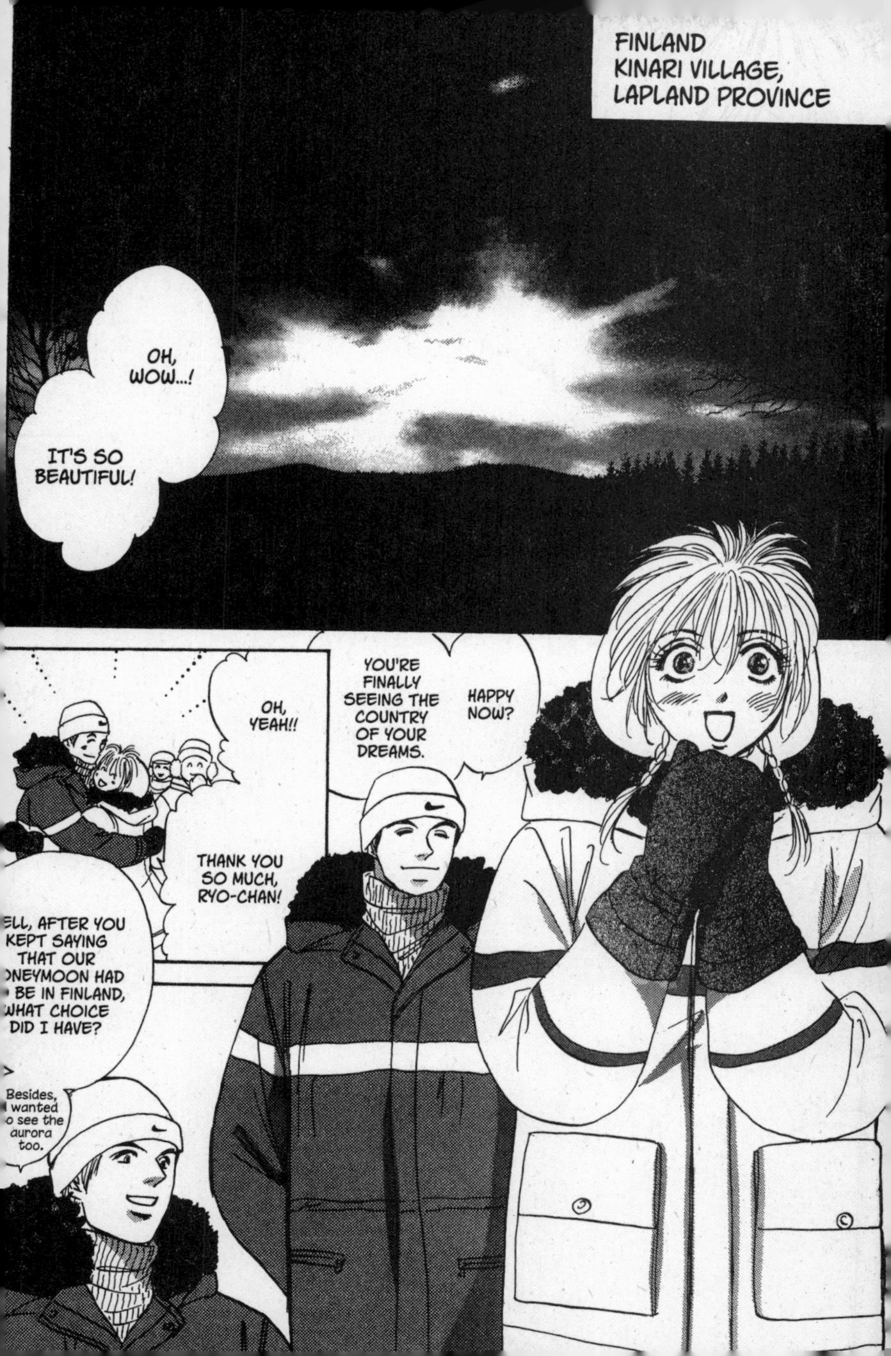
FINLAND
KINARI VILLAGE, LAPLAND PROVINCE
OH, WOW...!
IT'S SO BEAUTIFUL!
HAPPY NOW?
YOU'RE FINALLY SEEING THE COUNTRY OF YOUR DREAMS.
OH, YEAH!!
THANK YOU SO MUCH, RYO-CHAN!
ELL, AFTER YOU KEPT SAYING THAT OUR ONEYMOON HAD BE IN FINLAND, WHAT CHOICE DID I HAVE?
Besides, wanted o see the aurora too.

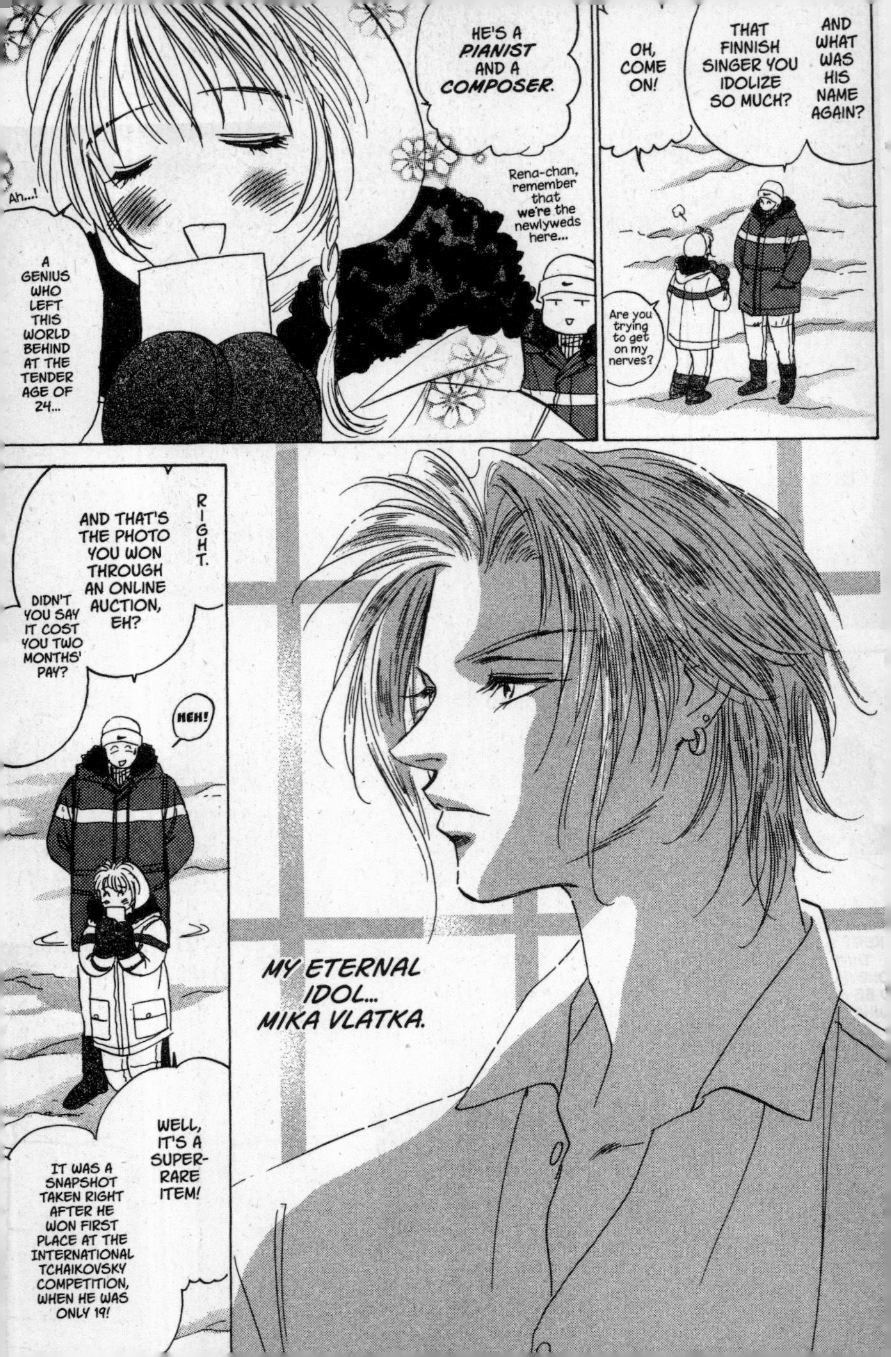

OH, COME ON!
THAT FINNISH SINGER YOU IDOLIZE SO MUCH?
AND WHAT WAS HIS NAME AGAIN?
Are you trying to get on my nerves?
HE'S A PIANIST AND A COMPOSER.
Rena-chan, remember that we're the newlyweds here...
Ah...!
A GENIUS WHO LEFT THIS WORLD BEHIND AT THE TENDER AGE OF 24...
MY ETERNAL IDOL... MIKA VLATKA.
RIGHT.
AND THAT'S THE PHOTO YOU WON THROUGH AN ONLINE AUCTION, EH?
DIDN'T YOU SAY IT COST YOU TWO MONTHS' PAY?
HEH!
WELL, IT'S A SUPER-RARE ITEM!
IT WAS A SNAPSHOT TAKEN RIGHT AFTER HE WON FIRST PLACE AT THE INTERNATIONAL TCHAIKOVSKY COMPETITION, WHEN HE WAS ONLY 19!

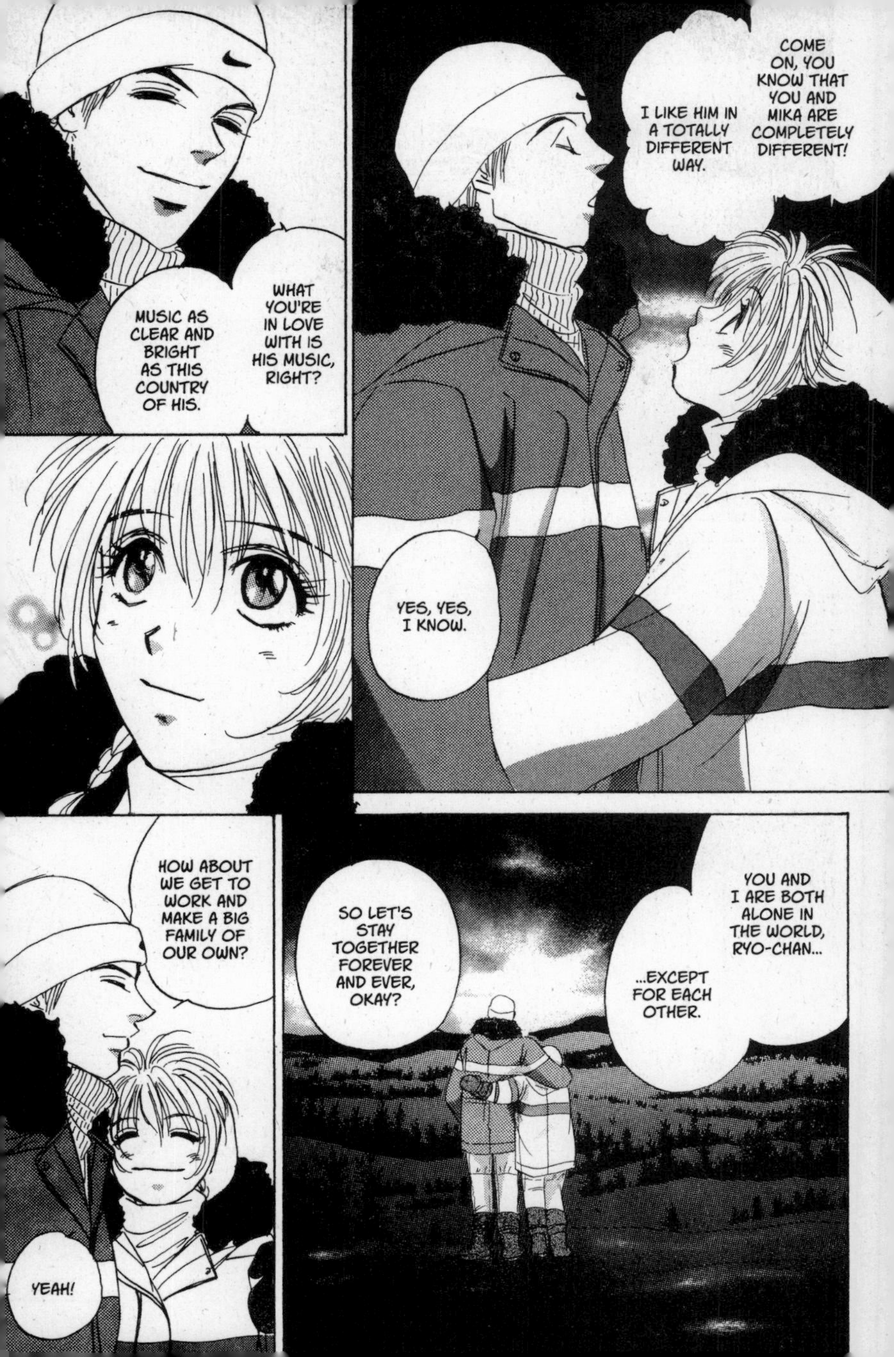
COME ON, YOU KNOW THAT YOU AND MIKA ARE COMPLETELY DIFFERENT!
I LIKE HIM IN A TOTALLY DIFFERENT WAY.
YES, YES, I KNOW.
WHAT YOU'RE IN LOVE WITH IS HIS MUSIC, RIGHT?
MUSIC AS CLEAR AND BRIGHT AS THIS COUNTRY OF HIS.
YOU AND I ARE BOTH ALONE IN THE WORLD, RYO-CHAN...
...EXCEPT FOR EACH OTHER.
SO LET'S STAY TOGETHER FOREVER AND EVER, OKAY?
HOW ABOUT WE GET TO WORK AND MAKE A BIG FAMILY OF OUR OWN?
YEAH!

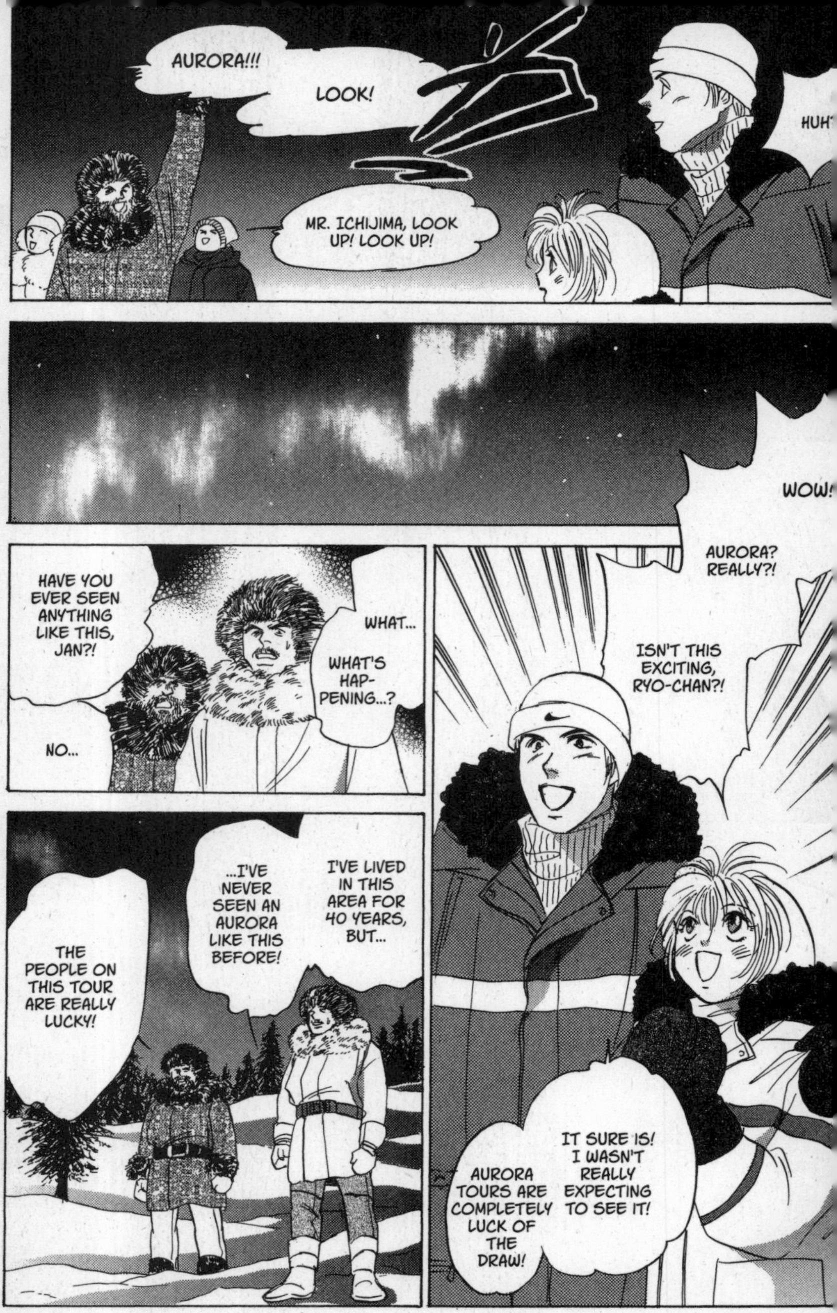
HUH
AURORA!!!
LOOK!
MR. ICHIJIMA, LOOK UP! LOOK UP!
WOW!
AURORA? REALLY?!
ISN'T THIS EXCITING, RYO-CHAN?!
IT SURE IS! I WASN'T REALLY EXPECTING TO SEE IT!
AURORA TOURS ARE COMPLETELY LUCK OF THE DRAW!
WHAT...
WHAT'S HAP-PENING...?
HAVE YOU EVER SEEN ANYTHING LIKE THIS, JAN?!
NO...
I'VE LIVED IN THIS AREA FOR 40 YEARS, BUT...
...I'VE NEVER SEEN AN AURORA LIKE THIS BEFORE!
THE PEOPLE ON THIS TOUR ARE REALLY LUCKY!

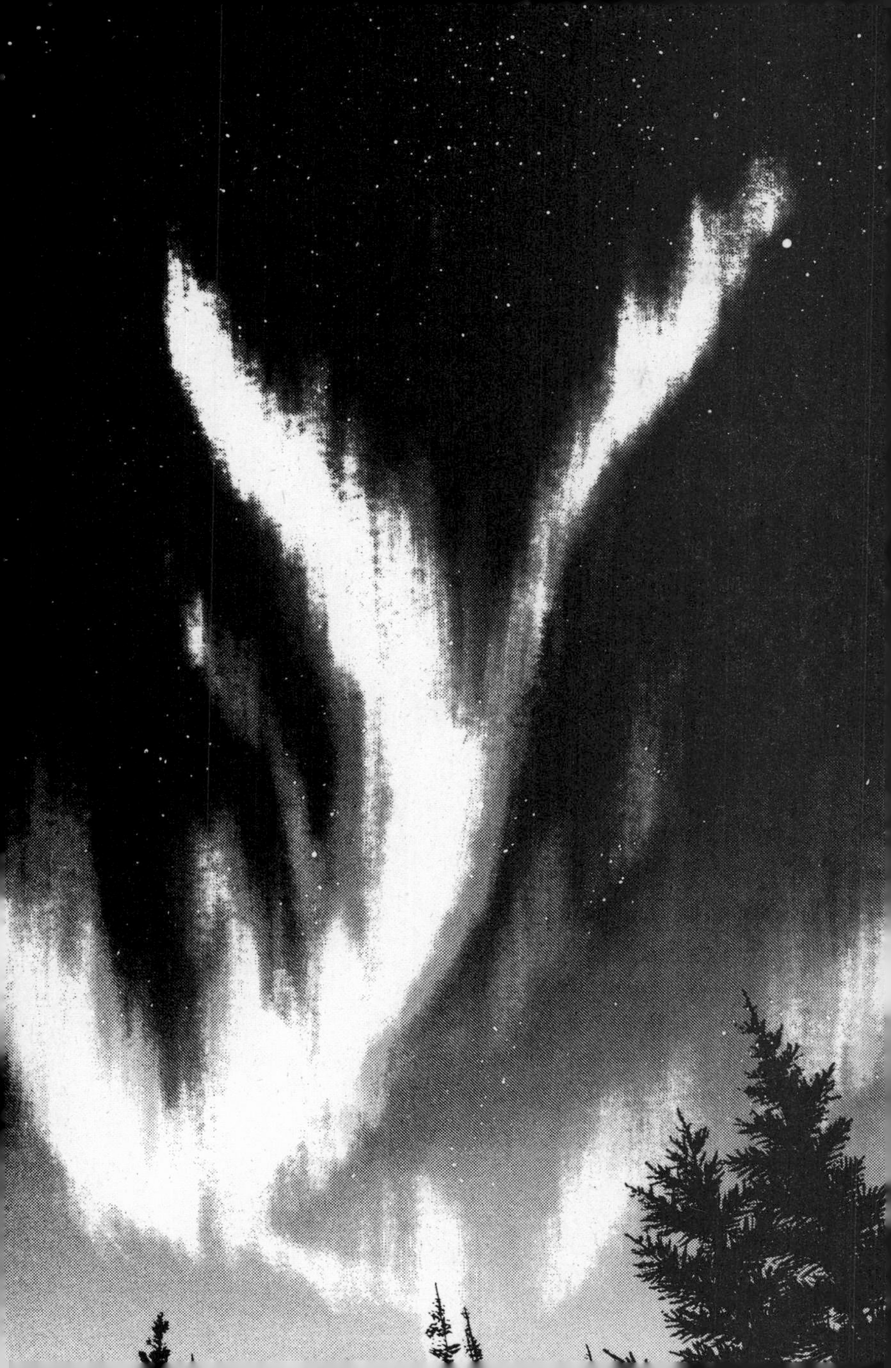

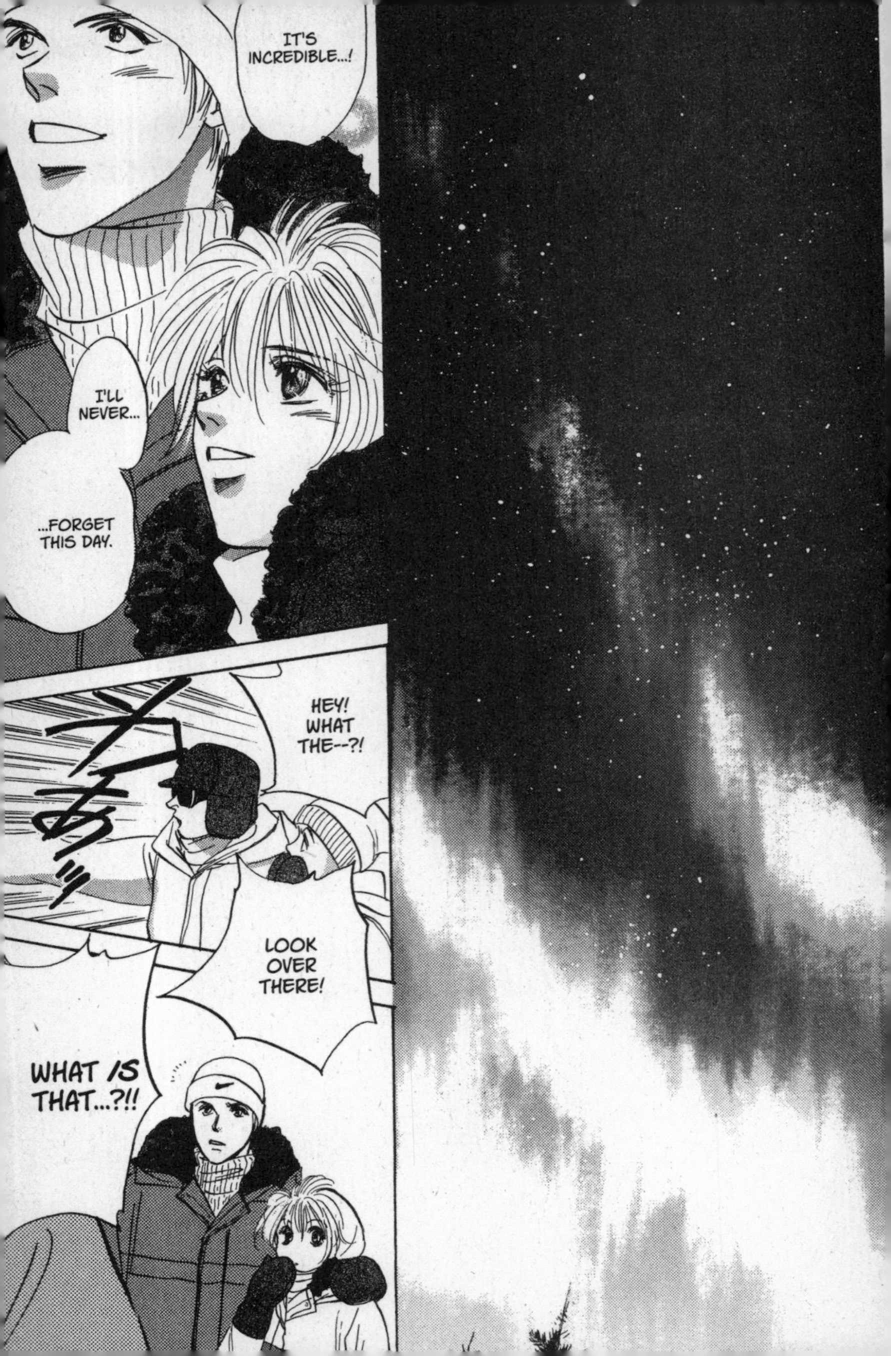
IT'S INCREDIBLE...!
I'LL NEVER...
...FORGET THIS DAY.
HEY! WHAT THE--?!
LOOK OVER THERE!
WHAT IS THAT...?!!

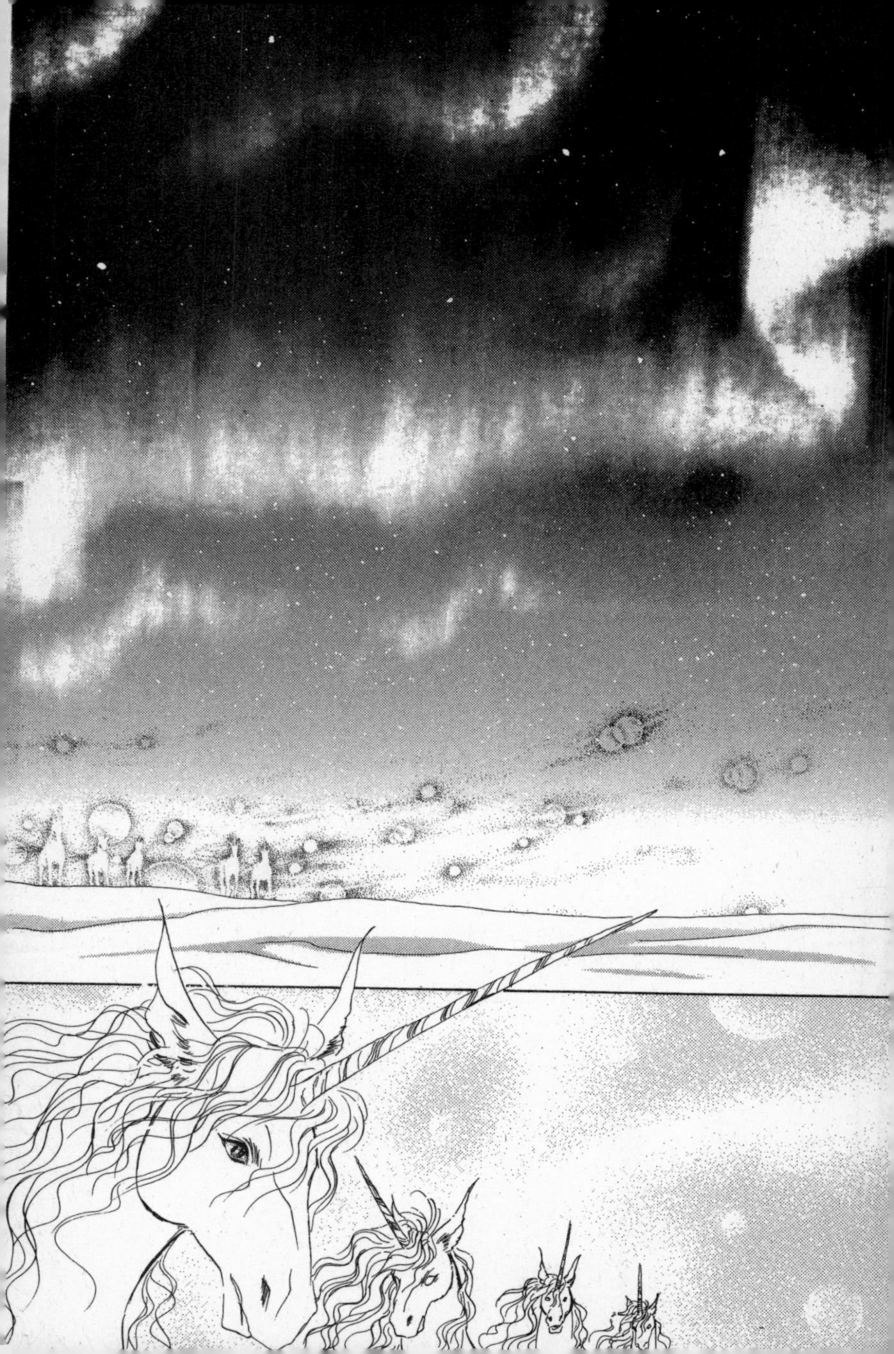

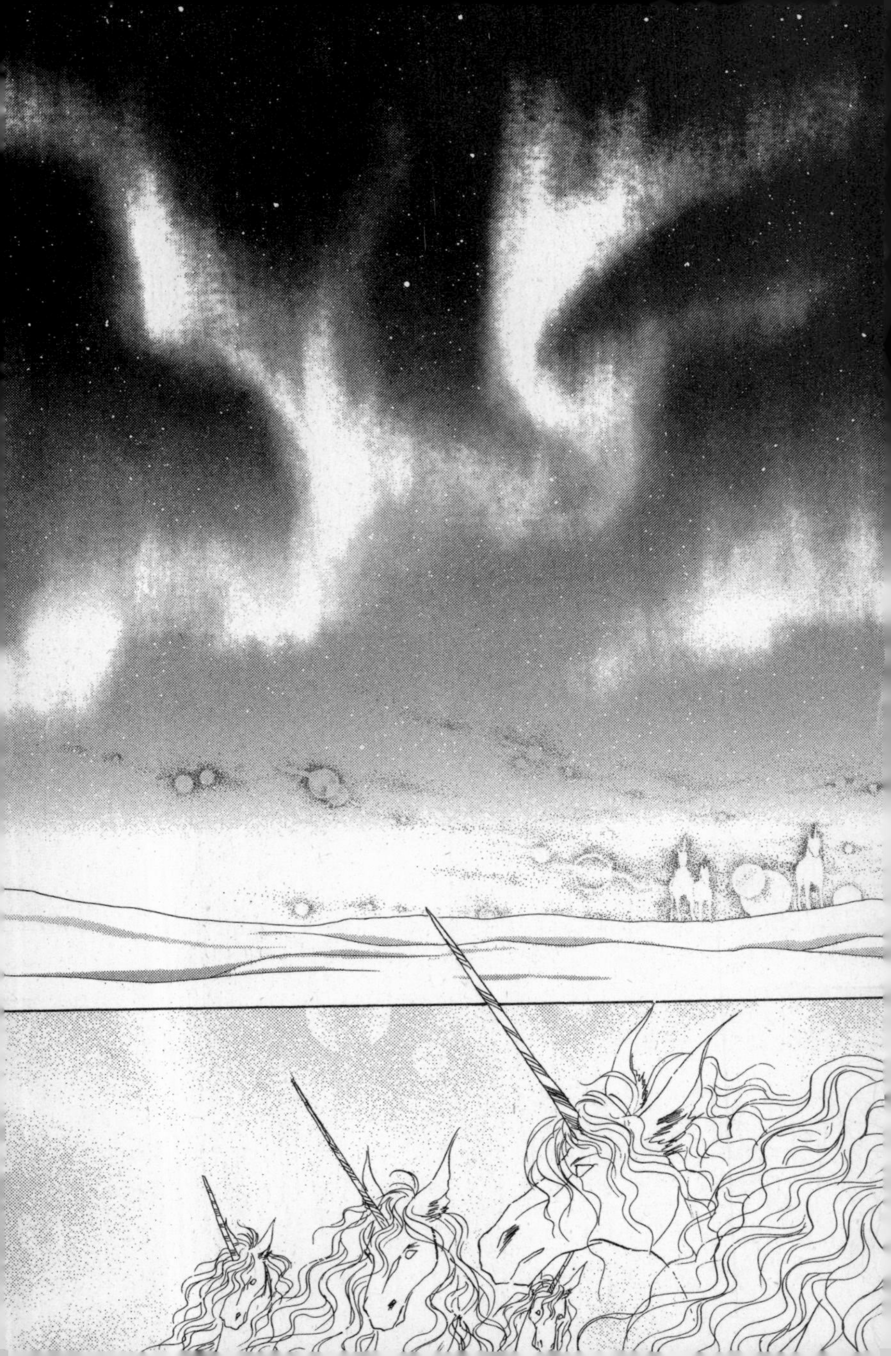

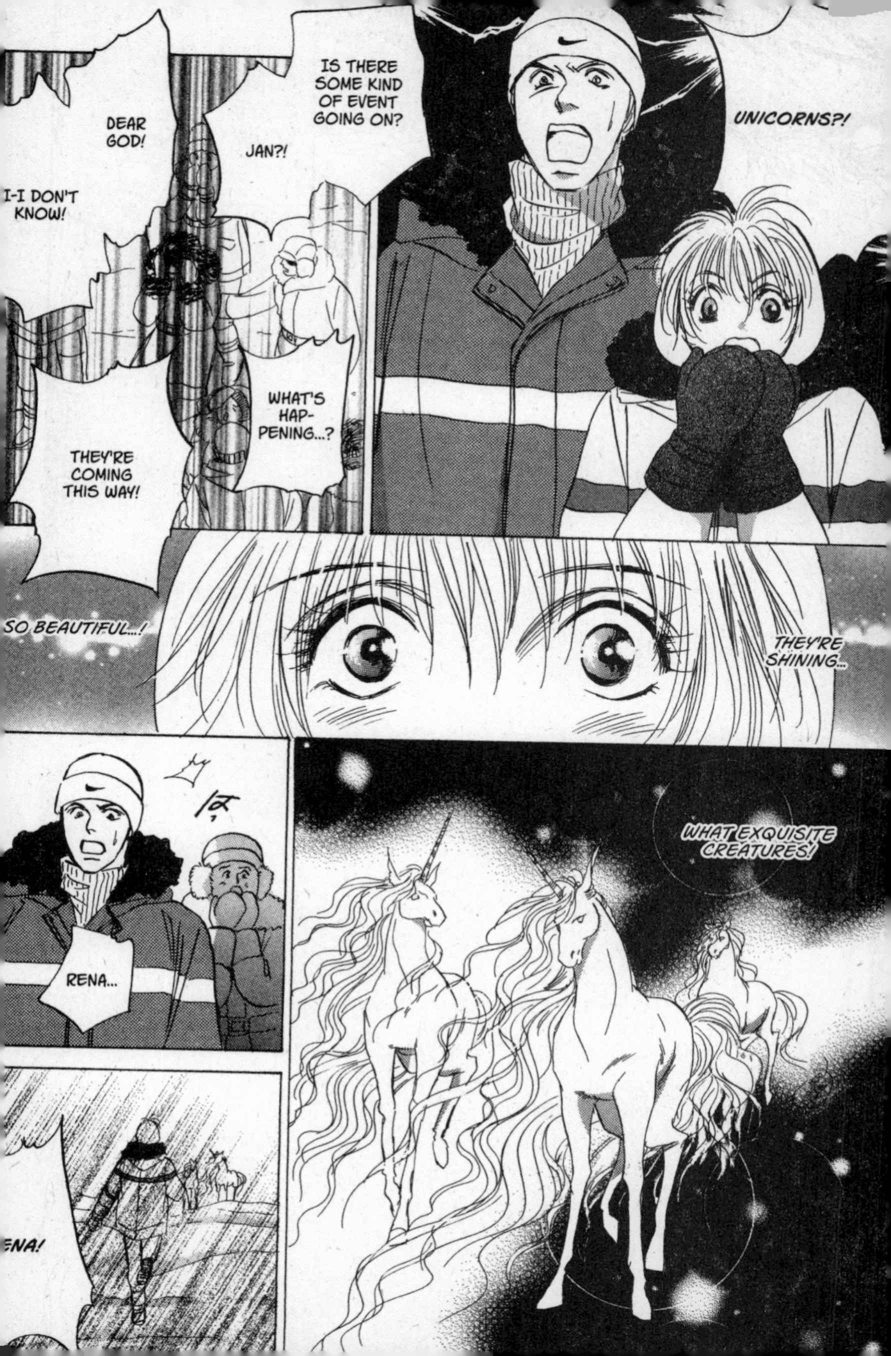
UNICORNS?!
IS THERE SOME KIND OF EVENT GOING ON?
JAN?!
WHAT'S HAP-PENING...?
DEAR GOD!
I-I DON'T KNOW!
THEY'RE COMING THIS WAY!
THEY'RE SHINING...
SO BEAUTIFUL...!
WHAT EXQUISITE CREATURES!
は
RENA...
ENA!

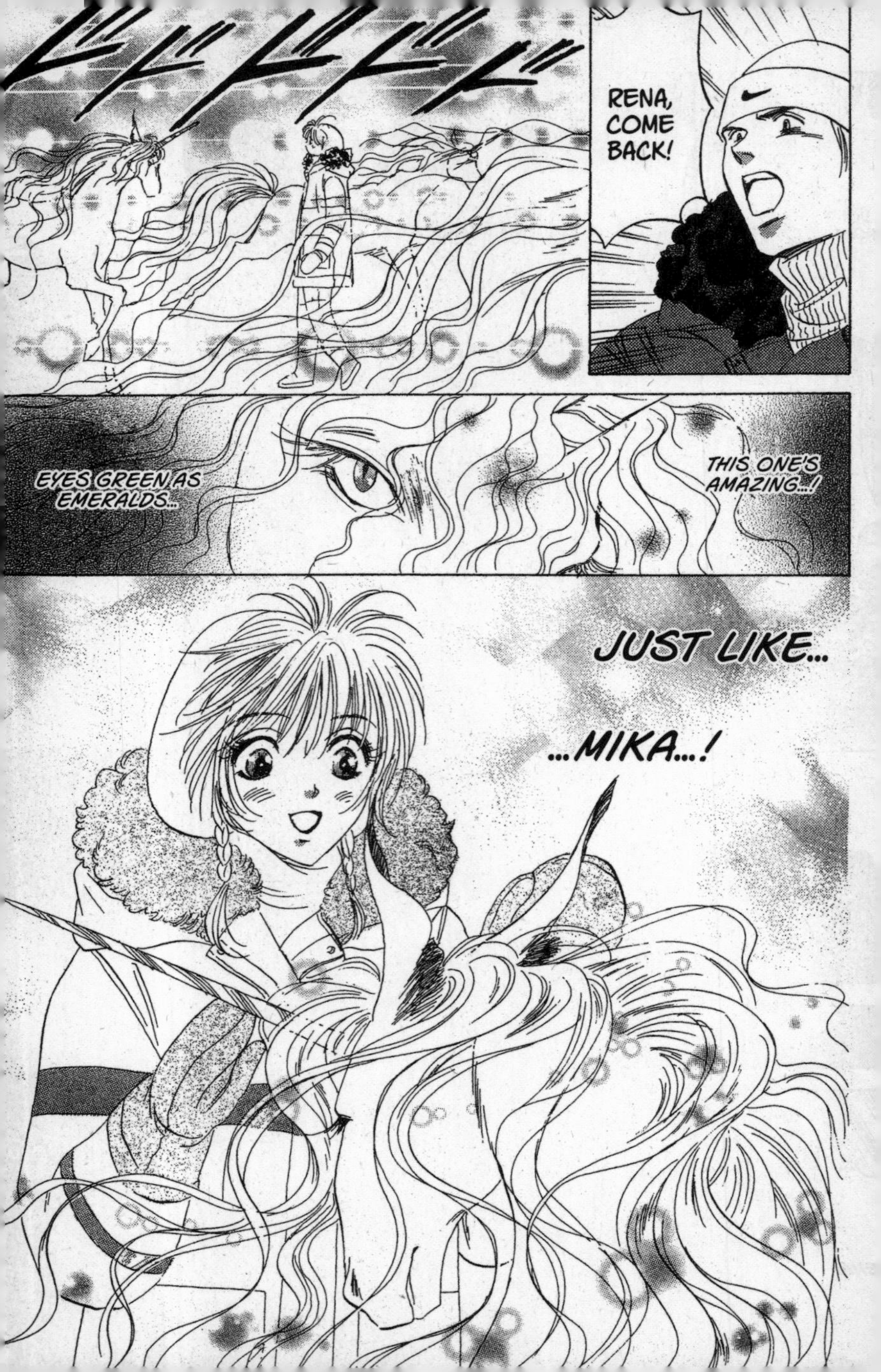
RENA, COME BACK!
THIS ONE'S AMAZING...!
EYES GREEN AS EMERALDS...
JUST LIKE...
...MIKA...!

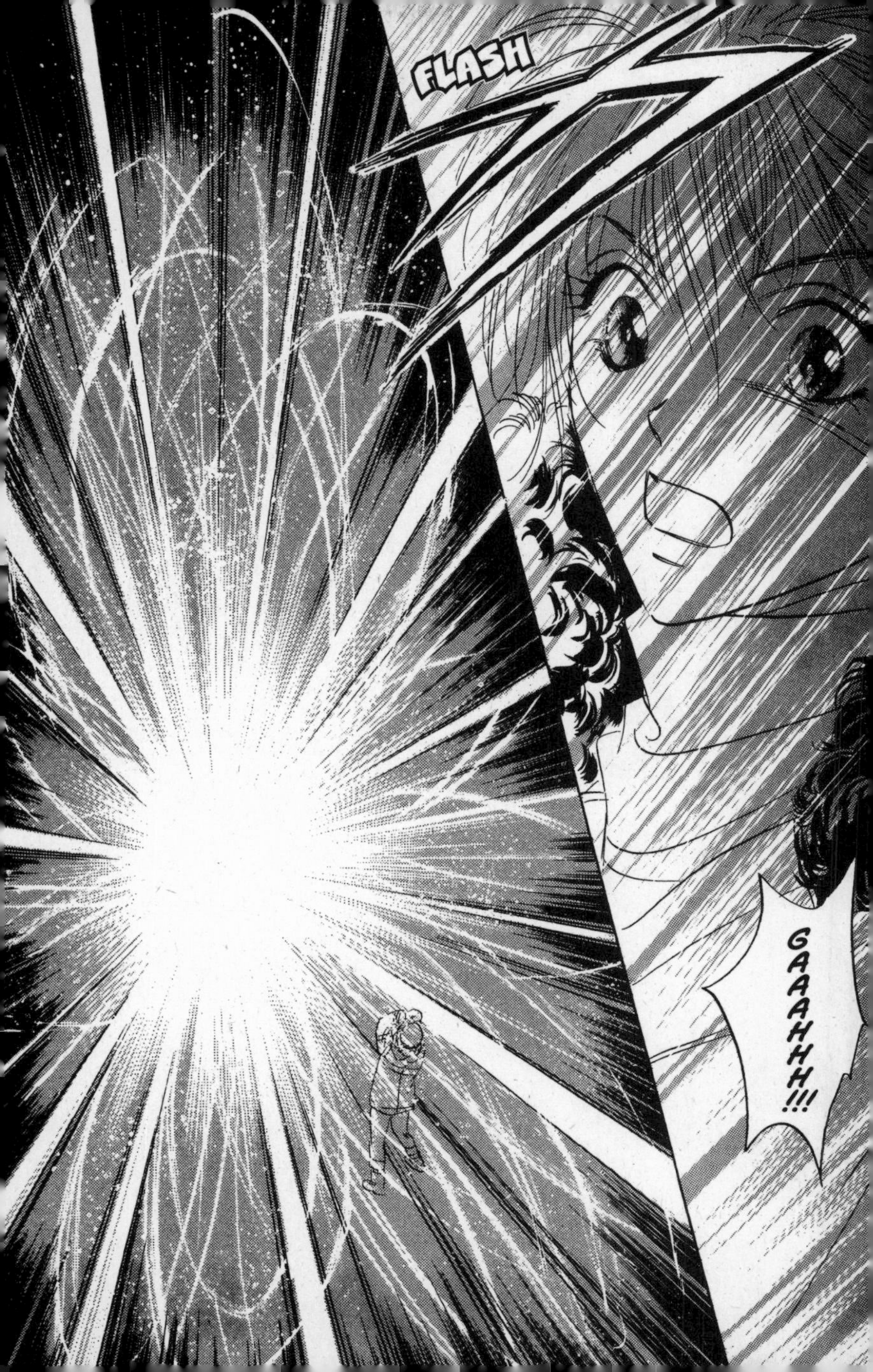
FLASH
GAAAHHH!!!

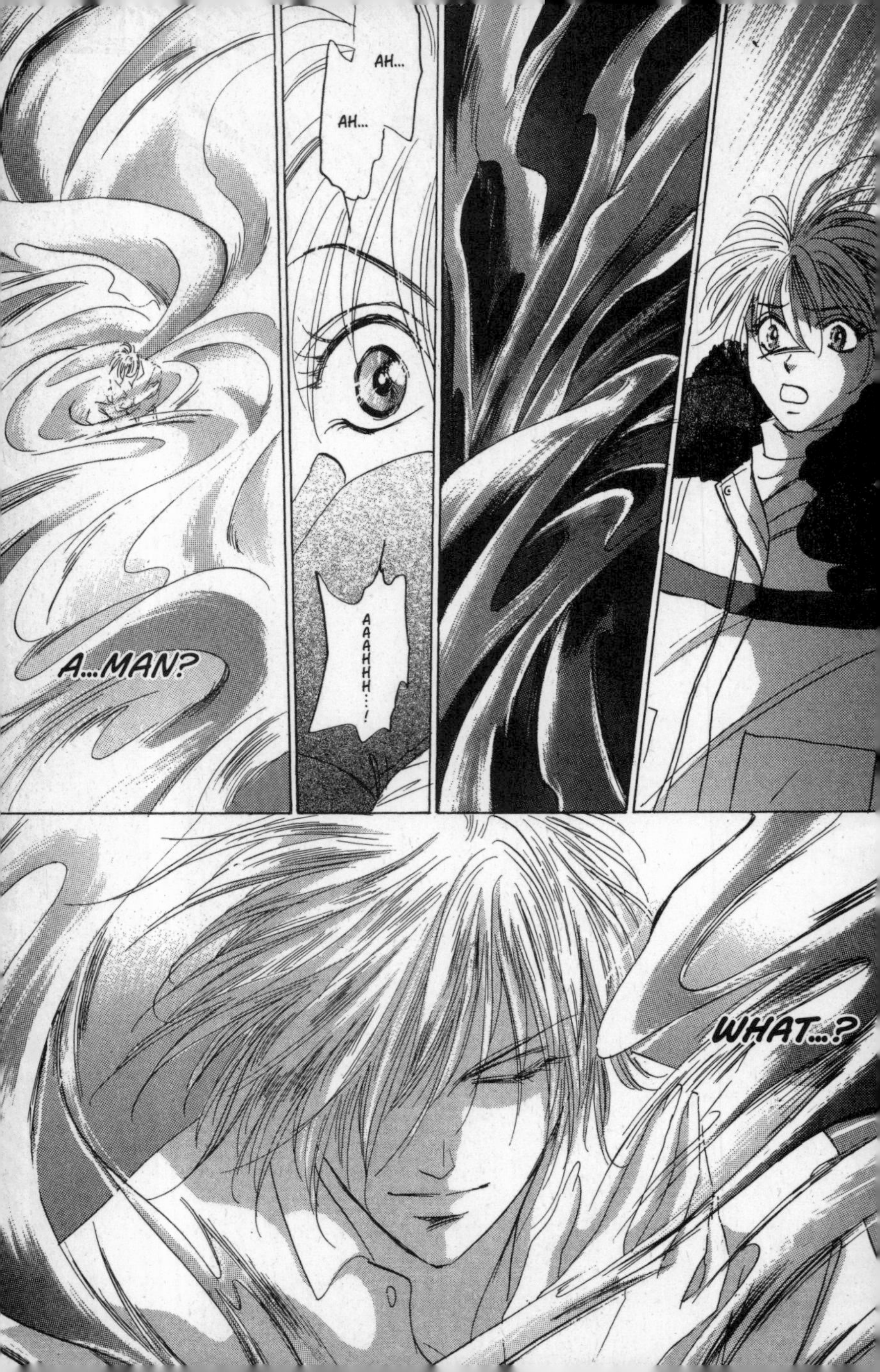
AH...
AH...
AAAHHH...!
A...MAN?
WHAT...?

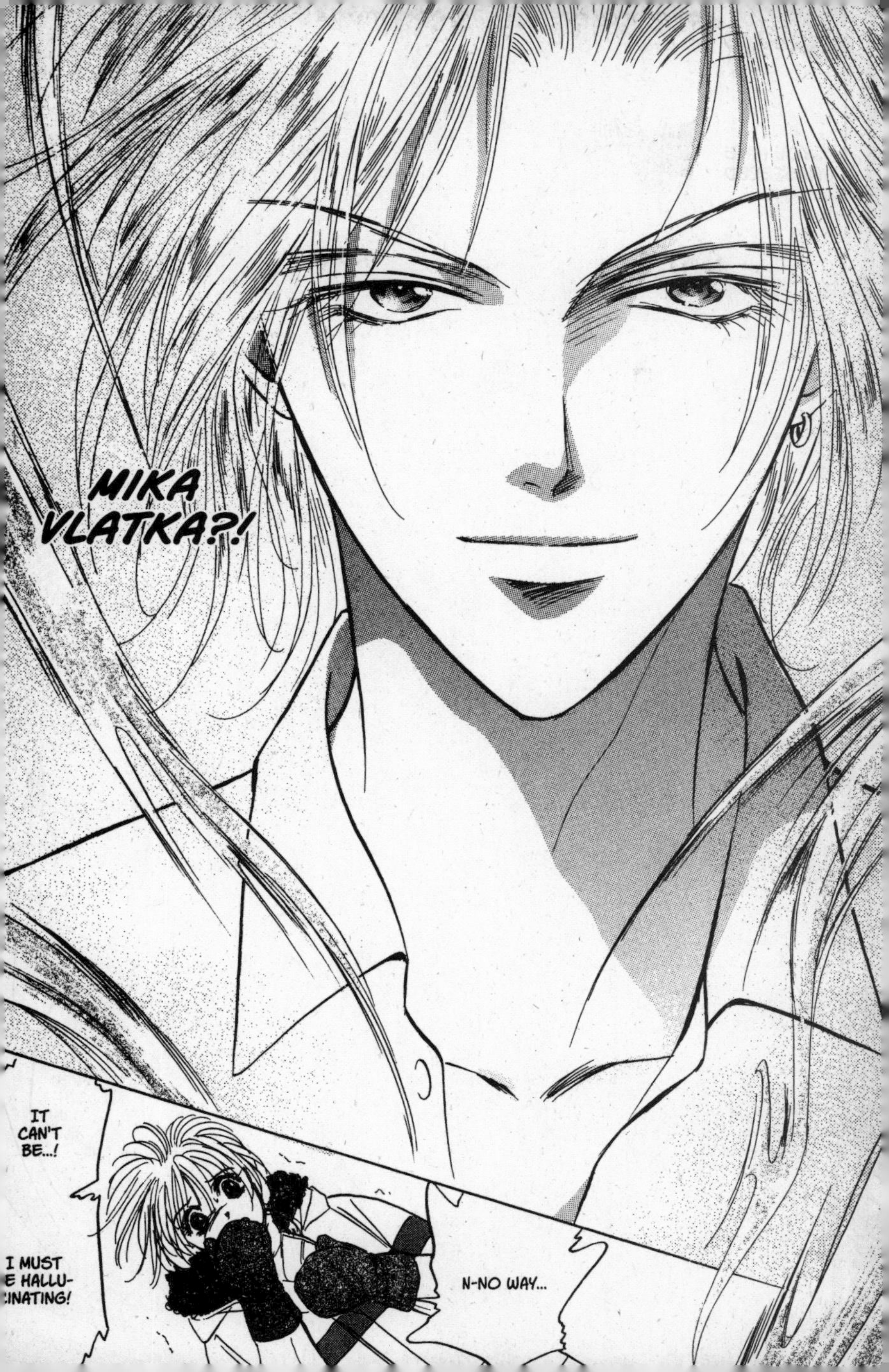
MIKA VLATKA?!
N-NO WAY...
IT CAN'T BE...!
I MUST E HALLU-INATING!

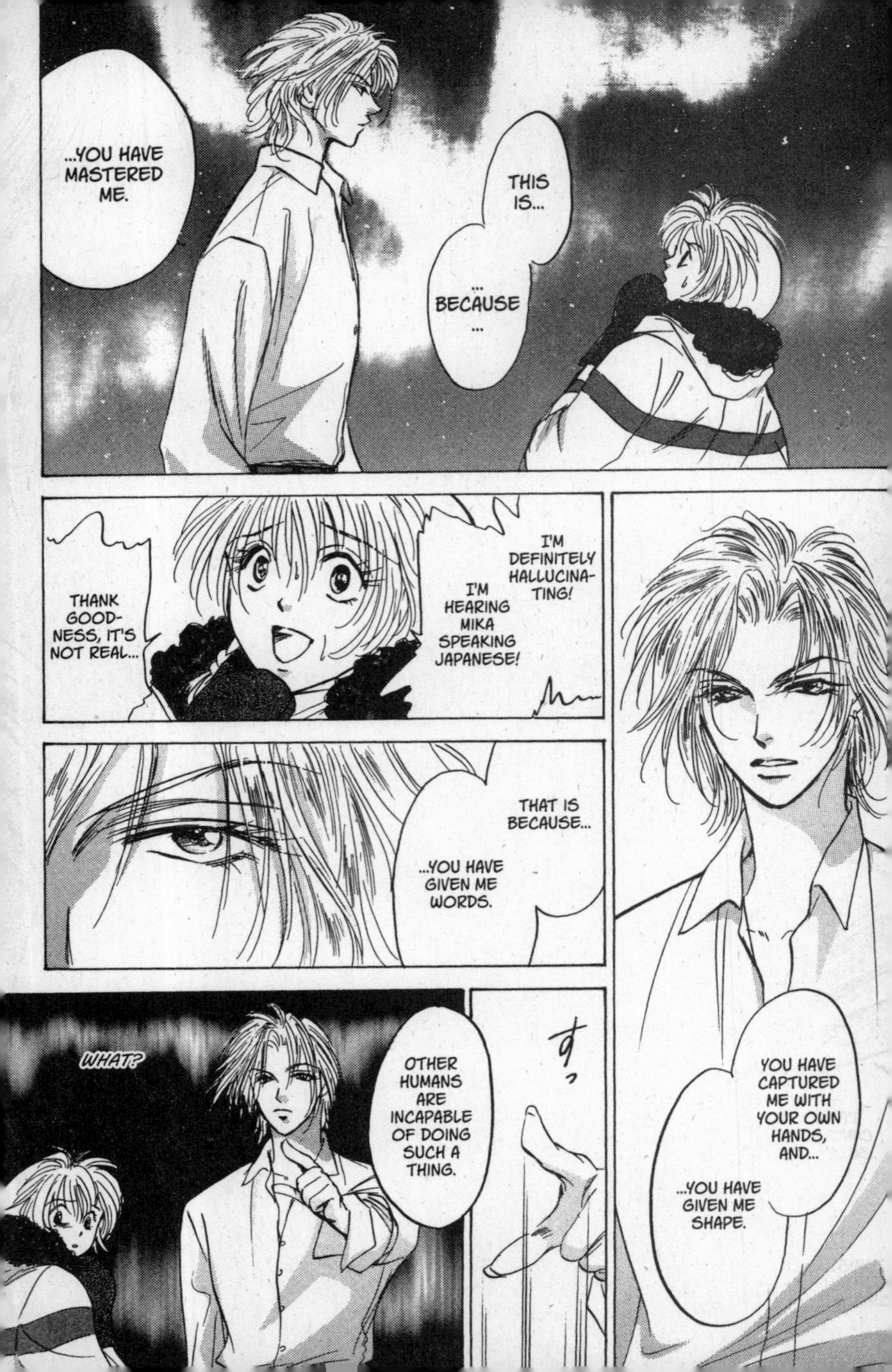
THIS IS...
...BECAUSE...
...YOU HAVE MASTERED ME.
YOU HAVE CAPTURED ME WITH YOUR OWN HANDS, AND...
...YOU HAVE GIVEN ME SHAPE.
I'M DEFINITELY HALLUCINATING!
I'M HEARING MIKA SPEAKING JAPANESE!
THANK GOODNESS, IT'S NOT REAL...
THAT IS BECAUSE...
...YOU HAVE GIVEN ME WORDS.
すっ
OTHER HUMANS ARE INCAPABLE OF DOING SUCH A THING.
WHAT?

WHAT...?!
WH...
WHAT'S...
...GOING ON...?

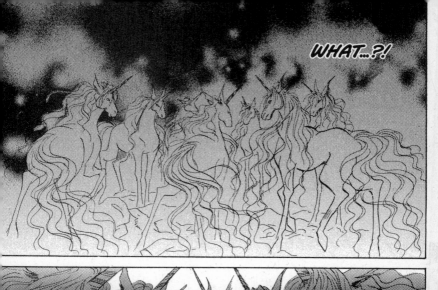

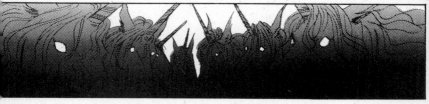

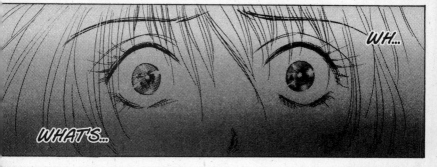

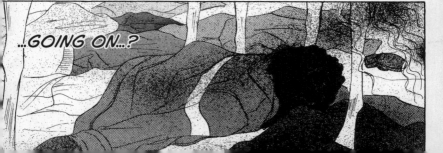

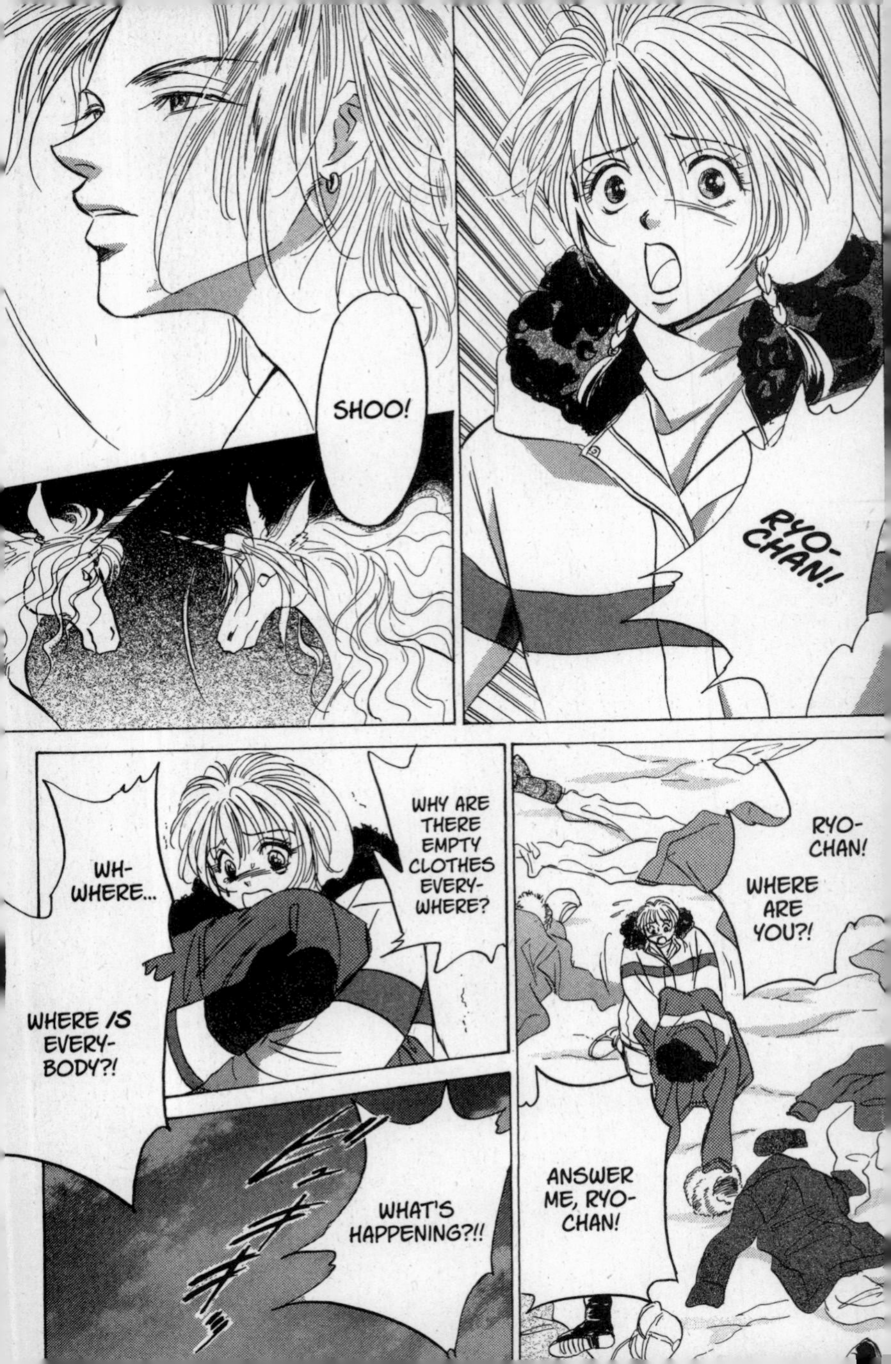
RYO-CHAN!
SHOO!
RYO-CHAN!
WHERE ARE YOU?!
ANSWER ME, RYO-CHAN!
WHY ARE THERE EMPTY CLOTHES EVERYWHERE?
WH-WHERE...
WHERE IS EVERYBODY?!
WHAT'S HAPPENING?!!

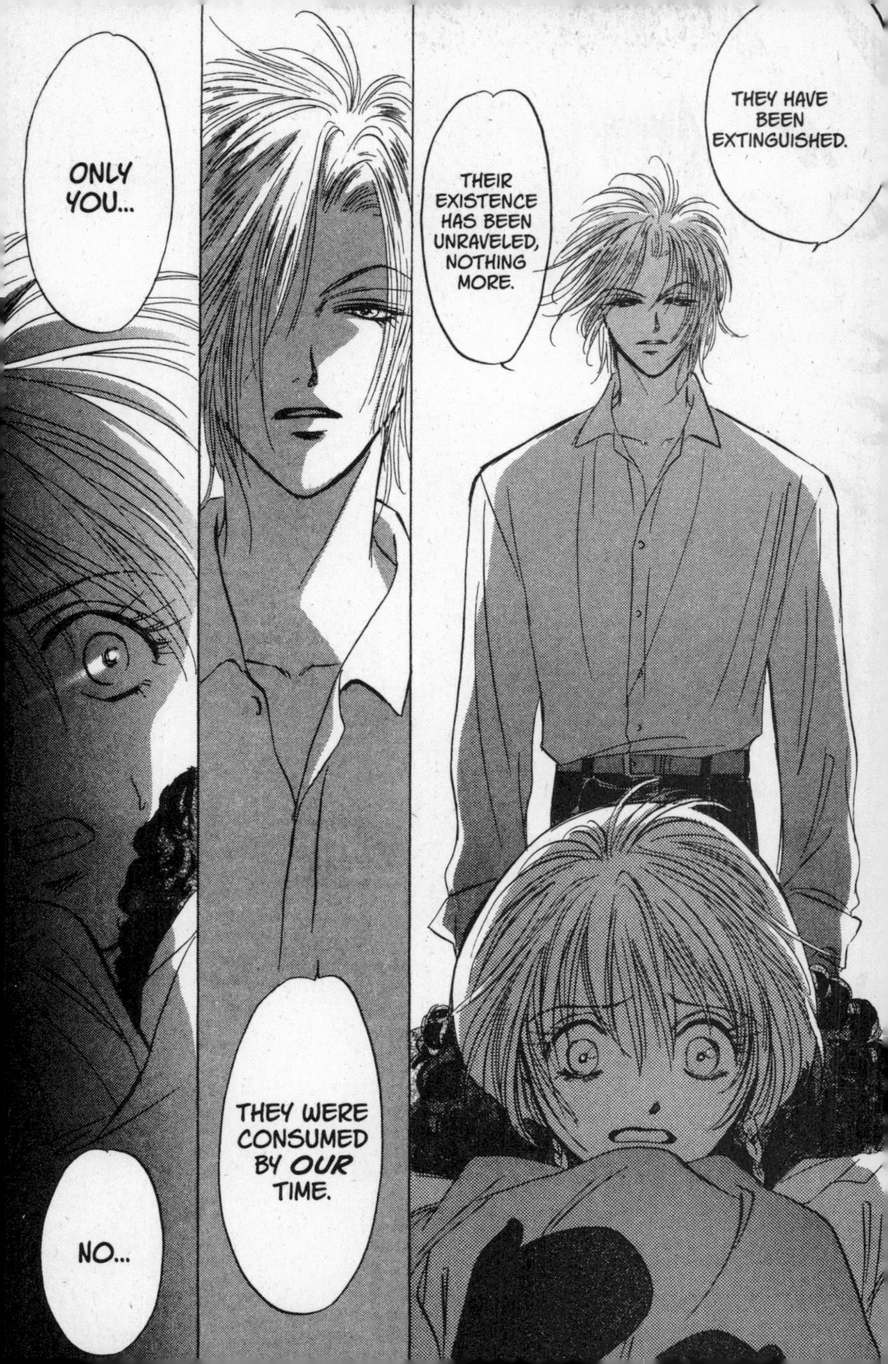
THEY HAVE BEEN EXTINGUISHED.
THEIR EXISTENCE HAS BEEN UNRAVELED, NOTHING MORE.
THEY WERE CONSUMED BY *OUR* TIME.
ONLY YOU...
NO...

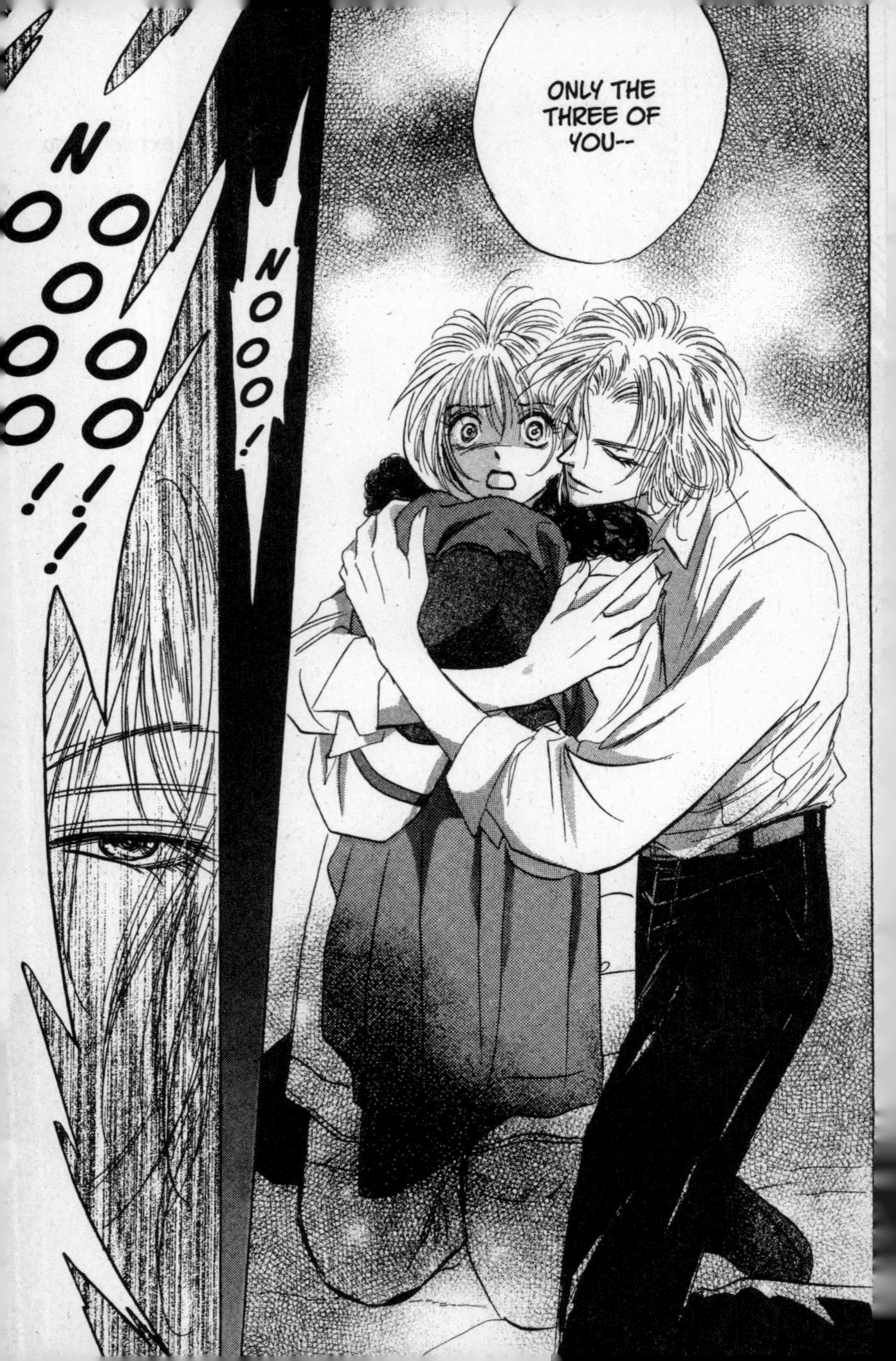

ONLY THE THREE OF YOU--
NOOOO!
NOOOO!!
OOOO!!

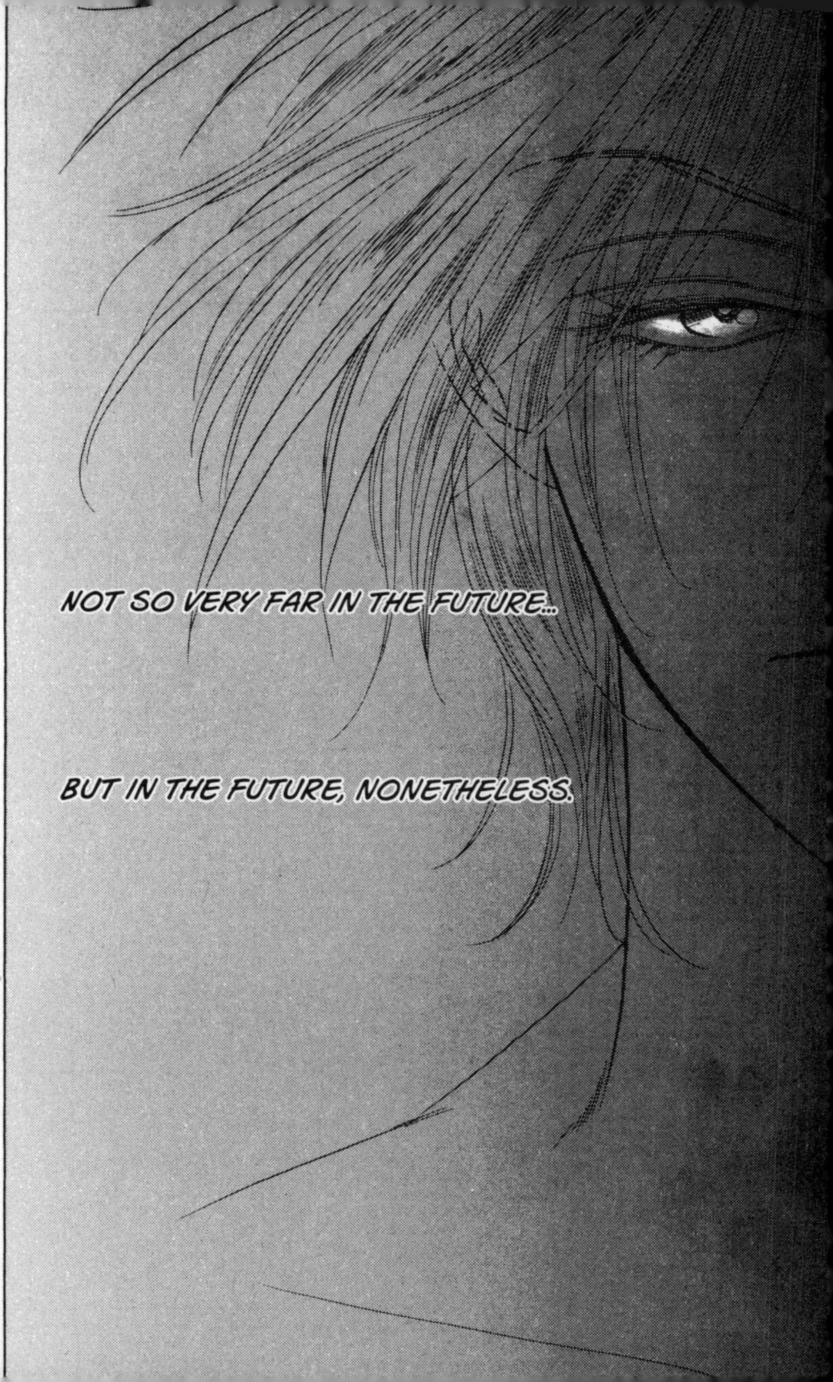
NOT SO VERY FAR IN THE FUTURE...
BUT IN THE FUTURE, NONETHELESS.

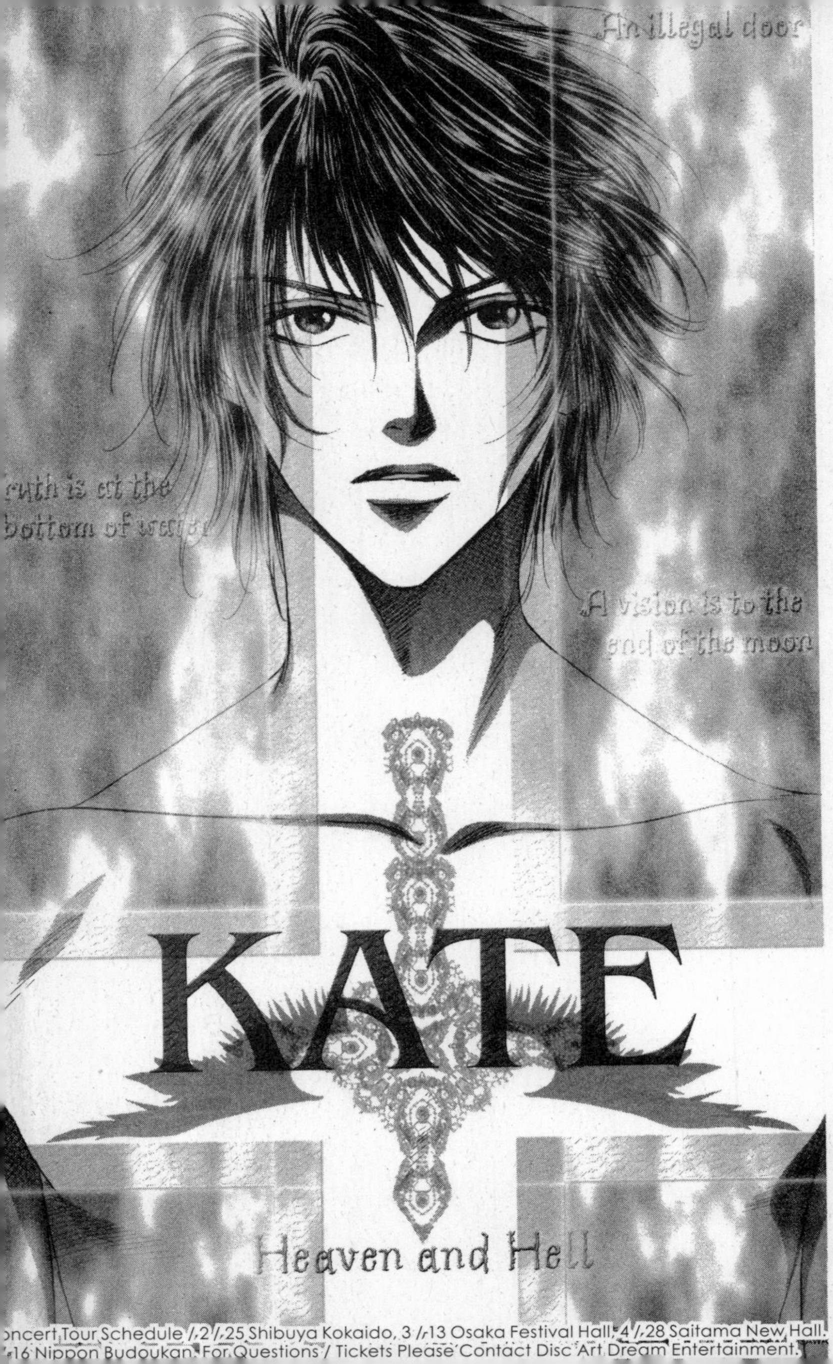
An illegal door
ruth is at the bottom of water
A vision is to the end of the moon
KATE
Heaven and Hell
oncert Tour Schedule / 2 / 25 Shibuya Kokaido, 3 / 13 Osaka Festival Hall, 4 / 28 Saitama New Hall.
16 Nippon Budoukan. For Questions / Tickets Please Contact Disc Art Dream Entertainment.

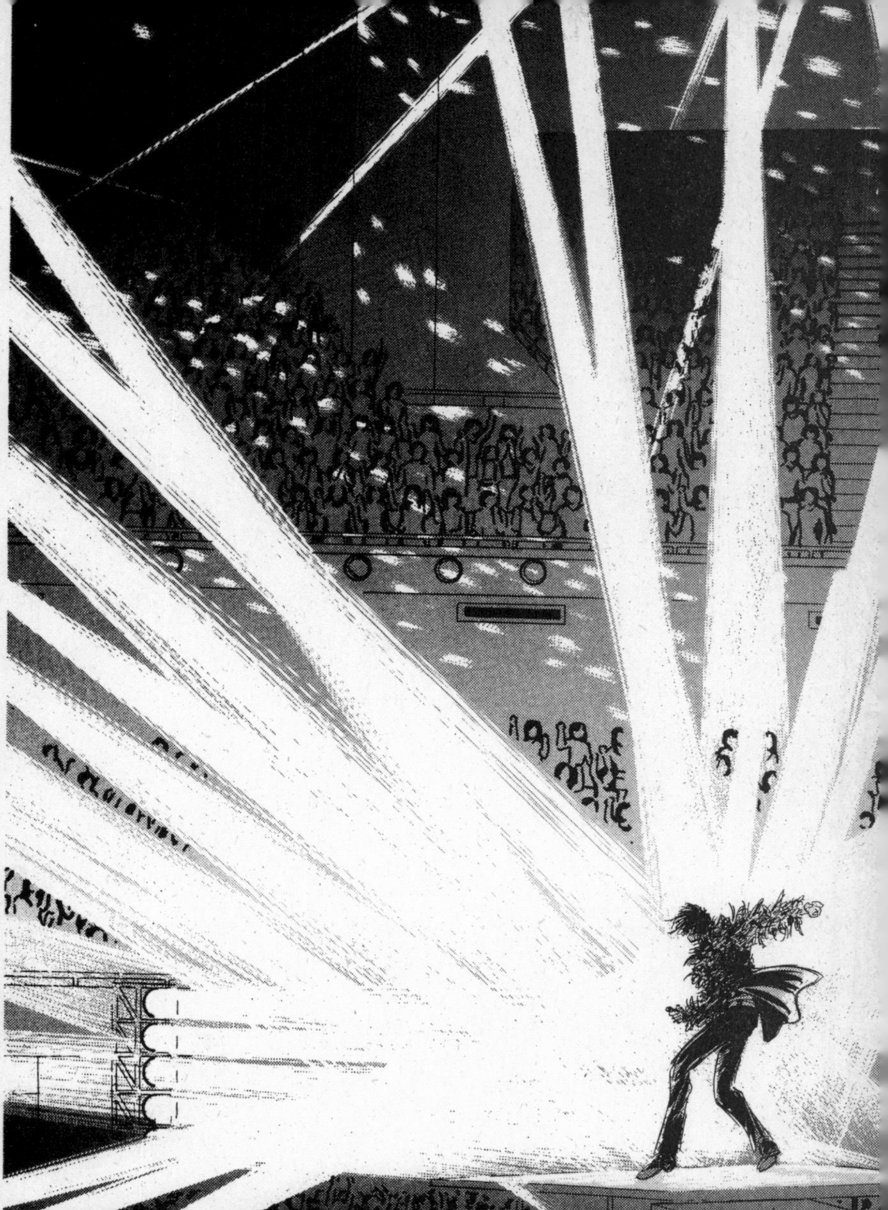

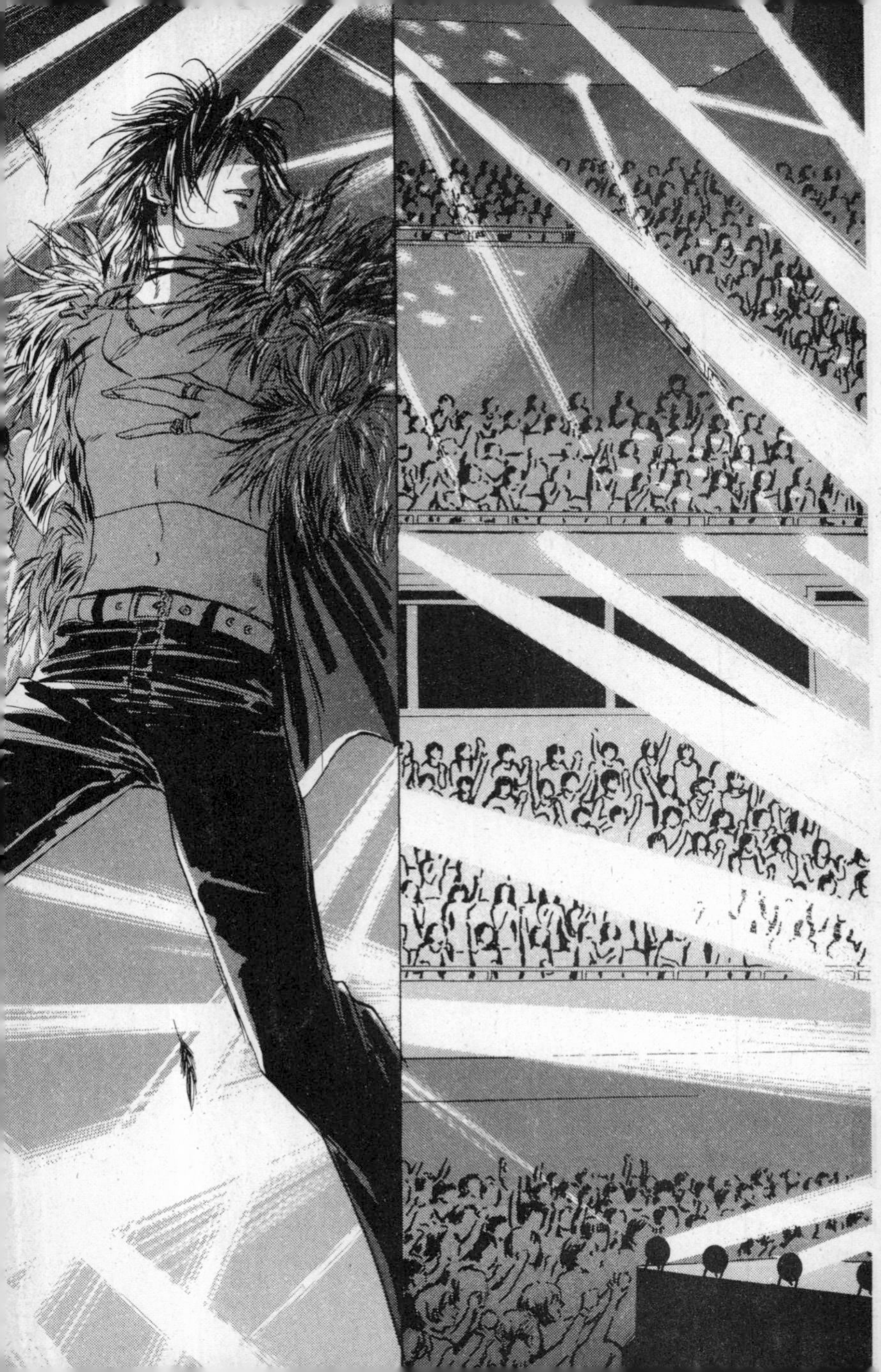

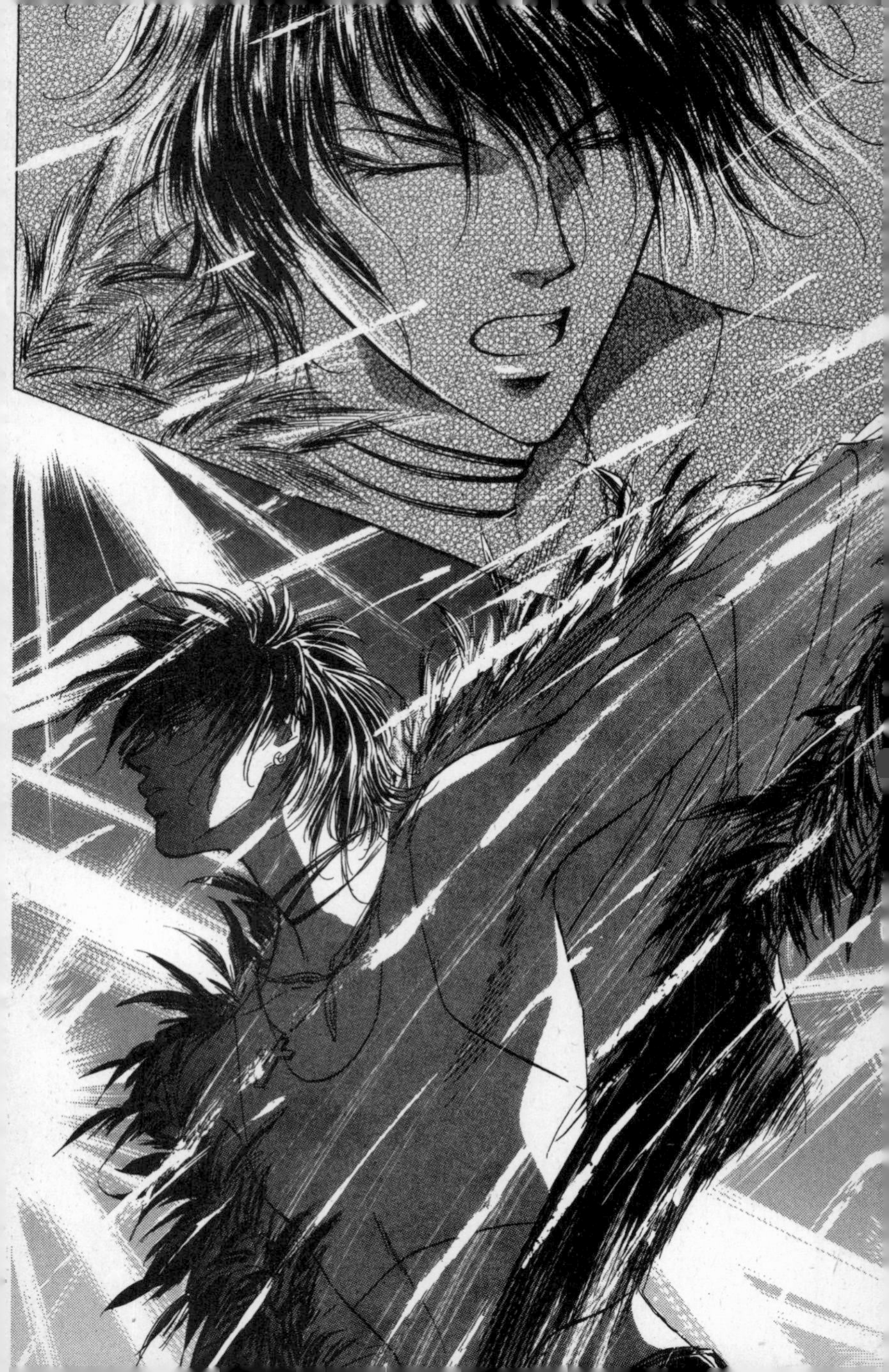

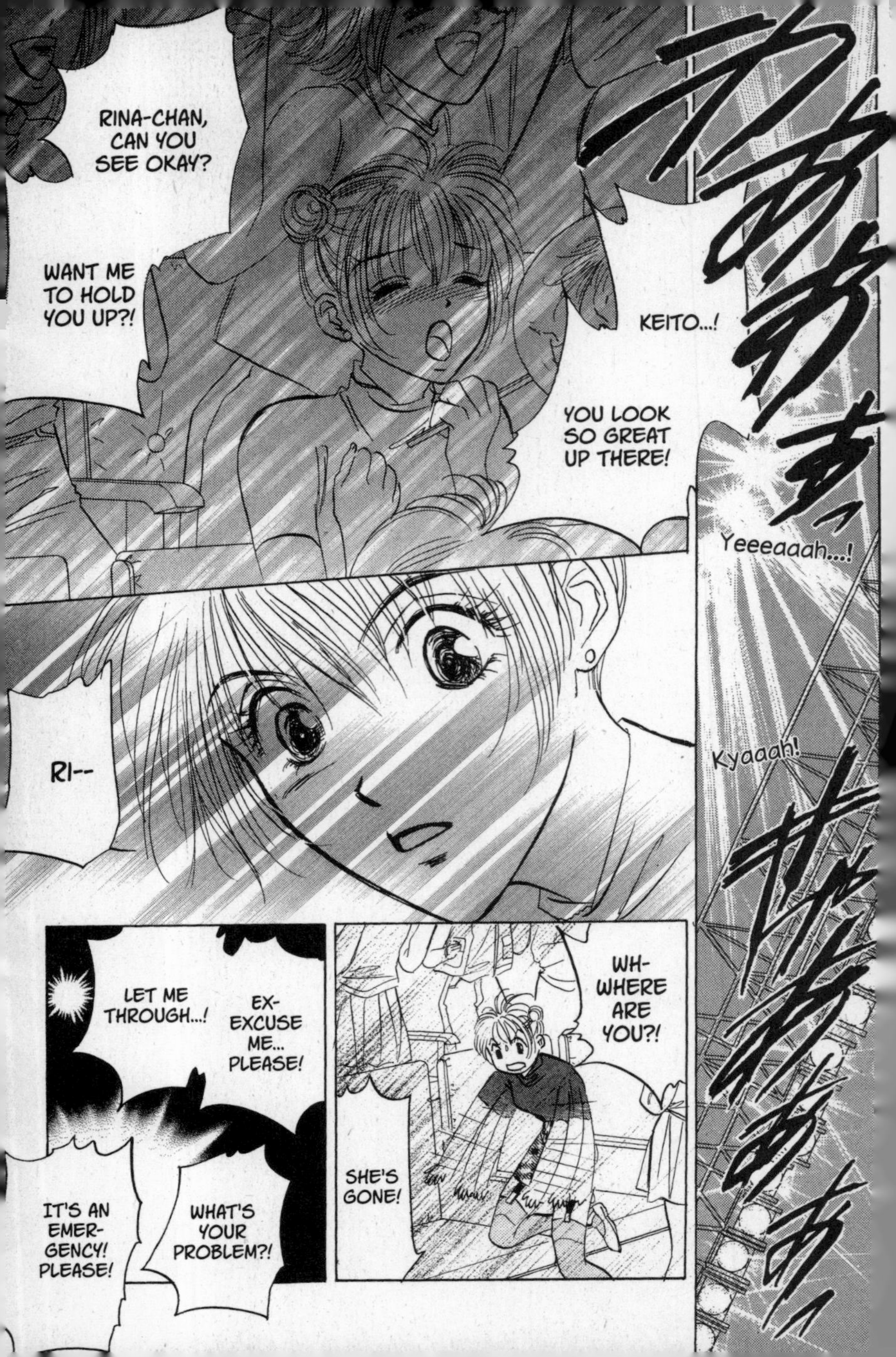
Yeeeaaah...!
Kyaaah!
KEITO...!
YOU LOOK SO GREAT UP THERE!
RINA-CHAN, CAN YOU SEE OKAY?
WANT ME TO HOLD YOU UP?!
RI--
WH- WHERE ARE YOU?!
SHE'S GONE!
EX- EXCUSE ME... PLEASE!
LET ME THROUGH...!
WHAT'S YOUR PROBLEM?!
IT'S AN EMER- GENCY! PLEASE!

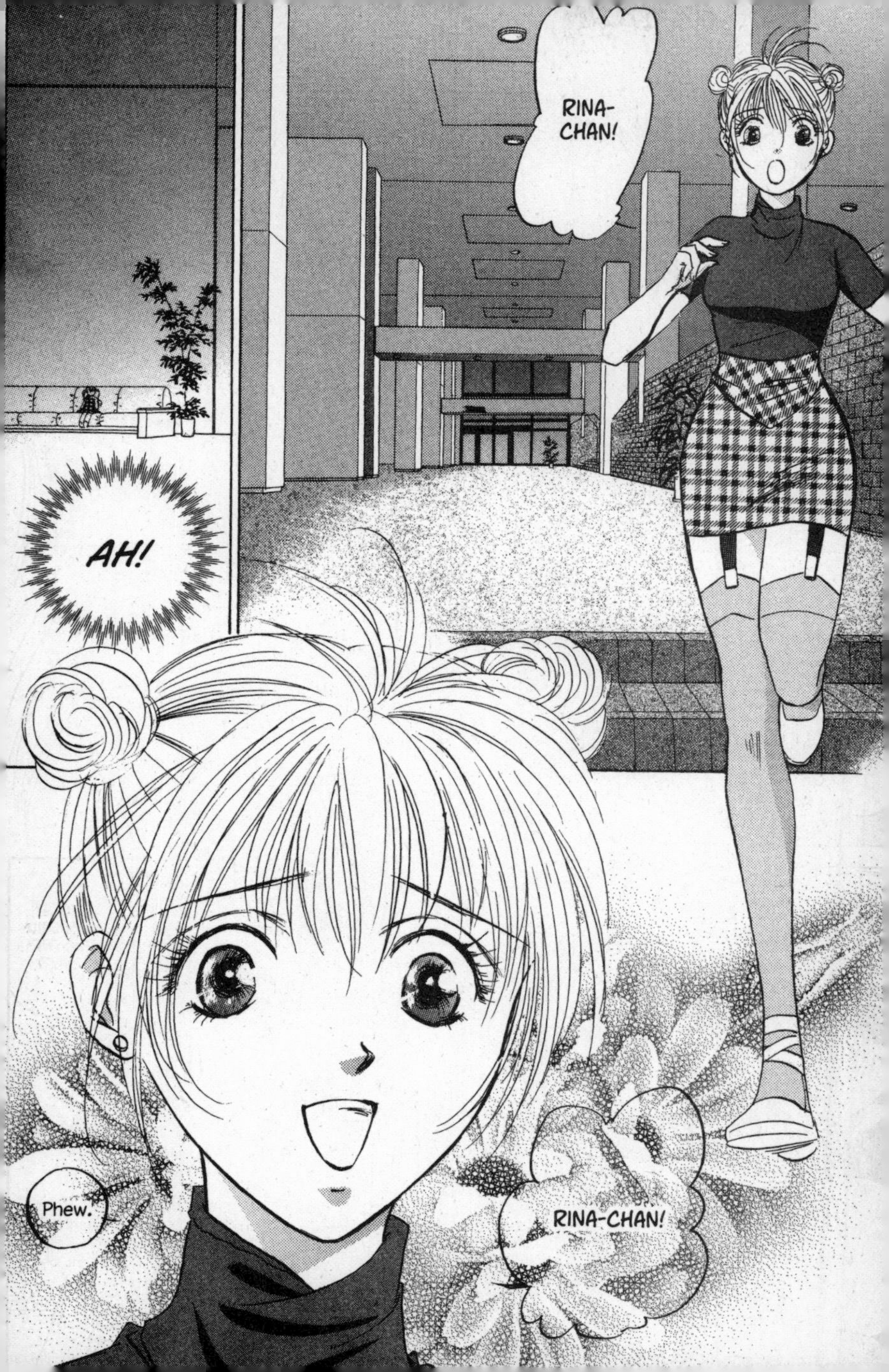
RINA-CHAN!
AH!
RINA-CHAN!
Phew.

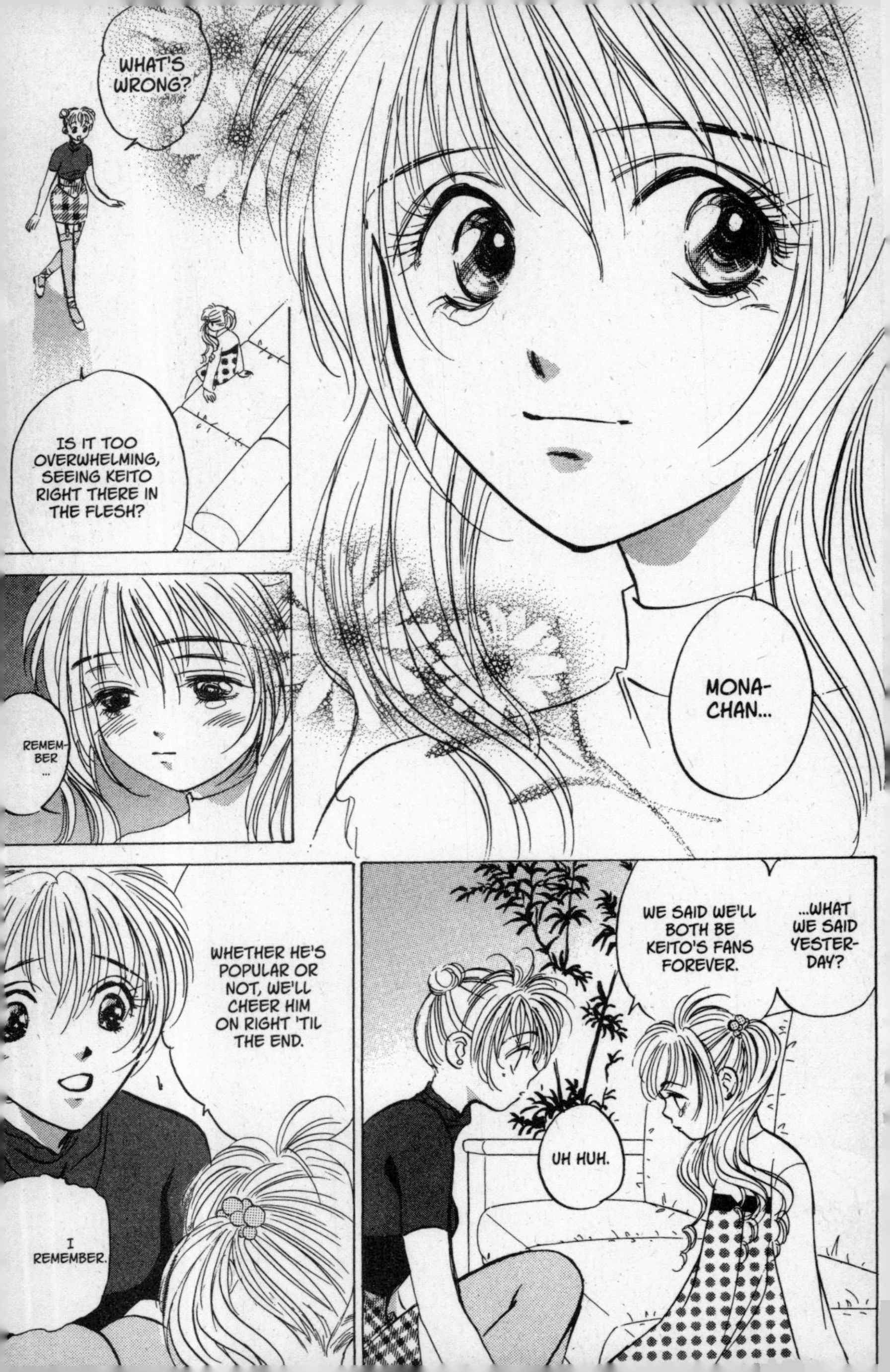
MONA-CHAN...
WHAT'S WRONG?
IS IT TOO OVERWHELMING, SEEING KEITO RIGHT THERE IN THE FLESH?
REMEMBER...
...WHAT WE SAID YESTERDAY?
WE SAID WE'LL BOTH BE KEITO'S FANS FOREVER.
UH HUH.
WHETHER HE'S POPULAR OR NOT, WE'LL CHEER HIM ON RIGHT 'TIL THE END.
I REMEMBER.

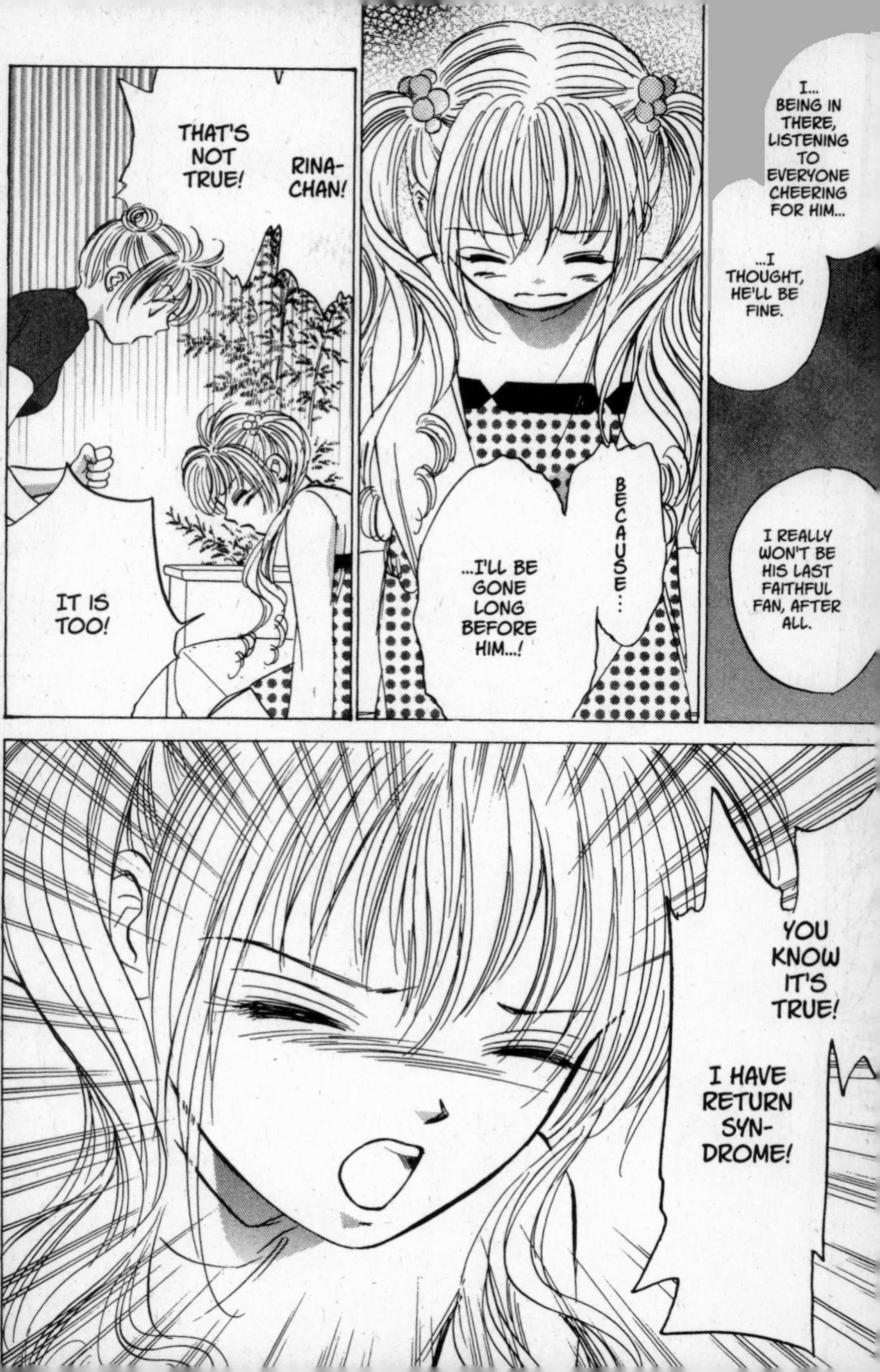
I... BEING IN THERE, LISTENING TO EVERYONE CHEERING FOR HIM...
...I THOUGHT, HE'LL BE FINE.
I REALLY WON'T BE HIS LAST FAITHFUL FAN, AFTER ALL.
BECAUSE...
...I'LL BE GONE LONG BEFORE HIM...!
RINA-CHAN!
THAT'S NOT TRUE!
IT IS TOO!
YOU KNOW IT'S TRUE!
I HAVE RETURN SYN-DROME!

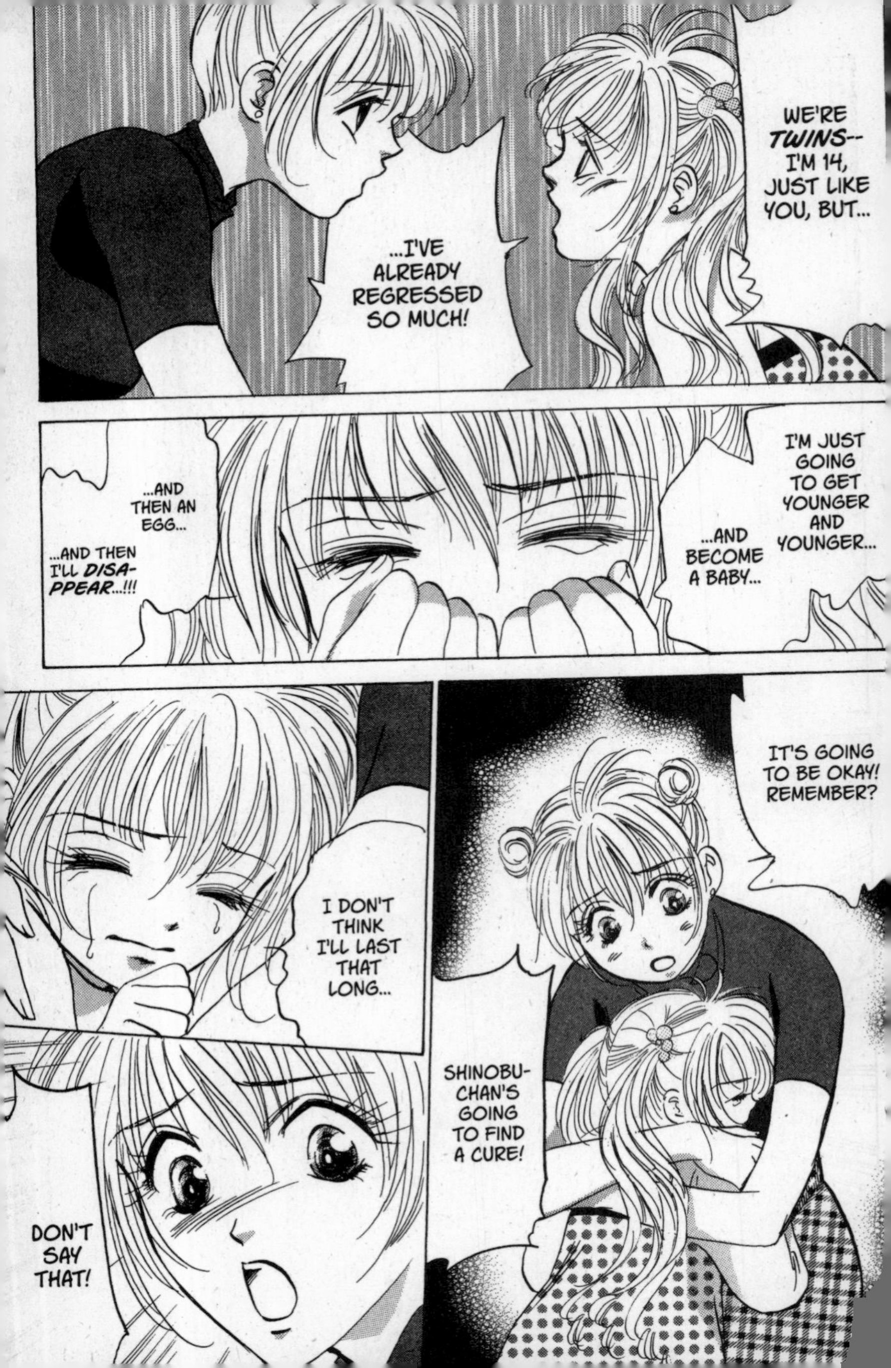
WE'RE *TWINS*-- I'M 14, JUST LIKE YOU, BUT...
...I'VE ALREADY REGRESSED SO MUCH!
I'M JUST GOING TO GET YOUNGER AND YOUNGER...
...AND BECOME A BABY...
...AND THEN AN EGG...
...AND THEN I'LL *DISAPPEAR*...!!!
IT'S GOING TO BE OKAY! REMEMBER?
SHINOBU-CHAN'S GOING TO FIND A CURE!
I DON'T THINK I'LL LAST THAT LONG...
DON'T SAY THAT!

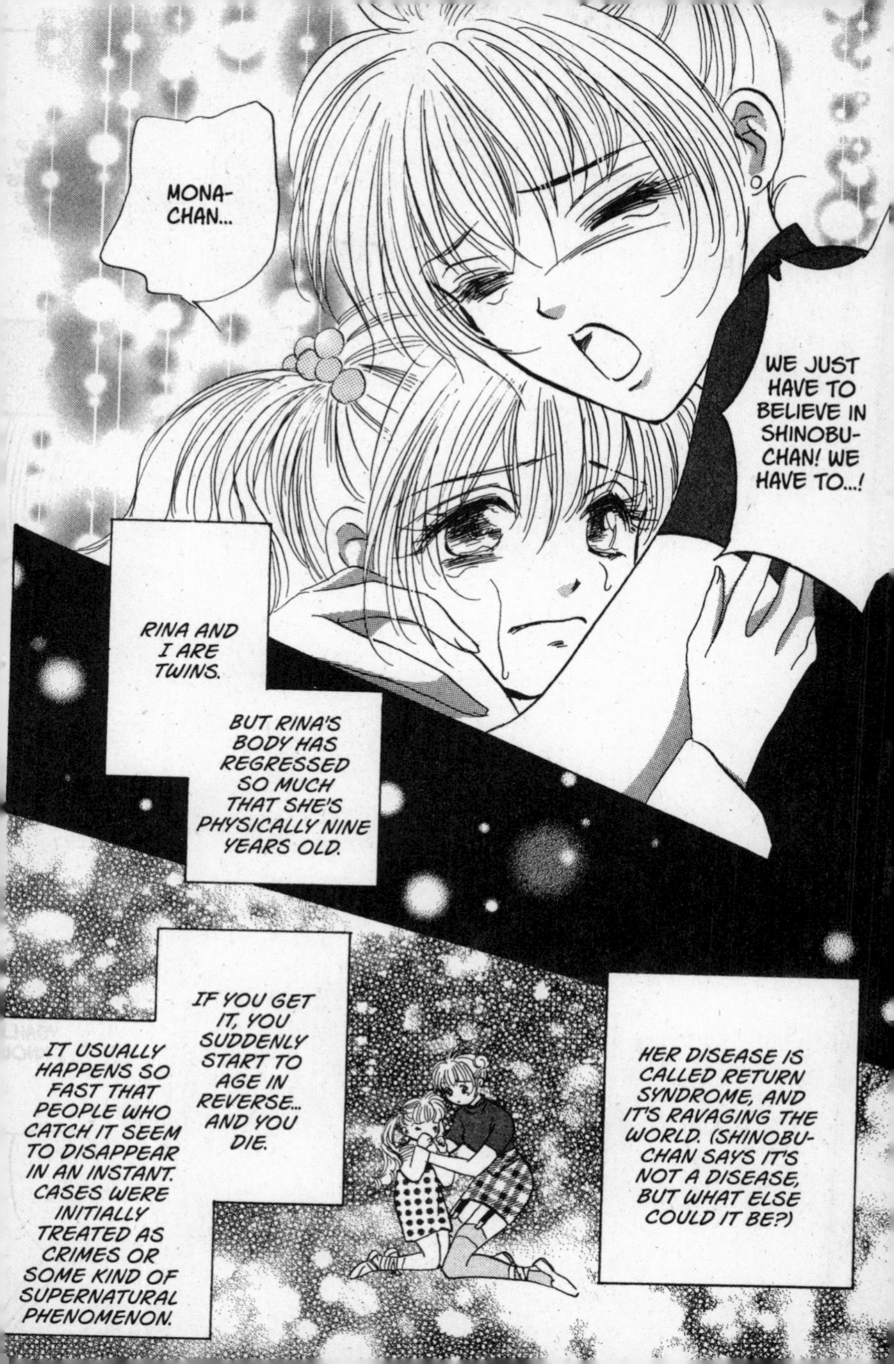
WE JUST HAVE TO BELIEVE IN SHINOBU-CHAN! WE HAVE TO...!
MONA-CHAN...
RINA AND I ARE TWINS.
BUT RINA'S BODY HAS REGRESSED SO MUCH THAT SHE'S PHYSICALLY NINE YEARS OLD.
HER DISEASE IS CALLED RETURN SYNDROME, AND IT'S RAVAGING THE WORLD. (SHINOBU-CHAN SAYS IT'S NOT A DISEASE, BUT WHAT ELSE COULD IT BE?)
IF YOU GET IT, YOU SUDDENLY START TO AGE IN REVERSE... AND YOU DIE.
IT USUALLY HAPPENS SO FAST THAT PEOPLE WHO CATCH IT SEEM TO DISAPPEAR IN AN INSTANT. CASES WERE INITIALLY TREATED AS CRIMES OR SOME KIND OF SUPERNATURAL PHENOMENON.

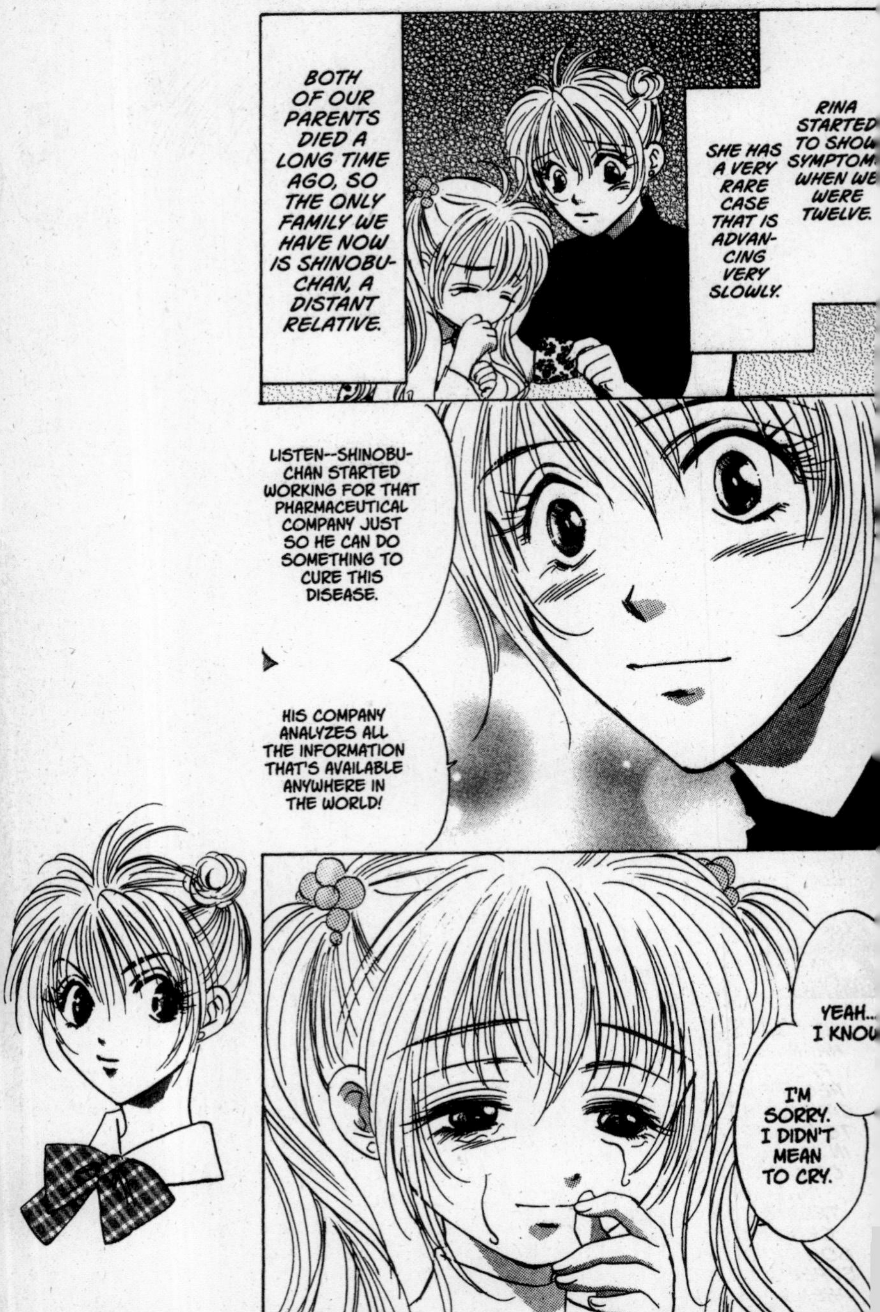
RINA STARTED TO SHOW SYMPTOMS WHEN WE WERE TWELVE.
SHE HAS A VERY RARE CASE THAT IS ADVANCING VERY SLOWLY.
BOTH OF OUR PARENTS DIED A LONG TIME AGO, SO THE ONLY FAMILY WE HAVE NOW IS SHINOBU-CHAN, A DISTANT RELATIVE.
LISTEN--SHINOBU-CHAN STARTED WORKING FOR THAT PHARMACEUTICAL COMPANY JUST SO HE CAN DO SOMETHING TO CURE THIS DISEASE.
HIS COMPANY ANALYZES ALL THE INFORMATION THAT'S AVAILABLE ANYWHERE IN THE WORLD!
YEAH... I KNOW
I'M SORRY. I DIDN'T MEAN TO CRY.

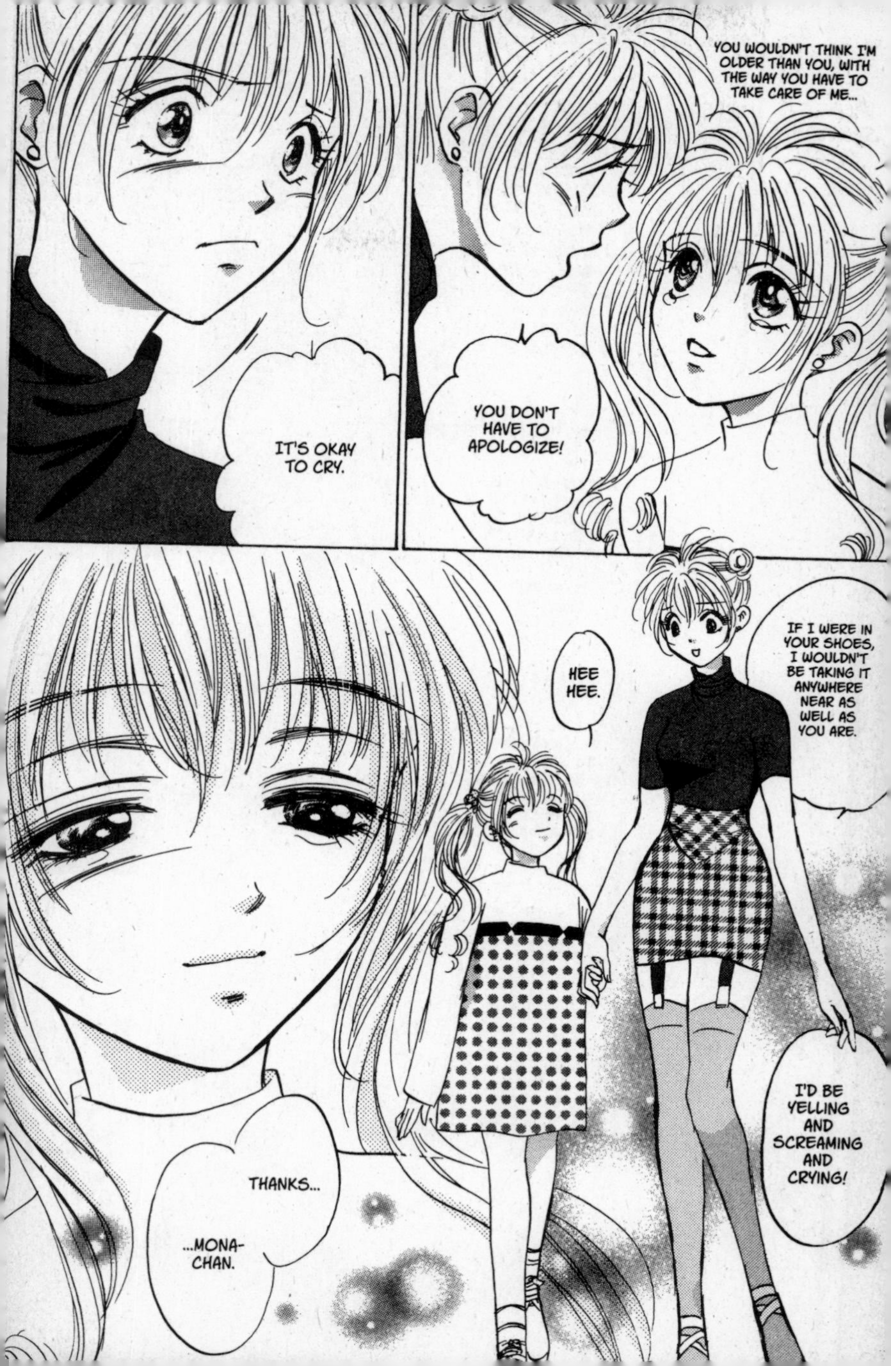
YOU WOULDN'T THINK I'M OLDER THAN YOU, WITH THE WAY YOU HAVE TO TAKE CARE OF ME...
YOU DON'T HAVE TO APOLOGIZE!
IT'S OKAY TO CRY.
IF I WERE IN YOUR SHOES, I WOULDN'T BE TAKING IT ANYWHERE NEAR AS WELL AS YOU ARE.
HEE HEE.
I'D BE YELLING AND SCREAMING AND CRYING!
THANKS...
...MONA-CHAN.

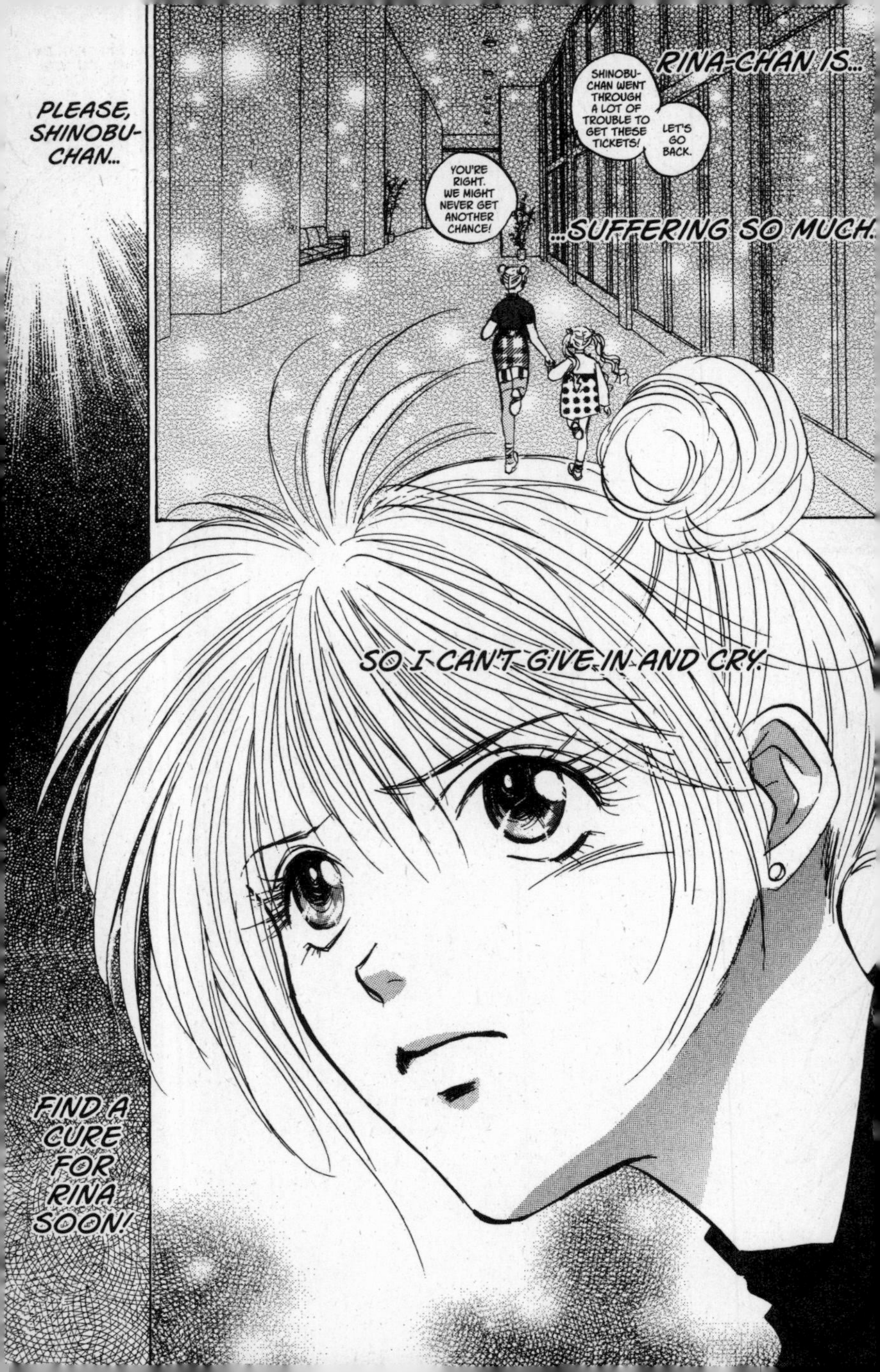
RINA-CHAN IS...
LET'S GO BACK.
SHINOBU-CHAN WENT THROUGH A LOT OF TROUBLE TO GET THESE TICKETS!
YOU'RE RIGHT. WE MIGHT NEVER GET ANOTHER CHANCE!
...SUFFERING SO MUCH.
SO I CAN'T GIVE IN AND CRY.
PLEASE, SHINOBU-CHAN...
FIND A CURE FOR RINA SOON!

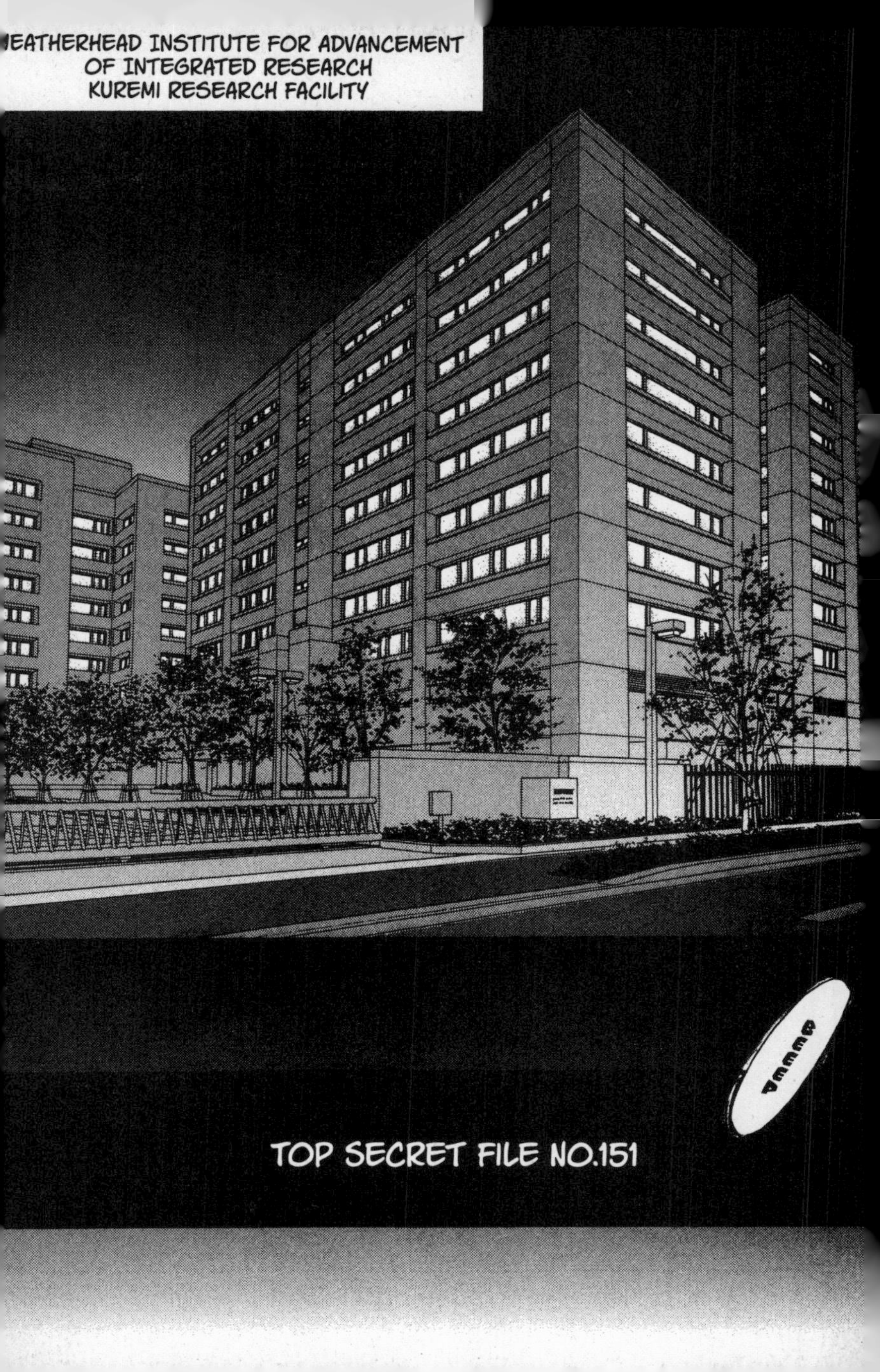
EATHERHEAD INSTITUTE FOR ADVANCEMENT OF INTEGRATED RESEARCH
KUREMI RESEARCH FACILITY
BEEEEP
TOP SECRET FILE NO.151

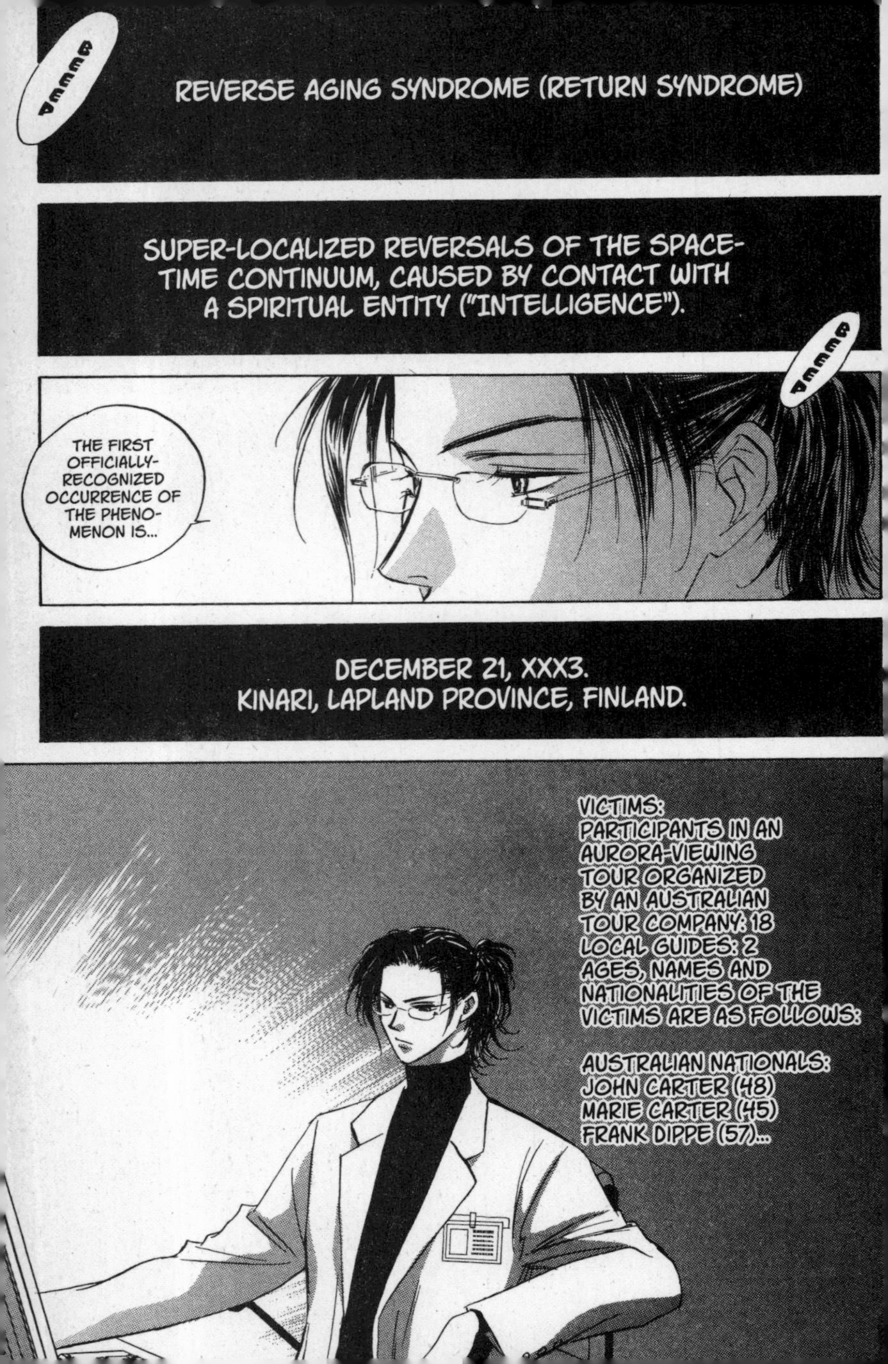
REVERSE AGING SYNDROME (RETURN SYNDROME)
BEEEP
SUPER-LOCALIZED REVERSALS OF THE SPACE-TIME CONTINUUM, CAUSED BY CONTACT WITH A SPIRITUAL ENTITY ("INTELLIGENCE").
BEEEP
THE FIRST OFFICIALLY-RECOGNIZED OCCURRENCE OF THE PHENOMENON IS...
DECEMBER 21, XXX3.
KINARI, LAPLAND PROVINCE, FINLAND.
VICTIMS: PARTICIPANTS IN AN AURORA-VIEWING TOUR ORGANIZED BY AN AUSTRALIAN TOUR COMPANY: 18 LOCAL GUIDES: 2 AGES, NAMES AND NATIONALITIES OF THE VICTIMS ARE AS FOLLOWS:
AUSTRALIAN NATIONALS: JOHN CARTER (48) MARIE CARTER (45) FRANK DIPPE (57)...

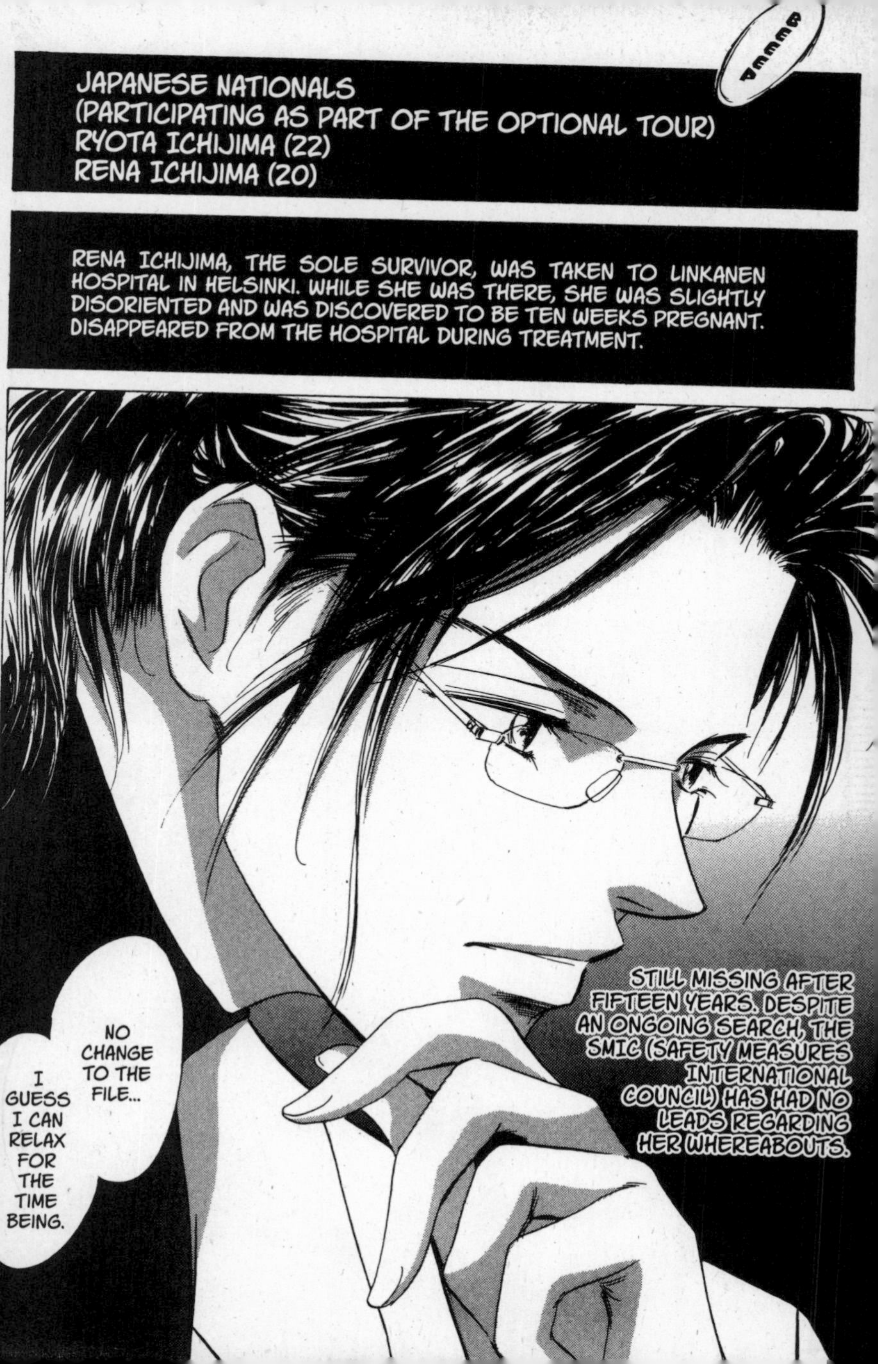

BEEEEP
JAPANESE NATIONALS
(PARTICIPATING AS PART OF THE OPTIONAL TOUR)
RYOTA ICHIJIMA (22)
RENA ICHIJIMA (20)
RENA ICHIJIMA, THE SOLE SURVIVOR, WAS TAKEN TO LINKANEN HOSPITAL IN HELSINKI. WHILE SHE WAS THERE, SHE WAS SLIGHTLY DISORIENTED AND WAS DISCOVERED TO BE TEN WEEKS PREGNANT. DISAPPEARED FROM THE HOSPITAL DURING TREATMENT.
STILL MISSING AFTER FIFTEEN YEARS. DESPITE AN ONGOING SEARCH, THE SMIC (SAFETY MEASURES INTERNATIONAL COUNCIL) HAS HAD NO LEADS REGARDING HER WHEREABOUTS.
NO CHANGE TO THE FILE...
I GUESS I CAN RELAX FOR THE TIME BEING.

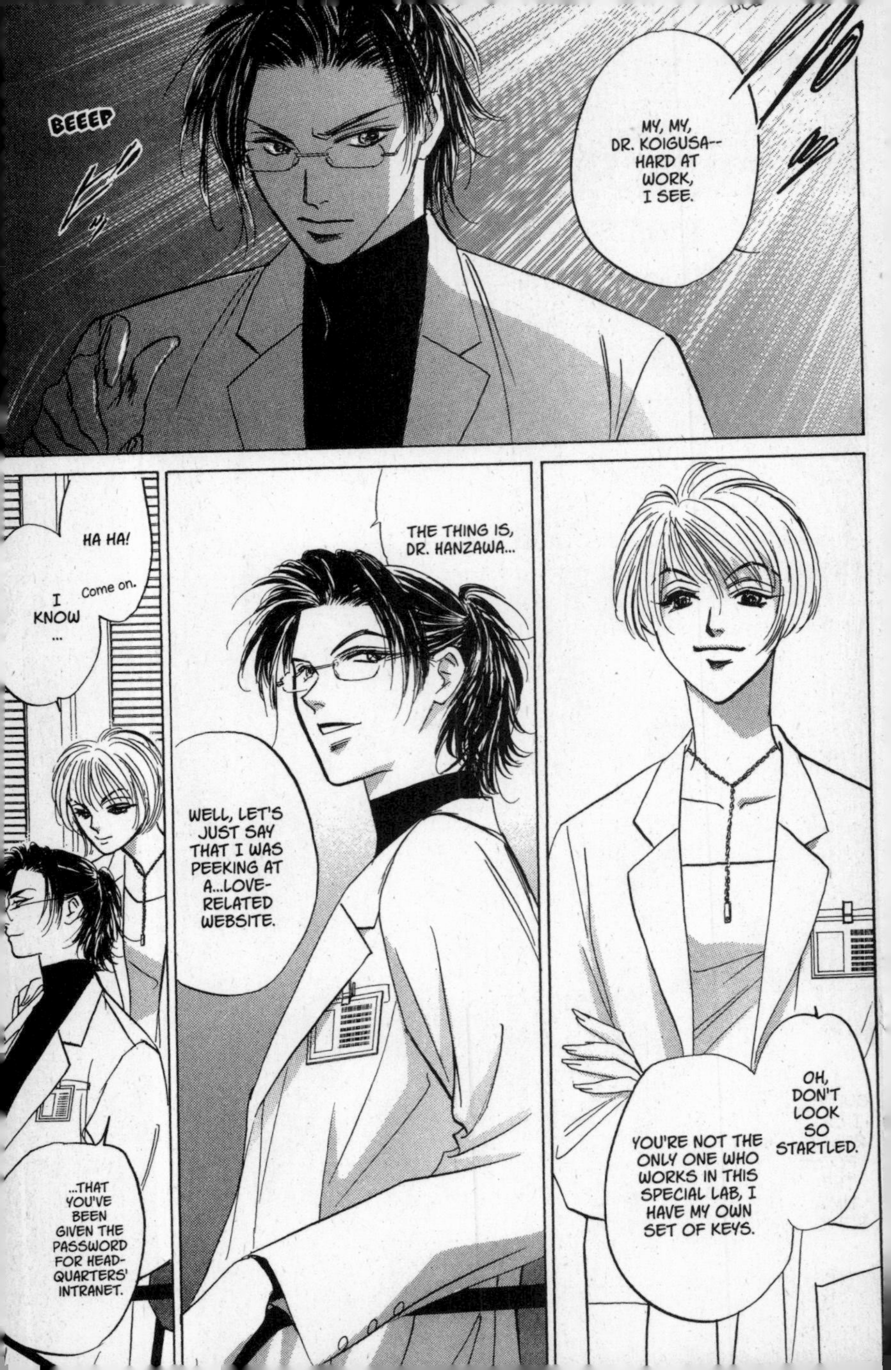
MY, MY, DR. KOIGUSA--HARD AT WORK, I SEE.
BEEEP
OH, DON'T LOOK SO STARTLED.
YOU'RE NOT THE ONLY ONE WHO WORKS IN THIS SPECIAL LAB, I HAVE MY OWN SET OF KEYS.
THE THING IS, DR. HANZAWA...
WELL, LET'S JUST SAY THAT I WAS PEEKING AT A...LOVE-RELATED WEBSITE.
HA HA!
Come on.
I KNOW...
...THAT YOU'VE BEEN GIVEN THE PASSWORD FOR HEAD-QUARTERS' INTRANET.

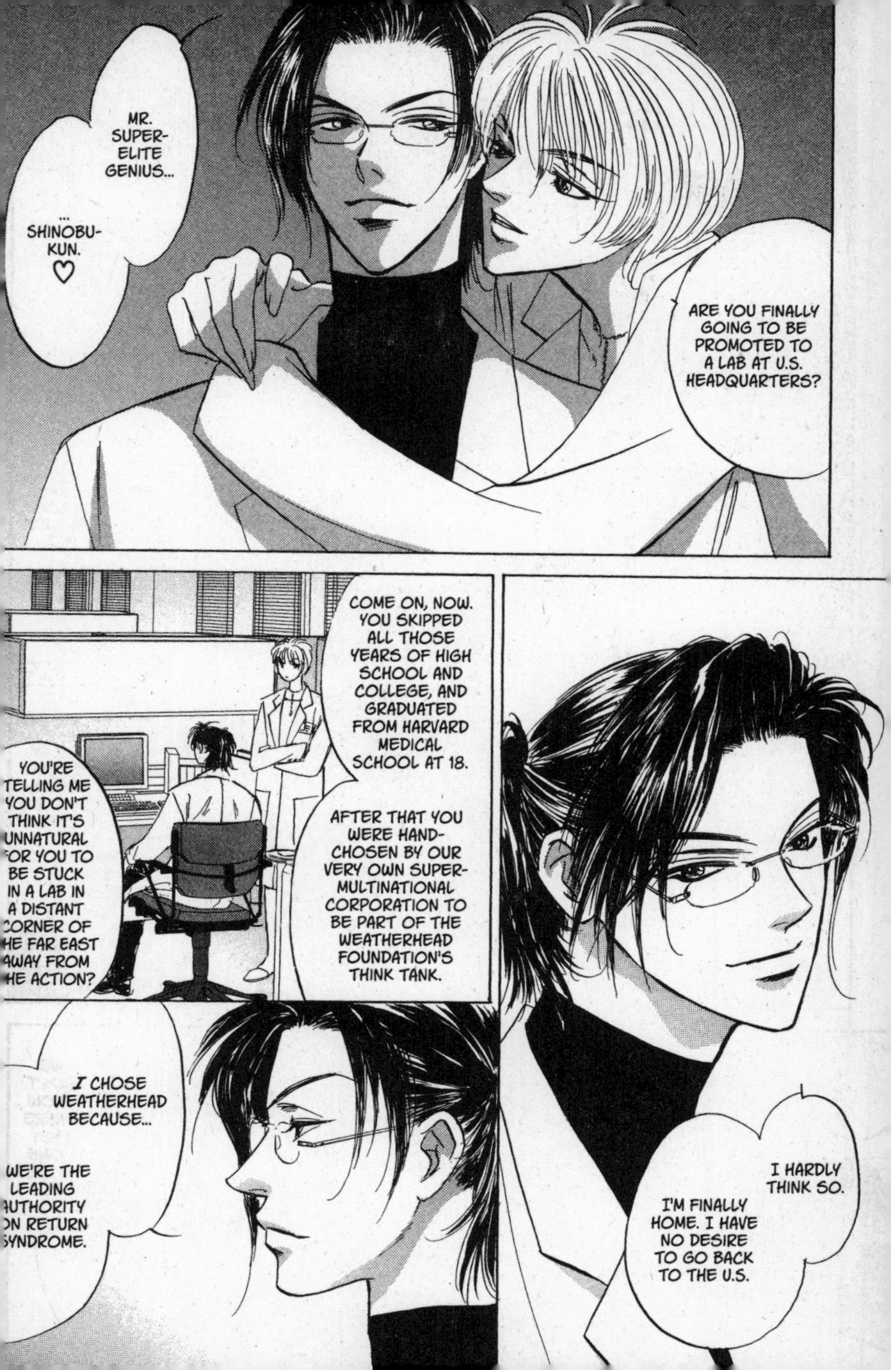
MR. SUPER-ELITE GENIUS...
...SHINOBU-KUN. ♡
ARE YOU FINALLY GOING TO BE PROMOTED TO A LAB AT U.S. HEADQUARTERS?
I HARDLY THINK SO.
I'M FINALLY HOME. I HAVE NO DESIRE TO GO BACK TO THE U.S.
COME ON, NOW. YOU SKIPPED ALL THOSE YEARS OF HIGH SCHOOL AND COLLEGE, AND GRADUATED FROM HARVARD MEDICAL SCHOOL AT 18.
AFTER THAT YOU WERE HAND-CHOSEN BY OUR VERY OWN SUPER-MULTINATIONAL CORPORATION TO BE PART OF THE WEATHERHEAD FOUNDATION'S THINK TANK.
YOU'RE TELLING ME YOU DON'T THINK IT'S UNNATURAL FOR YOU TO BE STUCK IN A LAB IN A DISTANT CORNER OF HE FAR EAST AWAY FROM HE ACTION?
I CHOSE WEATHERHEAD BECAUSE...
WE'RE THE LEADING AUTHORITY ON RETURN SYNDROME.

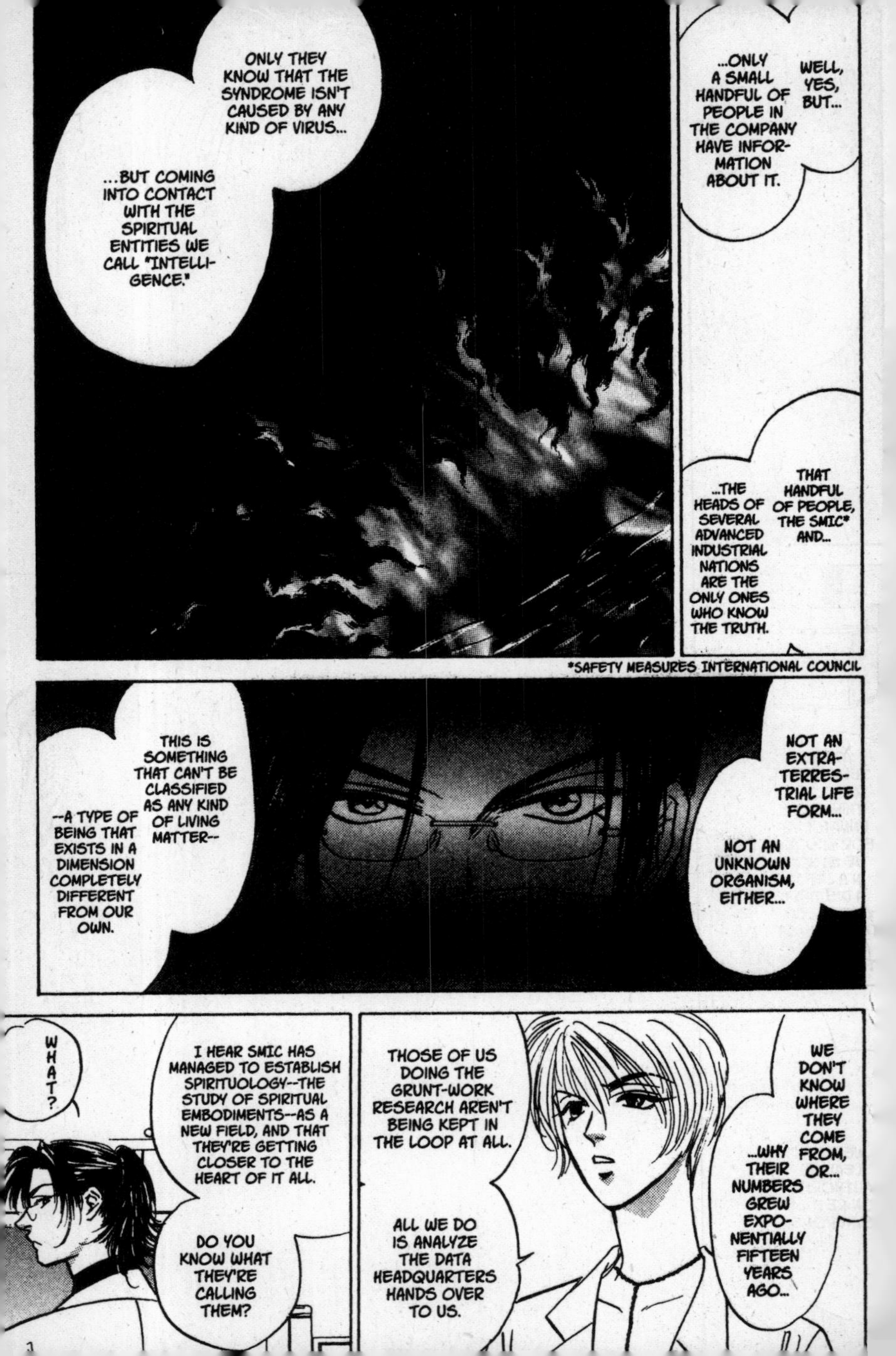
WELL, YES, BUT...
...ONLY A SMALL HANDFUL OF PEOPLE IN THE COMPANY HAVE INFORMATION ABOUT IT.
THAT HANDFUL OF PEOPLE, THE SMIC* AND...
...THE HEADS OF SEVERAL ADVANCED INDUSTRIAL NATIONS ARE THE ONLY ONES WHO KNOW THE TRUTH.
ONLY THEY KNOW THAT THE SYNDROME ISN'T CAUSED BY ANY KIND OF VIRUS...
...BUT COMING INTO CONTACT WITH THE SPIRITUAL ENTITIES WE CALL "INTELLIGENCE."
*SAFETY MEASURES INTERNATIONAL COUNCIL
NOT AN EXTRA-TERRESTRIAL LIFE FORM...
NOT AN UNKNOWN ORGANISM, EITHER...
THIS IS SOMETHING THAT CAN'T BE CLASSIFIED AS ANY KIND OF LIVING MATTER--
--A TYPE OF BEING THAT EXISTS IN A DIMENSION COMPLETELY DIFFERENT FROM OUR OWN.
WE DON'T KNOW WHERE THEY COME FROM, OR...
...WHY THEIR NUMBERS GREW EXPONENTIALLY FIFTEEN YEARS AGO...
THOSE OF US DOING THE GRUNT-WORK RESEARCH AREN'T BEING KEPT IN THE LOOP AT ALL.
ALL WE DO IS ANALYZE THE DATA HEADQUARTERS HANDS OVER TO US.
I HEAR SMIC HAS MANAGED TO ESTABLISH SPIRITUOLOGY--THE STUDY OF SPIRITUAL EMBODIMENTS--AS A NEW FIELD, AND THAT THEY'RE GETTING CLOSER TO THE HEART OF IT ALL.
DO YOU KNOW WHAT THEY'RE CALLING THEM?
WHAT?

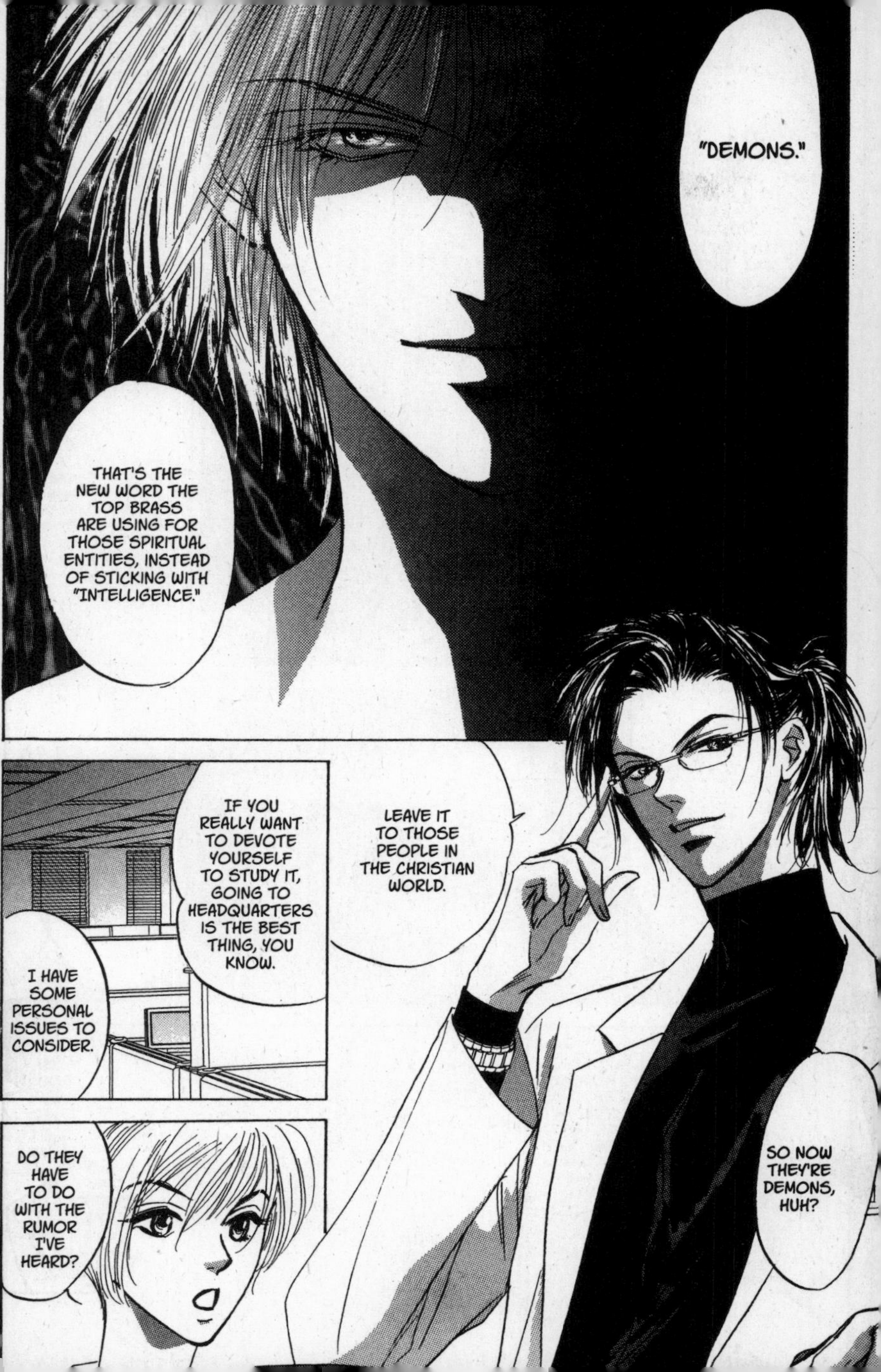
"DEMONS."
THAT'S THE NEW WORD THE TOP BRASS ARE USING FOR THOSE SPIRITUAL ENTITIES, INSTEAD OF STICKING WITH "INTELLIGENCE."
SO NOW THEY'RE DEMONS, HUH?
LEAVE IT TO THOSE PEOPLE IN THE CHRISTIAN WORLD.
IF YOU REALLY WANT TO DEVOTE YOURSELF TO STUDY IT, GOING TO HEADQUARTERS IS THE BEST THING, YOU KNOW.
I HAVE SOME PERSONAL ISSUES TO CONSIDER.
DO THEY HAVE TO DO WITH THE RUMOR I'VE HEARD?

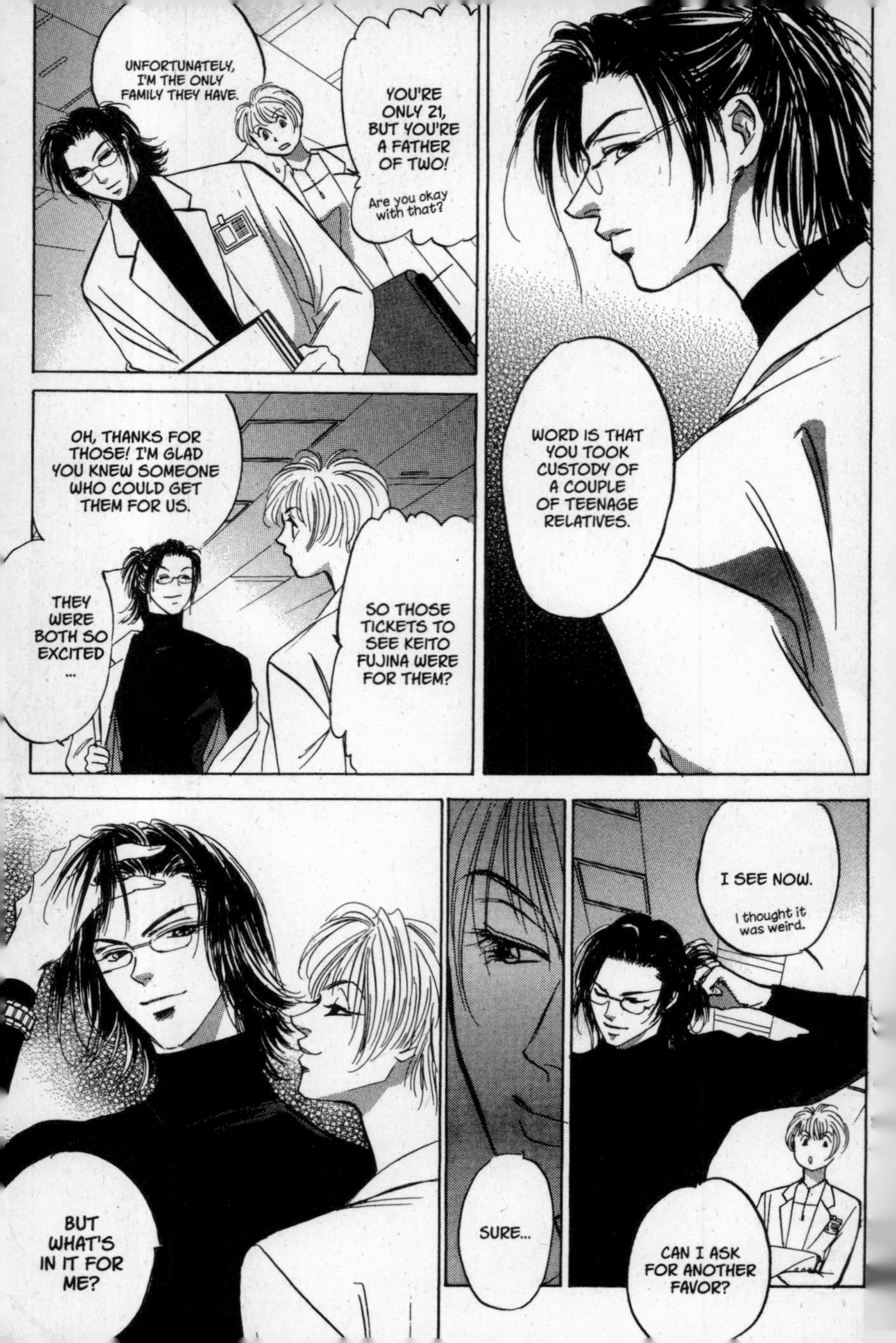
WORD IS THAT YOU TOOK CUSTODY OF A COUPLE OF TEENAGE RELATIVES.
YOU'RE ONLY 21, BUT YOU'RE A FATHER OF TWO!
Are you okay with that?
UNFORTUNATELY, I'M THE ONLY FAMILY THEY HAVE.
SO THOSE TICKETS TO SEE KEITO FUJINA WERE FOR THEM?
OH, THANKS FOR THOSE! I'M GLAD YOU KNEW SOMEONE WHO COULD GET THEM FOR US.
THEY WERE BOTH SO EXCITED ...
I SEE NOW.
I thought it was weird.
CAN I ASK FOR ANOTHER FAVOR?
SURE...
BUT WHAT'S IN IT FOR ME?

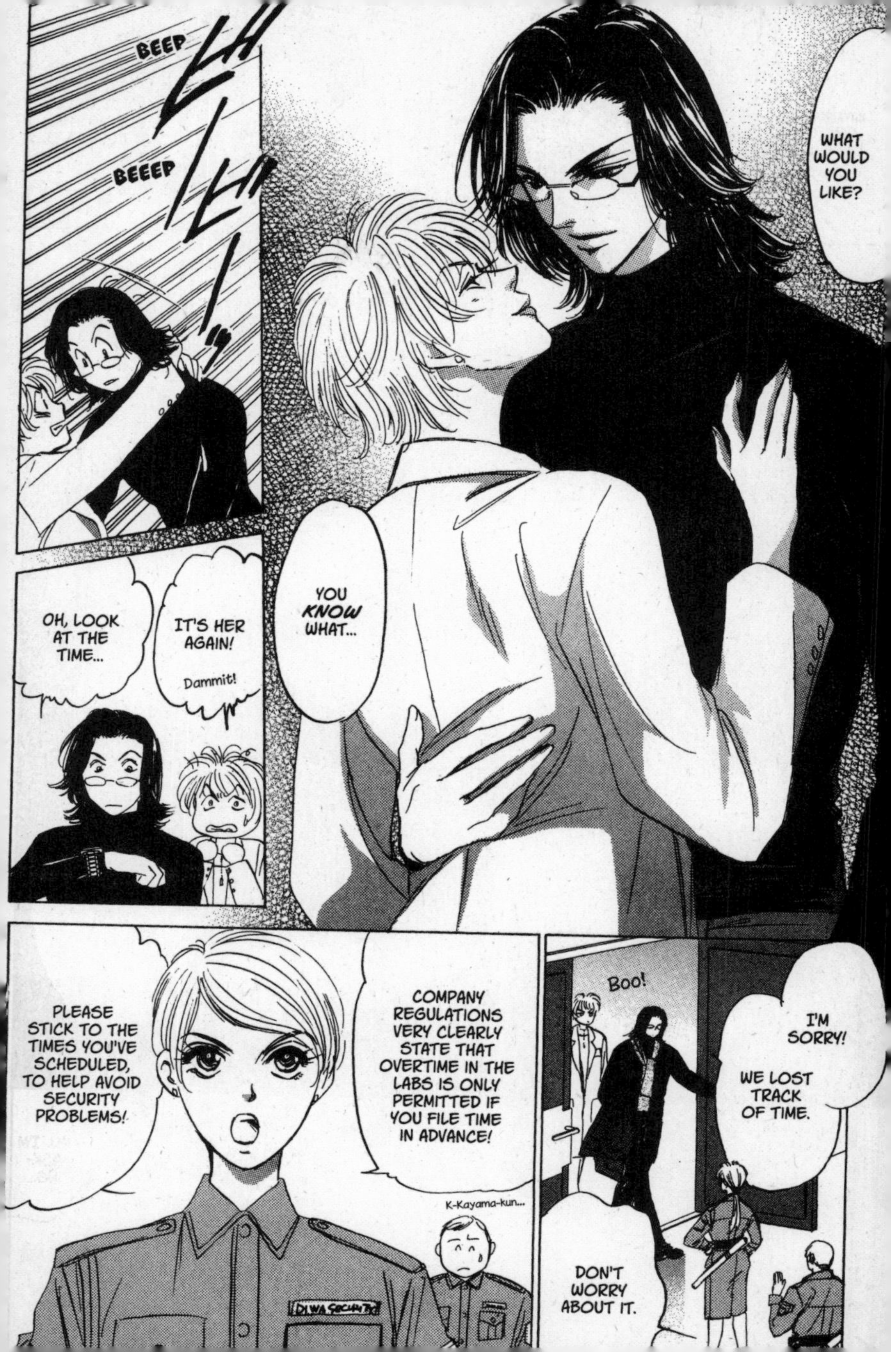
WHAT WOULD YOU LIKE?
YOU *KNOW* WHAT...
BEEP
BEEEP
IT'S HER AGAIN!
Dammit!
OH, LOOK AT THE TIME...
Boo!
I'M SORRY!
WE LOST TRACK OF TIME.
DON'T WORRY ABOUT IT.
COMPANY REGULATIONS VERY CLEARLY STATE THAT OVERTIME IN THE LABS IS ONLY PERMITTED IF YOU FILE TIME IN ADVANCE!
PLEASE STICK TO THE TIMES YOU'VE SCHEDULED, TO HELP AVOID SECURITY PROBLEMS!
K-Kayama-kun...

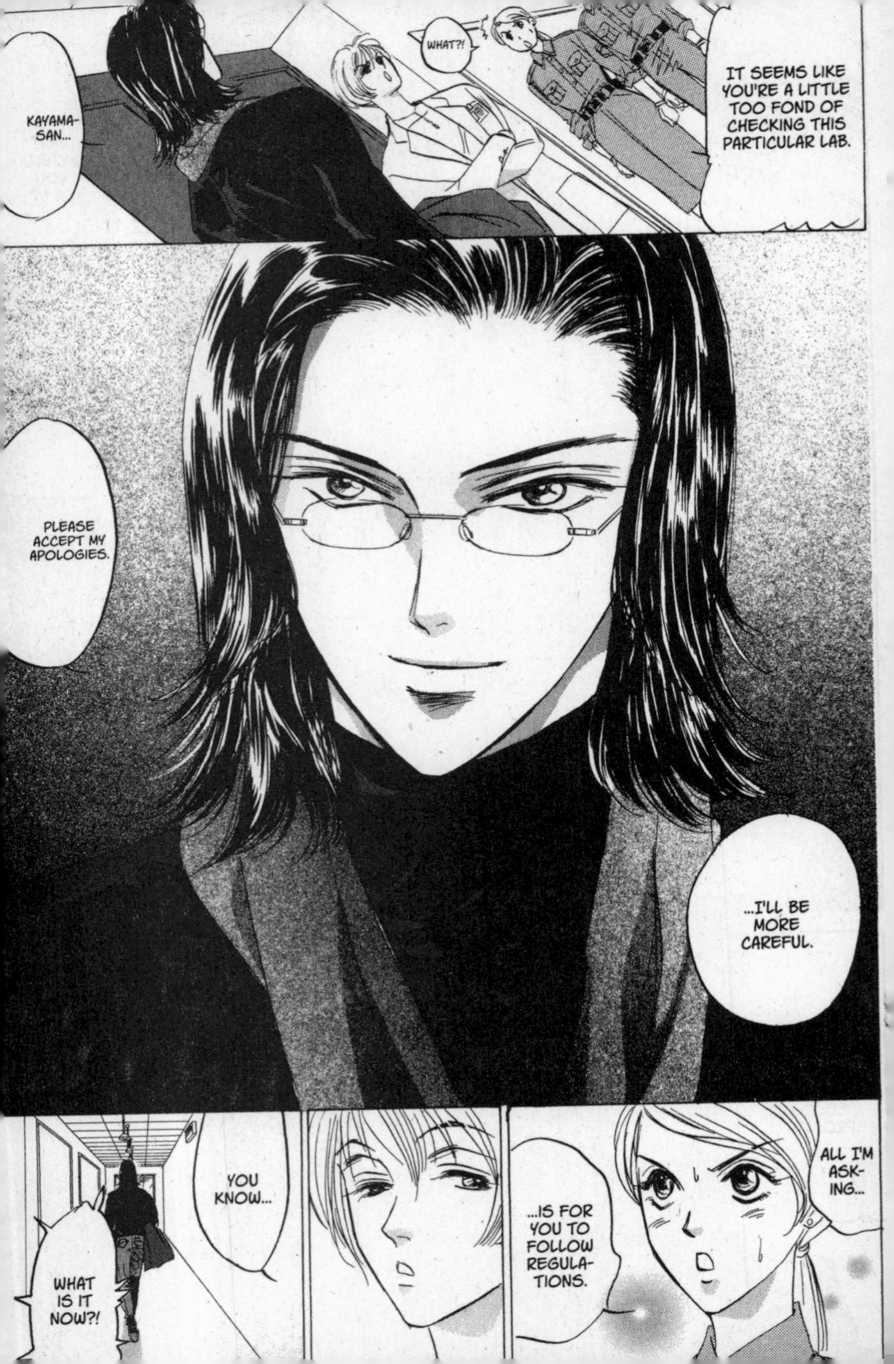

IT SEEMS LIKE YOU'RE A LITTLE TOO FOND OF CHECKING THIS PARTICULAR LAB.
WHAT?!
KAYAMA-SAN...
PLEASE ACCEPT MY APOLOGIES.
...I'LL BE MORE CAREFUL.
ALL I'M ASKING...
...IS FOR YOU TO FOLLOW REGULATIONS.
YOU KNOW...
WHAT IS IT NOW?!

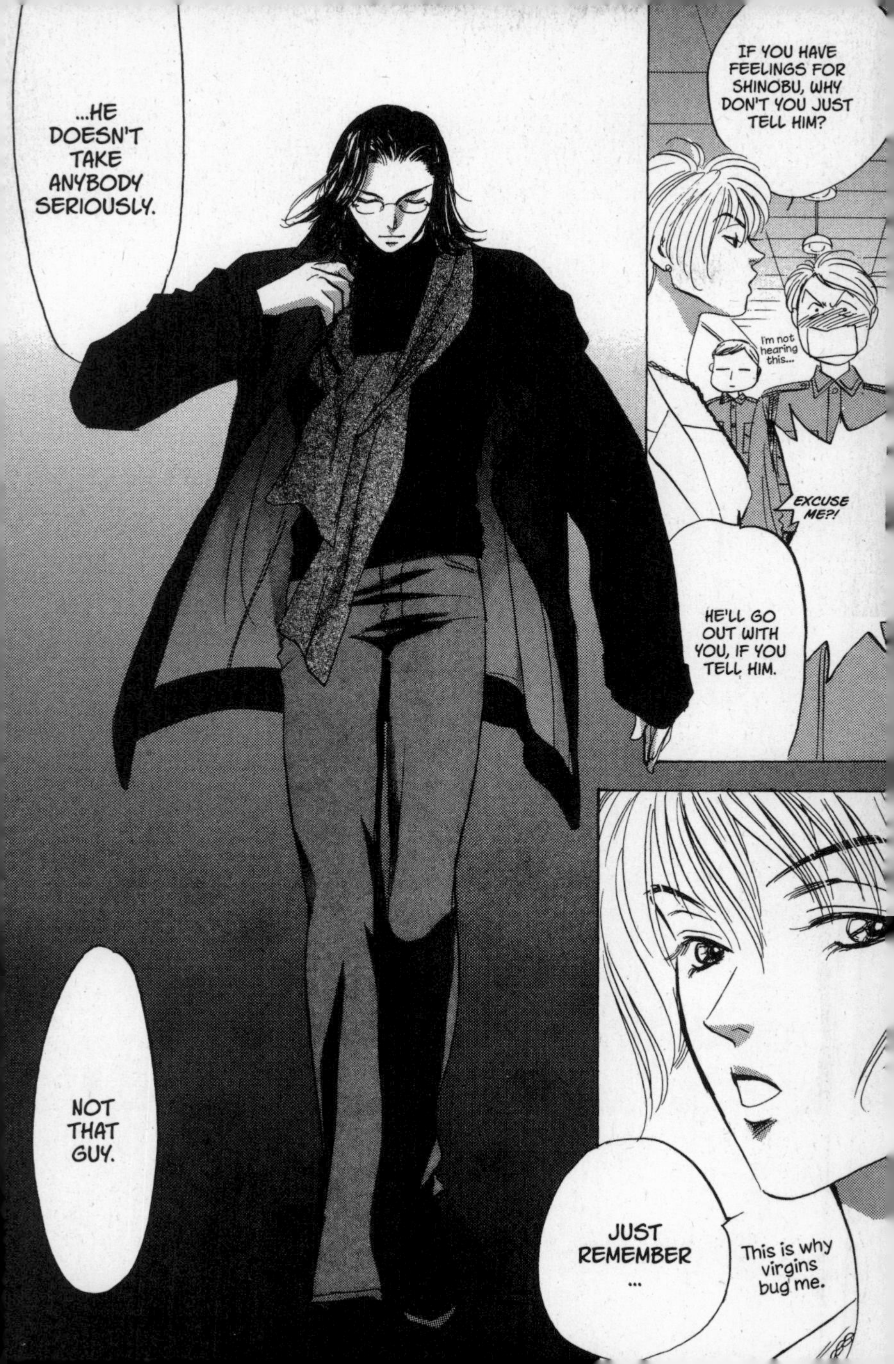
IF YOU HAVE FEELINGS FOR SHINOBU, WHY DON'T YOU JUST TELL HIM?
I'm not hearing this...
EXCUSE ME?!
HE'LL GO OUT WITH YOU, IF YOU TELL HIM.
This is why virgins bug me.
JUST REMEMBER ...
...HE DOESN'T TAKE ANYBODY SERIOUSLY.
NOT THAT GUY.

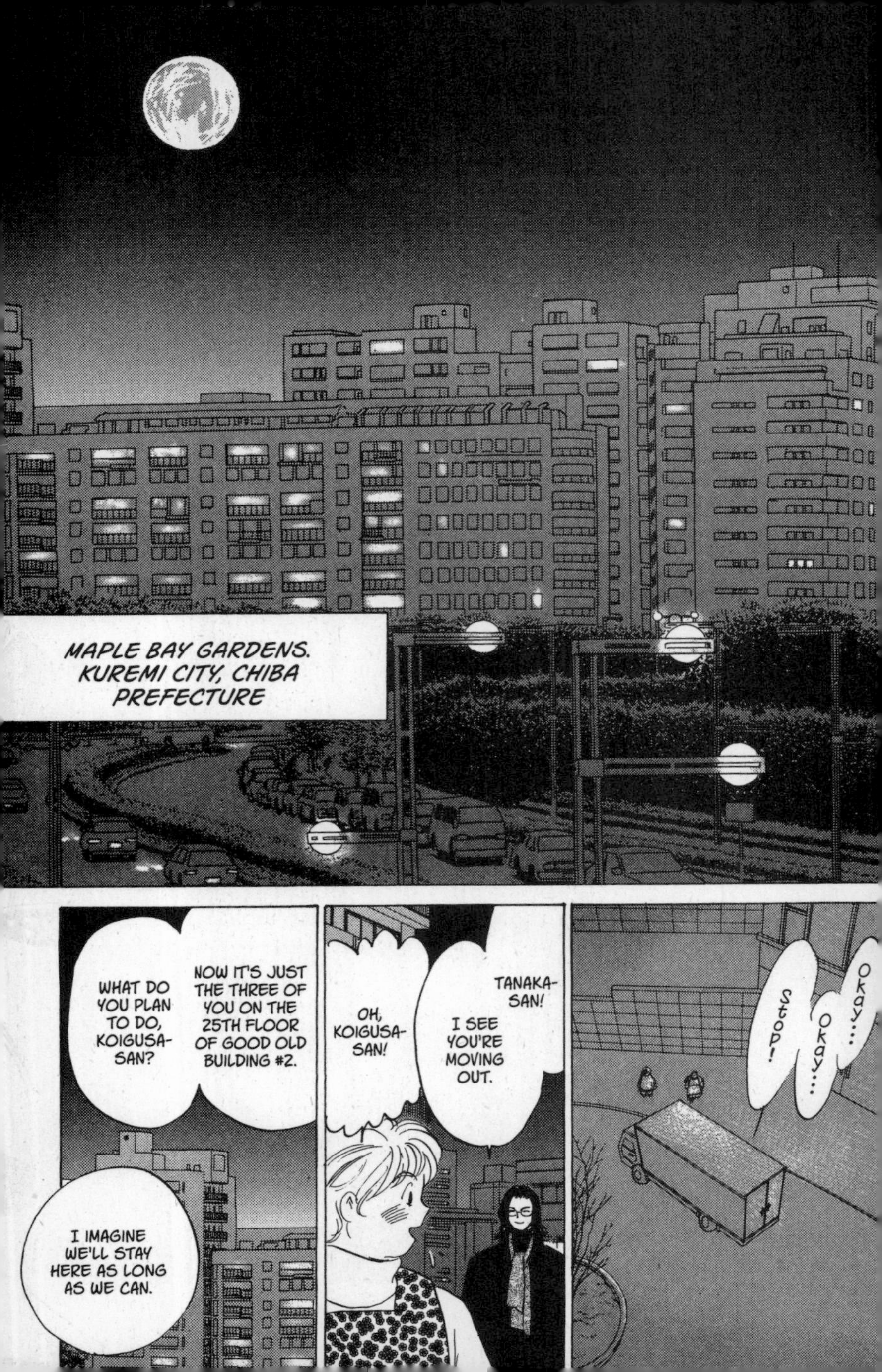
MAPLE BAY GARDENS. KUREMI CITY, CHIBA PREFECTURE
Okay...
Okay...
Stop!
TANAKA-SAN!
I SEE YOU'RE MOVING OUT.
OH, KOIGUSA-SAN!
NOW IT'S JUST THE THREE OF YOU ON THE 25TH FLOOR OF GOOD OLD BUILDING #2.
WHAT DO YOU PLAN TO DO, KOIGUSA-SAN?
I IMAGINE WE'LL STAY HERE AS LONG AS WE CAN.

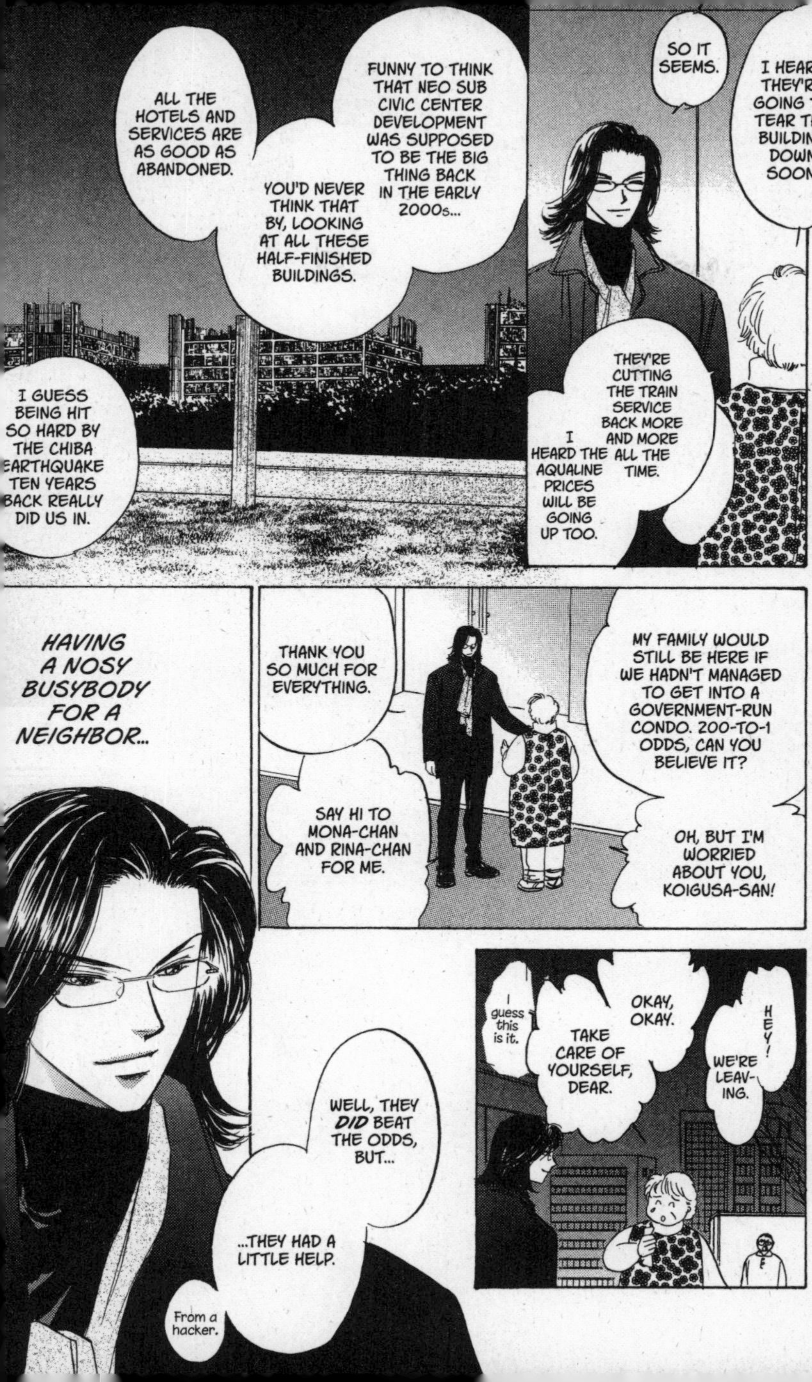
I HEARD THEY'RE GOING TO TEAR THE BUILDING DOWN SOON.
SO IT SEEMS.
THEY'RE CUTTING THE TRAIN SERVICE BACK MORE AND MORE ALL THE TIME.
I HEARD THE AQUALINE PRICES WILL BE GOING UP TOO.
FUNNY TO THINK THAT NEO SUB CIVIC CENTER DEVELOPMENT WAS SUPPOSED TO BE THE BIG THING BACK IN THE EARLY 2000s...
ALL THE HOTELS AND SERVICES ARE AS GOOD AS ABANDONED.
YOU'D NEVER THINK THAT BY, LOOKING AT ALL THESE HALF-FINISHED BUILDINGS.
I GUESS BEING HIT SO HARD BY THE CHIBA EARTHQUAKE TEN YEARS BACK REALLY DID US IN.
MY FAMILY WOULD STILL BE HERE IF WE HADN'T MANAGED TO GET INTO A GOVERNMENT-RUN CONDO. 200-TO-1 ODDS, CAN YOU BELIEVE IT?
THANK YOU SO MUCH FOR EVERYTHING.
OH, BUT I'M WORRIED ABOUT YOU, KOIGUSA-SAN!
SAY HI TO MONA-CHAN AND RINA-CHAN FOR ME.
HEY!
WE'RE LEAV-ING.
OKAY, OKAY.
TAKE CARE OF YOURSELF, DEAR.
I guess this is it.
HAVING A NOSY BUSYBODY FOR A NEIGHBOR...
WELL, THEY *DID* BEAT THE ODDS, BUT...
...THEY HAD A LITTLE HELP.
From a hacker.

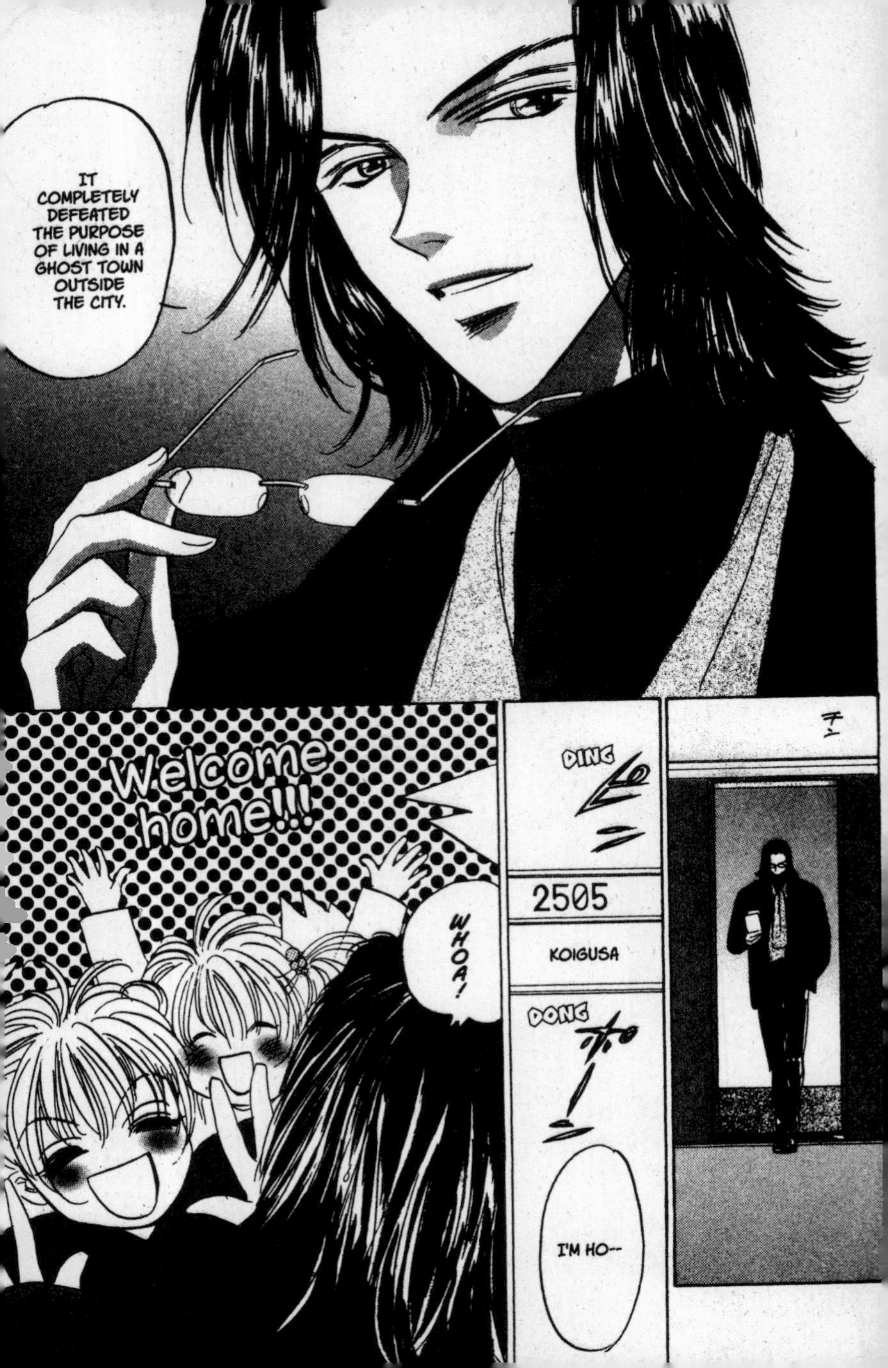
IT COMPLETELY DEFEATED THE PURPOSE OF LIVING IN A GHOST TOWN OUTSIDE THE CITY.
DING
2505
KOIGUSA
DONG
I'M HO--
Welcome home!!!
WHOA!

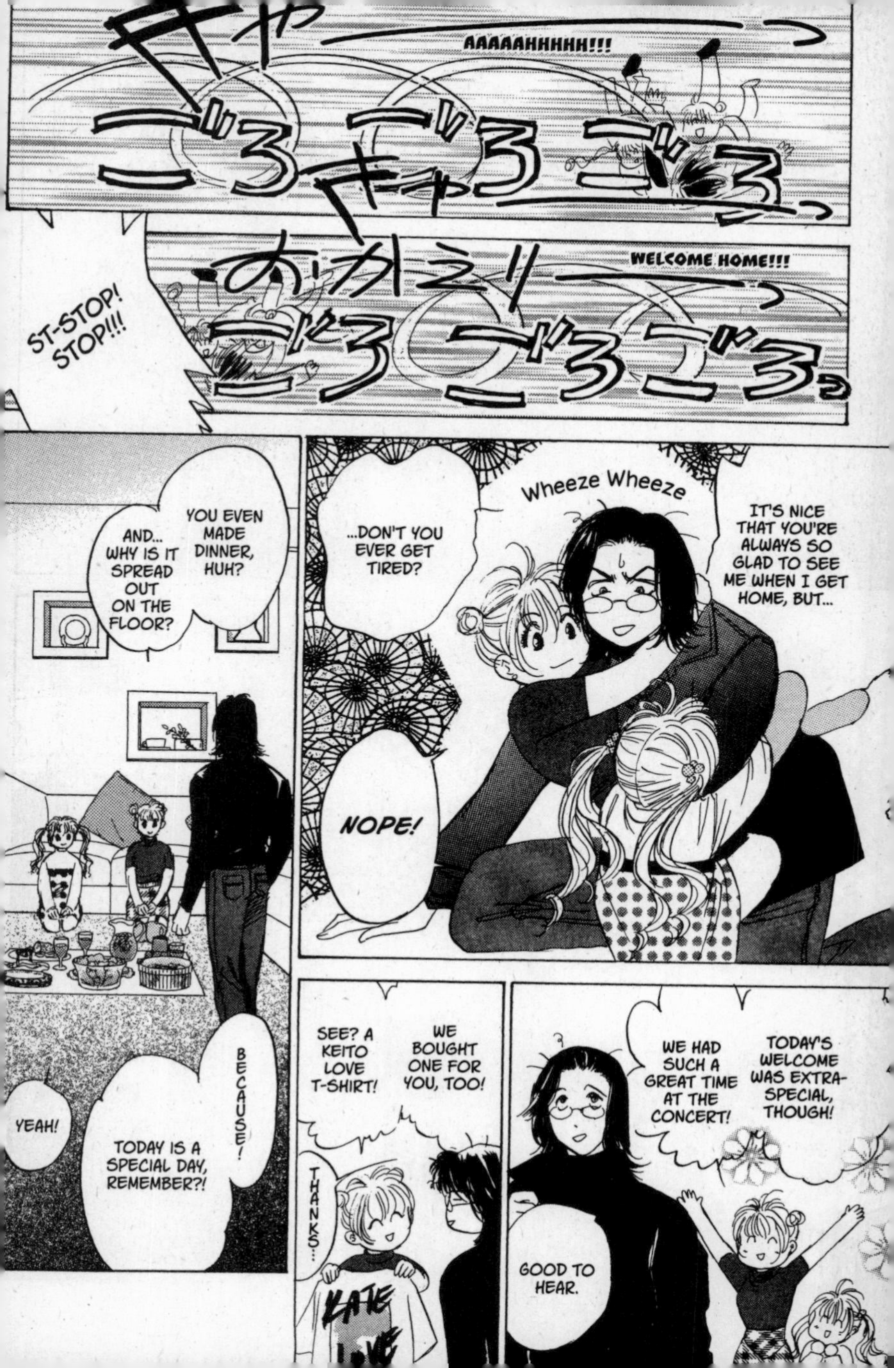
ギャーーっ
AAAAAHHHHH!!!
ごろ
ぎゃ
ごろ
ごろっ
おかえりーっ
WELCOME HOME!!!
ごろ
ごろ
ごろっ
ST-STOP! STOP!!!
Wheeze Wheeze
IT'S NICE THAT YOU'RE ALWAYS SO GLAD TO SEE ME WHEN I GET HOME, BUT...
...DON'T YOU EVER GET TIRED?
NOPE!
TODAY'S WELCOME WAS EXTRA-SPECIAL, THOUGH!
WE HAD SUCH A GREAT TIME AT THE CONCERT!
GOOD TO HEAR.
WE BOUGHT ONE FOR YOU, TOO!
SEE? A KEITO LOVE T-SHIRT!
THANKS...
YOU EVEN MADE DINNER, HUH?
AND... WHY IS IT SPREAD OUT ON THE FLOOR?
BECAUSE!
TODAY IS A SPECIAL DAY, REMEMBER?!
YEAH!

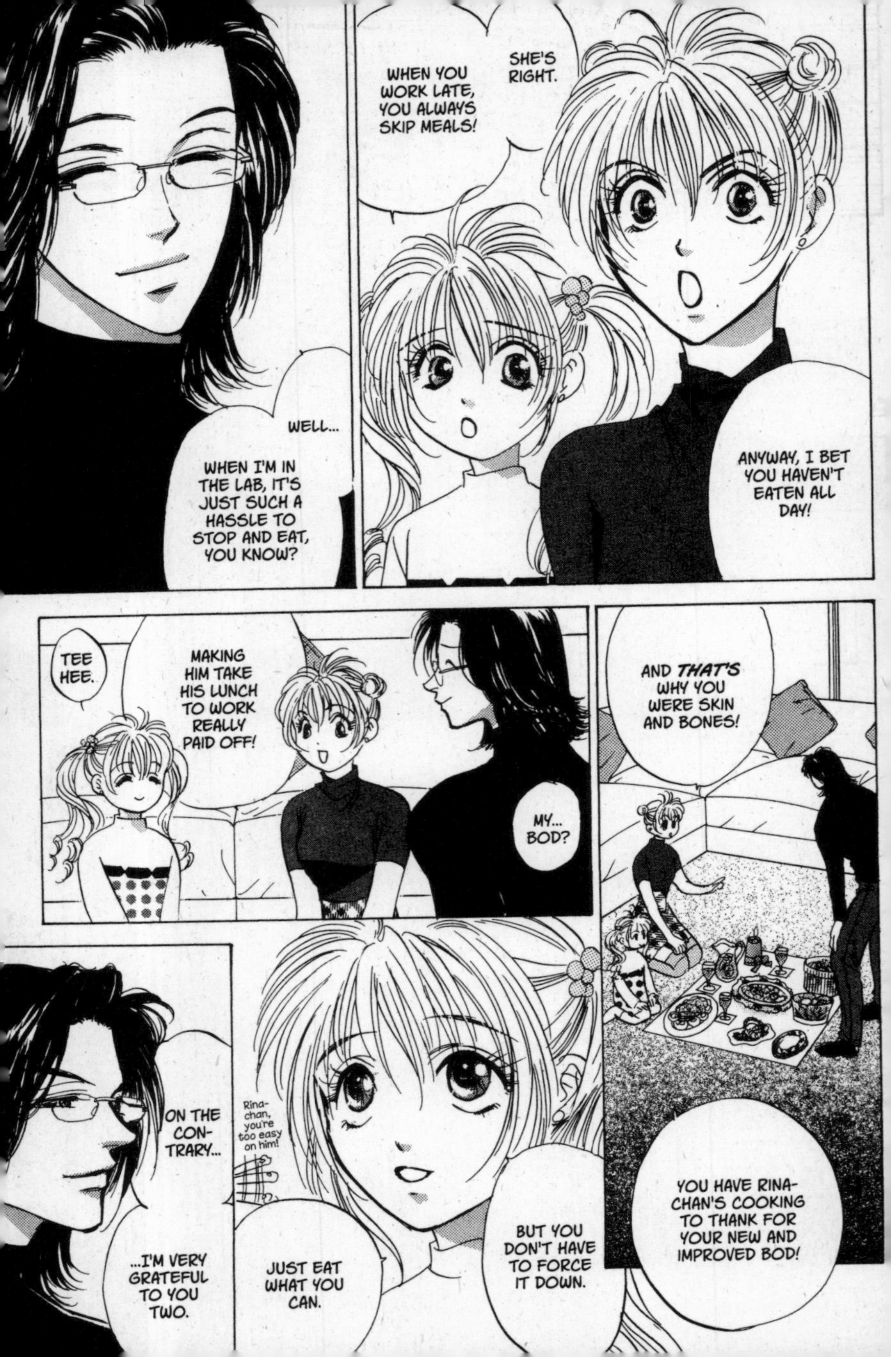
ANYWAY, I BET YOU HAVEN'T EATEN ALL DAY!
SHE'S RIGHT.
WHEN YOU WORK LATE, YOU ALWAYS SKIP MEALS!
WELL...
WHEN I'M IN THE LAB, IT'S JUST SUCH A HASSLE TO STOP AND EAT, YOU KNOW?
AND *THAT'S* WHY YOU WERE SKIN AND BONES!
YOU HAVE RINA-CHAN'S COOKING TO THANK FOR YOUR NEW AND IMPROVED BOD!
MY... BOD?
MAKING HIM TAKE HIS LUNCH TO WORK REALLY PAID OFF!
TEE HEE.
BUT YOU DON'T HAVE TO FORCE IT DOWN.
JUST EAT WHAT YOU CAN.
Rina-chan, you're too easy on him!
ON THE CON-TRARY...
...I'M VERY GRATEFUL TO YOU TWO.

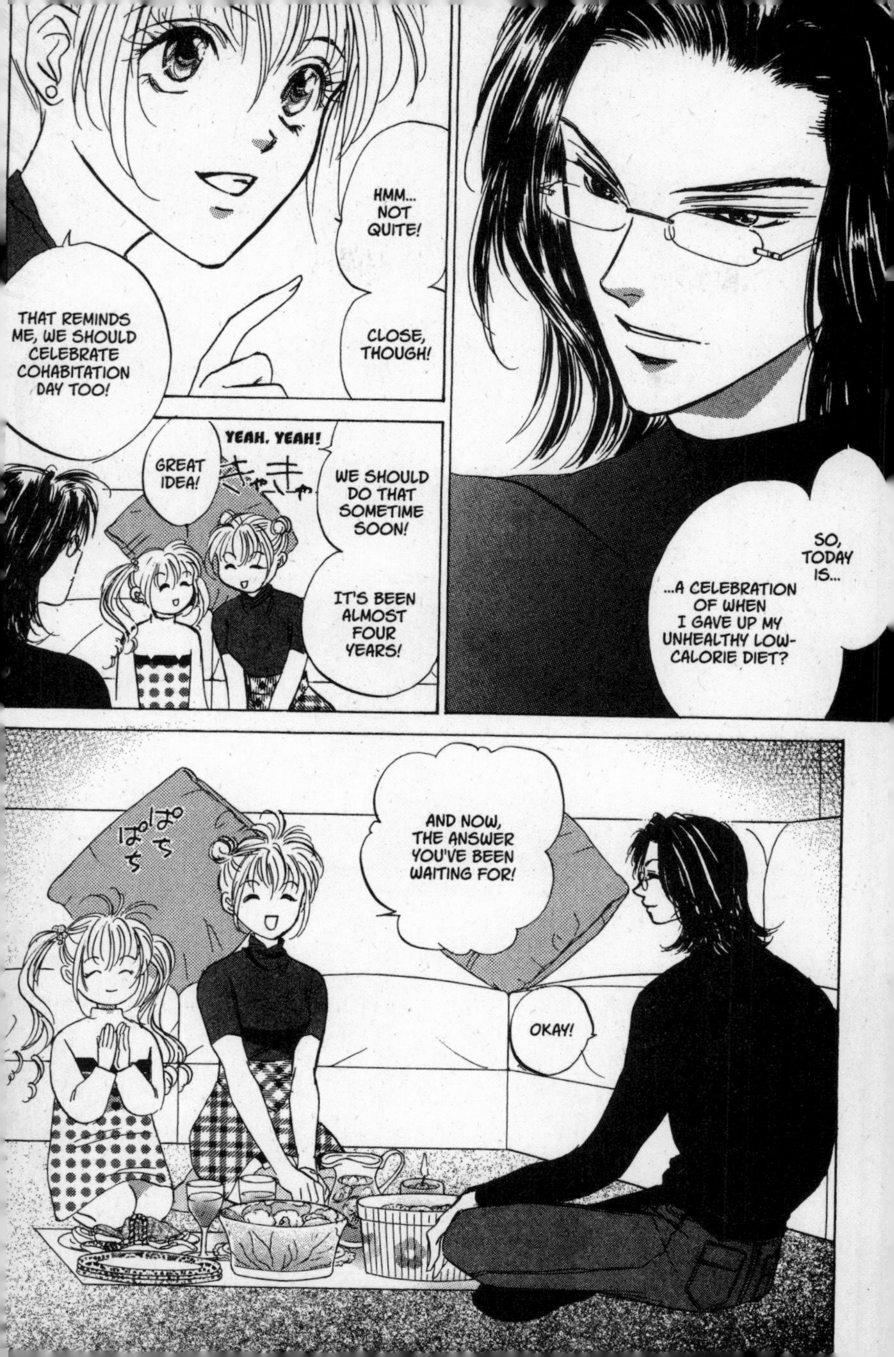
SO, TODAY IS...
...A CELEBRATION OF WHEN I GAVE UP MY UNHEALTHY LOW-CALORIE DIET?
HMM... NOT QUITE!
CLOSE, THOUGH!
THAT REMINDS ME, WE SHOULD CELEBRATE COHABITATION DAY TOO!
WE SHOULD DO THAT SOMETIME SOON!
IT'S BEEN ALMOST FOUR YEARS!
YEAH, YEAH!
GREAT IDEA!
AND NOW, THE ANSWER YOU'VE BEEN WAITING FOR!
OKAY!
ぱちぱち

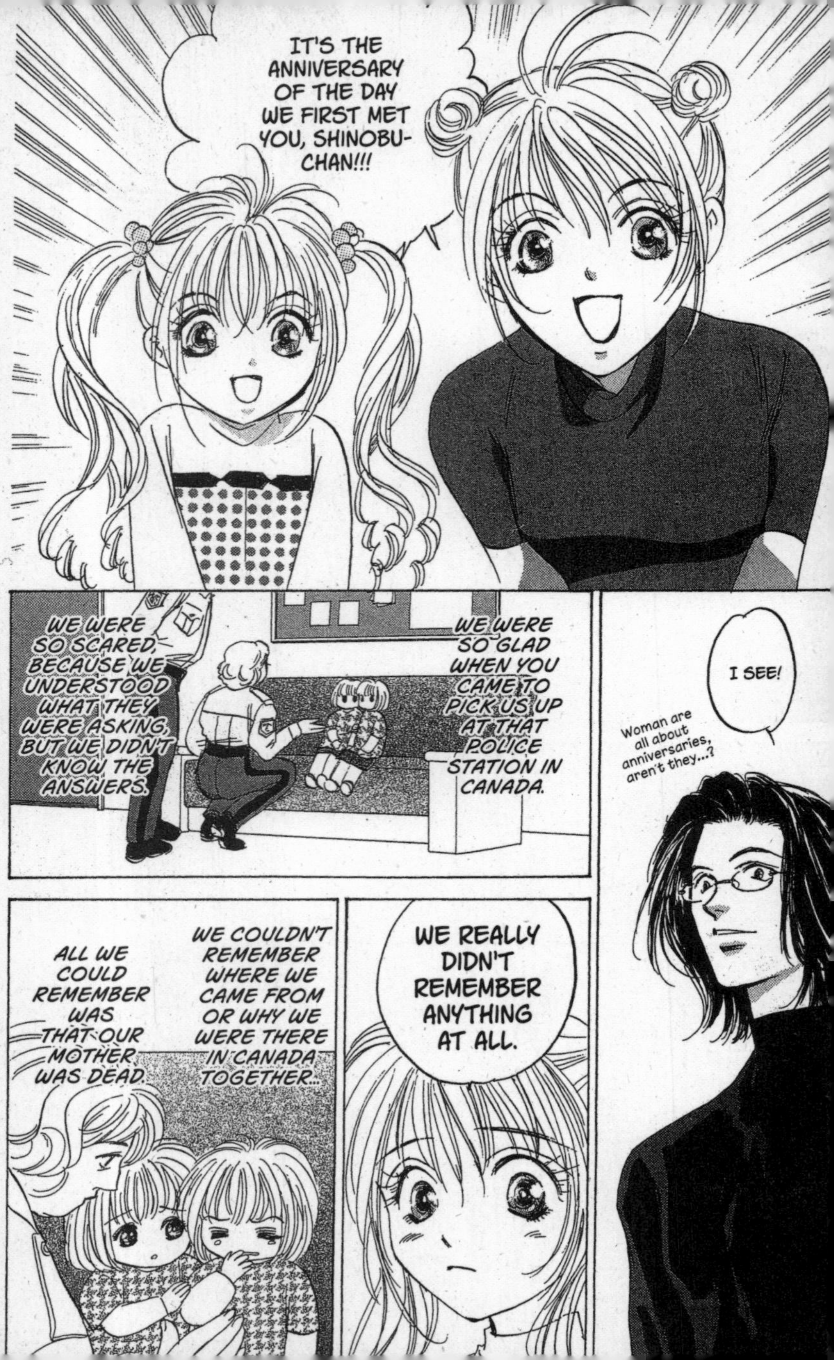
IT'S THE ANNIVERSARY OF THE DAY WE FIRST MET YOU, SHINOBU-CHAN!!!
I SEE!
Woman are all about anniversaries, aren't they...?
WE WERE SO GLAD WHEN YOU CAME TO PICK US UP AT THAT POLICE STATION IN CANADA.
WE WERE SO SCARED, BECAUSE WE UNDERSTOOD WHAT THEY WERE ASKING, BUT WE DIDN'T KNOW THE ANSWERS.
WE REALLY DIDN'T REMEMBER ANYTHING AT ALL.
WE COULDN'T REMEMBER WHERE WE CAME FROM OR WHY WE WERE THERE IN CANADA TOGETHER...
ALL WE COULD REMEMBER WAS THAT OUR MOTHER WAS DEAD.

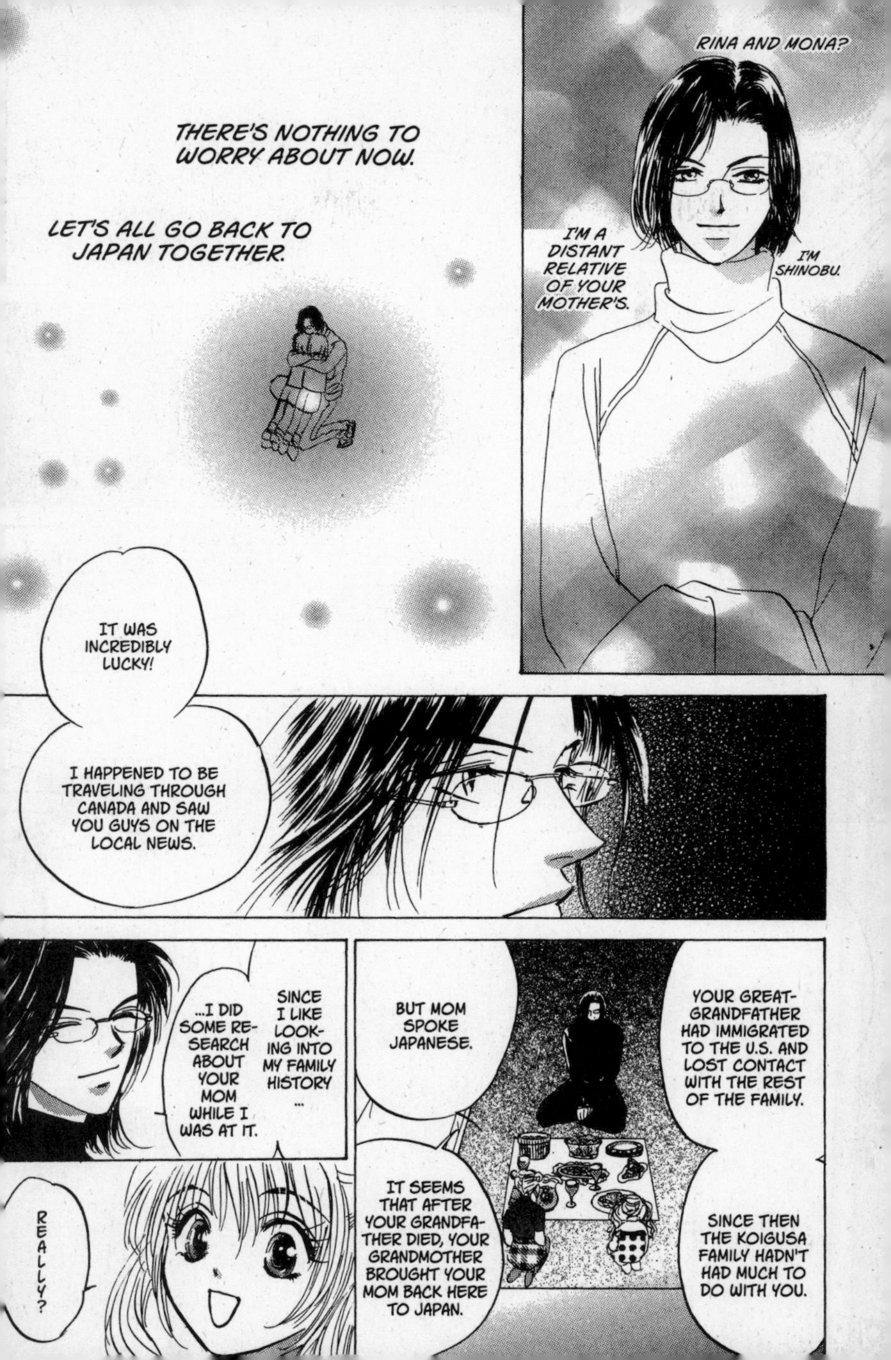
RINA AND MONA?
I'M SHINOBU.
I'M A DISTANT RELATIVE OF YOUR MOTHER'S.
THERE'S NOTHING TO WORRY ABOUT NOW.
LET'S ALL GO BACK TO JAPAN TOGETHER.
IT WAS INCREDIBLY LUCKY!
I HAPPENED TO BE TRAVELING THROUGH CANADA AND SAW YOU GUYS ON THE LOCAL NEWS.
YOUR GREAT-GRANDFATHER HAD IMMIGRATED TO THE U.S. AND LOST CONTACT WITH THE REST OF THE FAMILY.
SINCE THEN THE KOIGUSA FAMILY HADN'T HAD MUCH TO DO WITH YOU.
BUT MOM SPOKE JAPANESE.
IT SEEMS THAT AFTER YOUR GRANDFATHER DIED, YOUR GRANDMOTHER BROUGHT YOUR MOM BACK HERE TO JAPAN.
SINCE I LIKE LOOKING INTO MY FAMILY HISTORY...
...I DID SOME RESEARCH ABOUT YOUR MOM WHILE I WAS AT IT.
REALLY?

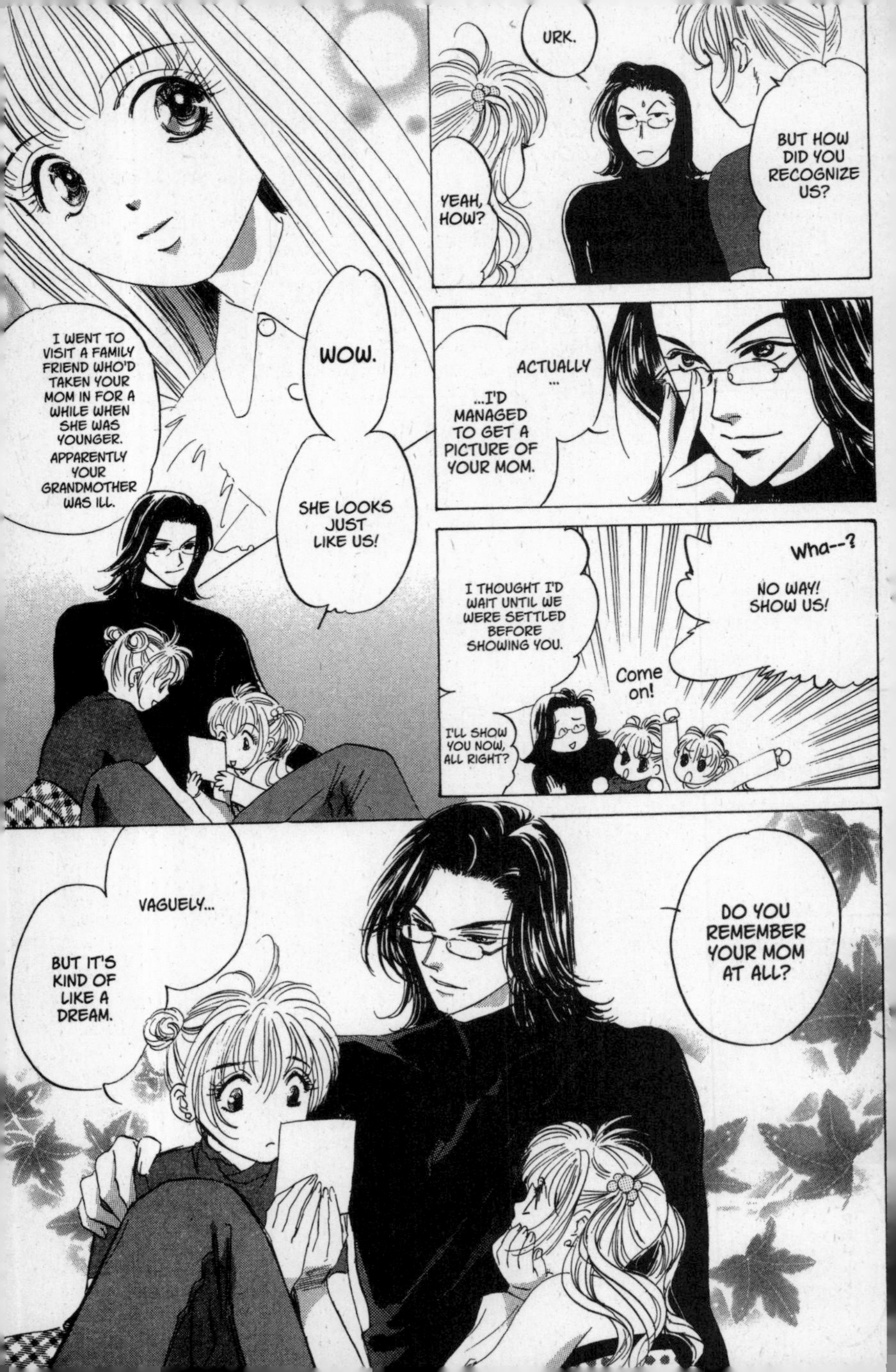
URK.
BUT HOW DID YOU RECOGNIZE US?
YEAH, HOW?
ACTUALLY ...
...I'D MANAGED TO GET A PICTURE OF YOUR MOM.
Wha--?
NO WAY! SHOW US!
I THOUGHT I'D WAIT UNTIL WE WERE SETTLED BEFORE SHOWING YOU.
Come on!
I'LL SHOW YOU NOW, ALL RIGHT?
WOW.
SHE LOOKS JUST LIKE US!
I WENT TO VISIT A FAMILY FRIEND WHO'D TAKEN YOUR MOM IN FOR A WHILE WHEN SHE WAS YOUNGER. APPARENTLY YOUR GRANDMOTHER WAS ILL.
DO YOU REMEMBER YOUR MOM AT ALL?
VAGUELY...
BUT IT'S KIND OF LIKE A DREAM.

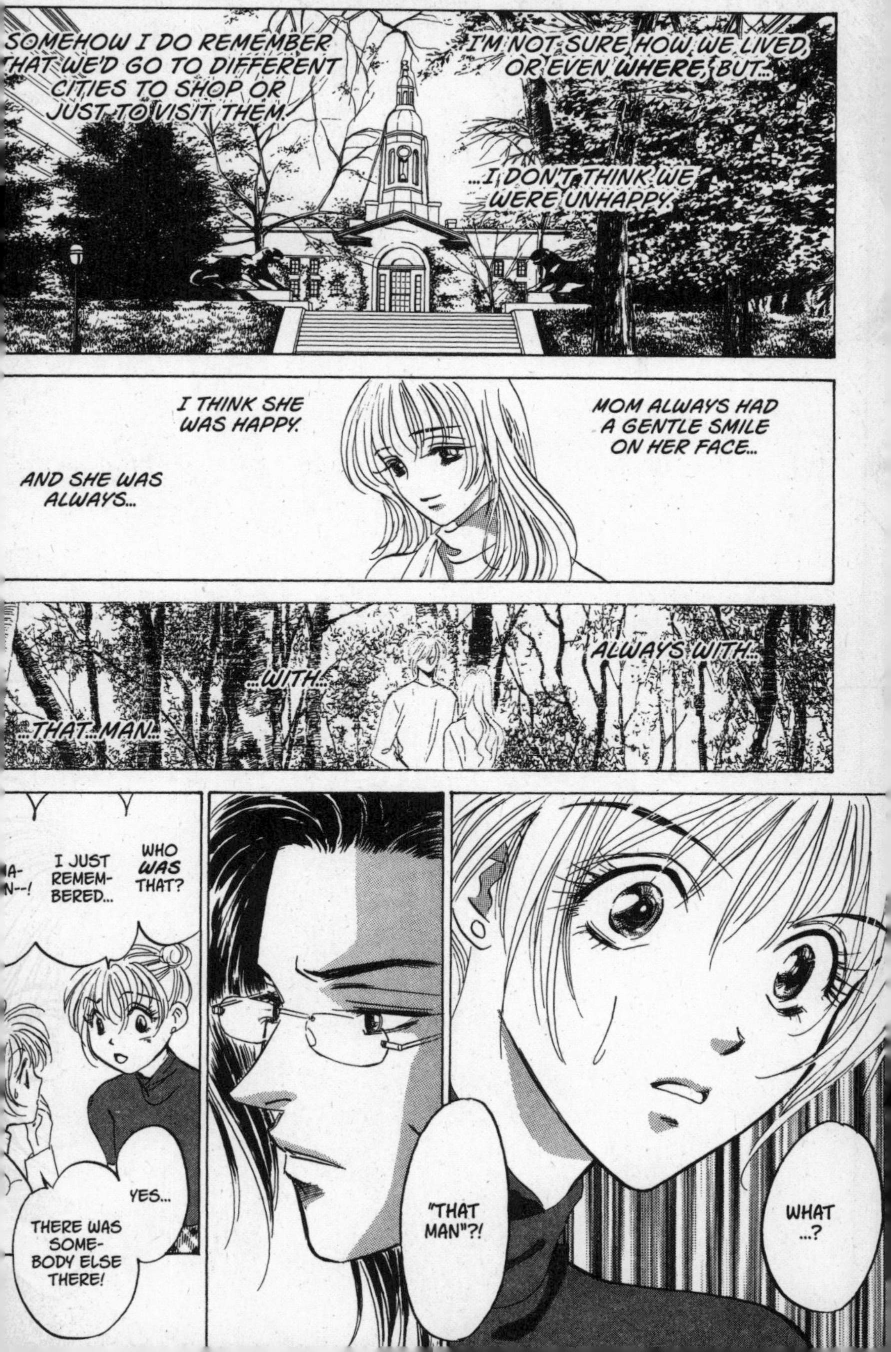
I'M NOT SURE HOW WE LIVED, OR EVEN WHERE, BUT...
...I DON'T THINK WE WERE UNHAPPY.
SOMEHOW I DO REMEMBER THAT WE'D GO TO DIFFERENT CITIES TO SHOP OR JUST TO VISIT THEM.
MOM ALWAYS HAD A GENTLE SMILE ON HER FACE...
I THINK SHE WAS HAPPY.
AND SHE WAS ALWAYS...
ALWAYS WITH...
...WITH...
...THAT...MAN...
WHAT ...?
"THAT MAN"?!
WHO WAS THAT?
I JUST REMEMBERED...
YES...
THERE WAS SOMEBODY ELSE THERE!

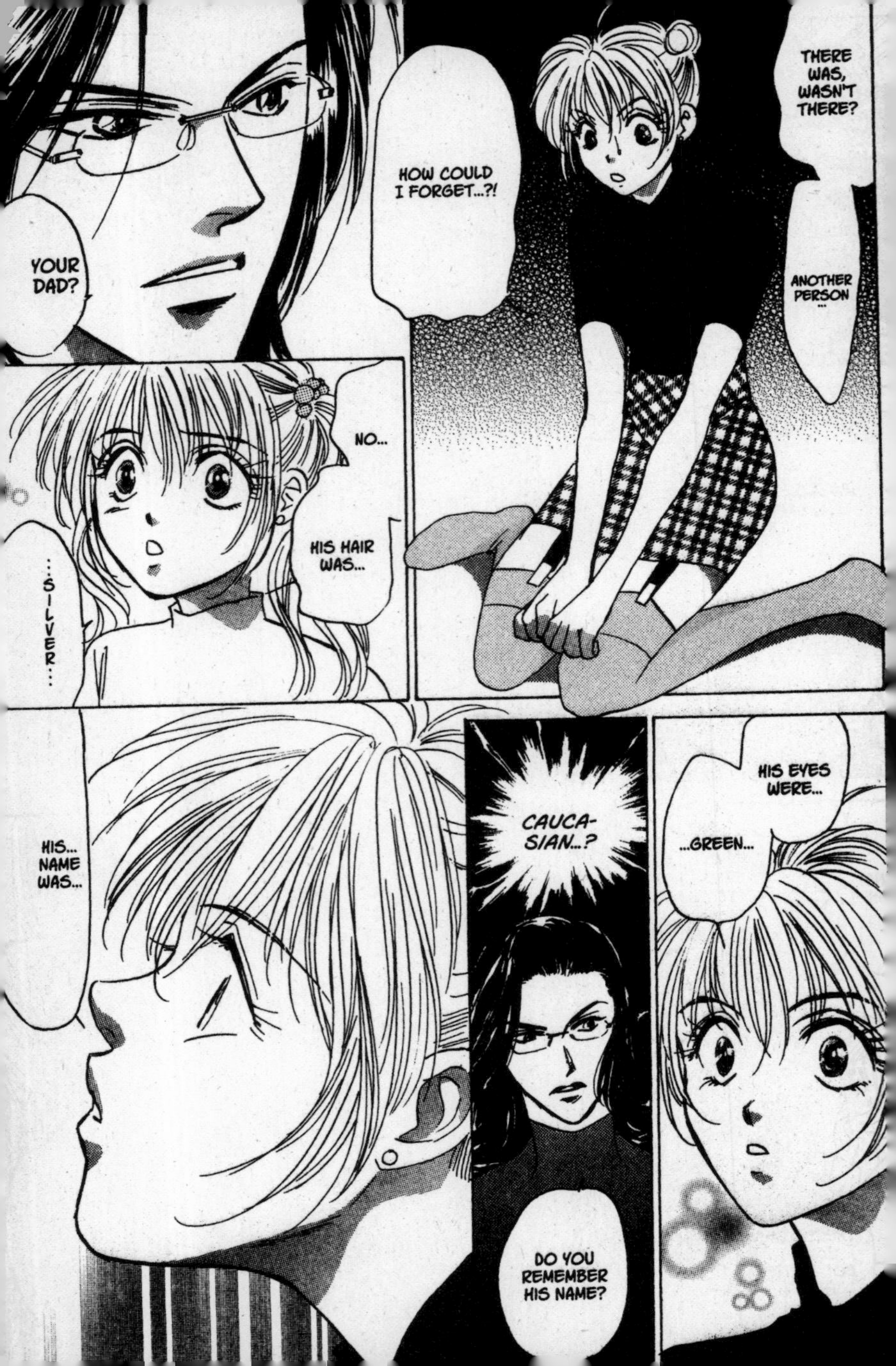
THERE WAS, WASN'T THERE?
ANOTHER PERSON...
HOW COULD I FORGET...?!
YOUR DAD?
NO...
HIS HAIR WAS...
...SILVER...
HIS EYES WERE...
...GREEN...
CAUCA-SIAN...?
DO YOU REMEMBER HIS NAME?
HIS... NAME WAS...

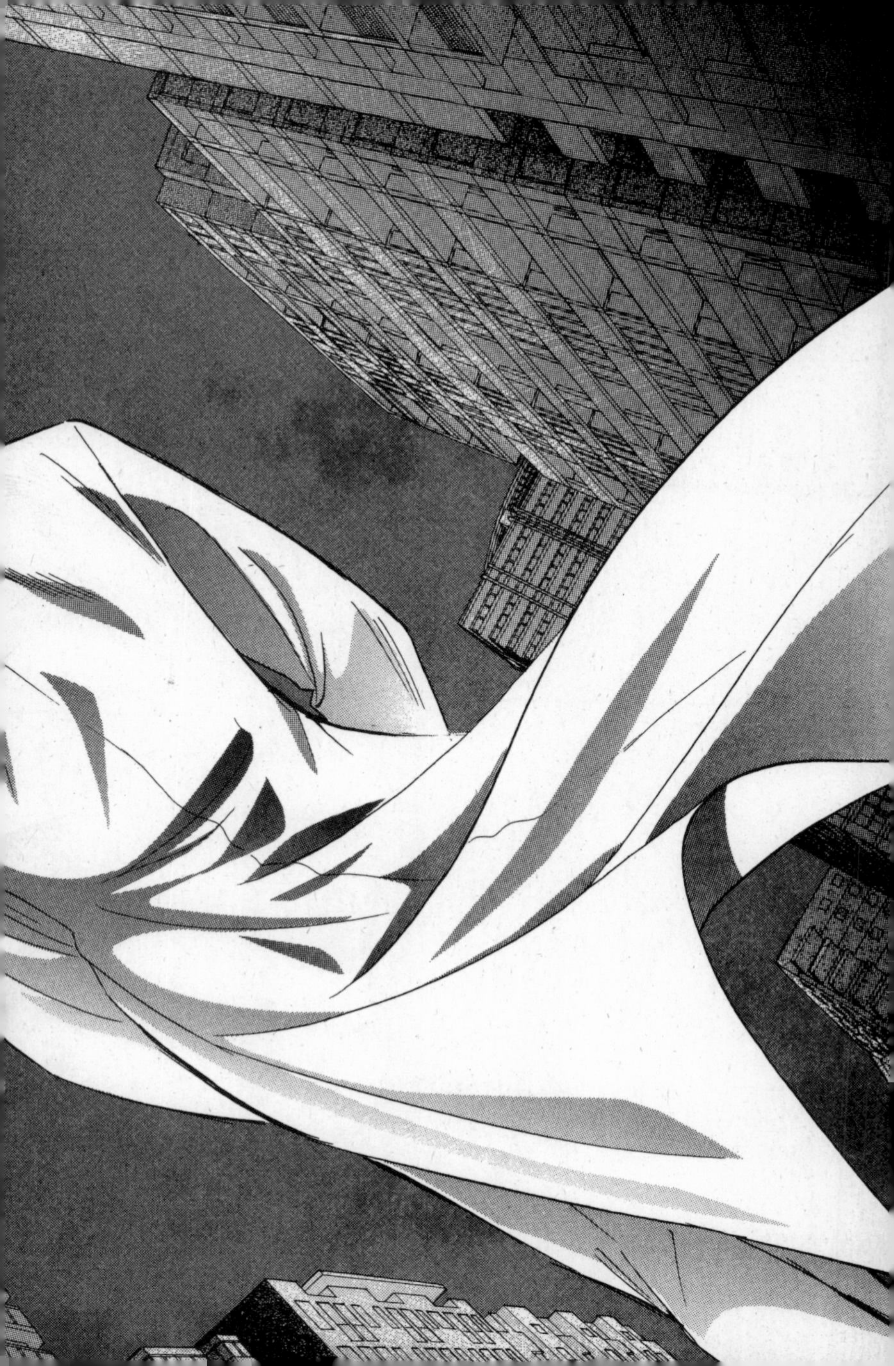

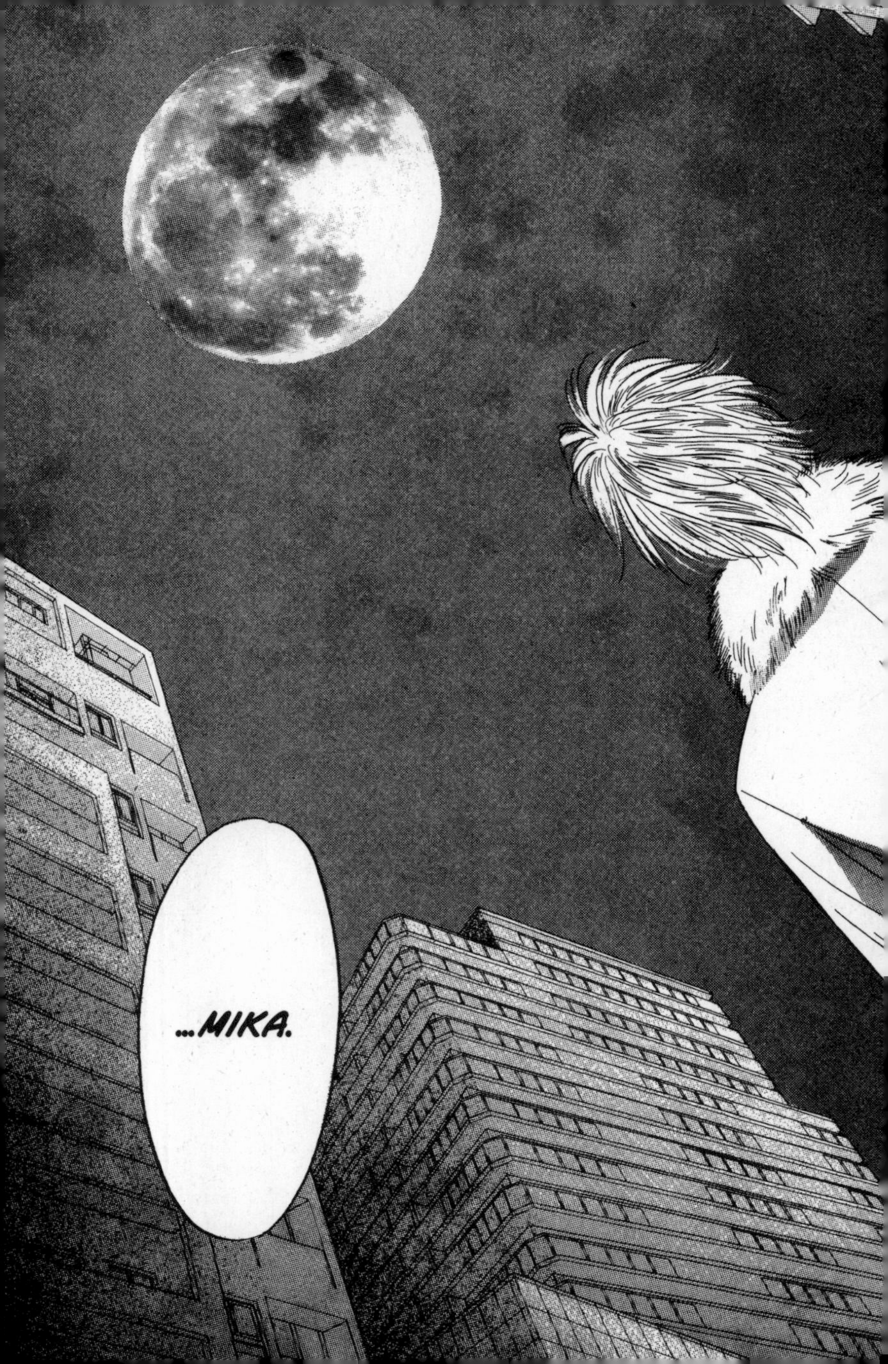
...MIKA.

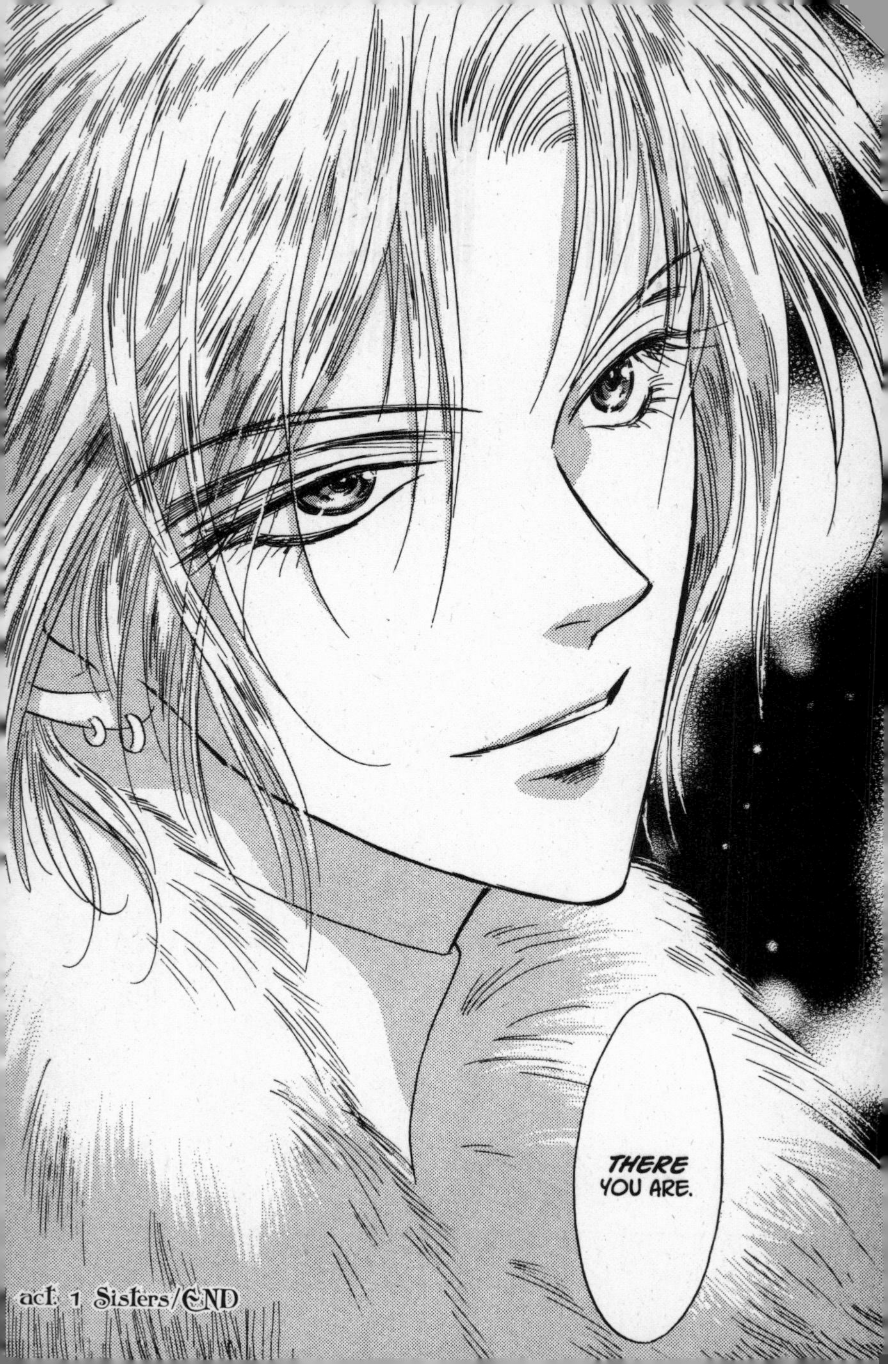
THERE YOU ARE.
act. 1 Sisters/END

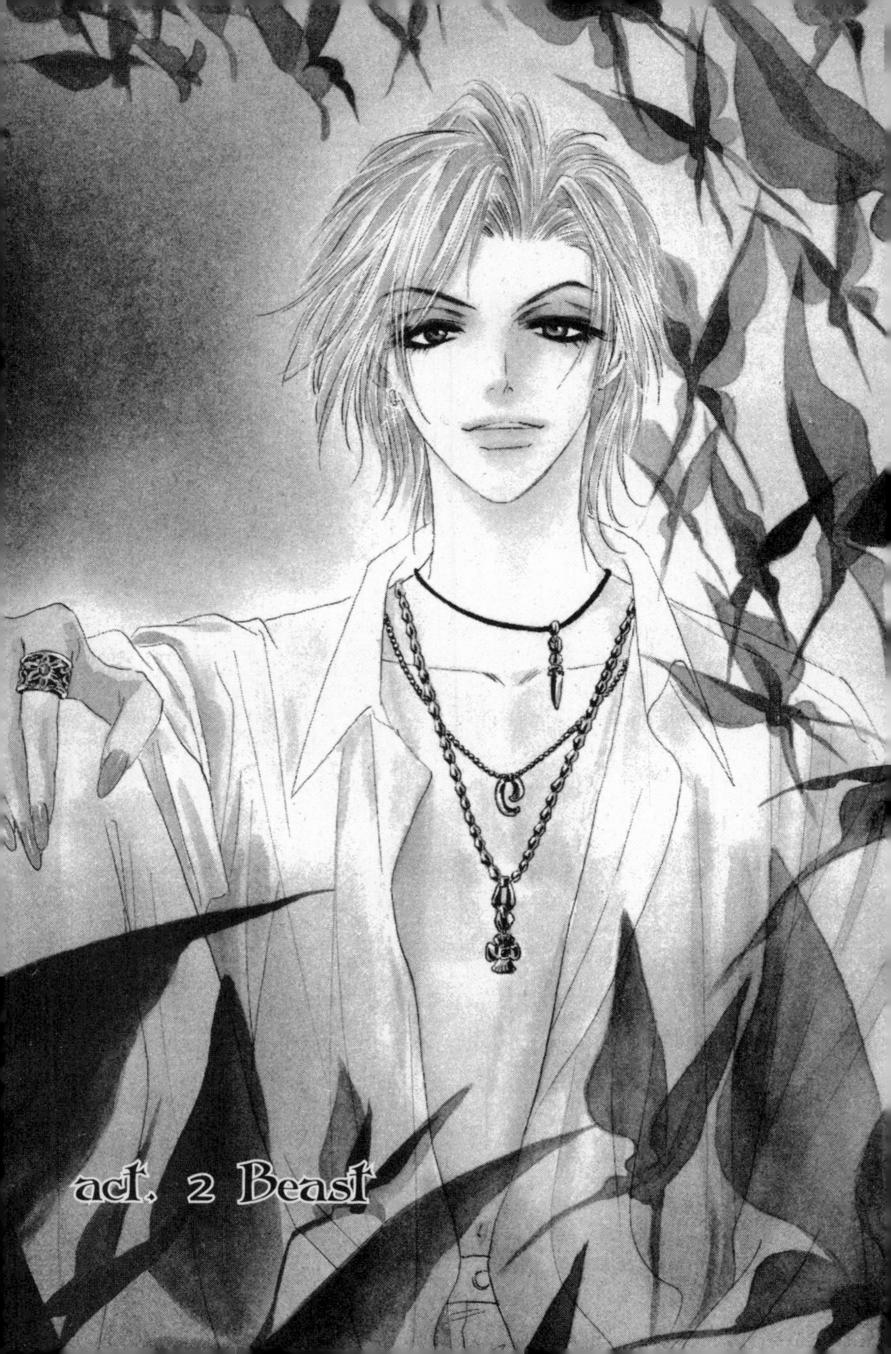
act. 2 Beast

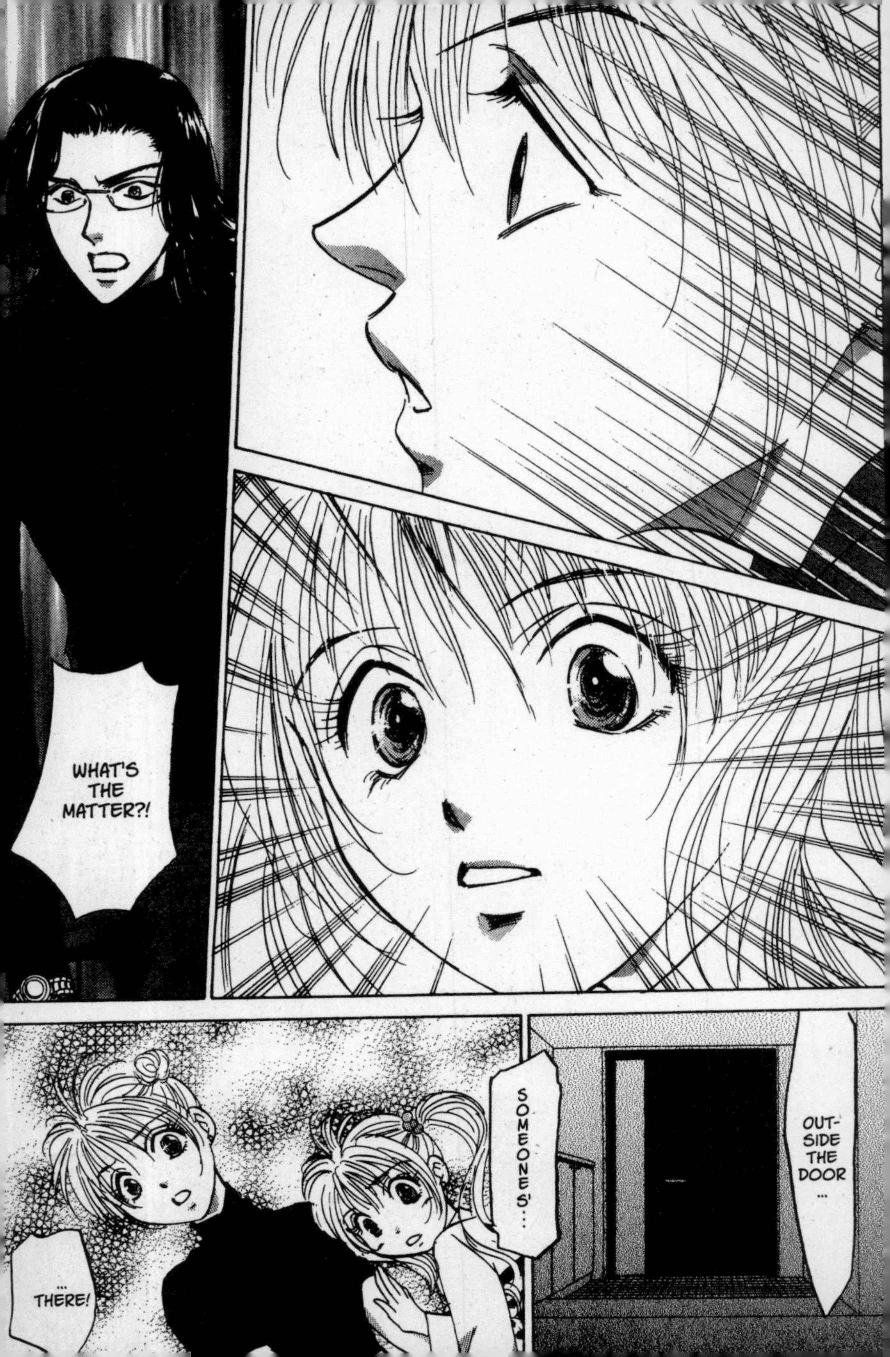
WHAT'S THE MATTER?!
OUT-SIDE THE DOOR ...
SOMEONE'S...
... THERE!

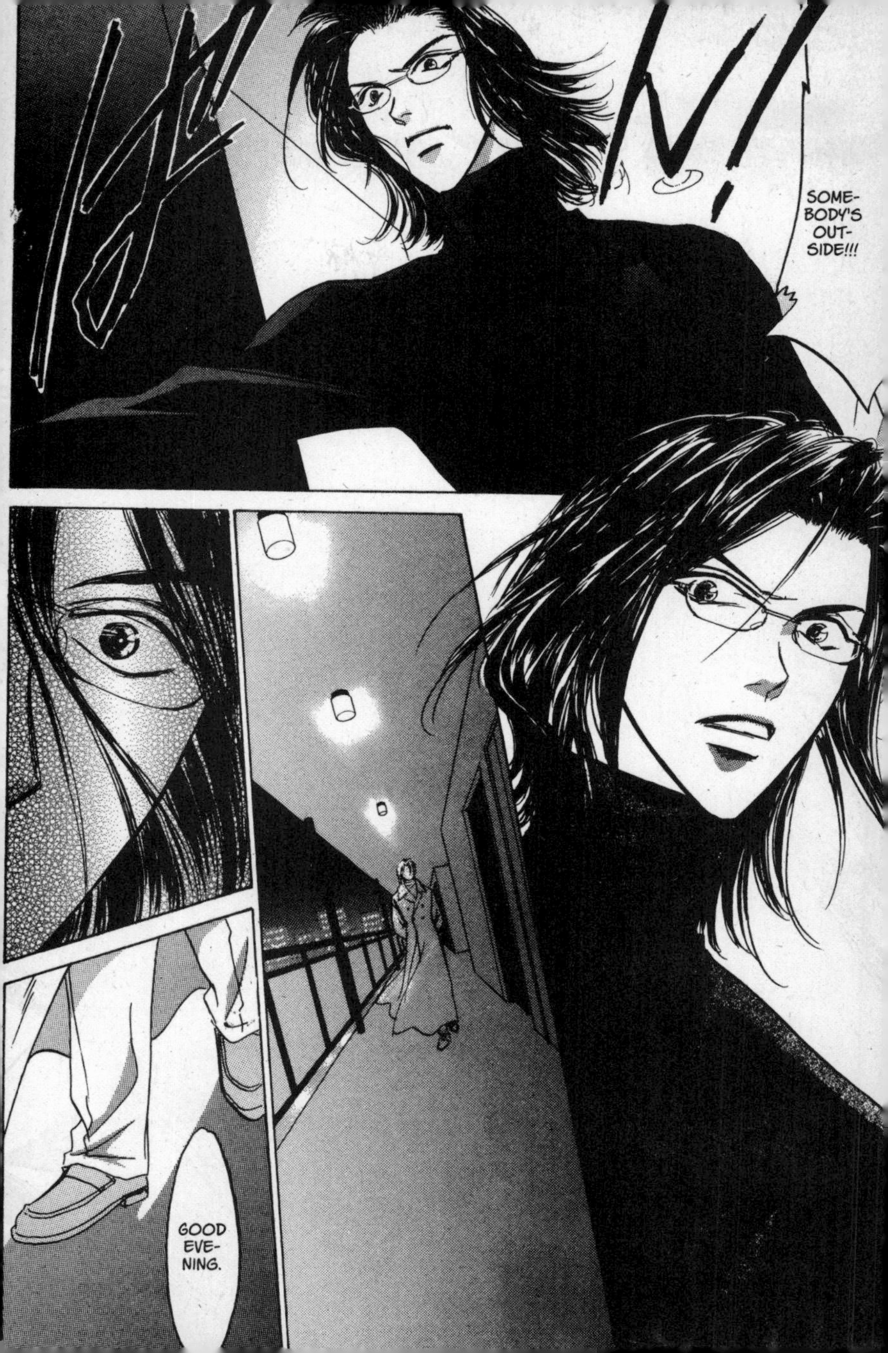
SOME-
BODY'S
OUT-
SIDE!!!
GOOD
EVE-
NING.

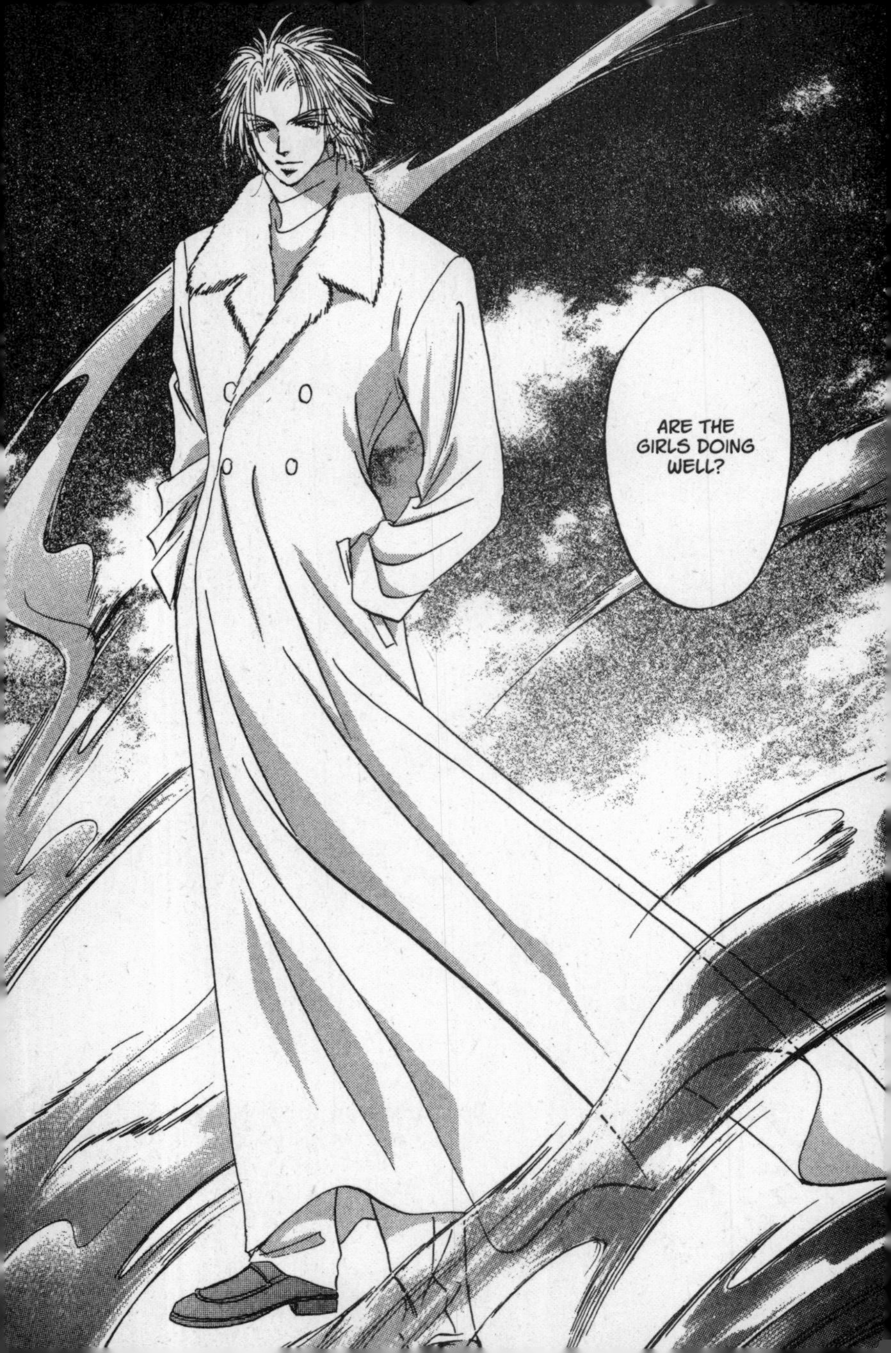
ARE THE GIRLS DOING WELL?

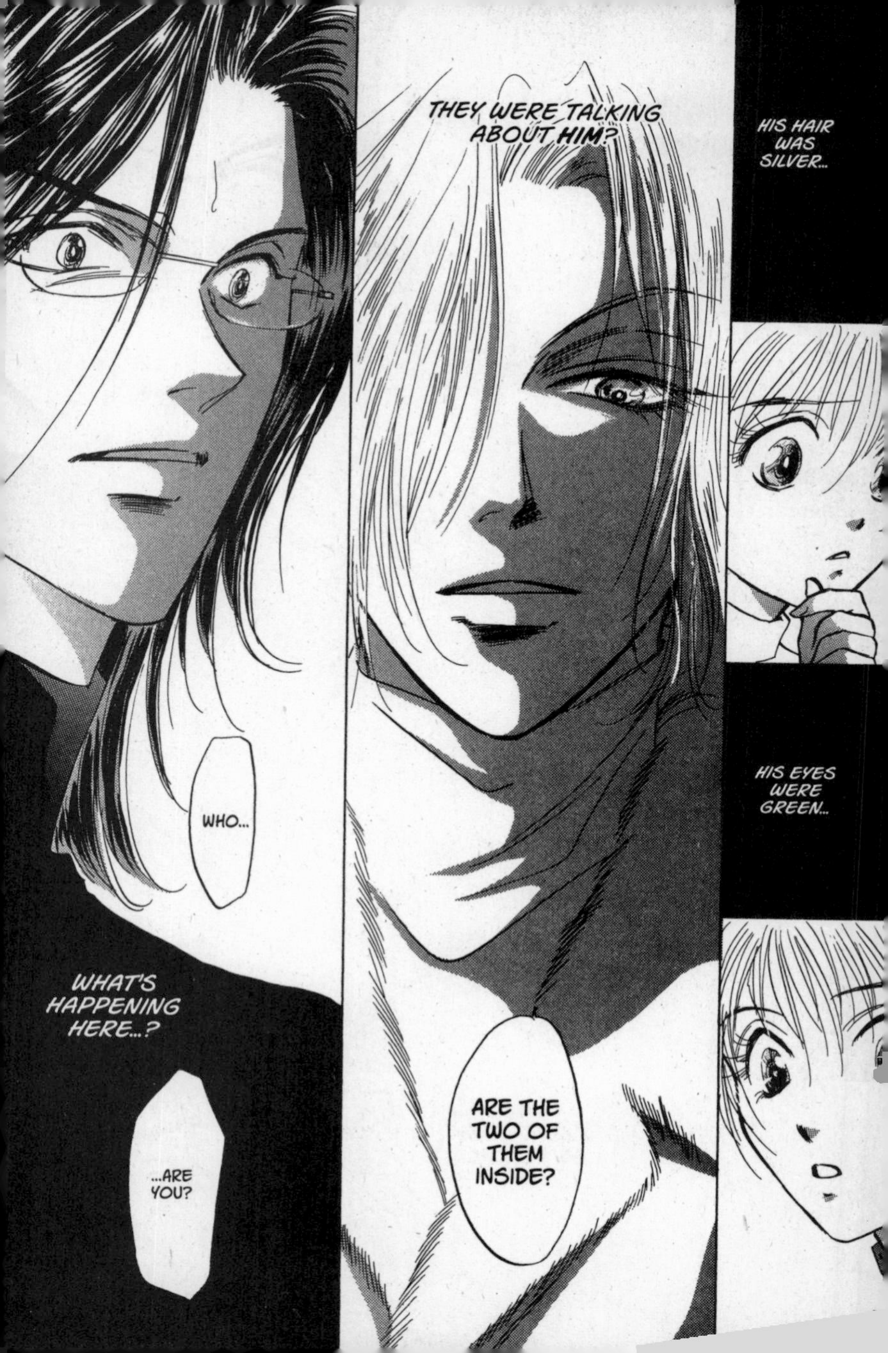
HIS HAIR WAS SILVER...
HIS EYES WERE GREEN...
THEY WERE TALKING ABOUT HIM?
ARE THE TWO OF THEM INSIDE?
WHO...
WHAT'S HAPPENING HERE...?
...ARE YOU?

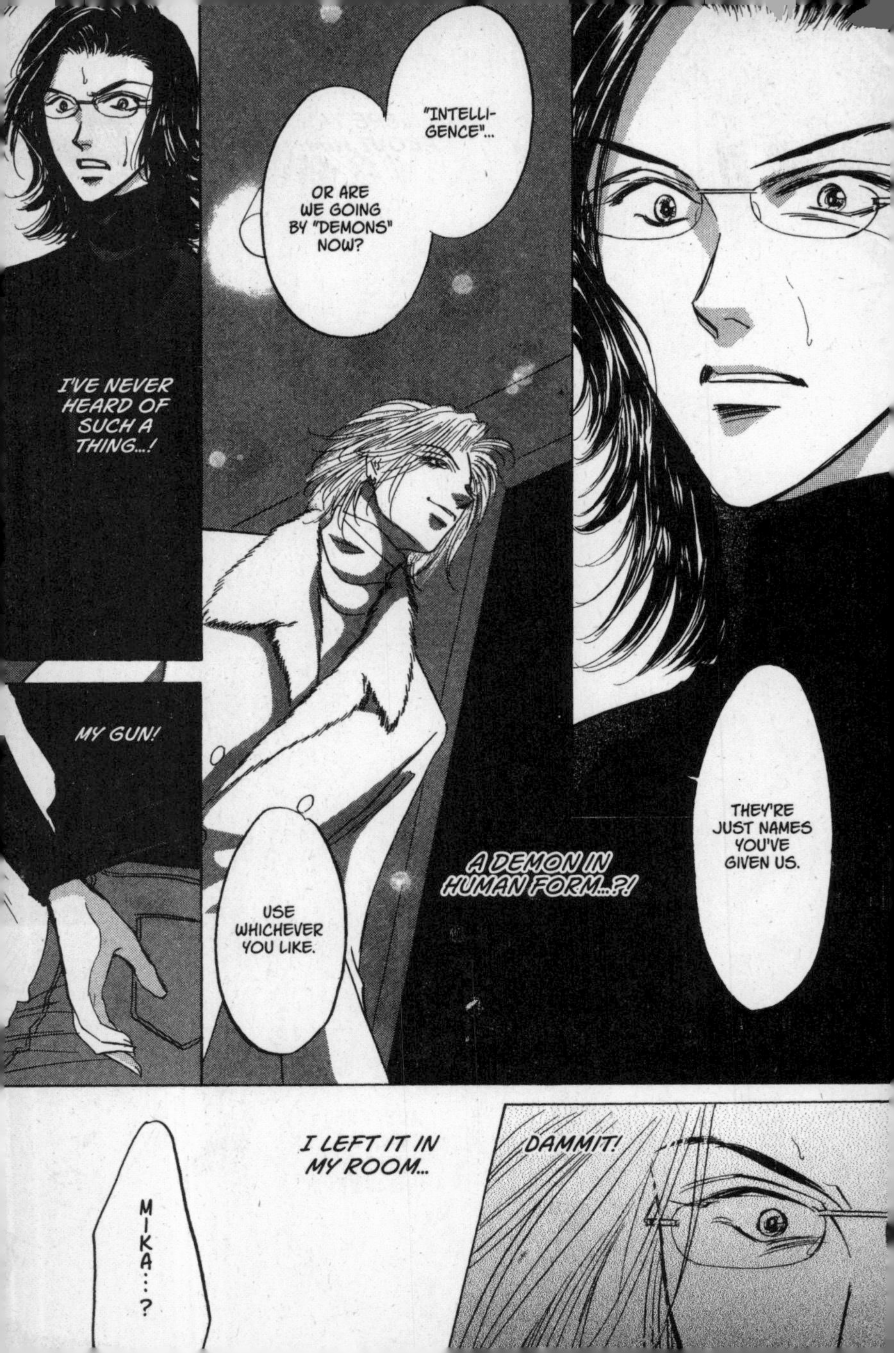
"INTELLIGENCE"...
OR ARE WE GOING BY "DEMONS" NOW?
THEY'RE JUST NAMES YOU'VE GIVEN US.
USE WHICHEVER YOU LIKE.
A DEMON IN HUMAN FORM...?!
I'VE NEVER HEARD OF SUCH A THING...!
MY GUN!
DAMMIT!
I LEFT IT IN MY ROOM...
MIKA...?

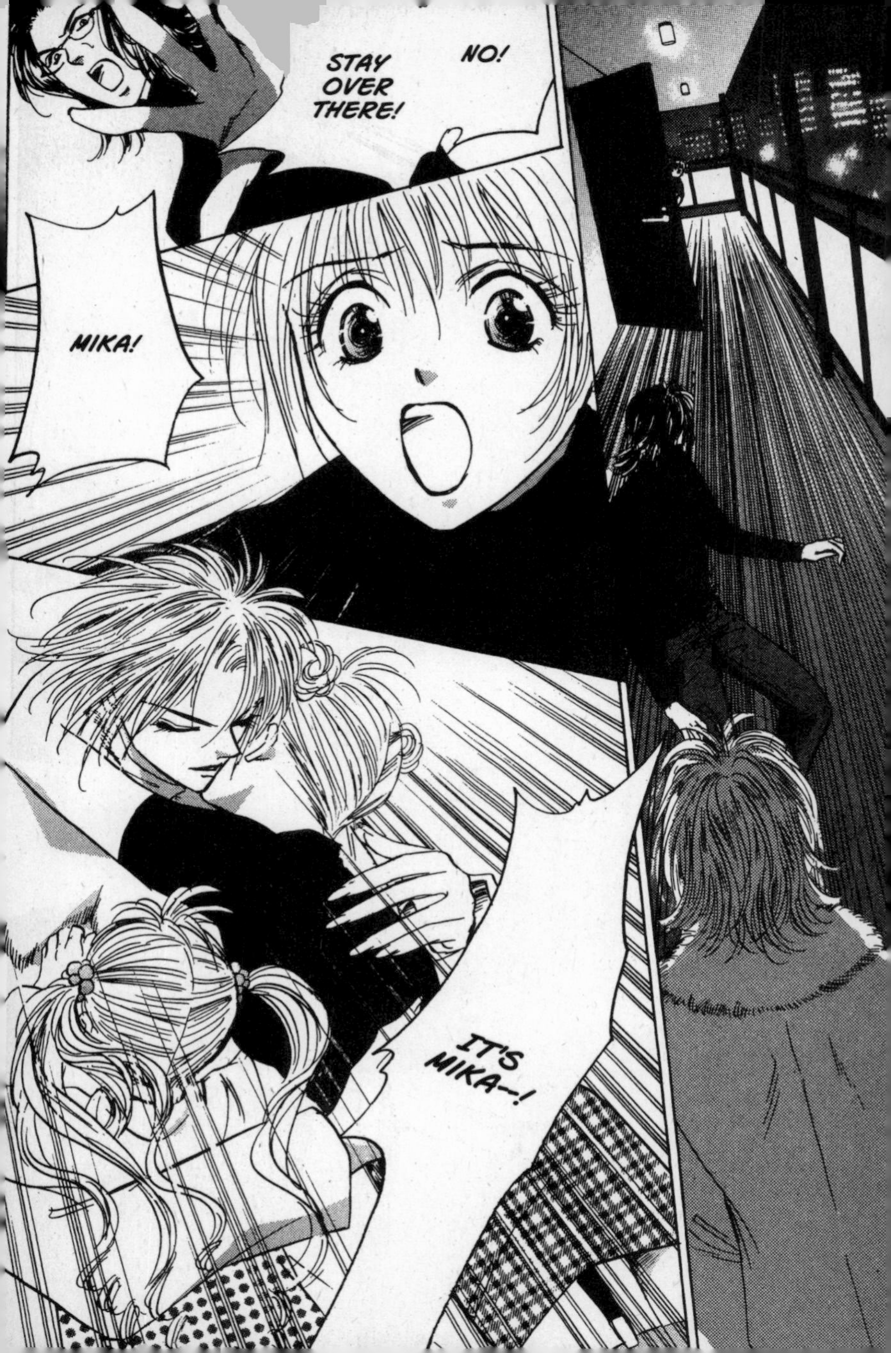
NO!
STAY OVER THERE!
MIKA!
IT'S MIKA--!

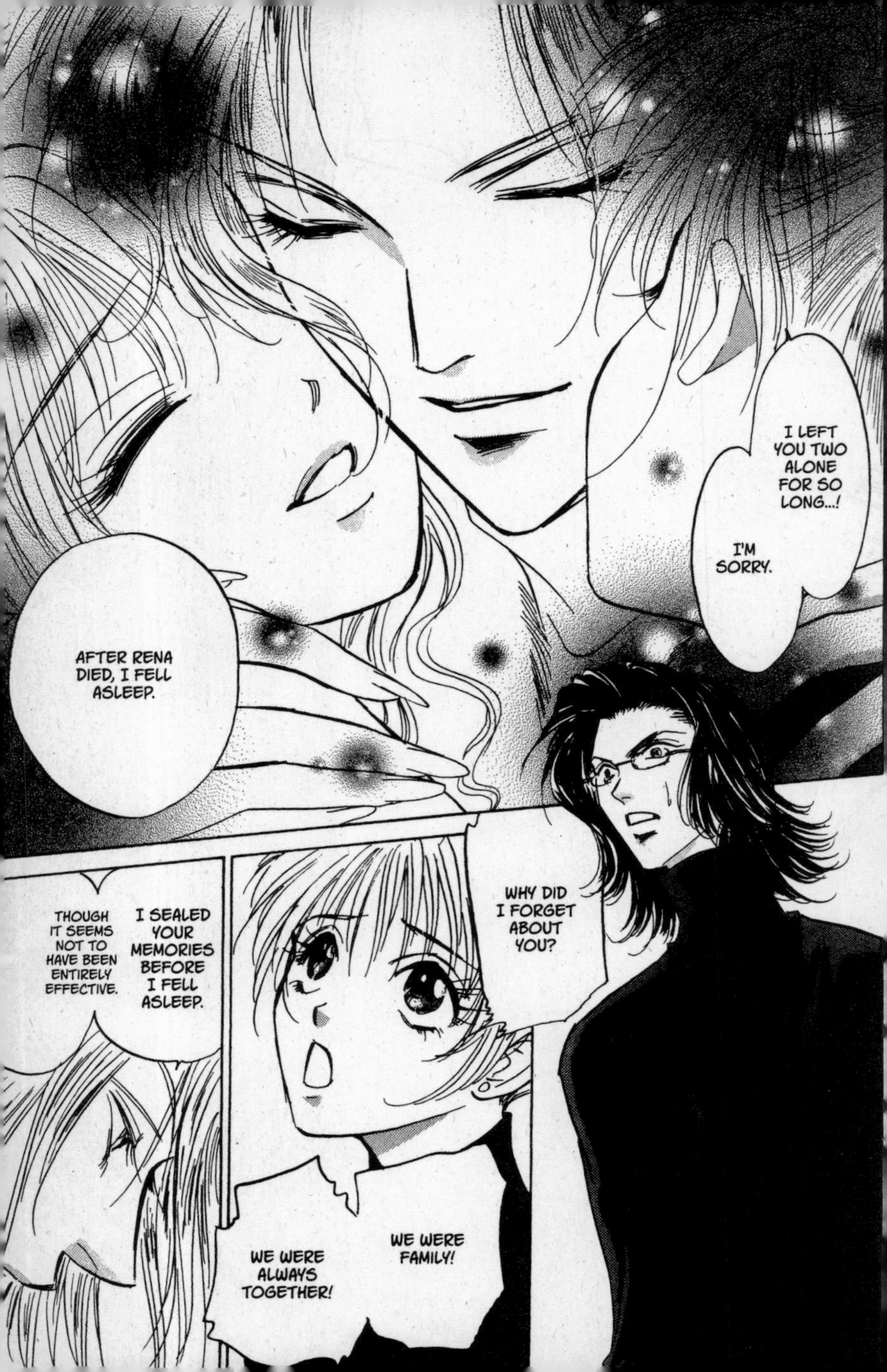

I LEFT YOU TWO ALONE FOR SO LONG...!
I'M SORRY.
AFTER RENA DIED, I FELL ASLEEP.
WHY DID I FORGET ABOUT YOU?
WE WERE FAMILY!
WE WERE ALWAYS TOGETHER!
I SEALED YOUR MEMORIES BEFORE I FELL ASLEEP.
THOUGH IT SEEMS NOT TO HAVE BEEN ENTIRELY EFFECTIVE.

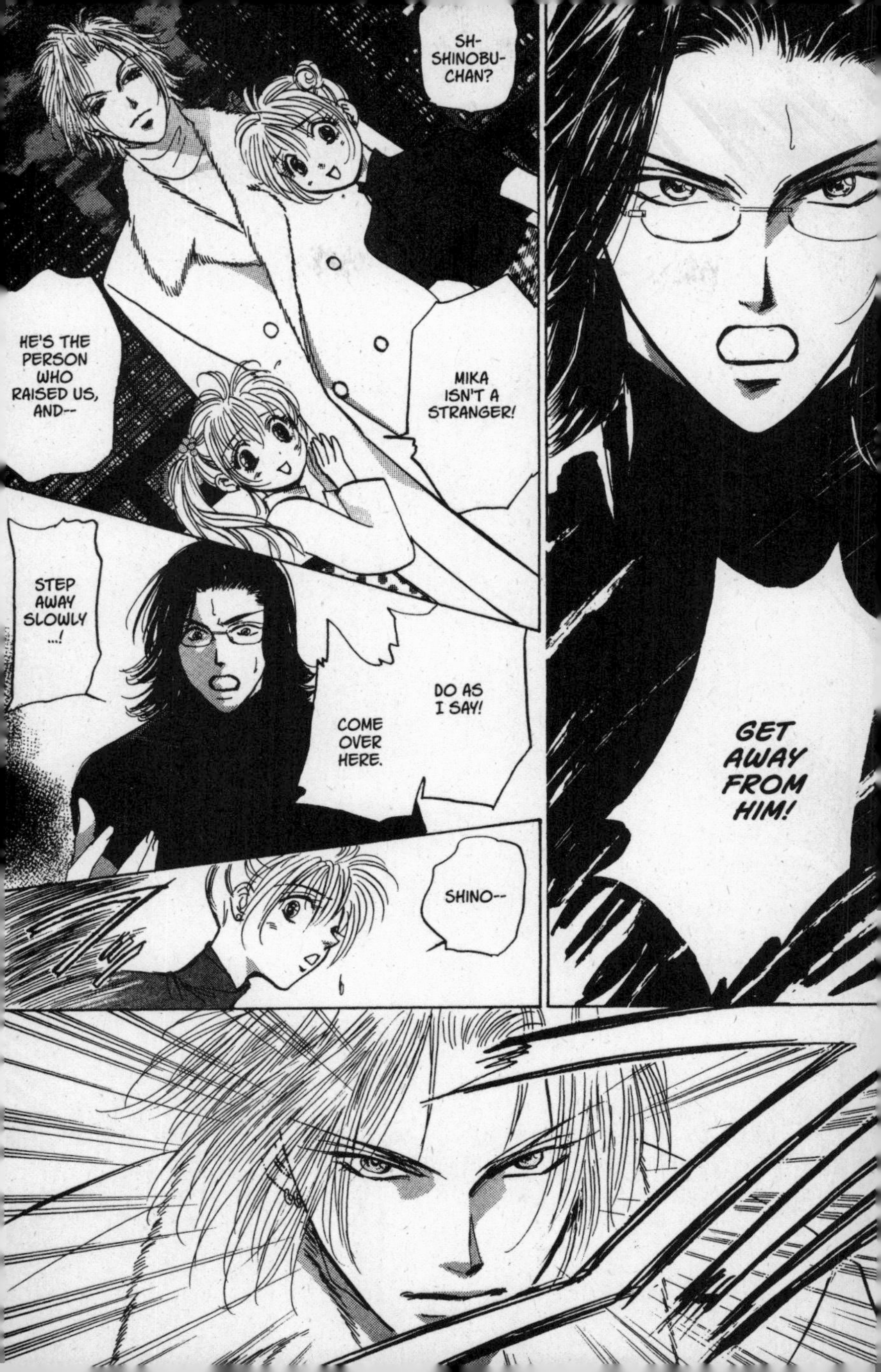
GET AWAY FROM HIM!
SH-SHINOBU-CHAN?
MIKA ISN'T A STRANGER!
HE'S THE PERSON WHO RAISED US, AND--
DO AS I SAY!
COME OVER HERE.
STEP AWAY SLOWLY ...!
SHINO--

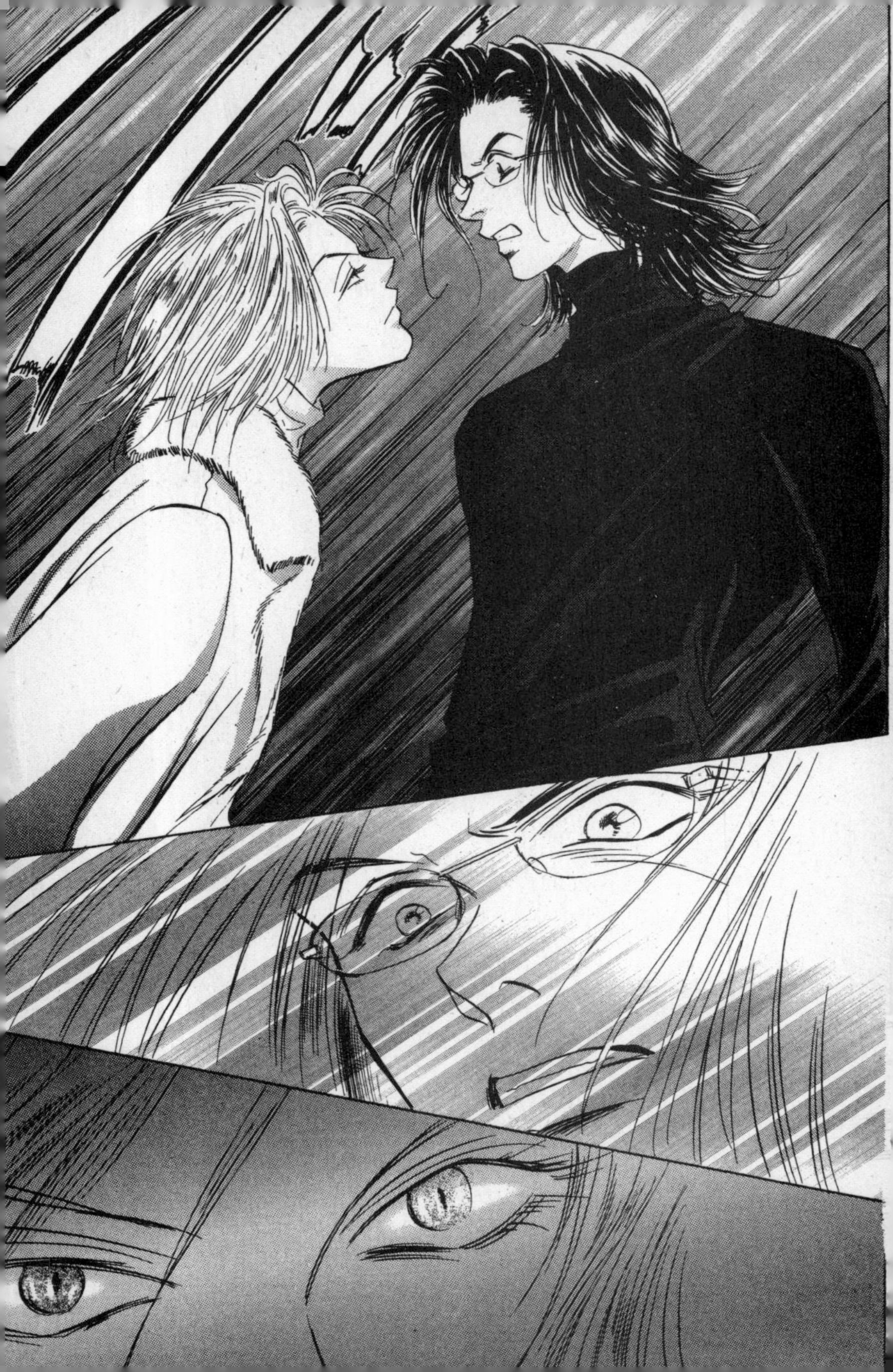

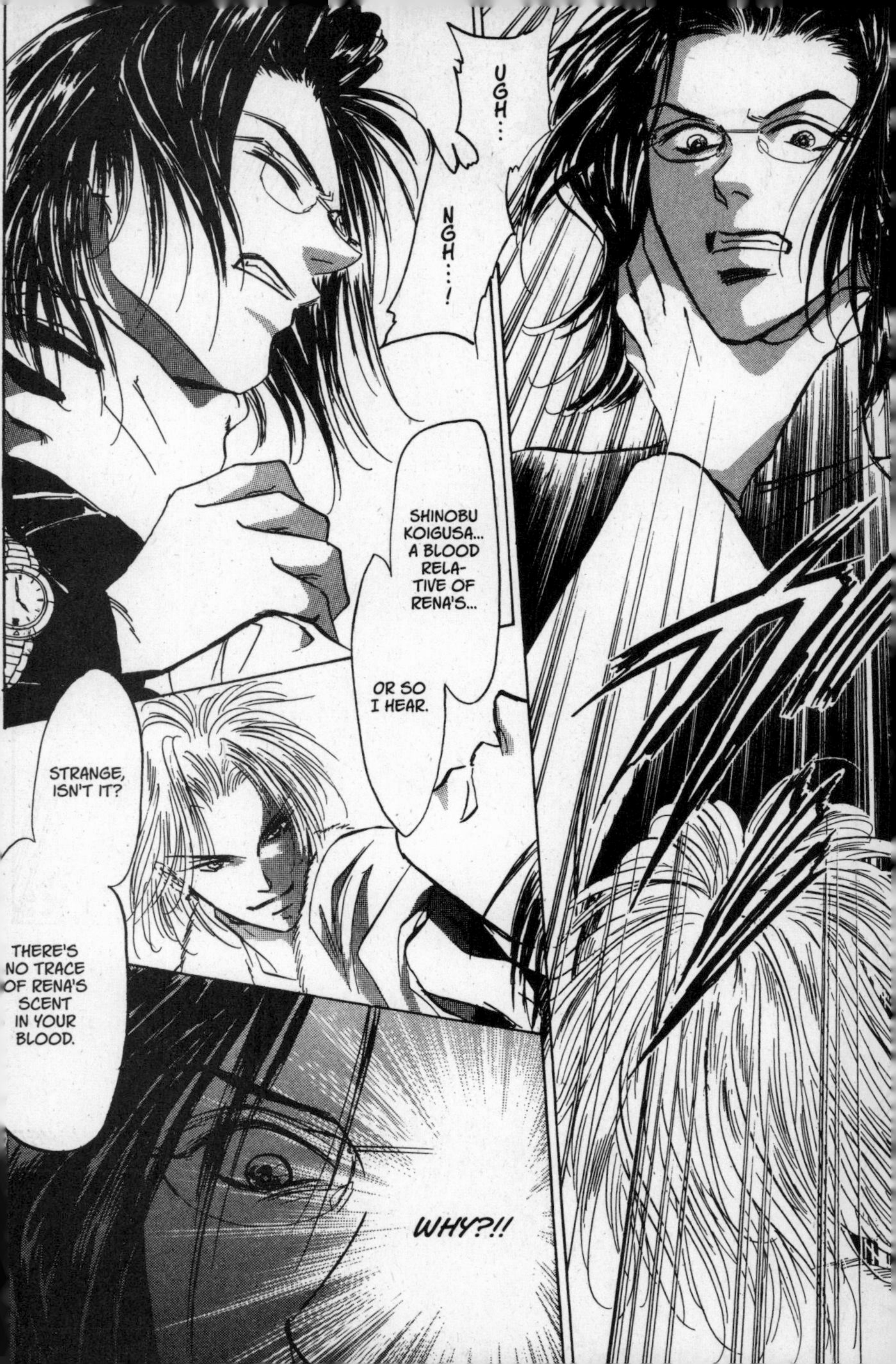
UGH...
NGH...!
SHINOBU KOIGUSA... A BLOOD RELATIVE OF RENA'S...
OR SO I HEAR.
STRANGE, ISN'T IT?
THERE'S NO TRACE OF RENA'S SCENT IN YOUR BLOOD.
WHY?!!

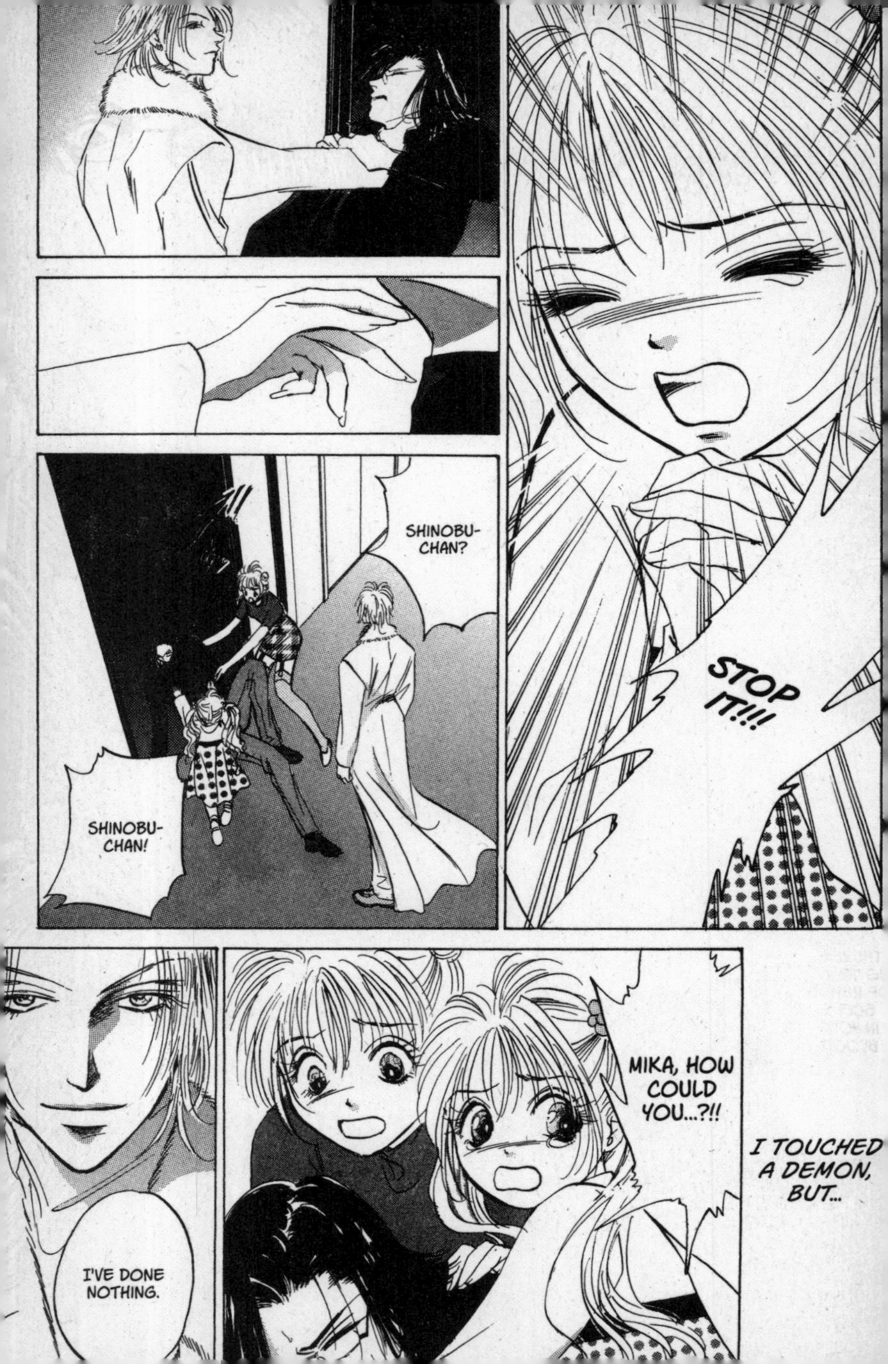
STOP IT!!!
SHINOBU-CHAN?
SHINOBU-CHAN!
MIKA, HOW COULD YOU...?!!
I TOUCHED A DEMON, BUT...
I'VE DONE NOTHING.

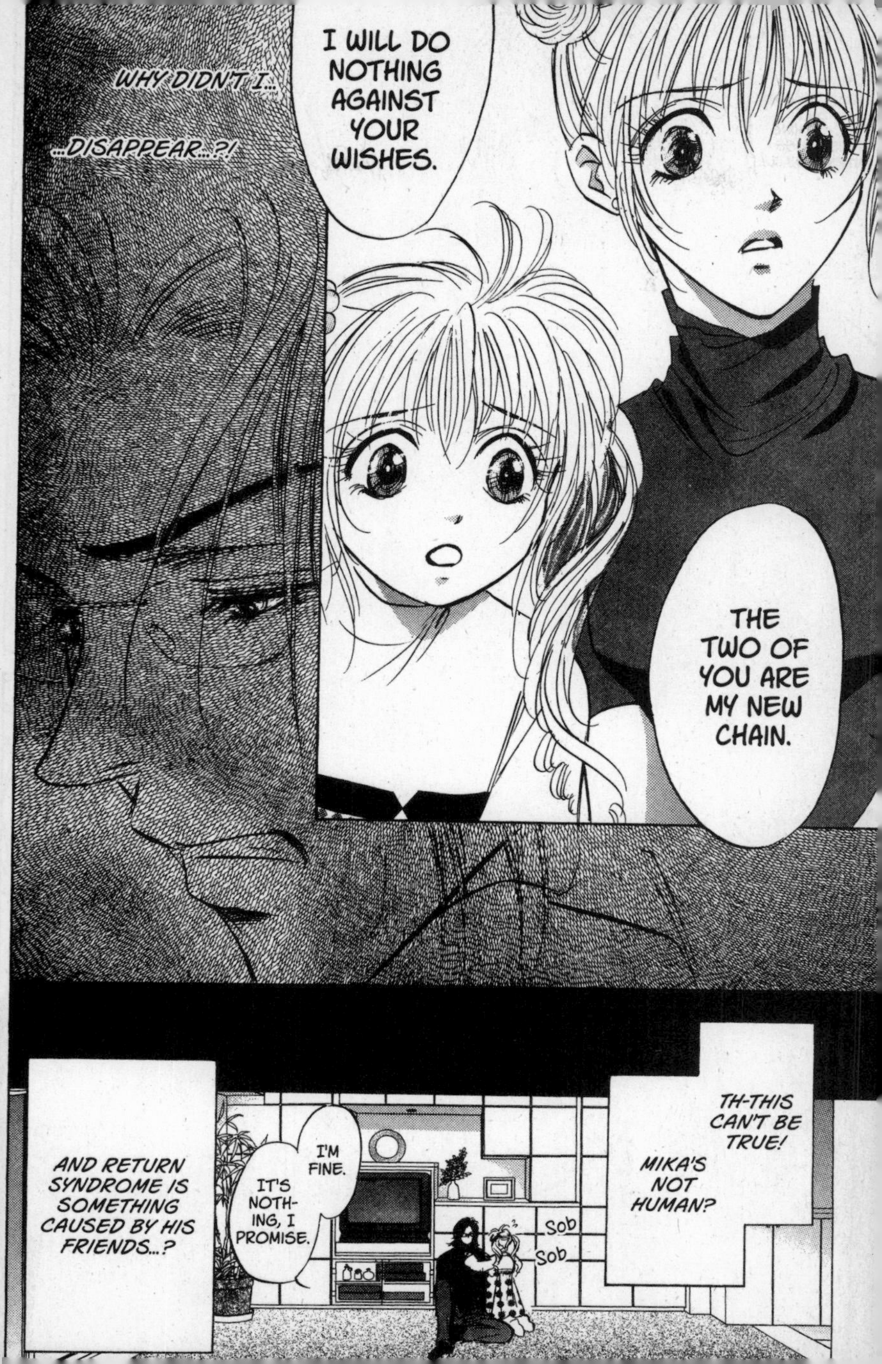
I WILL DO NOTHING AGAINST YOUR WISHES.
THE TWO OF YOU ARE MY NEW CHAIN.
WHY DIDN'T I...
...DISAPPEAR...?!
TH-THIS CAN'T BE TRUE!
MIKA'S NOT HUMAN?
Sob
Sob
I'M FINE.
IT'S NOTHING, I PROMISE.
AND RETURN SYNDROME IS SOMETHING CAUSED BY HIS FRIENDS...?

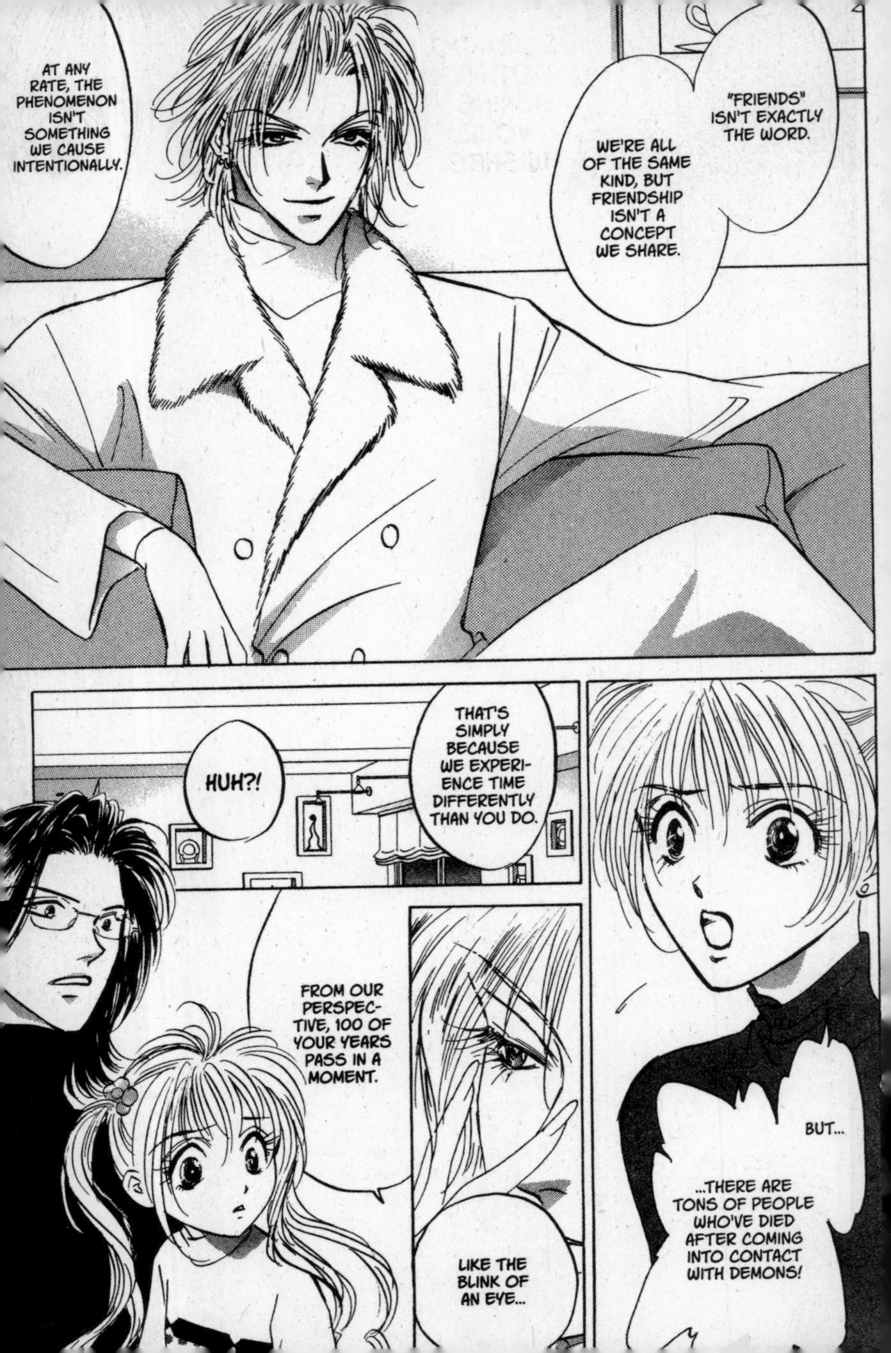
"FRIENDS" ISN'T EXACTLY THE WORD.
WE'RE ALL OF THE SAME KIND, BUT FRIENDSHIP ISN'T A CONCEPT WE SHARE.
AT ANY RATE, THE PHENOMENON ISN'T SOMETHING WE CAUSE INTENTIONALLY.
BUT...
...THERE ARE TONS OF PEOPLE WHO'VE DIED AFTER COMING INTO CONTACT WITH DEMONS!
THAT'S SIMPLY BECAUSE WE EXPERIENCE TIME DIFFERENTLY THAN YOU DO.
HUH?!
FROM OUR PERSPECTIVE, 100 OF YOUR YEARS PASS IN A MOMENT.
LIKE THE BLINK OF AN EYE...

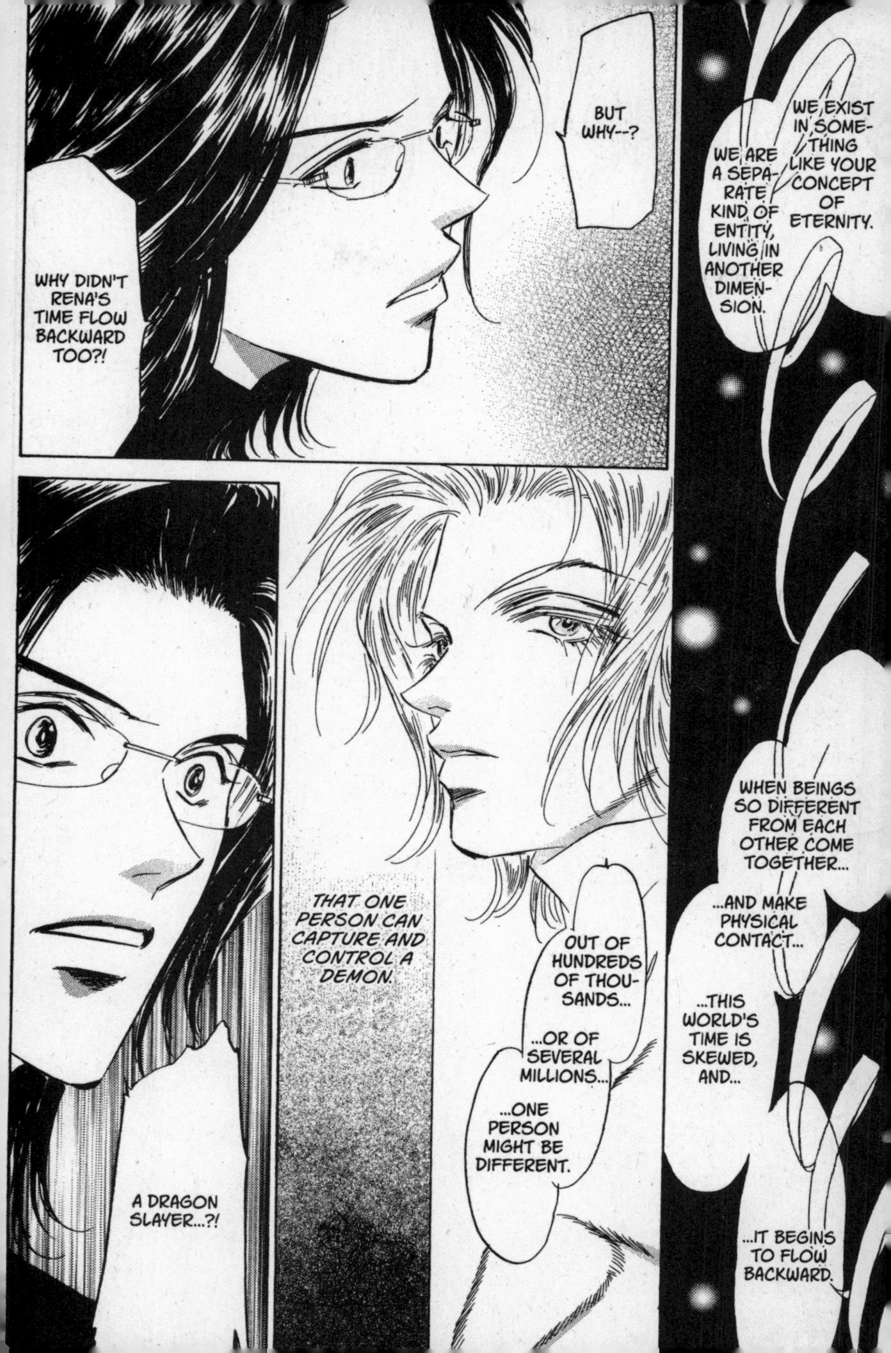
WE EXIST IN SOMETHING LIKE YOUR CONCEPT OF ETERNITY.
WE ARE A SEPARATE KIND OF ENTITY, LIVING IN ANOTHER DIMENSION.
WHEN BEINGS SO DIFFERENT FROM EACH OTHER COME TOGETHER...
...AND MAKE PHYSICAL CONTACT...
...THIS WORLD'S TIME IS SKEWED, AND...
...IT BEGINS TO FLOW BACKWARD.
BUT WHY--?
WHY DIDN'T RENA'S TIME FLOW BACKWARD TOO?!
OUT OF HUNDREDS OF THOUSANDS...
...OR OF SEVERAL MILLIONS...
...ONE PERSON MIGHT BE DIFFERENT.
THAT ONE PERSON CAN CAPTURE AND CONTROL A DEMON.
A DRAGON SLAYER...?!

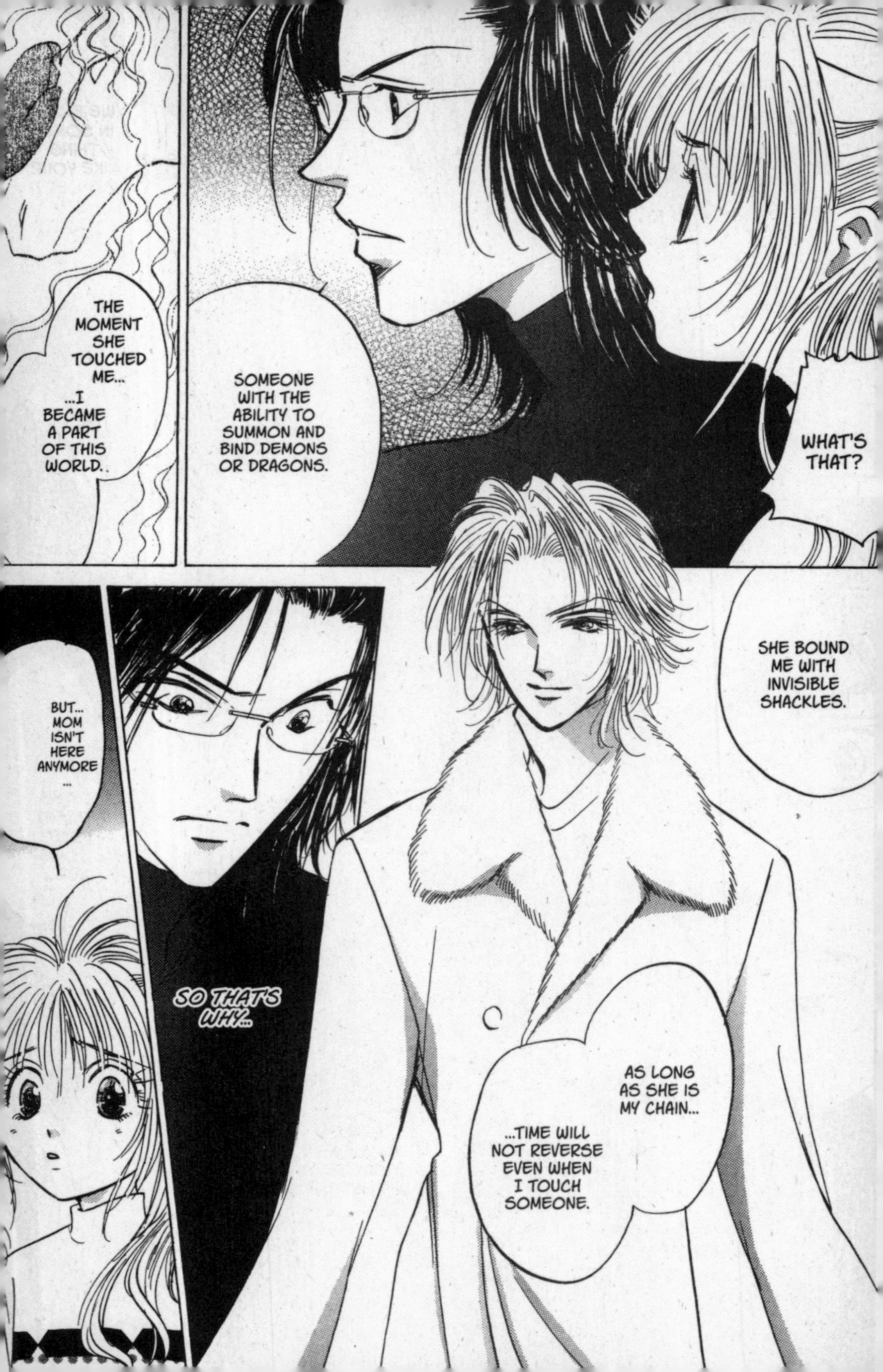
WHAT'S THAT?
SOMEONE WITH THE ABILITY TO SUMMON AND BIND DEMONS OR DRAGONS.
THE MOMENT SHE TOUCHED ME...
...I BECAME A PART OF THIS WORLD.
SHE BOUND ME WITH INVISIBLE SHACKLES.
AS LONG AS SHE IS MY CHAIN...
...TIME WILL NOT REVERSE EVEN WHEN I TOUCH SOMEONE.
SO THAT'S WHY...
BUT... MOM ISN'T HERE ANYMORE ...

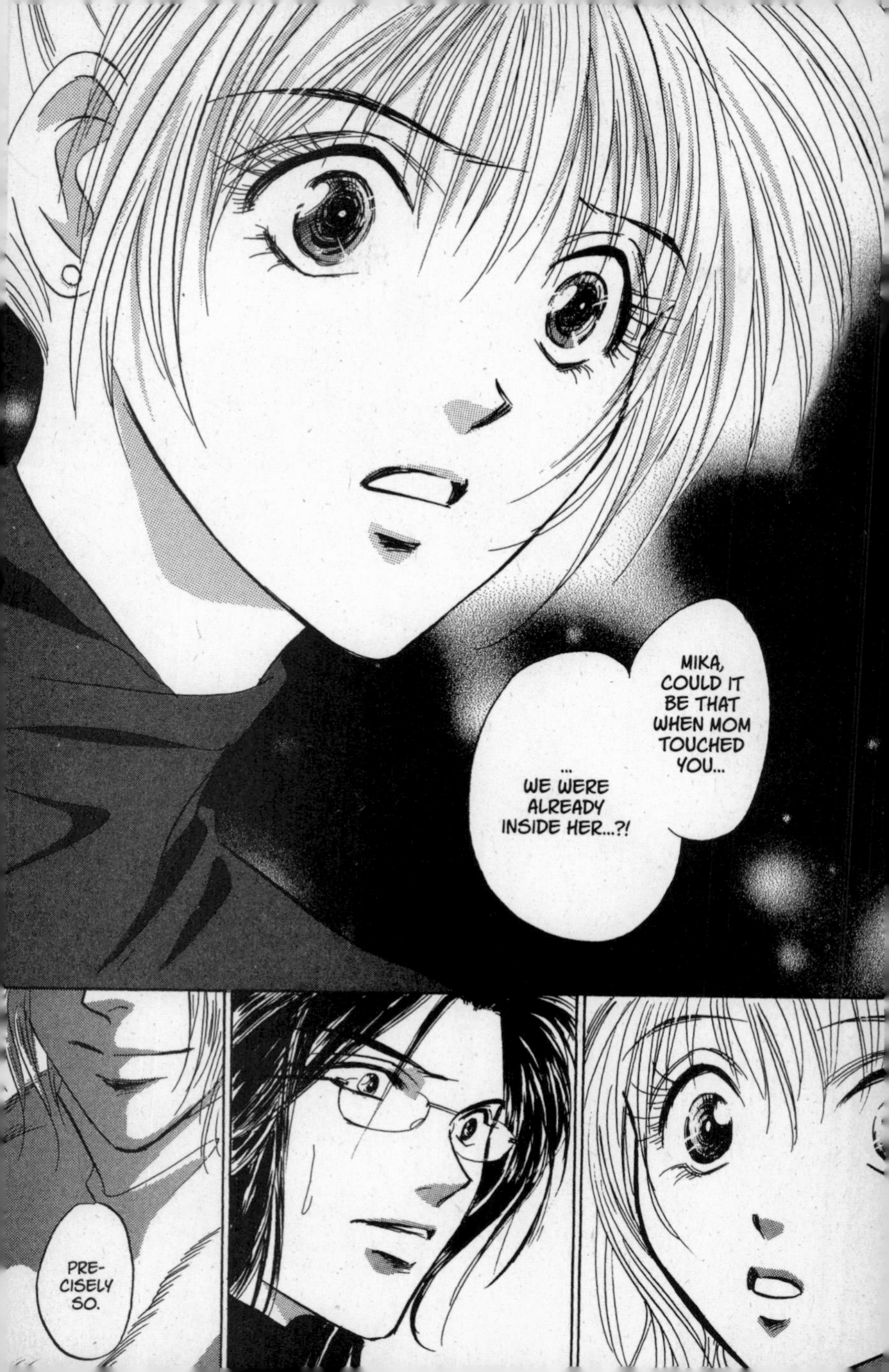
MIKA, COULD IT BE THAT WHEN MOM TOUCHED YOU...
... WE WERE ALREADY INSIDE HER...?!
PRE-CISELY SO.

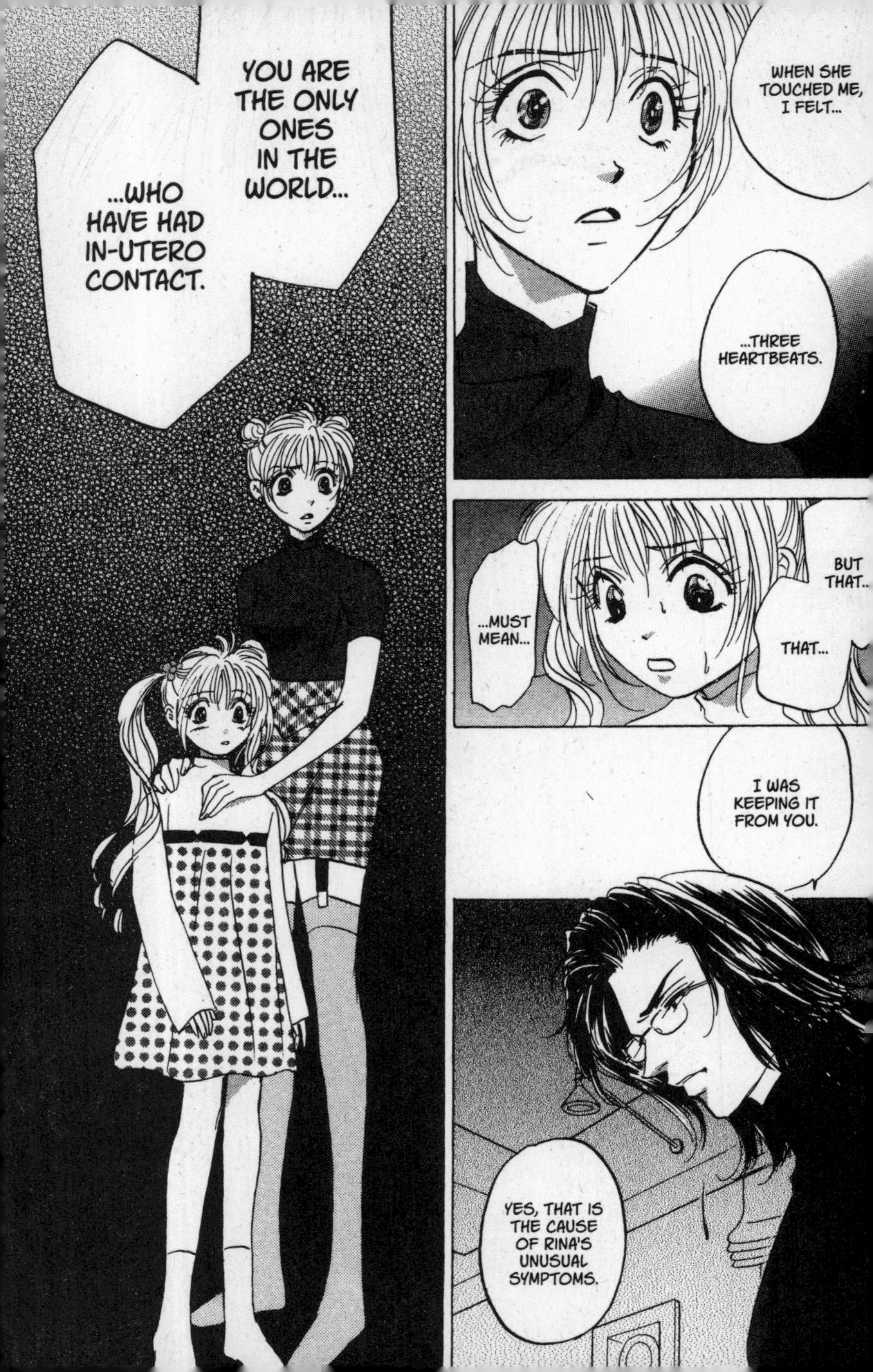
WHEN SHE TOUCHED ME, I FELT...
...THREE HEARTBEATS.
BUT THAT...
THAT...
...MUST MEAN...
I WAS KEEPING IT FROM YOU.
YES, THAT IS THE CAUSE OF RINA'S UNUSUAL SYMPTOMS.
YOU ARE THE ONLY ONES IN THE WORLD...
...WHO HAVE HAD IN-UTERO CONTACT.

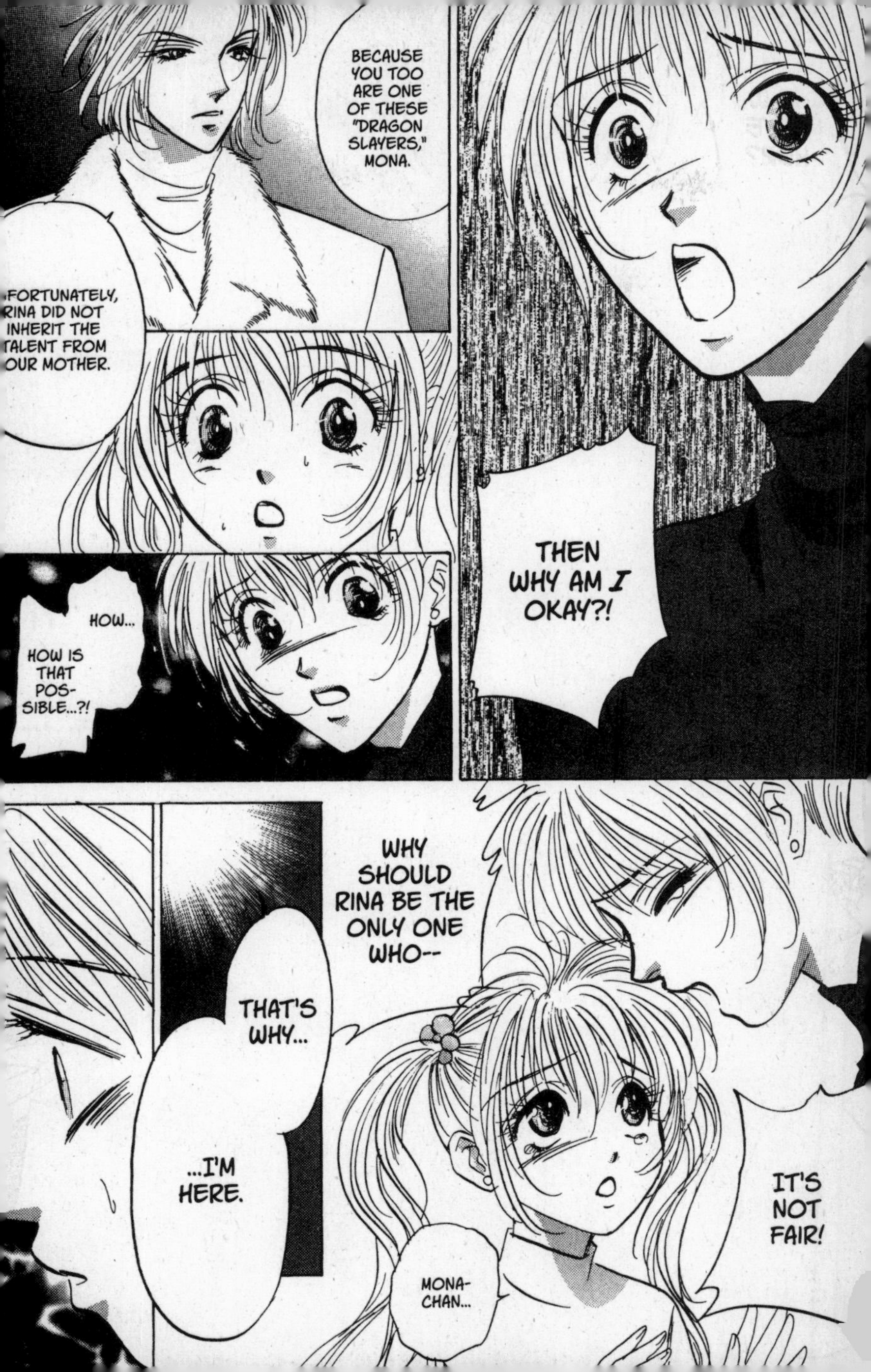
THEN WHY AM *I* OKAY?!
BECAUSE YOU TOO ARE ONE OF THESE "DRAGON SLAYERS," MONA.
FORTUNATELY, RINA DID NOT INHERIT THE TALENT FROM OUR MOTHER.
HOW...
HOW IS THAT POS-SIBLE...?!
WHY SHOULD RINA BE THE ONLY ONE WHO--
IT'S NOT FAIR!
MONA-CHAN...
THAT'S WHY...
...I'M HERE.

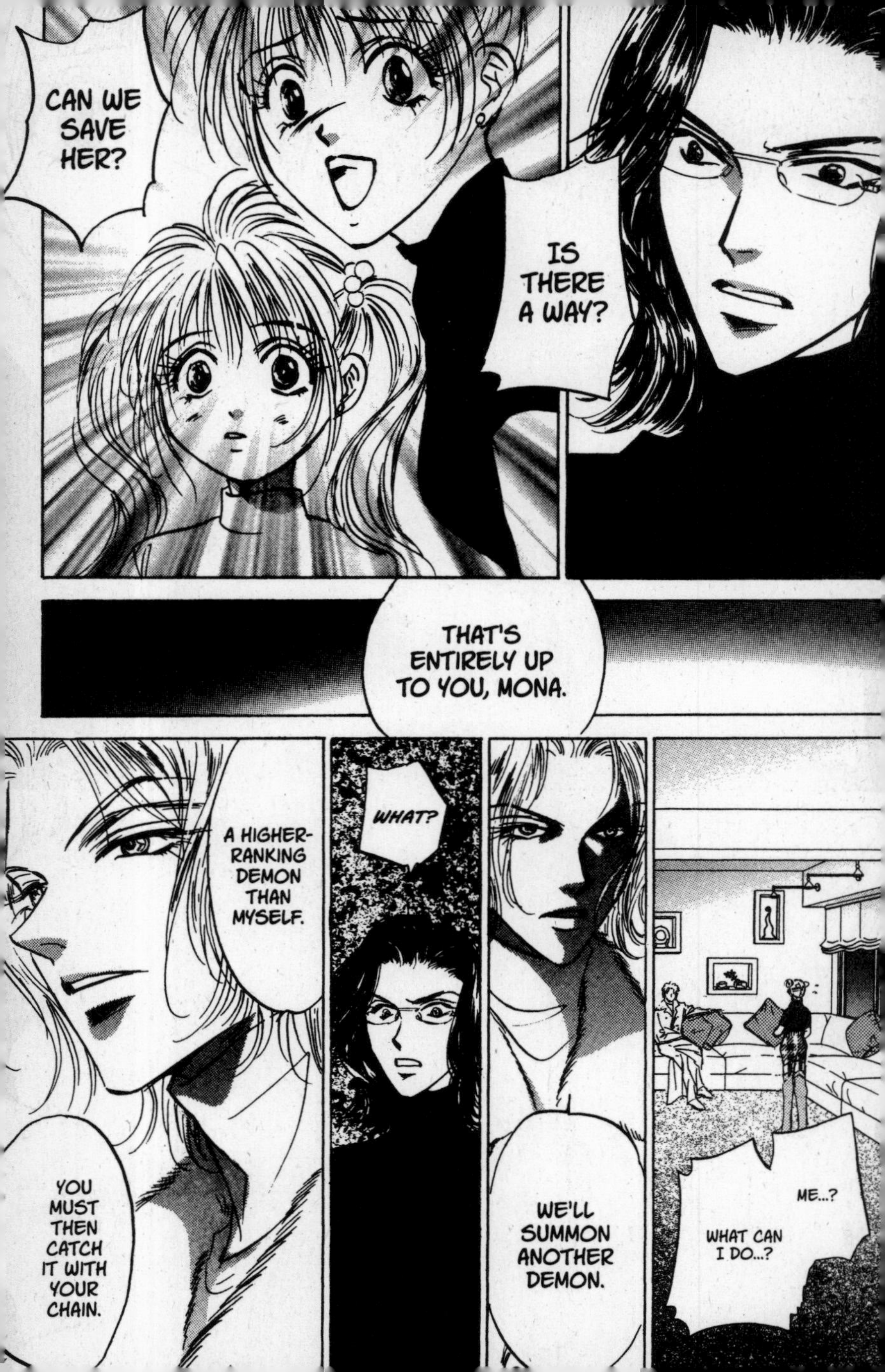
IS THERE A WAY?
CAN WE SAVE HER?
THAT'S ENTIRELY UP TO YOU, MONA.
ME...?
WHAT CAN I DO...?
WE'LL SUMMON ANOTHER DEMON.
WHAT?
A HIGHER-RANKING DEMON THAN MYSELF.
YOU MUST THEN CATCH IT WITH YOUR CHAIN.

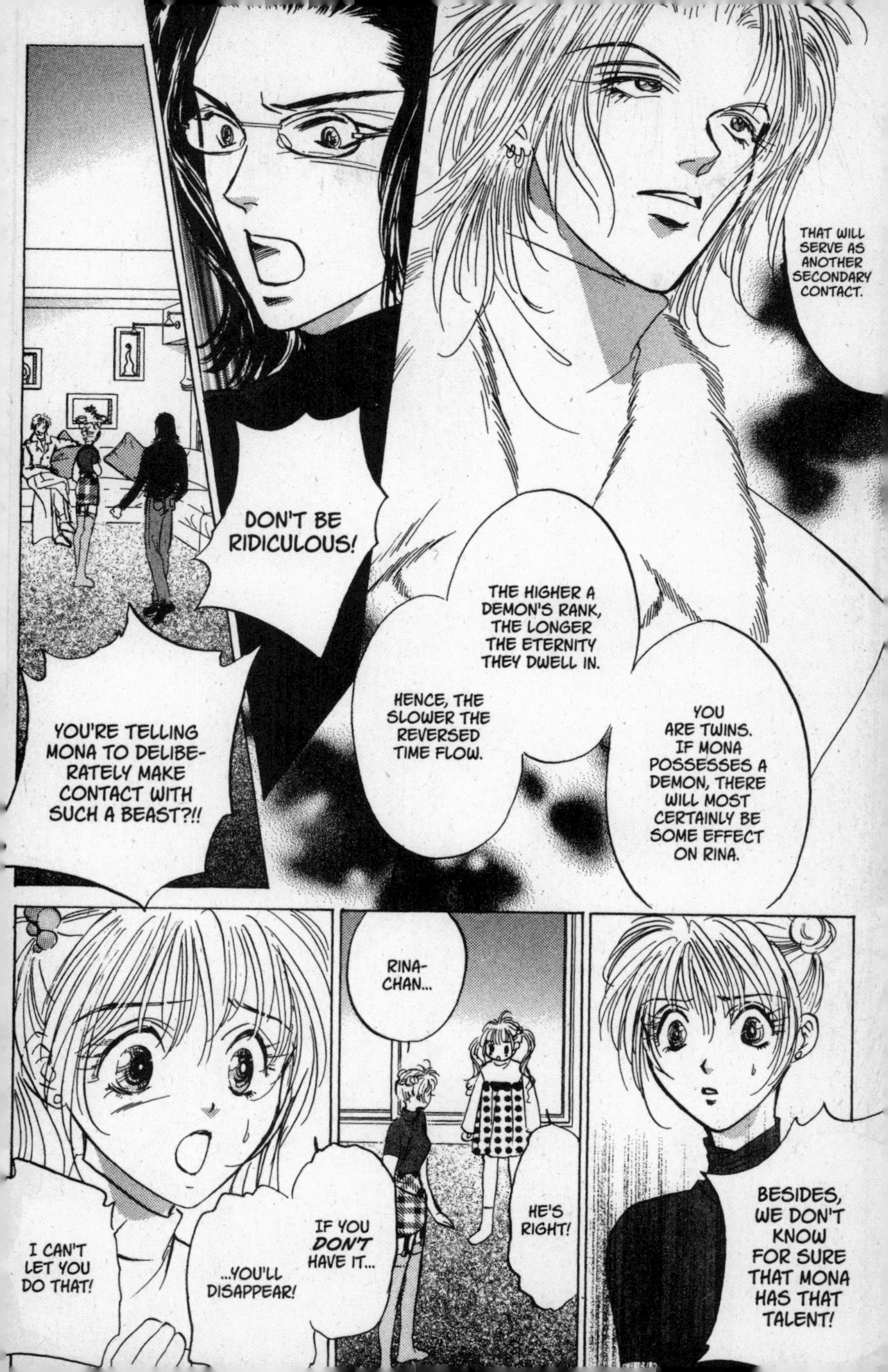
THAT WILL SERVE AS ANOTHER SECONDARY CONTACT.
THE HIGHER A DEMON'S RANK, THE LONGER THE ETERNITY THEY DWELL IN.
HENCE, THE SLOWER THE REVERSED TIME FLOW.
YOU ARE TWINS. IF MONA POSSESSES A DEMON, THERE WILL MOST CERTAINLY BE SOME EFFECT ON RINA.
DON'T BE RIDICULOUS!
YOU'RE TELLING MONA TO DELIBERATELY MAKE CONTACT WITH SUCH A BEAST?!!
BESIDES, WE DON'T KNOW FOR SURE THAT MONA HAS THAT TALENT!
RINA-CHAN...
HE'S RIGHT!
IF YOU *DON'T* HAVE IT...
...YOU'LL DISAPPEAR!
I CAN'T LET YOU DO THAT!

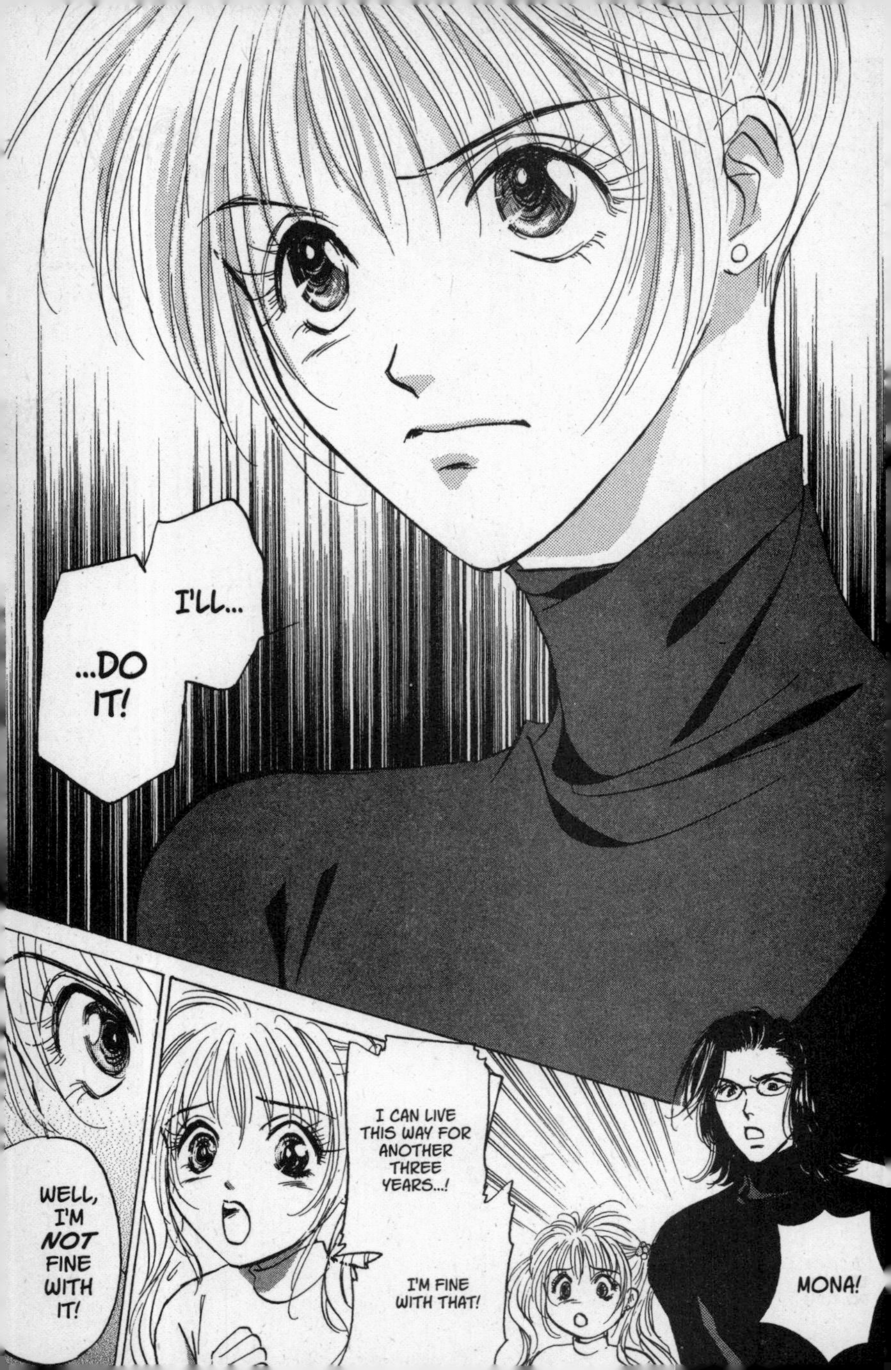
I'LL...
...DO IT!
I CAN LIVE THIS WAY FOR ANOTHER THREE YEARS...!
I'M FINE WITH THAT!
MONA!
WELL, I'M *NOT* FINE WITH IT!

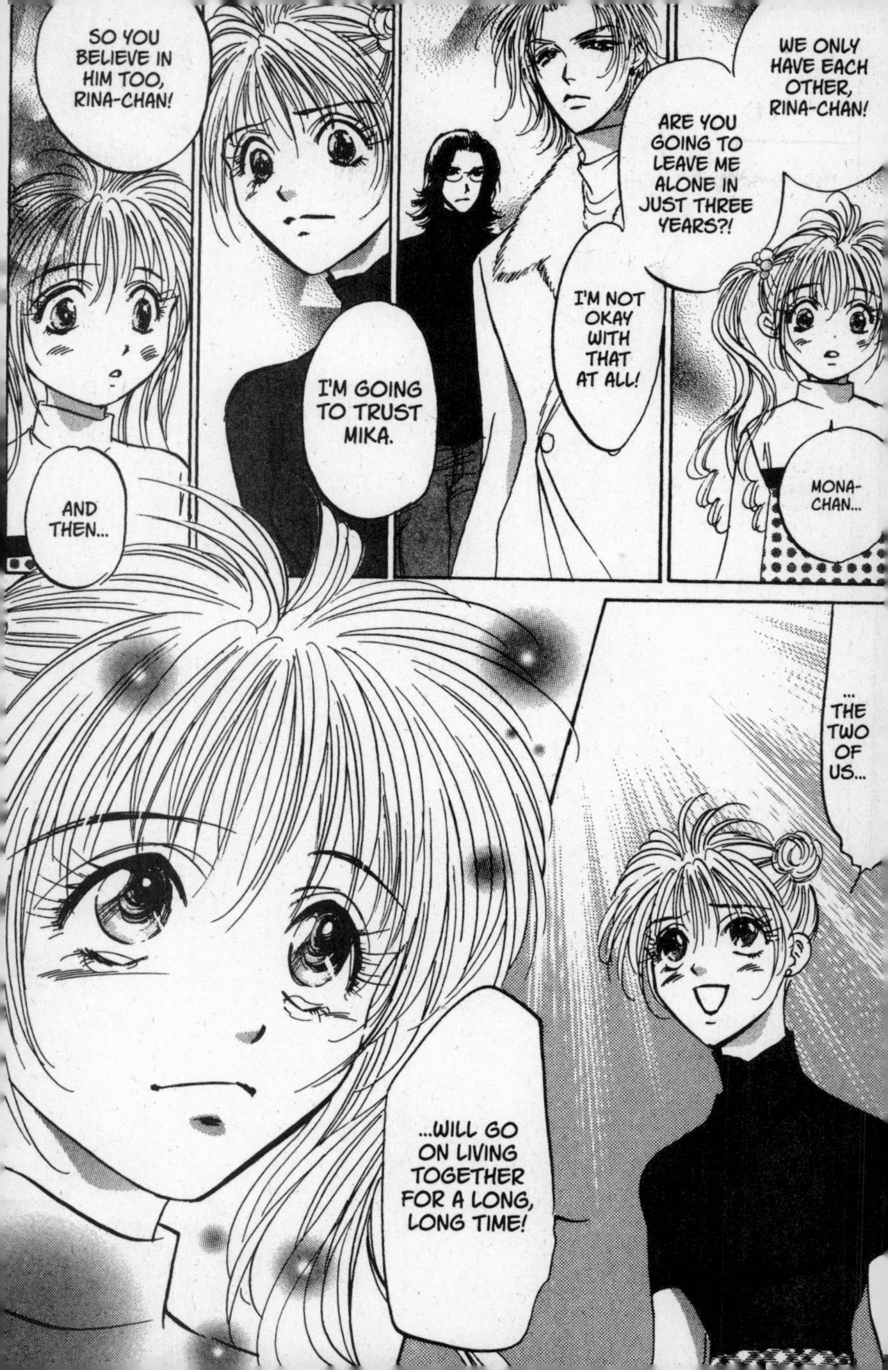
WE ONLY HAVE EACH OTHER, RINA-CHAN!
MONA-CHAN...
ARE YOU GOING TO LEAVE ME ALONE IN JUST THREE YEARS?!
I'M NOT OKAY WITH THAT AT ALL!
I'M GOING TO TRUST MIKA.
SO YOU BELIEVE IN HIM TOO, RINA-CHAN!
AND THEN...
...THE TWO OF US...
...WILL GO ON LIVING TOGETHER FOR A LONG, LONG TIME!

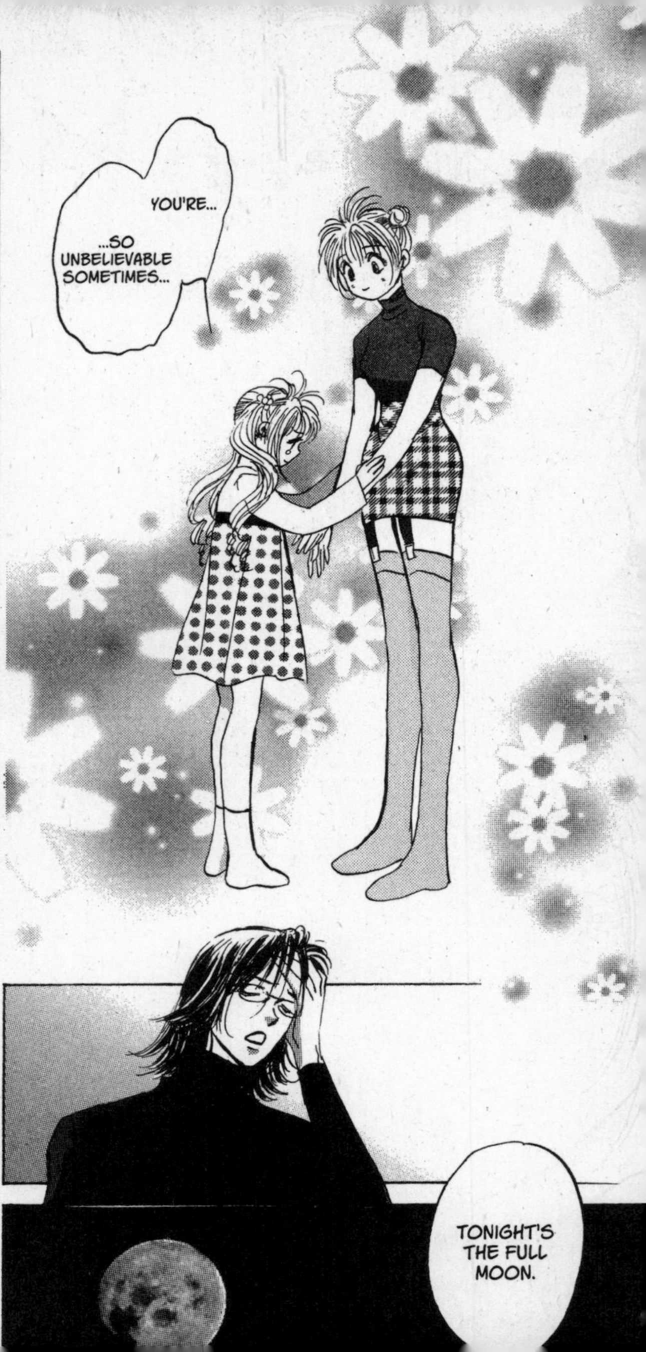
YOU'RE...
...SO UNBELIEVABLE SOMETIMES...
TONIGHT'S THE FULL MOON.

FREE TALK

⟨1⟩

Hello, everyone! To my new readers, how do you do?

Having just finished two previous series, Yakumotatsu and Ju-oh-sei, I'm finally beginning a new one!

This story is one of two proposals I submitted to a seinen magazine a few years ago. Given the nature of that magazine, I thought they'd surely choose to go with Demon Sacred, but it turned out that they wanted something a little different from their usual fare, so they went with Akatsuki no Musuko, my other proposal.

Each piece is organic, so this one changed a little while it was sitting on my desk and waiting for its time to come. If it had been developed for a men's magazine, it would likely be a little different than it is now.

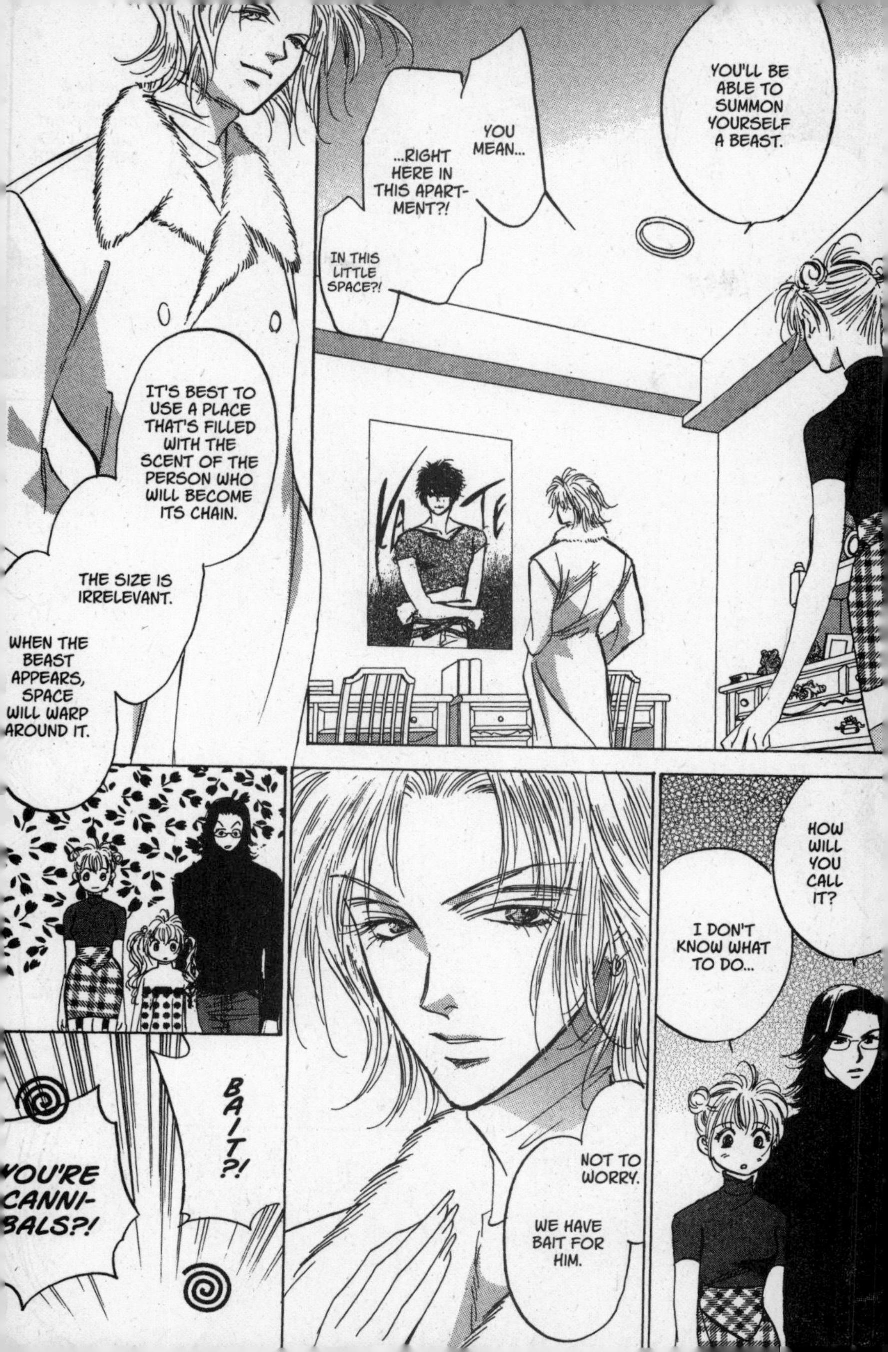

YOU'LL BE ABLE TO SUMMON YOURSELF A BEAST.
YOU MEAN...
...RIGHT HERE IN THIS APART-MENT?!
IN THIS LITTLE SPACE?!
IT'S BEST TO USE A PLACE THAT'S FILLED WITH THE SCENT OF THE PERSON WHO WILL BECOME ITS CHAIN.
THE SIZE IS IRRELEVANT.
WHEN THE BEAST APPEARS, SPACE WILL WARP AROUND IT.
HOW WILL YOU CALL IT?
I DON'T KNOW WHAT TO DO...
NOT TO WORRY.
WE HAVE BAIT FOR HIM.
BAIT?!
YOU'RE CANNI-BALS?!

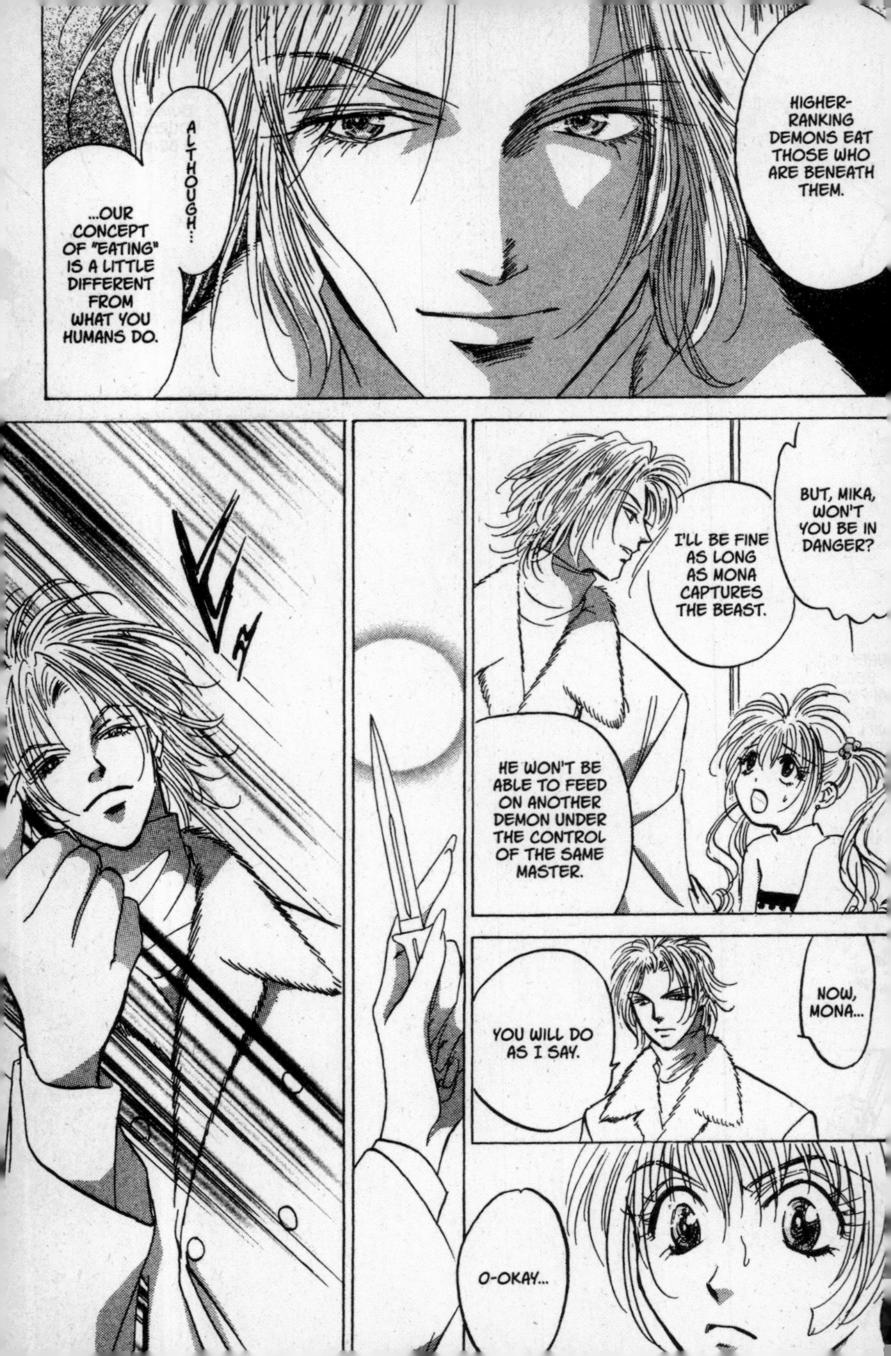
HIGHER-RANKING DEMONS EAT THOSE WHO ARE BENEATH THEM.
ALTHOUGH...
...OUR CONCEPT OF "EATING" IS A LITTLE DIFFERENT FROM WHAT YOU HUMANS DO.
BUT, MIKA, WON'T YOU BE IN DANGER?
I'LL BE FINE AS LONG AS MONA CAPTURES THE BEAST.
HE WON'T BE ABLE TO FEED ON ANOTHER DEMON UNDER THE CONTROL OF THE SAME MASTER.
NOW, MONA...
YOU WILL DO AS I SAY.
O-OKAY...

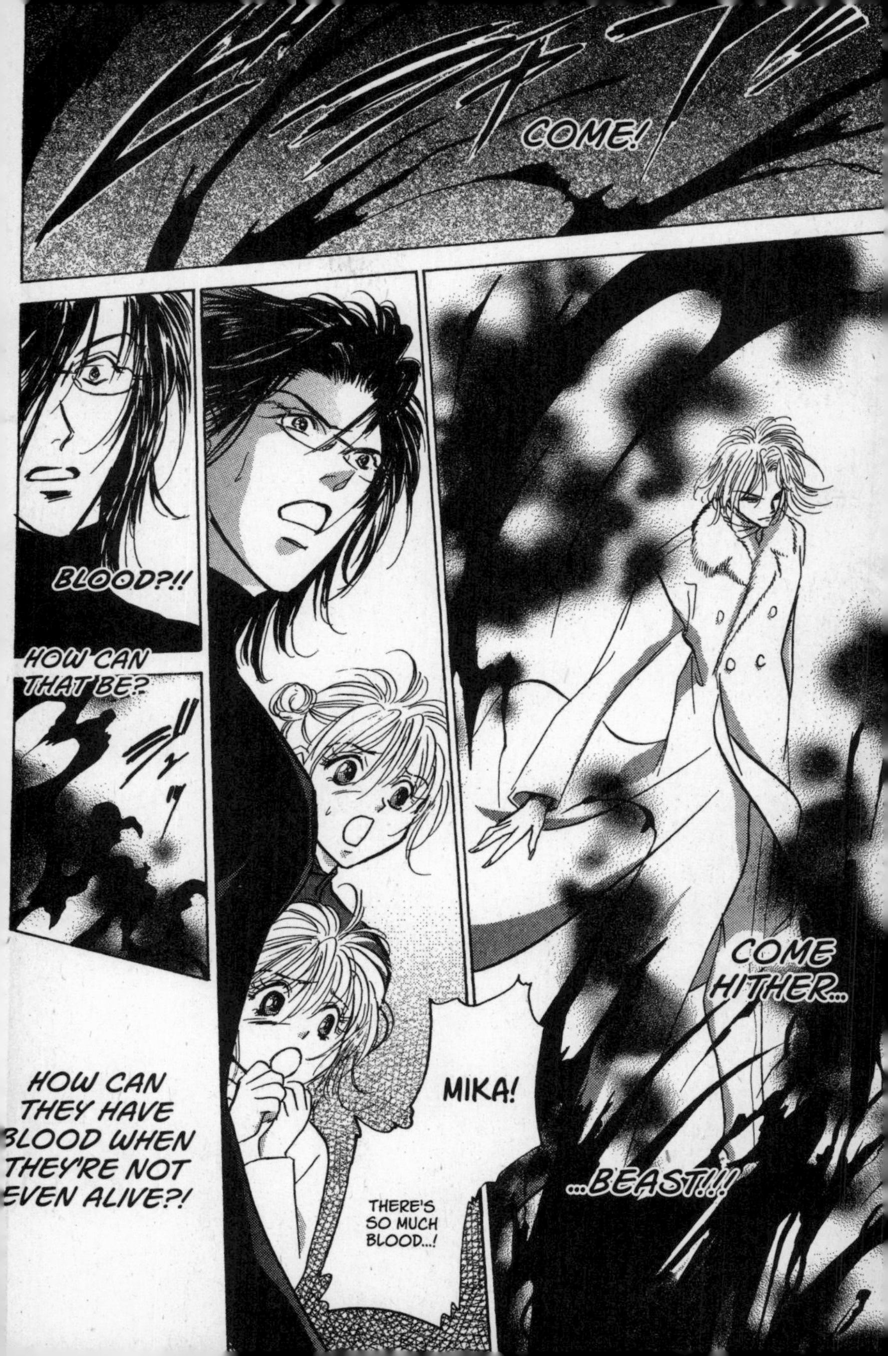
COME!
COME HITHER...
...BEAST!!!
MIKA!
THERE'S SO MUCH BLOOD...!
BLOOD?!!
HOW CAN THAT BE?
HOW CAN THEY HAVE BLOOD WHEN THEY'RE NOT EVEN ALIVE?!

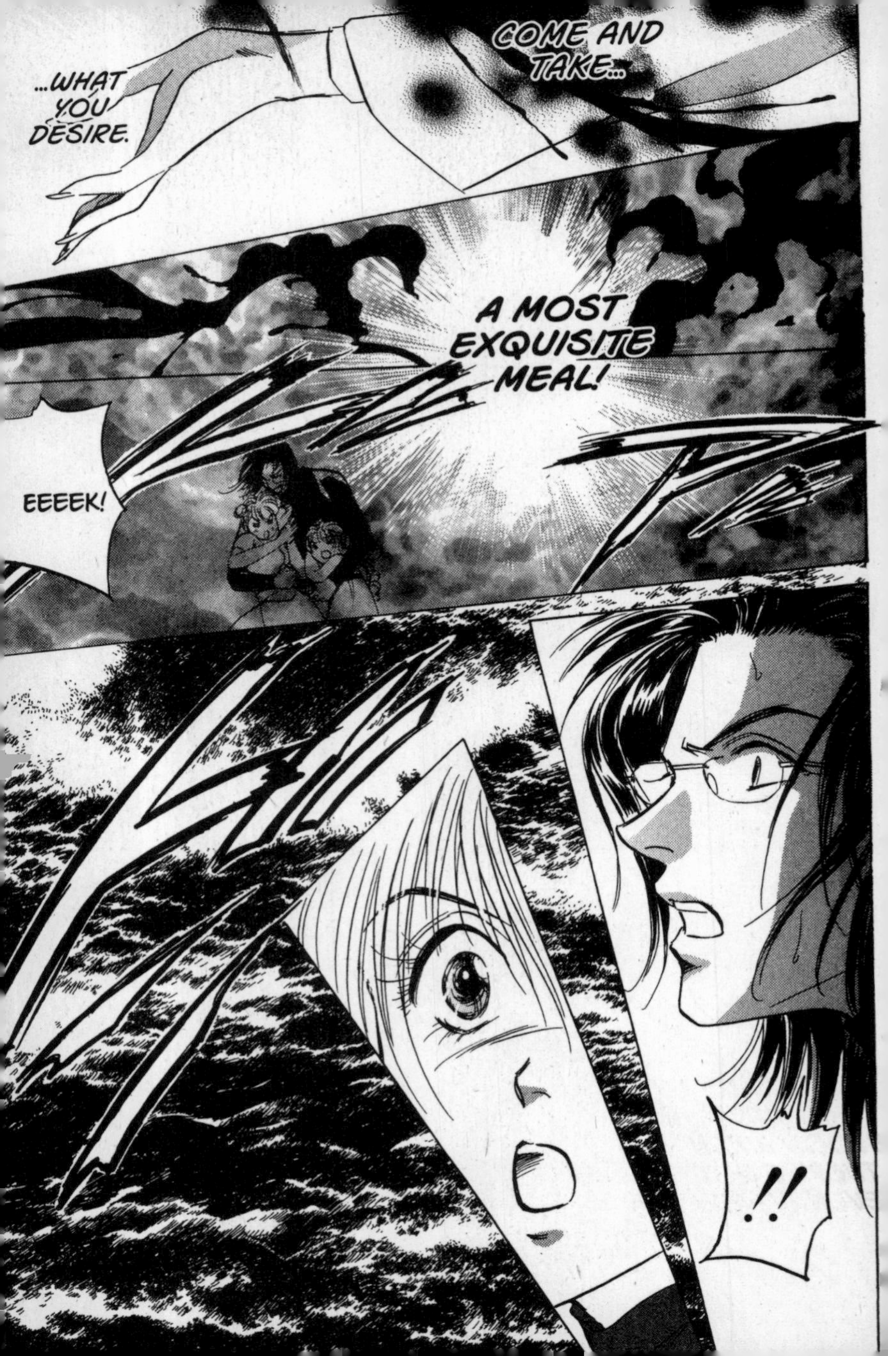
COME AND TAKE...
...WHAT YOU DESIRE.
A MOST EXQUISITE MEAL!
EEEEK!
!!

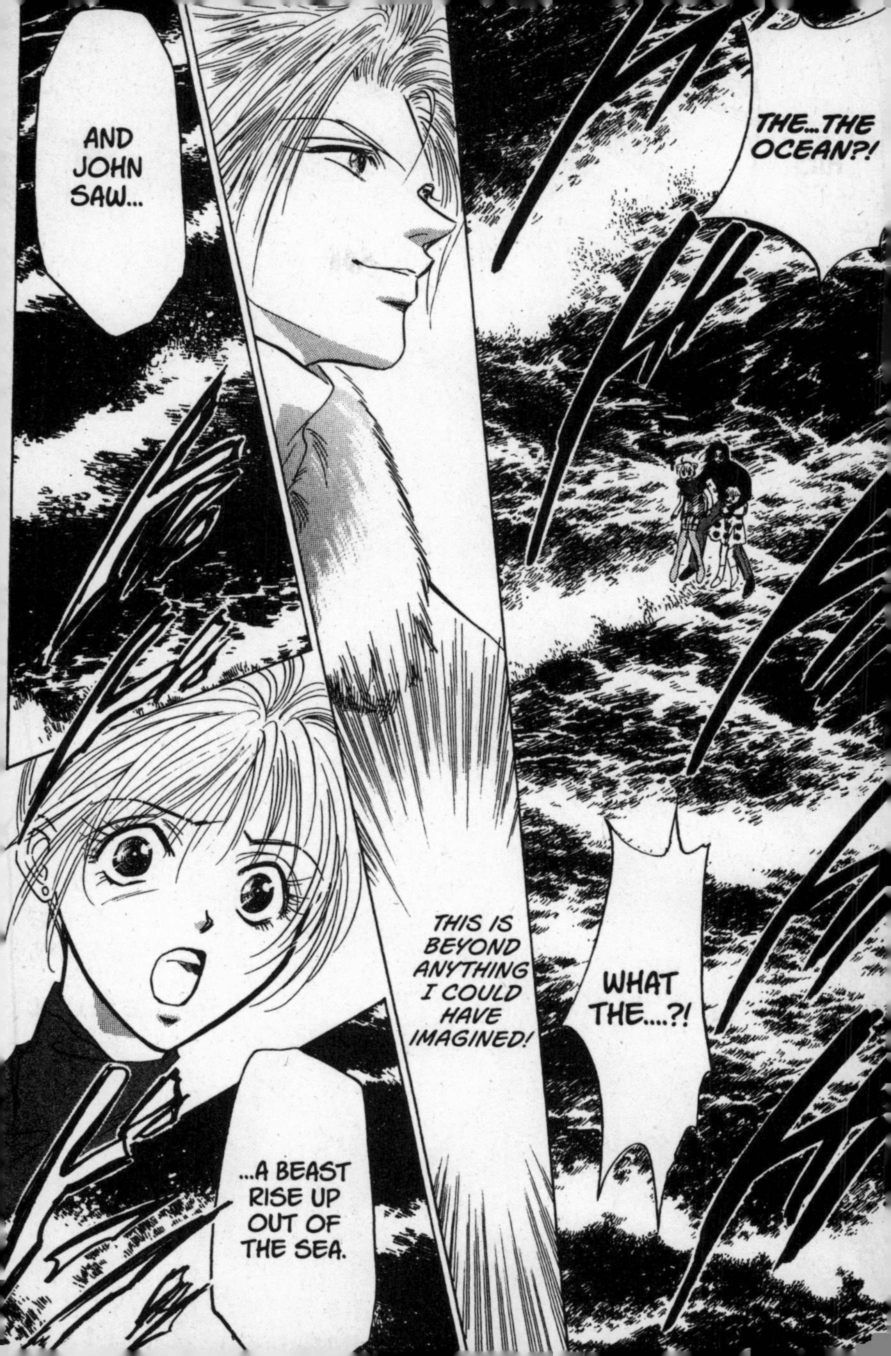
THE...THE OCEAN?!
WHAT THE....?!
THIS IS BEYOND ANYTHING I COULD HAVE IMAGINED!
AND JOHN SAW...
...A BEAST RISE UP OUT OF THE SEA.

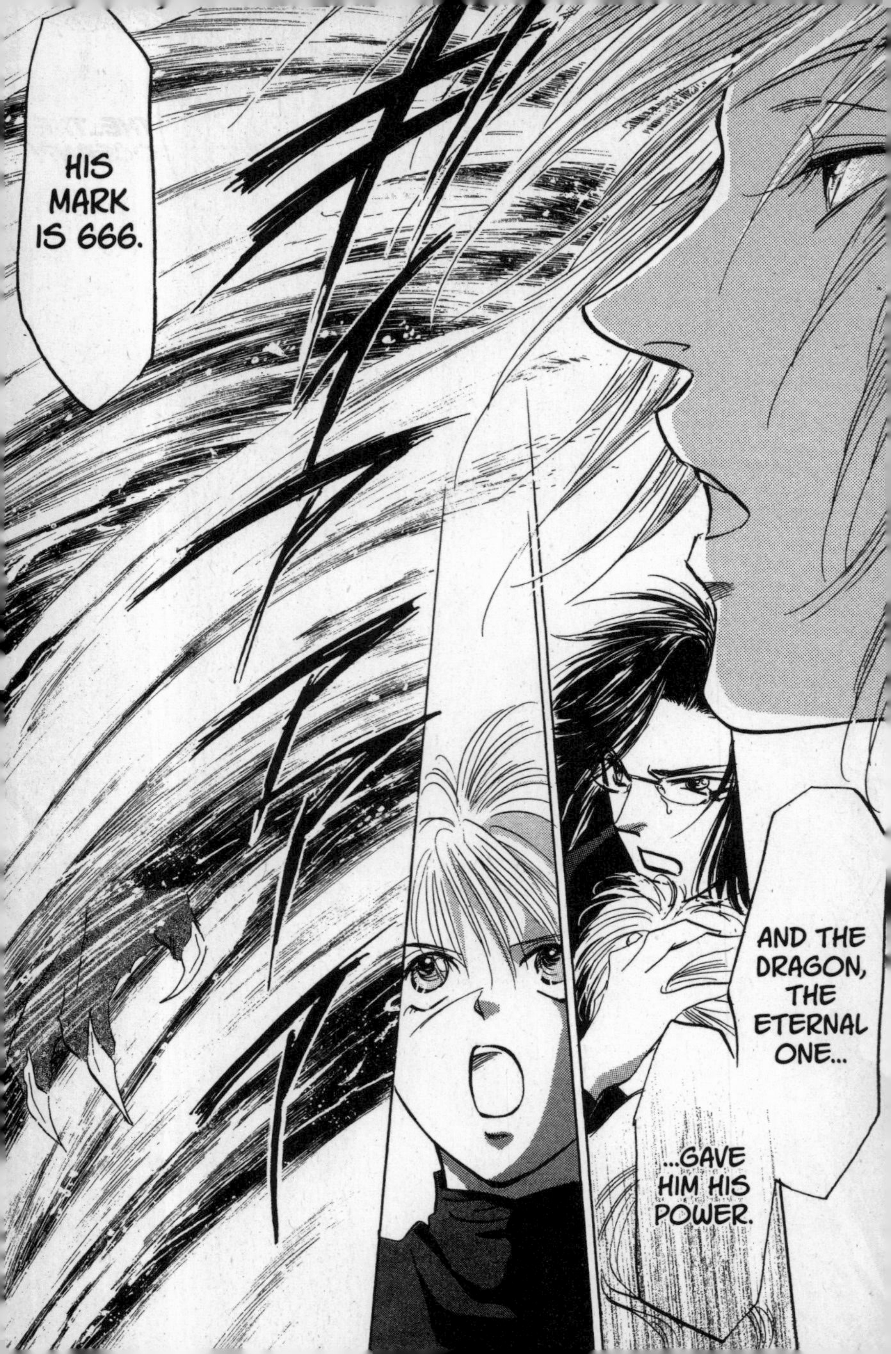
AND THE DRAGON, THE ETERNAL ONE...
...GAVE HIM HIS POWER.
HIS MARK IS 666.

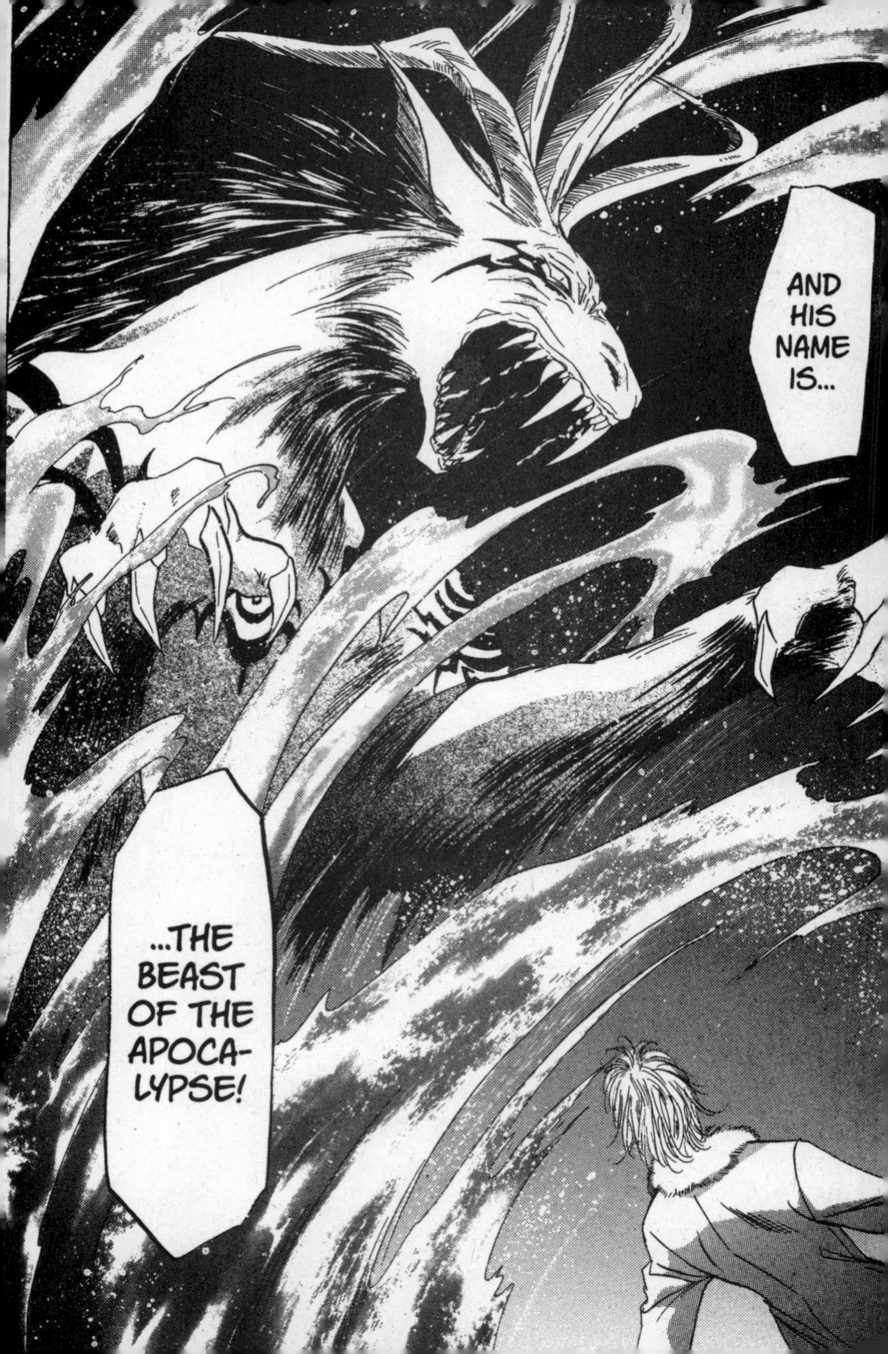
AND HIS NAME IS...
...THE BEAST OF THE APOCA-LYPSE!

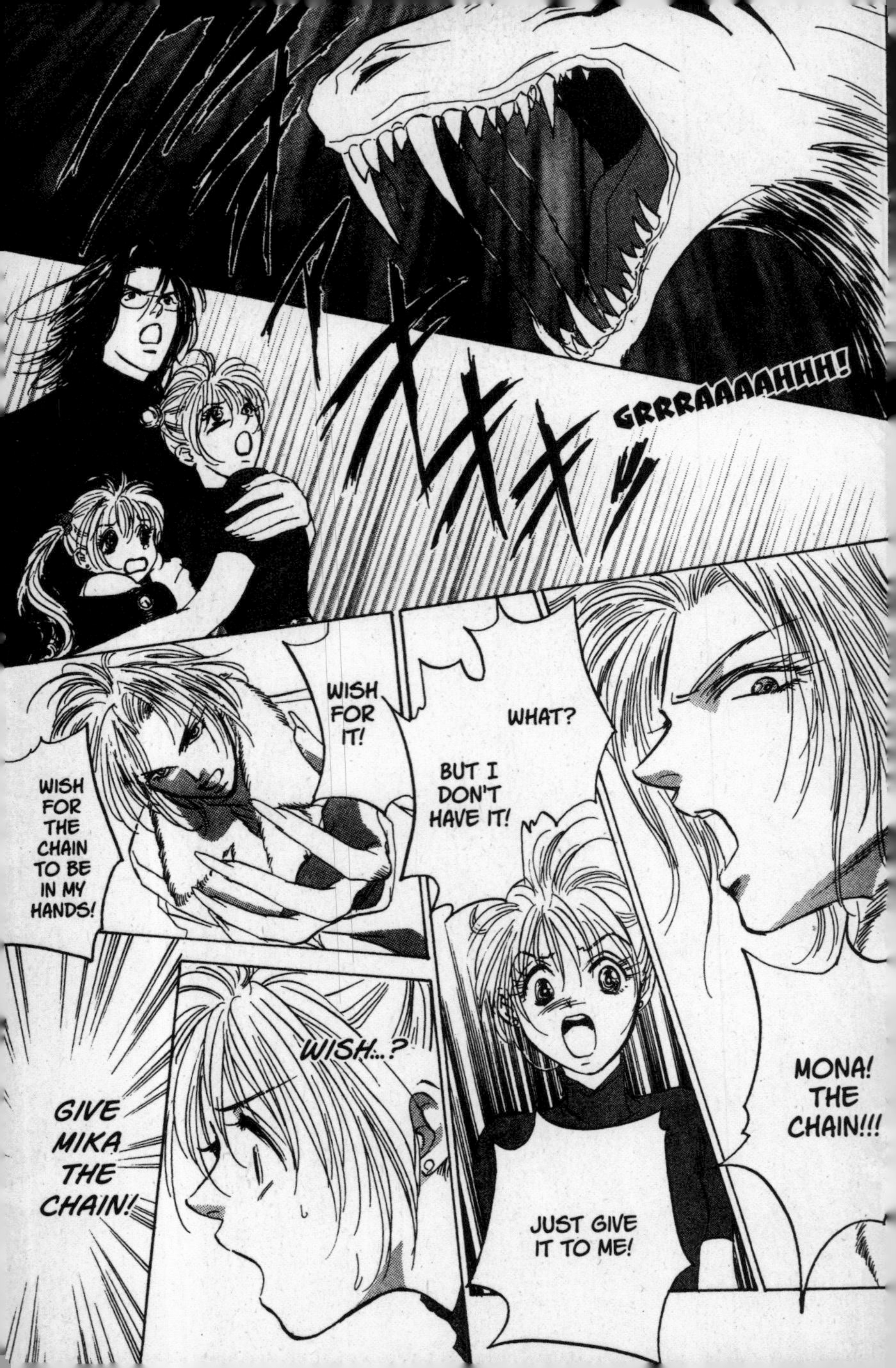

GRRRAAAAAHHH!
WHAT?
BUT I DON'T HAVE IT!
WISH FOR IT!
WISH FOR THE CHAIN TO BE IN MY HANDS!
MONA! THE CHAIN!!!
JUST GIVE IT TO ME!
WISH...?
GIVE MIKA THE CHAIN!

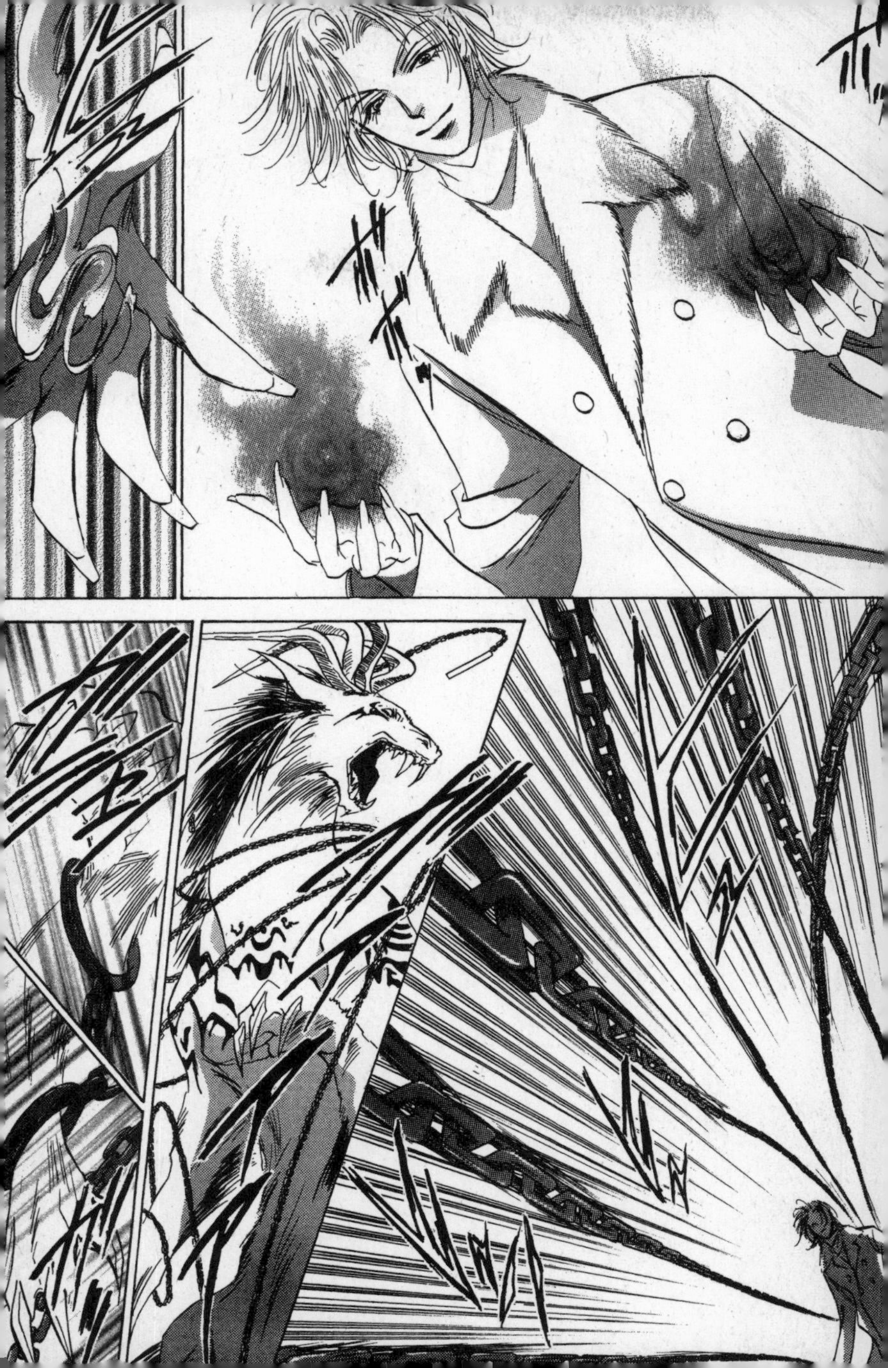

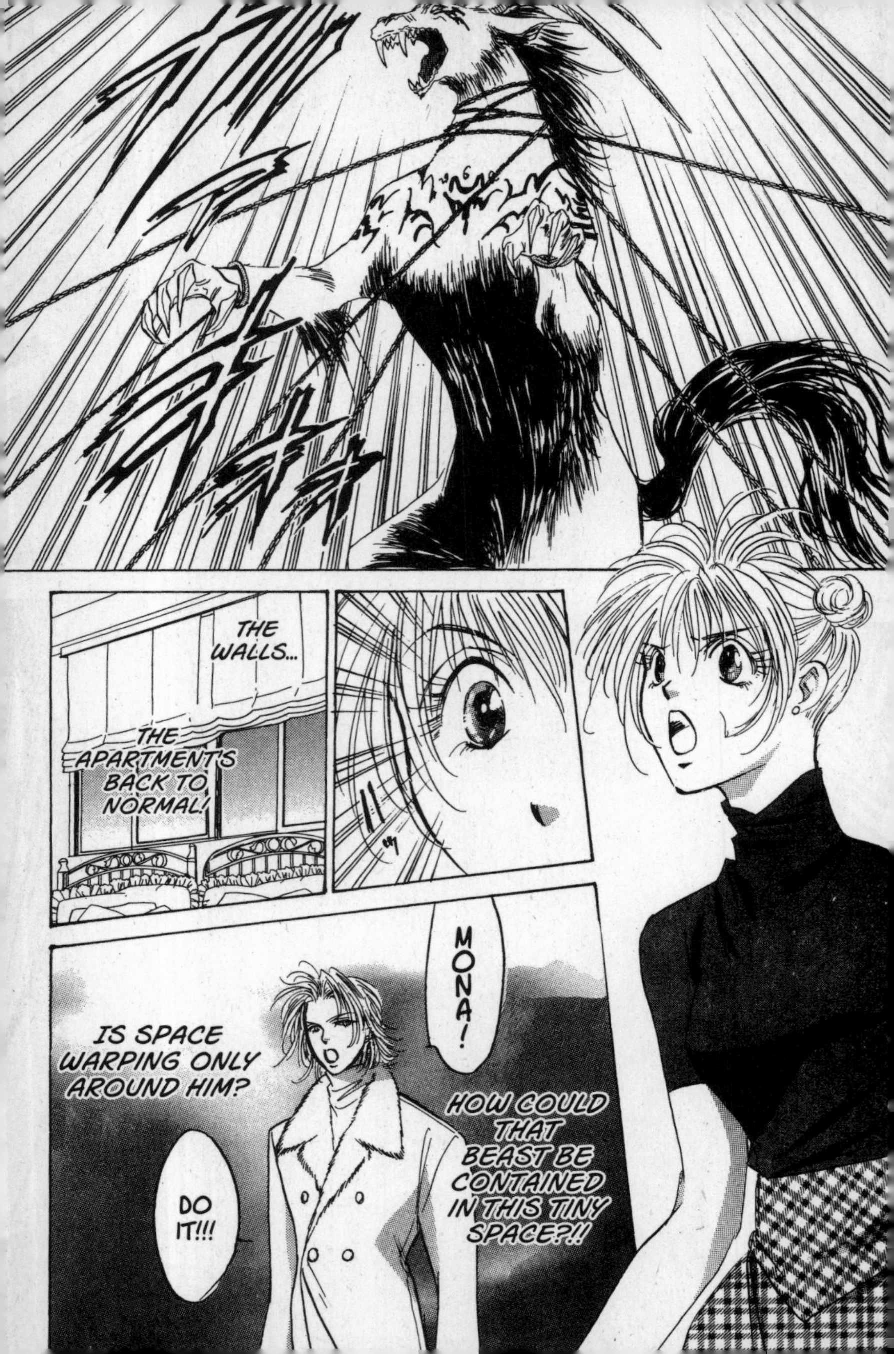
THE WALLS...
THE APARTMENT'S BACK TO NORMAL!
MONA!
IS SPACE WARPING ONLY AROUND HIM?
HOW COULD THAT BEAST BE CONTAINED IN THIS TINY SPACE?!
DO IT!!!

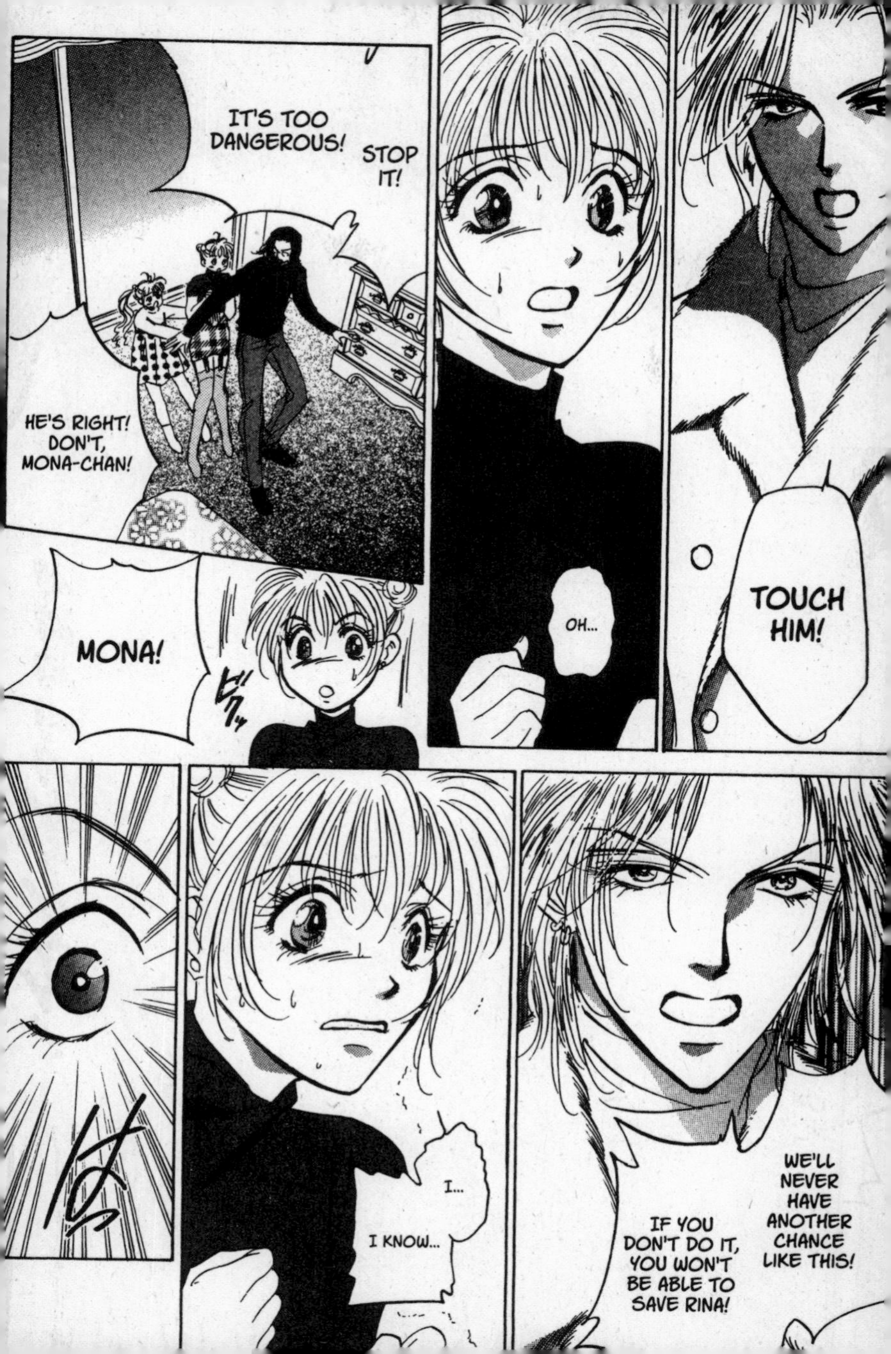
TOUCH HIM!
OH...
STOP IT!
IT'S TOO DANGEROUS!
HE'S RIGHT! DON'T, MONA-CHAN!
MONA!
WE'LL NEVER HAVE ANOTHER CHANCE LIKE THIS!
IF YOU DON'T DO IT, YOU WON'T BE ABLE TO SAVE RINA!
I...
I KNOW...

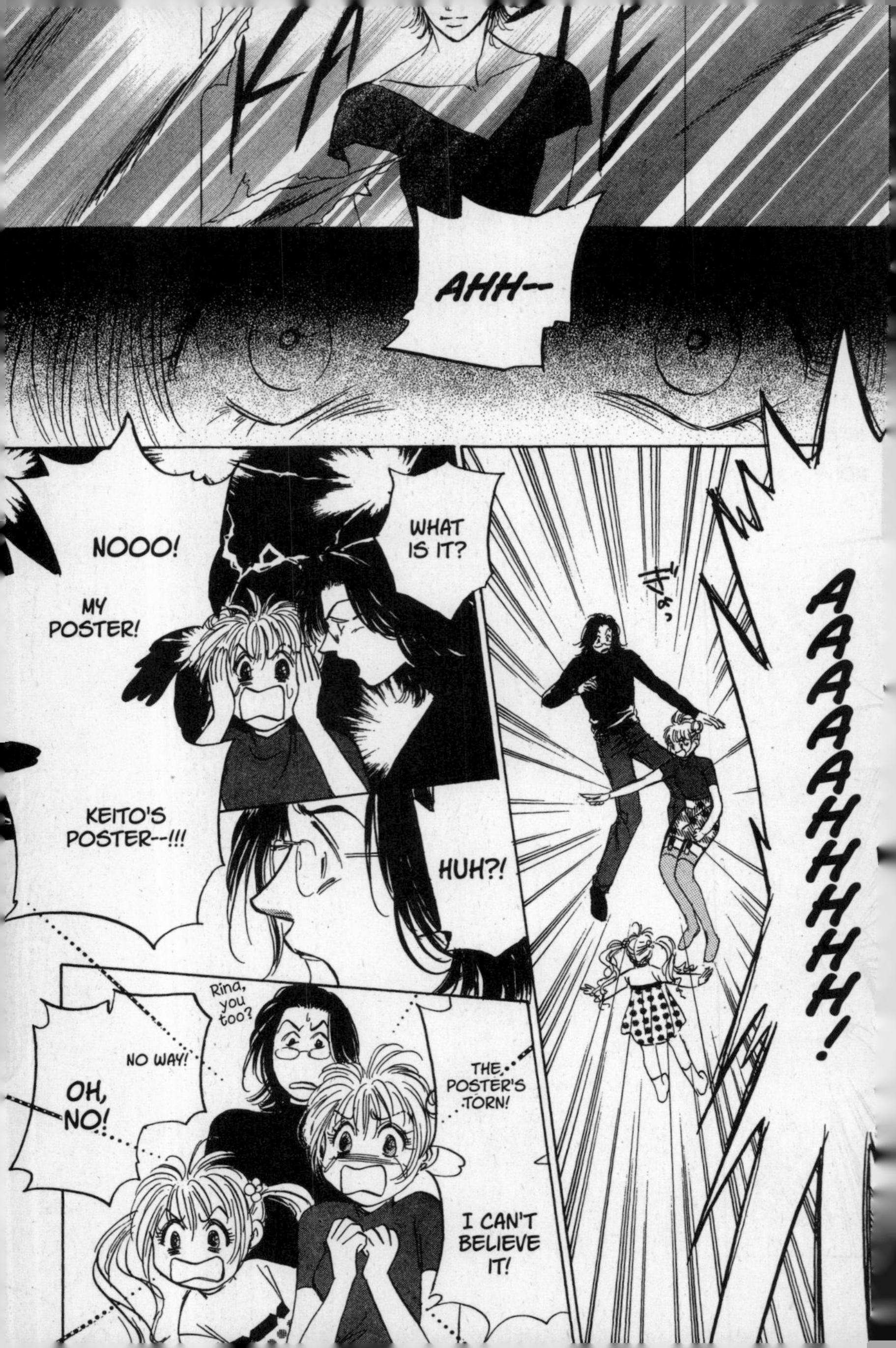
AHH--
AAAAAAHHHHHH!
WHAT IS IT?
NOOO!
MY POSTER!
KEITO'S POSTER--!!!
HUH?!
THE POSTER'S TORN!
I CAN'T BELIEVE IT!
Rina, you too?
NO WAY!
OH, NO!

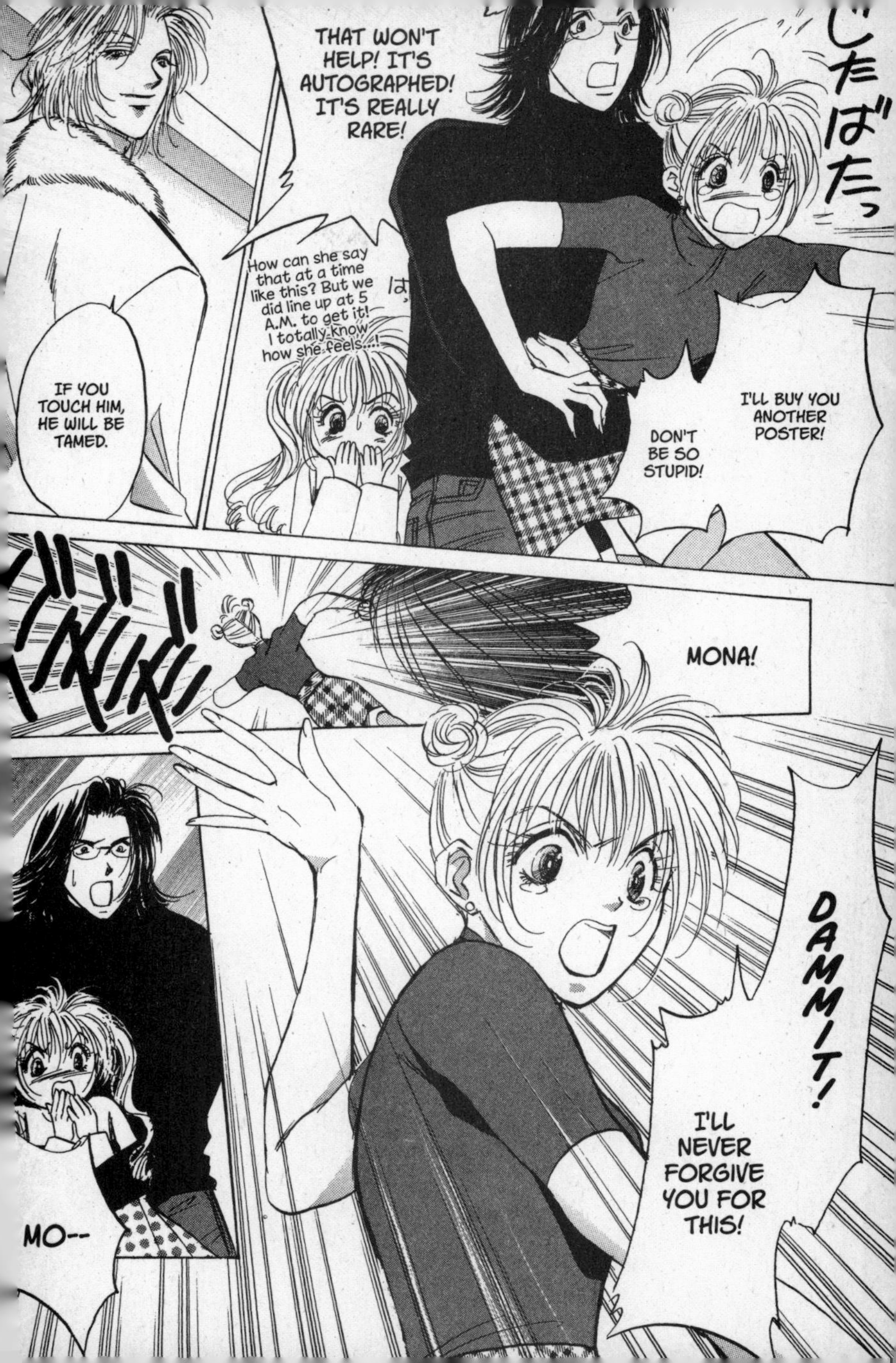
じたばたっ
I'LL BUY YOU ANOTHER POSTER!
DON'T BE SO STUPID!
THAT WON'T HELP! IT'S AUTOGRAPHED! IT'S REALLY RARE!
How can she say that at a time like this? But we did line up at 5 A.M. to get it! I totally know how she feels...!
は
IF YOU TOUCH HIM, HE WILL BE TAMED.
MONA!
DAMMIT!
I'LL NEVER FORGIVE YOU FOR THIS!
MO--

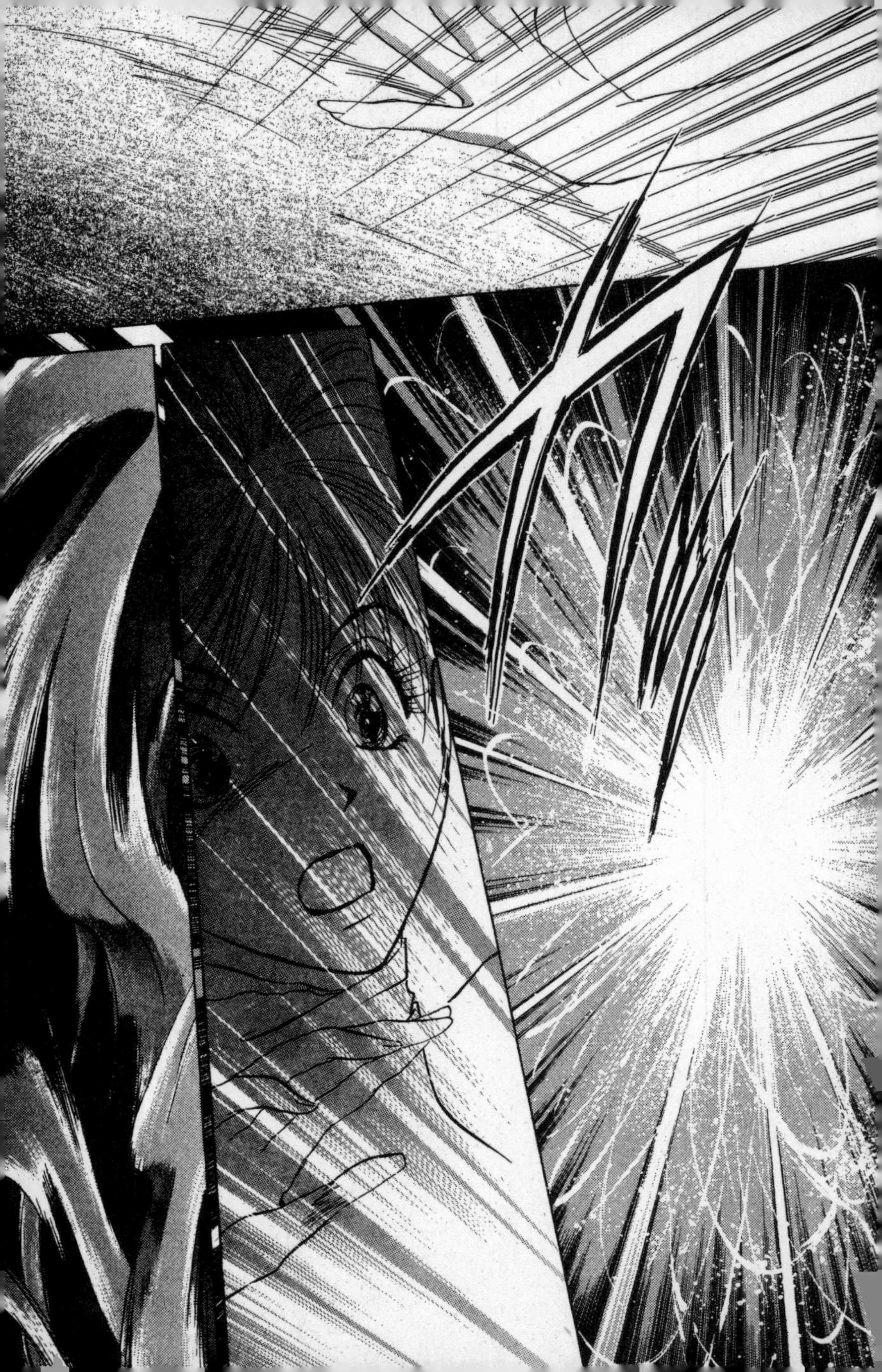

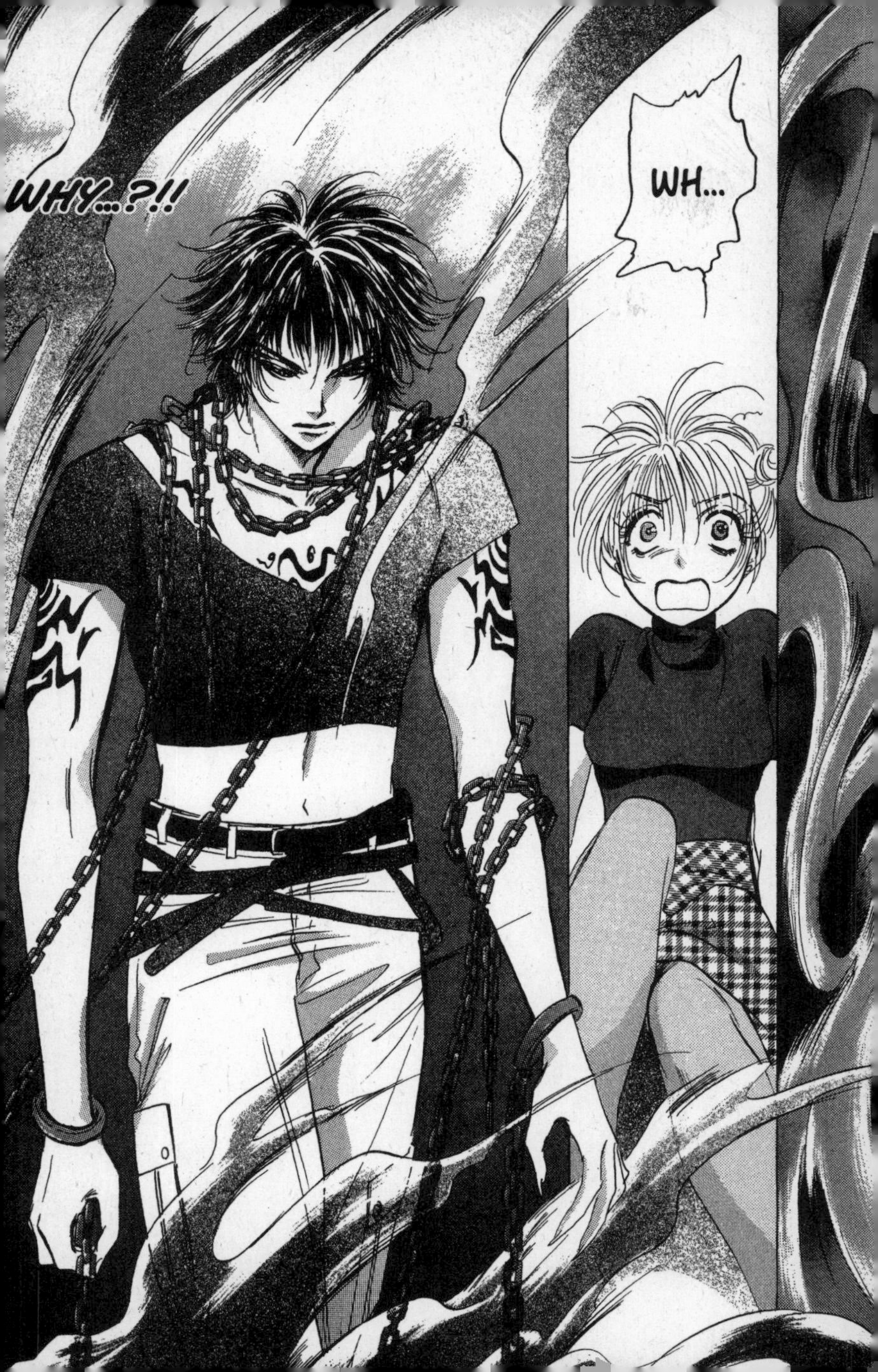
WH...
WHY...?!!

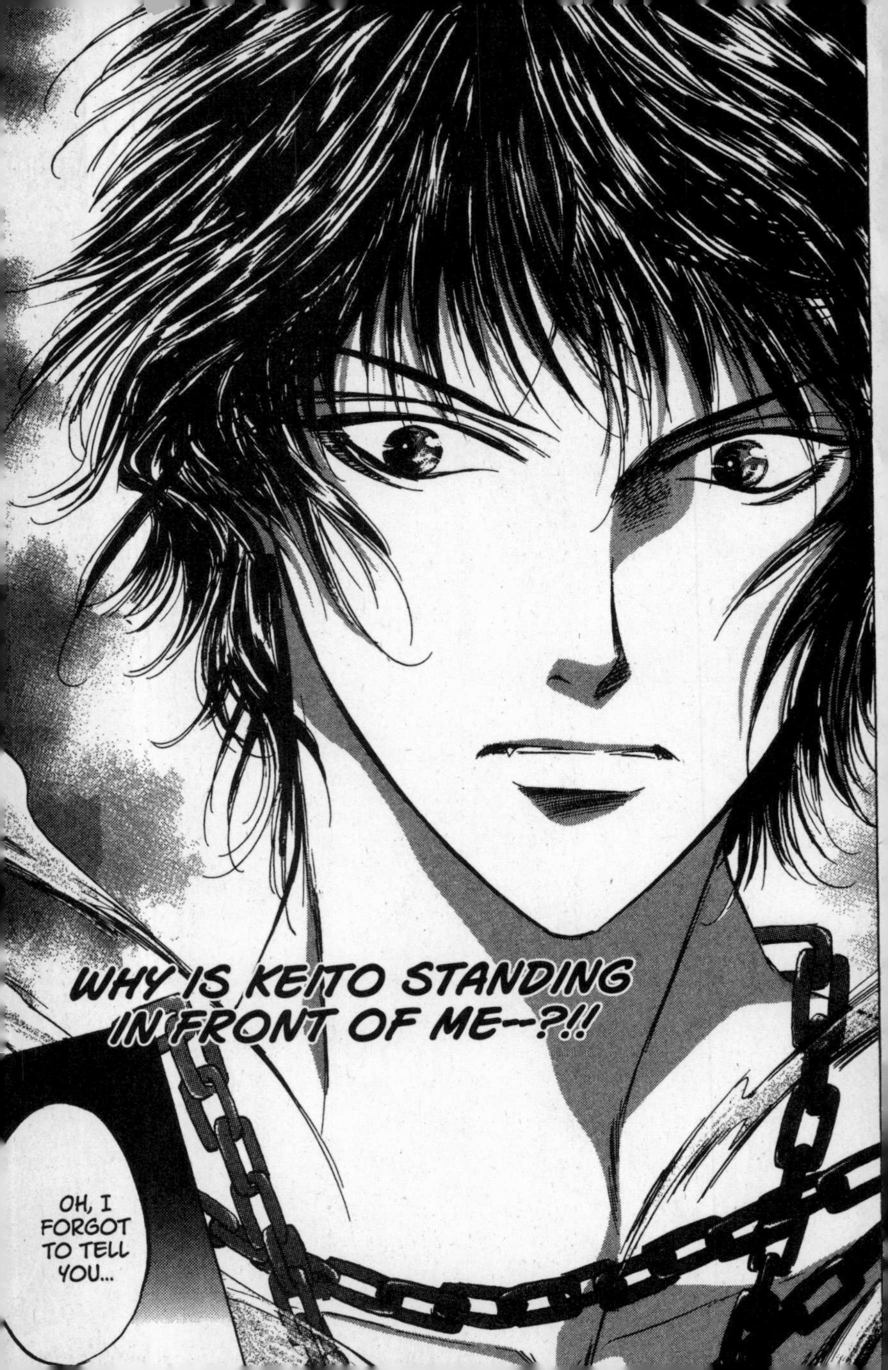
WHY IS KEITO STANDING IN FRONT OF ME--?!!
OH, I FORGOT TO TELL YOU...

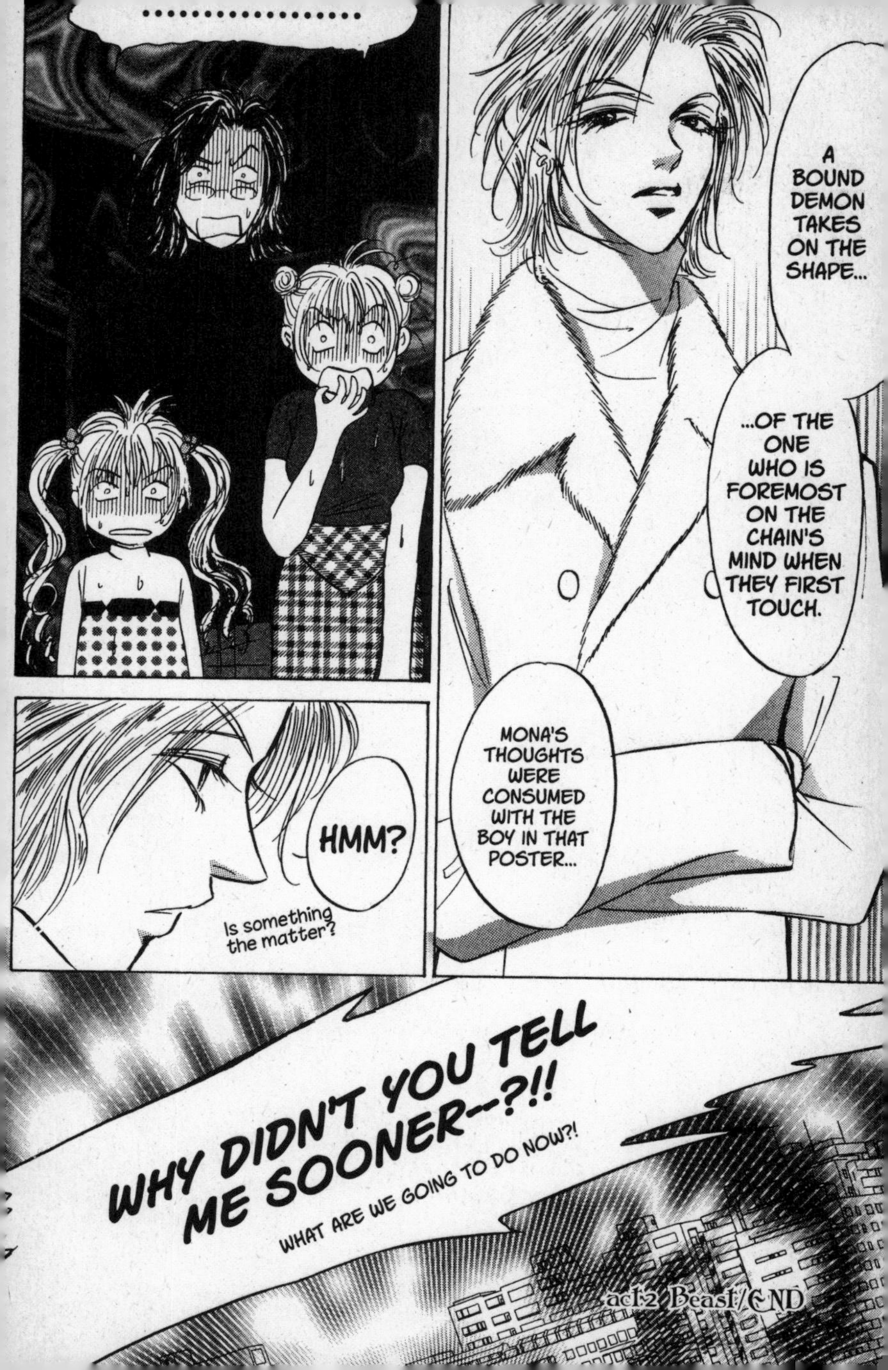
A BOUND DEMON TAKES ON THE SHAPE...
...OF THE ONE WHO IS FOREMOST ON THE CHAIN'S MIND WHEN THEY FIRST TOUCH.
MONA'S THOUGHTS WERE CONSUMED WITH THE BOY IN THAT POSTER...
....
HMM?
Is something the matter?
WHY DIDN'T YOU TELL ME SOONER--?!!
WHAT ARE WE GOING TO DO NOW?!
act.2 Beast/END

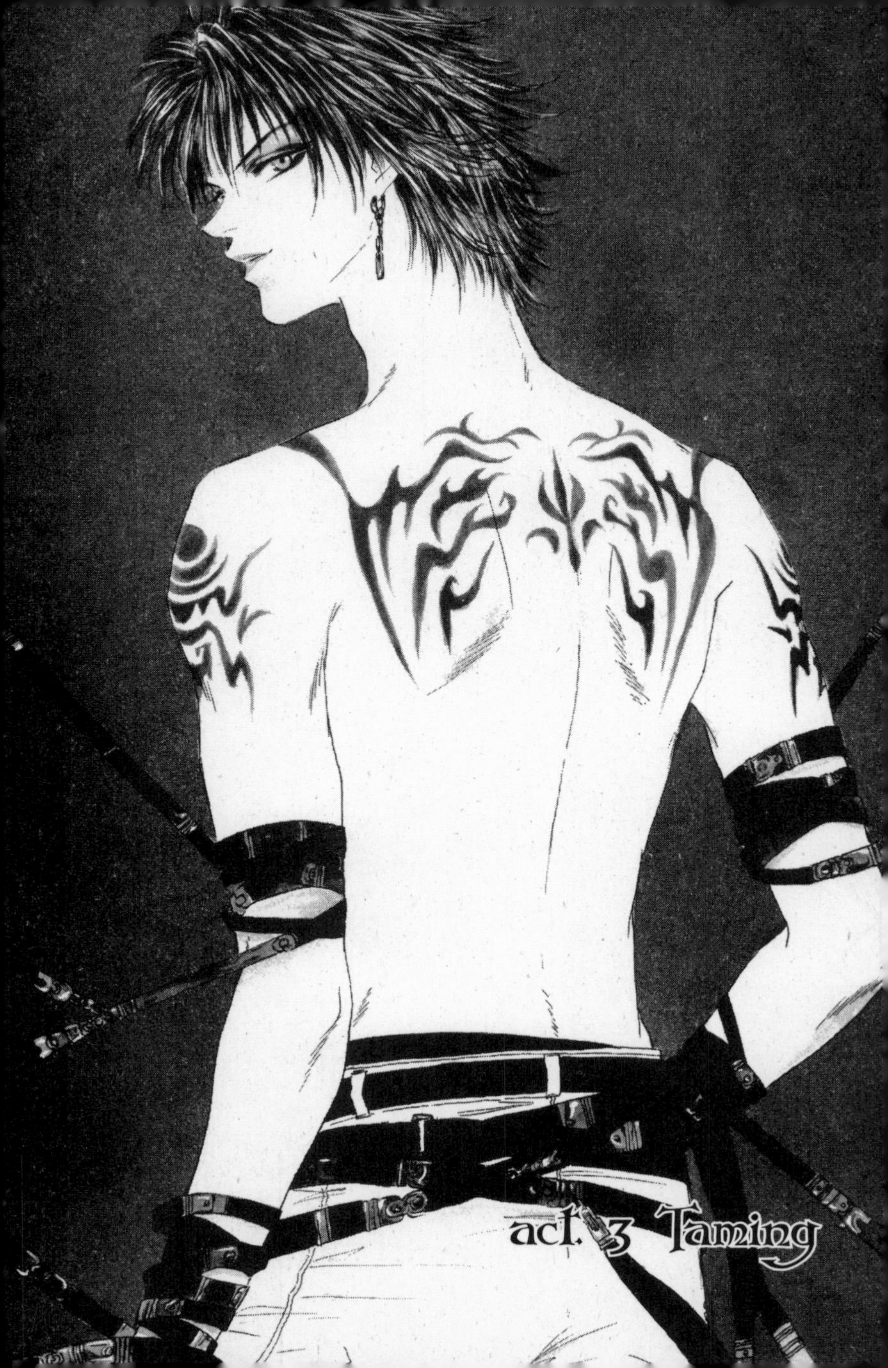
act. 3 Taming

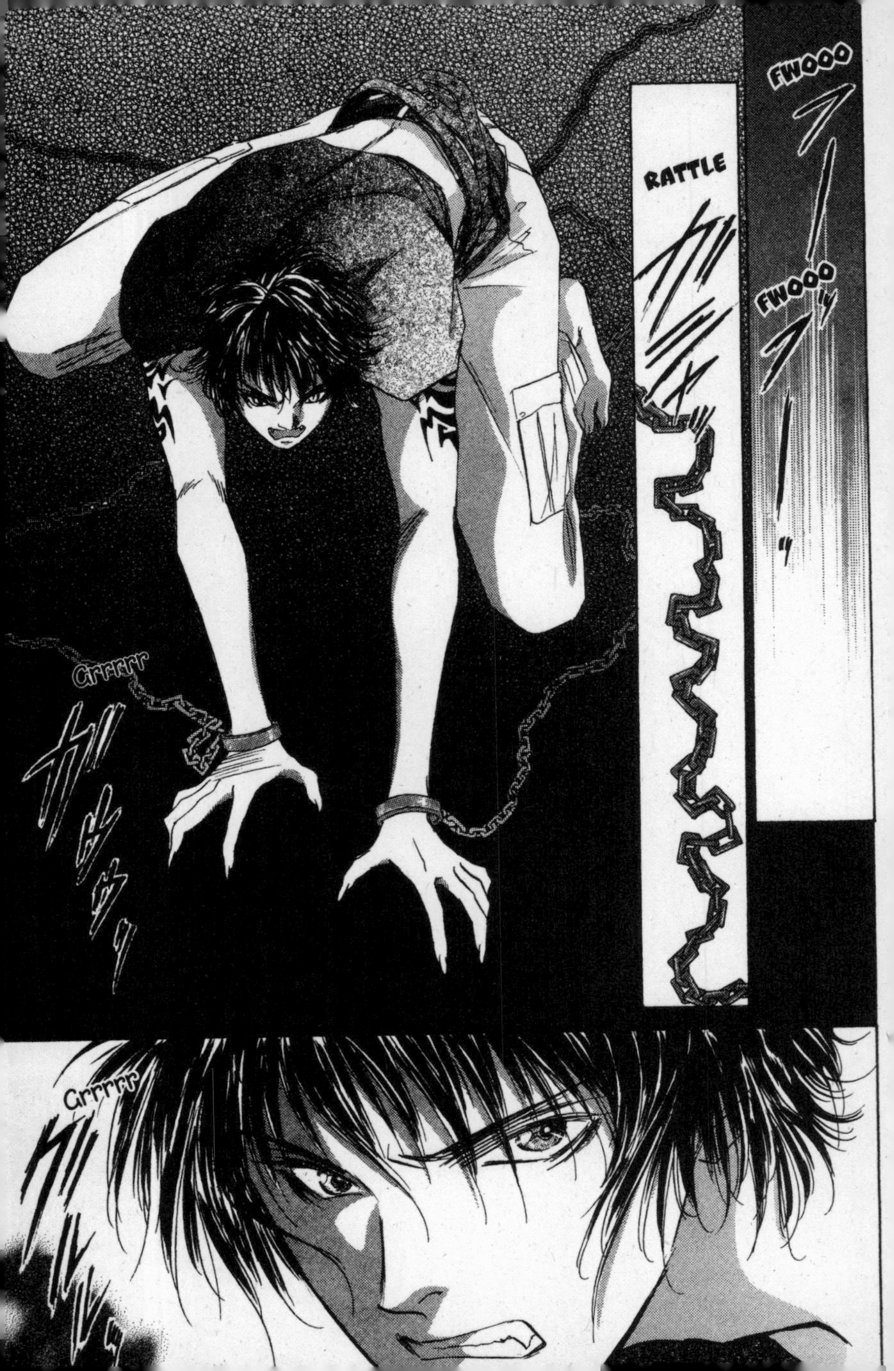
FWOOO
FWOOO
RATTLE
Grrrrr
Grrrrr

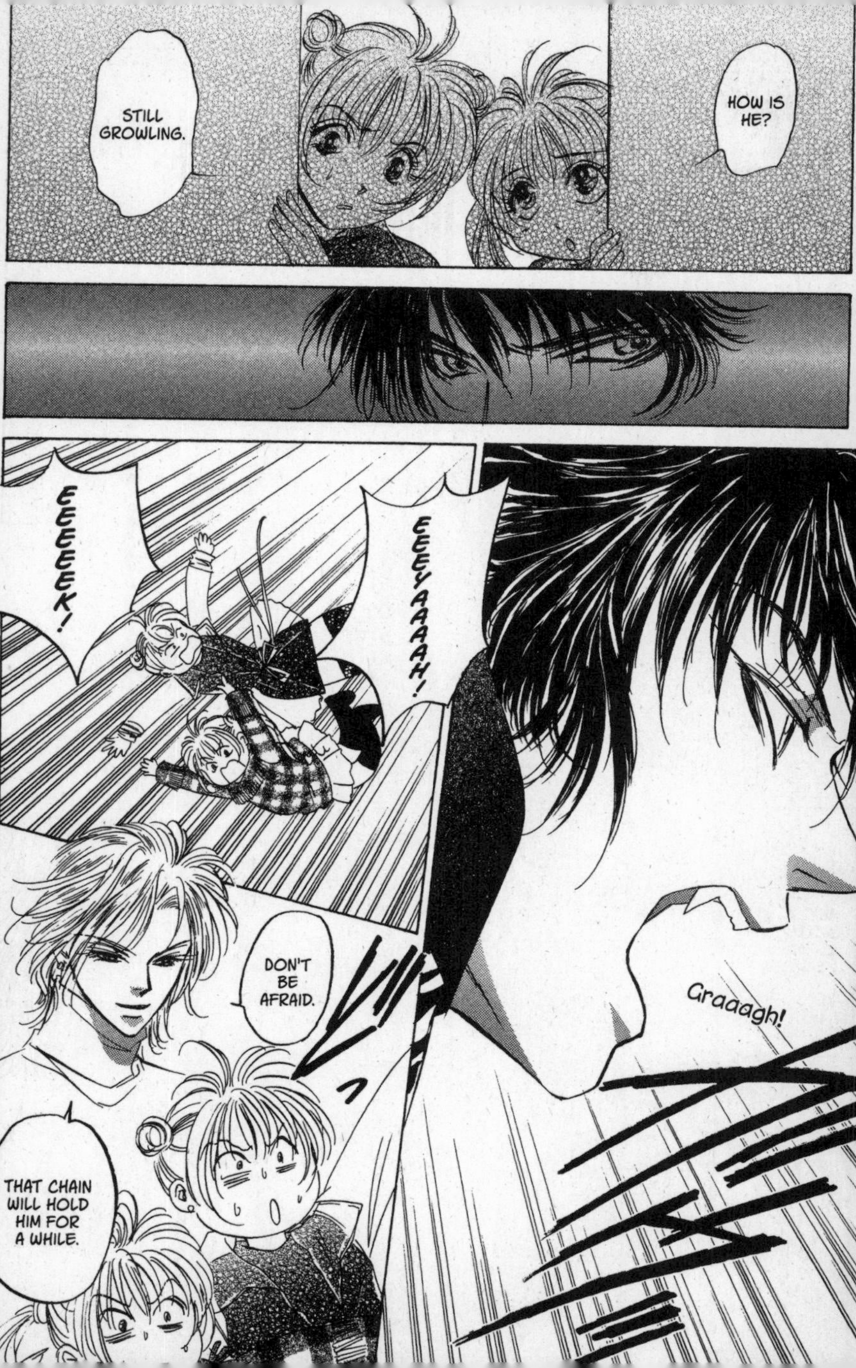
HOW IS HE?
STILL GROWLING.
Graaagh!
EEEYAAAAAH!
EEEEEK!
DON'T BE AFRAID.
THAT CHAIN WILL HOLD HIM FOR A WHILE.

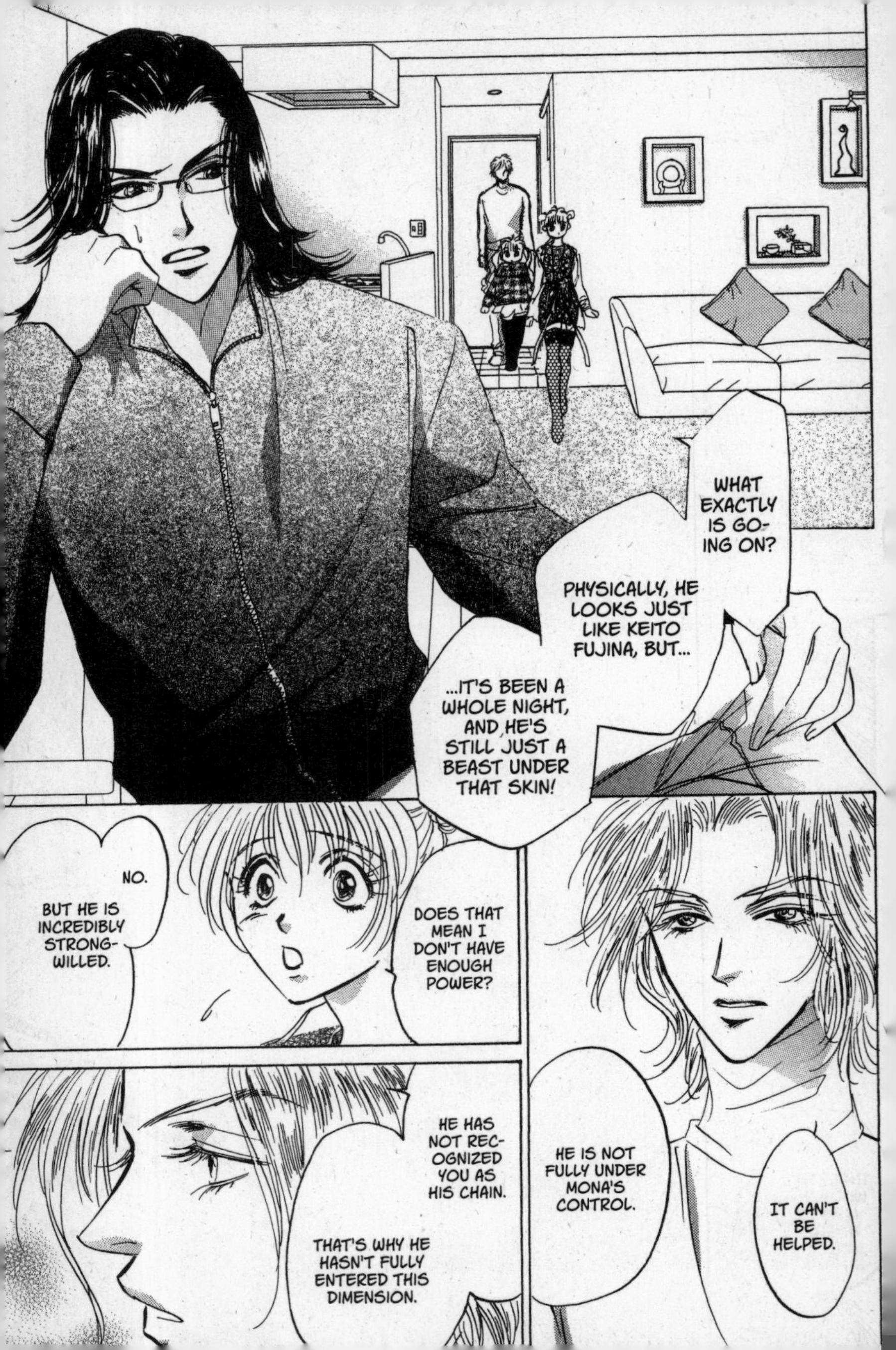
WHAT EXACTLY IS GO-ING ON?
PHYSICALLY, HE LOOKS JUST LIKE KEITO FUJINA, BUT...
...IT'S BEEN A WHOLE NIGHT, AND HE'S STILL JUST A BEAST UNDER THAT SKIN!
HE IS NOT FULLY UNDER MONA'S CONTROL.
IT CAN'T BE HELPED.
DOES THAT MEAN I DON'T HAVE ENOUGH POWER?
NO.
BUT HE IS INCREDIBLY STRONG-WILLED.
HE HAS NOT REC-OGNIZED YOU AS HIS CHAIN.
THAT'S WHY HE HASN'T FULLY ENTERED THIS DIMENSION.

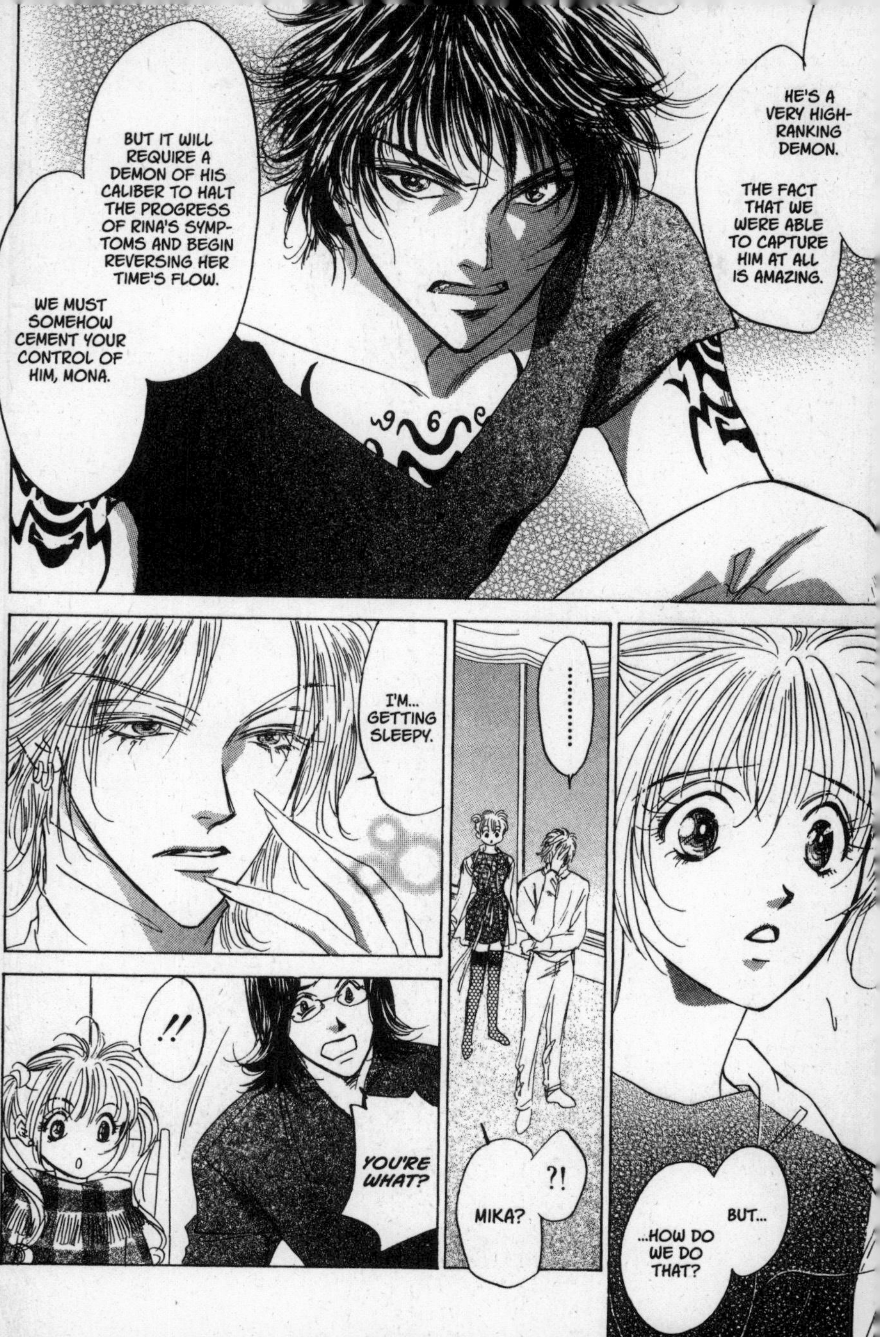
HE'S A VERY HIGH-RANKING DEMON.
THE FACT THAT WE WERE ABLE TO CAPTURE HIM AT ALL IS AMAZING.
BUT IT WILL REQUIRE A DEMON OF HIS CALIBER TO HALT THE PROGRESS OF RINA'S SYMP-TOMS AND BEGIN REVERSING HER TIME'S FLOW.
WE MUST SOMEHOW CEMENT YOUR CONTROL OF HIM, MONA.
BUT...
...HOW DO WE DO THAT?
....
?!
MIKA?
I'M... GETTING SLEEPY.
!!
YOU'RE WHAT?

FREE TALK
⟨2⟩

Here's what I've been up to lately, although the performances will be over by the time this book hits stores in August *OZ*, a piece I wrote over ten years ago, is being staged!

At this point I haven't seen it yet (it's May right now), but when they told me about the production, I was blown away. *OZ* is hardcore science fiction!

There are lots of action scenes and other things that are difficult to do on stage, but Studio Life's enthusiasm for the project finally convinced me to let them go ahead with it. I'm not a theater-goer, but I'm really looking forward to seeing it! Next time I'll report back and let you know how it went!

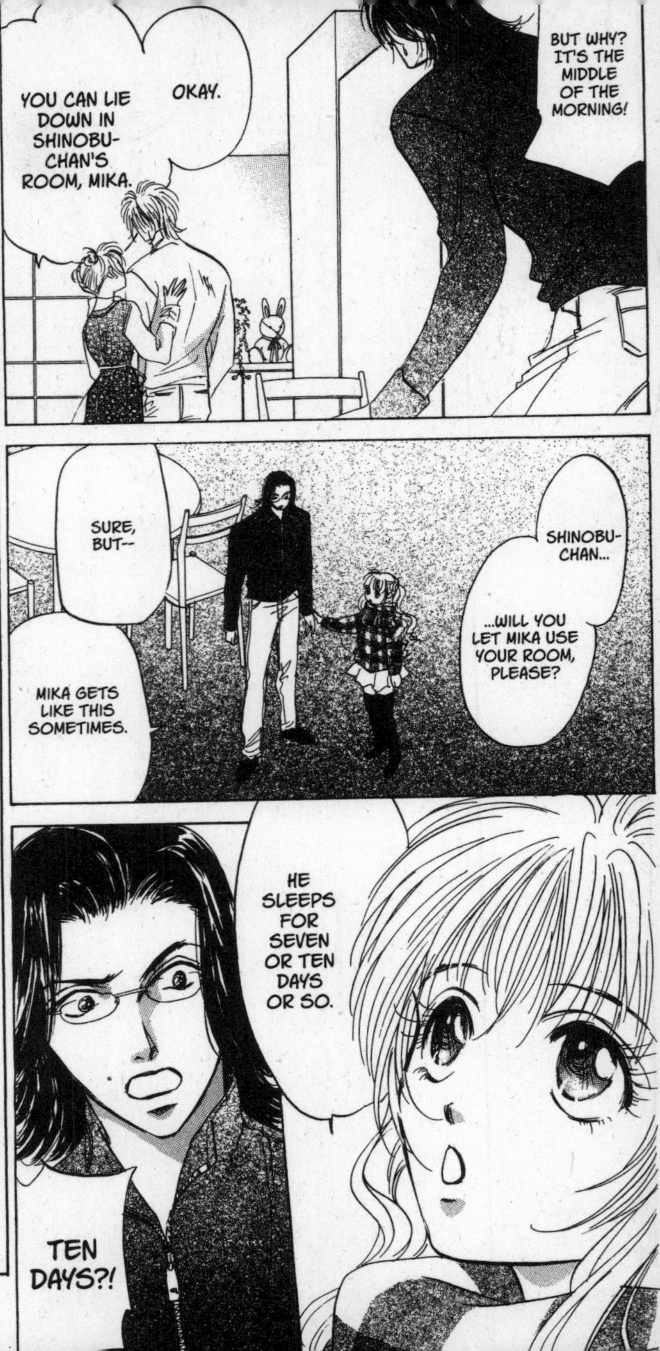
BUT WHY? IT'S THE MIDDLE OF THE MORNING!
OKAY.
YOU CAN LIE DOWN IN SHINOBU-CHAN'S ROOM, MIKA.
SHINOBU-CHAN...
...WILL YOU LET MIKA USE YOUR ROOM, PLEASE?
SURE, BUT--
MIKA GETS LIKE THIS SOMETIMES.
HE SLEEPS FOR SEVEN OR TEN DAYS OR SO.
TEN DAYS?!

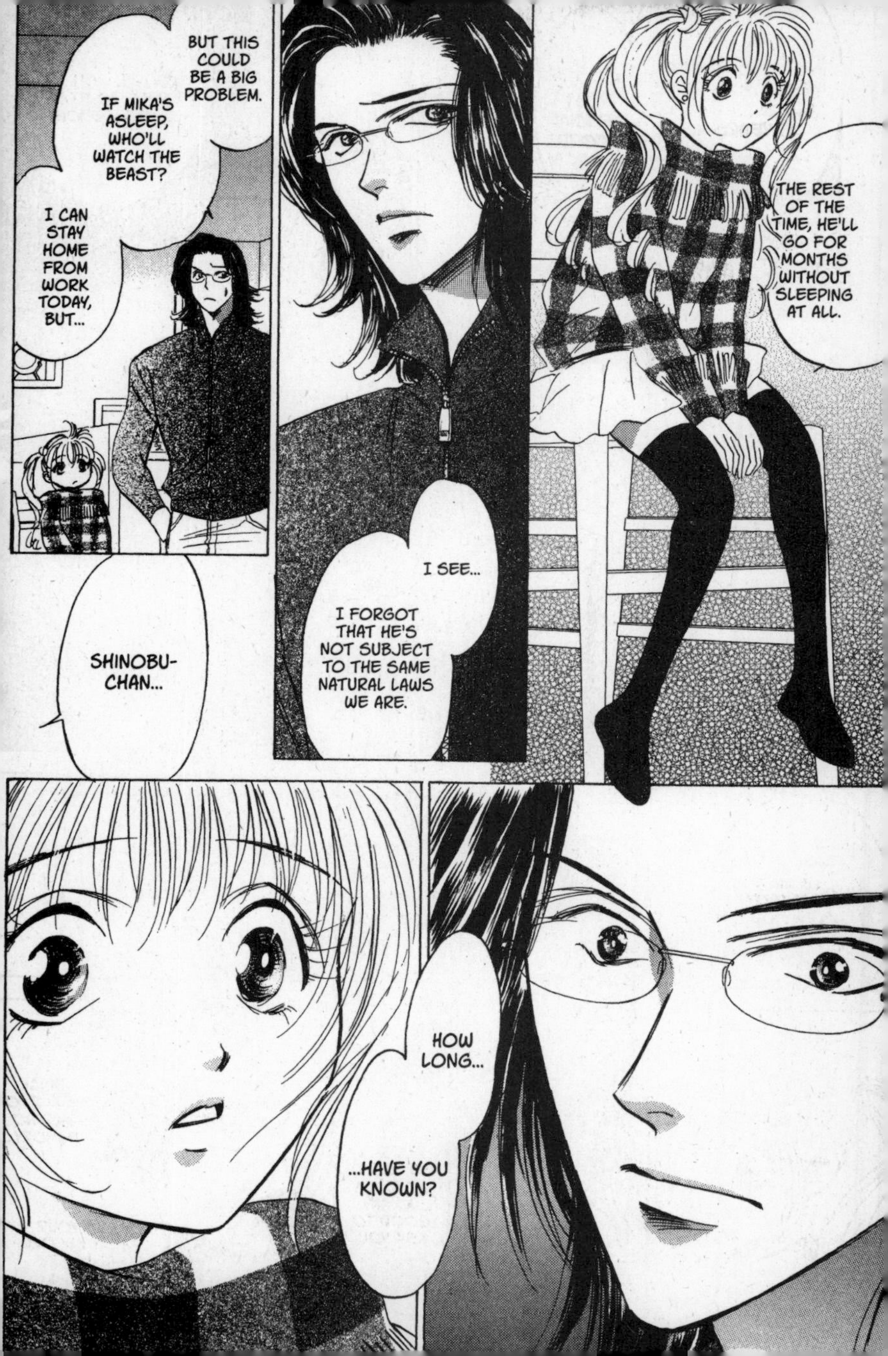
THE REST OF THE TIME, HE'LL GO FOR MONTHS WITHOUT SLEEPING AT ALL.
I SEE...
I FORGOT THAT HE'S NOT SUBJECT TO THE SAME NATURAL LAWS WE ARE.
BUT THIS COULD BE A BIG PROBLEM.
IF MIKA'S ASLEEP, WHO'LL WATCH THE BEAST?
I CAN STAY HOME FROM WORK TODAY, BUT...
SHINOBU-CHAN...
HOW LONG...
...HAVE YOU KNOWN?

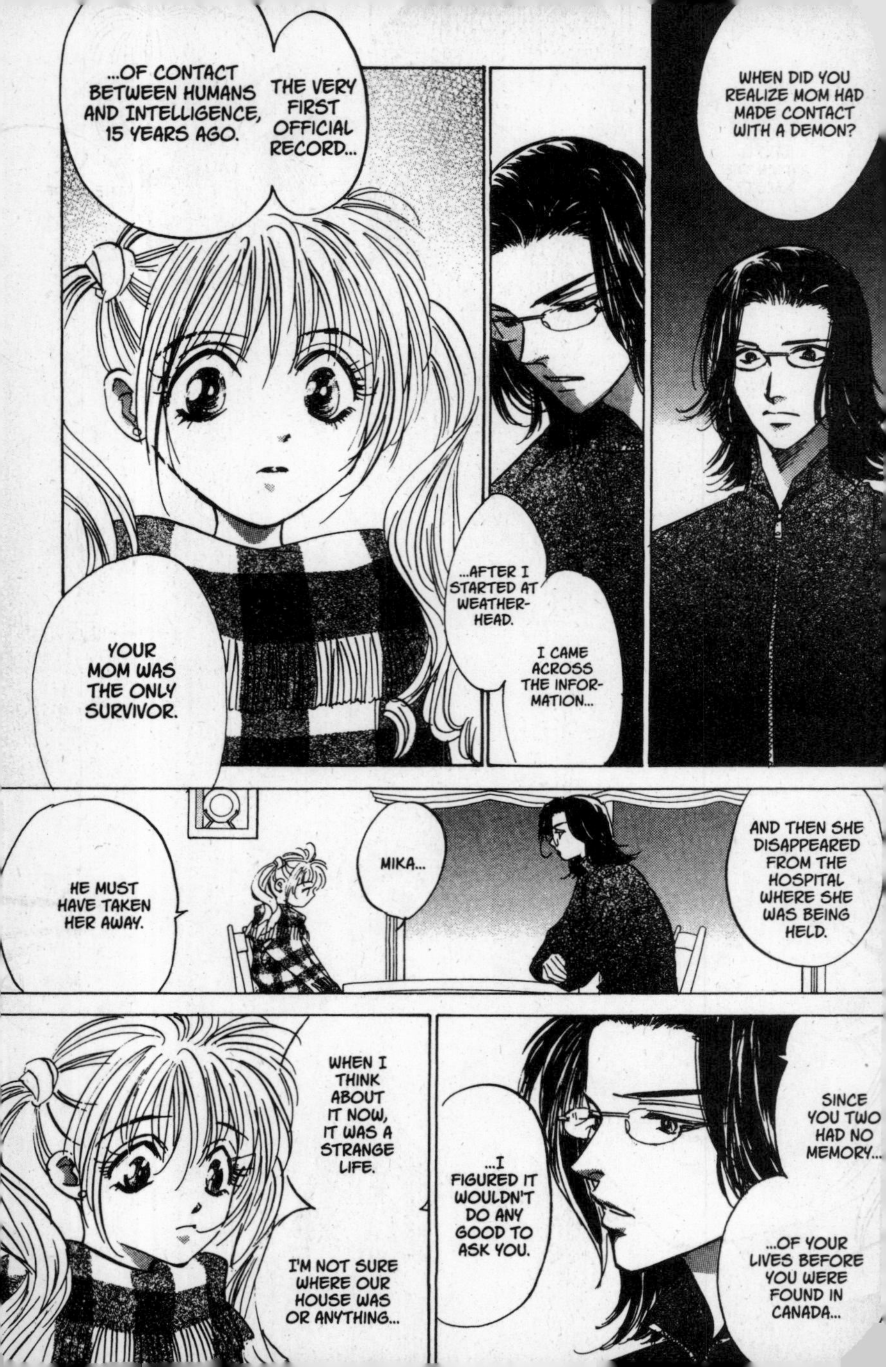
WHEN DID YOU REALIZE MOM HAD MADE CONTACT WITH A DEMON?
...AFTER I STARTED AT WEATHER-HEAD.
I CAME ACROSS THE INFORMATION...
THE VERY FIRST OFFICIAL RECORD...
...OF CONTACT BETWEEN HUMANS AND INTELLIGENCE, 15 YEARS AGO.
YOUR MOM WAS THE ONLY SURVIVOR.
AND THEN SHE DISAPPEARED FROM THE HOSPITAL WHERE SHE WAS BEING HELD.
MIKA...
HE MUST HAVE TAKEN HER AWAY.
SINCE YOU TWO HAD NO MEMORY...
...OF YOUR LIVES BEFORE YOU WERE FOUND IN CANADA...
...I FIGURED IT WOULDN'T DO ANY GOOD TO ASK YOU.
WHEN I THINK ABOUT IT NOW, IT WAS A STRANGE LIFE.
I'M NOT SURE WHERE OUR HOUSE WAS OR ANYTHING...

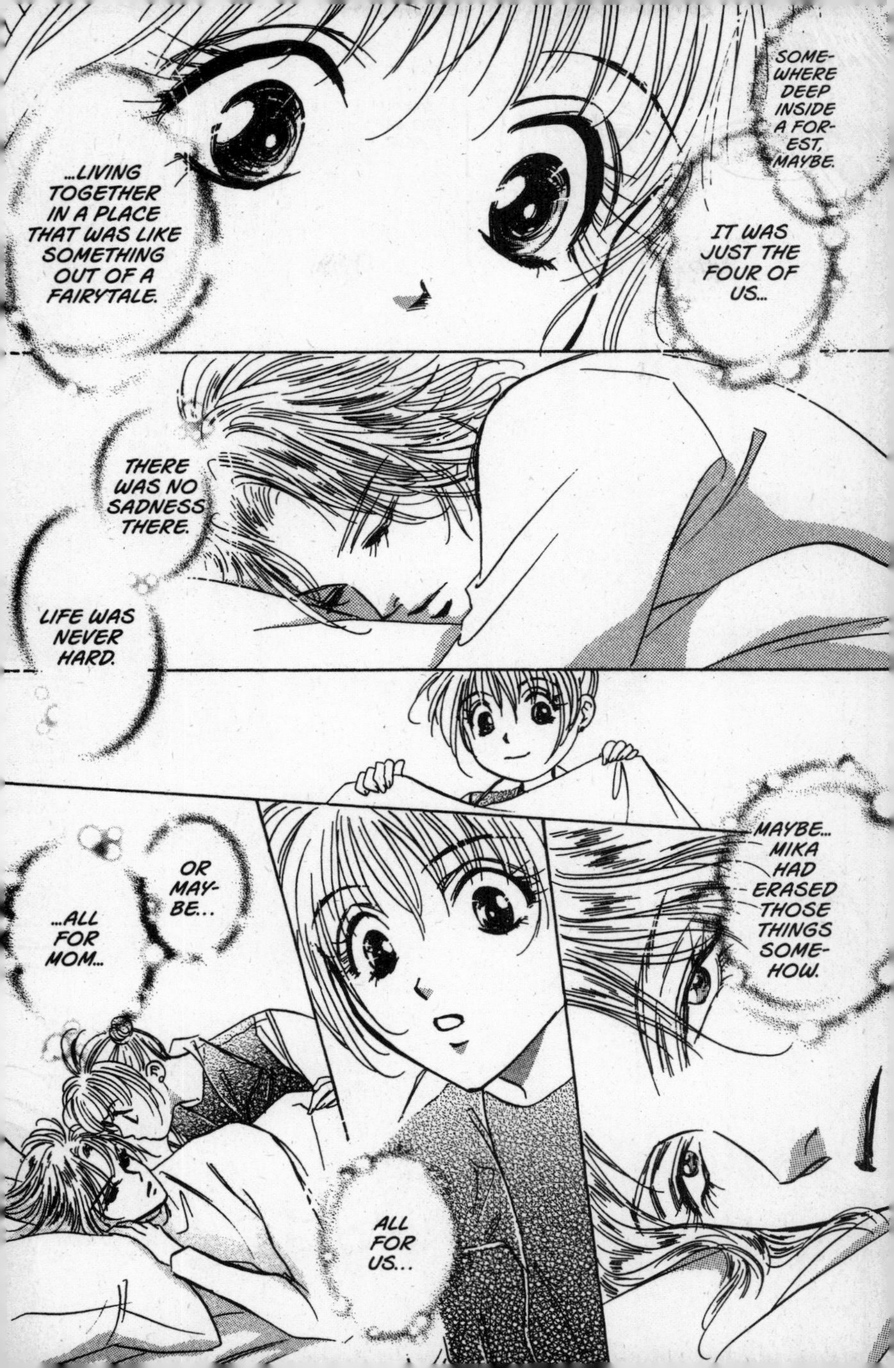
SOMEWHERE DEEP INSIDE A FOREST, MAYBE.
IT WAS JUST THE FOUR OF US...
...LIVING TOGETHER IN A PLACE THAT WAS LIKE SOMETHING OUT OF A FAIRYTALE.
THERE WAS NO SADNESS THERE.
LIFE WAS NEVER HARD.
MAYBE... MIKA HAD ERASED THOSE THINGS SOMEHOW.
OR MAYBE...
...ALL FOR MOM...
ALL FOR US...

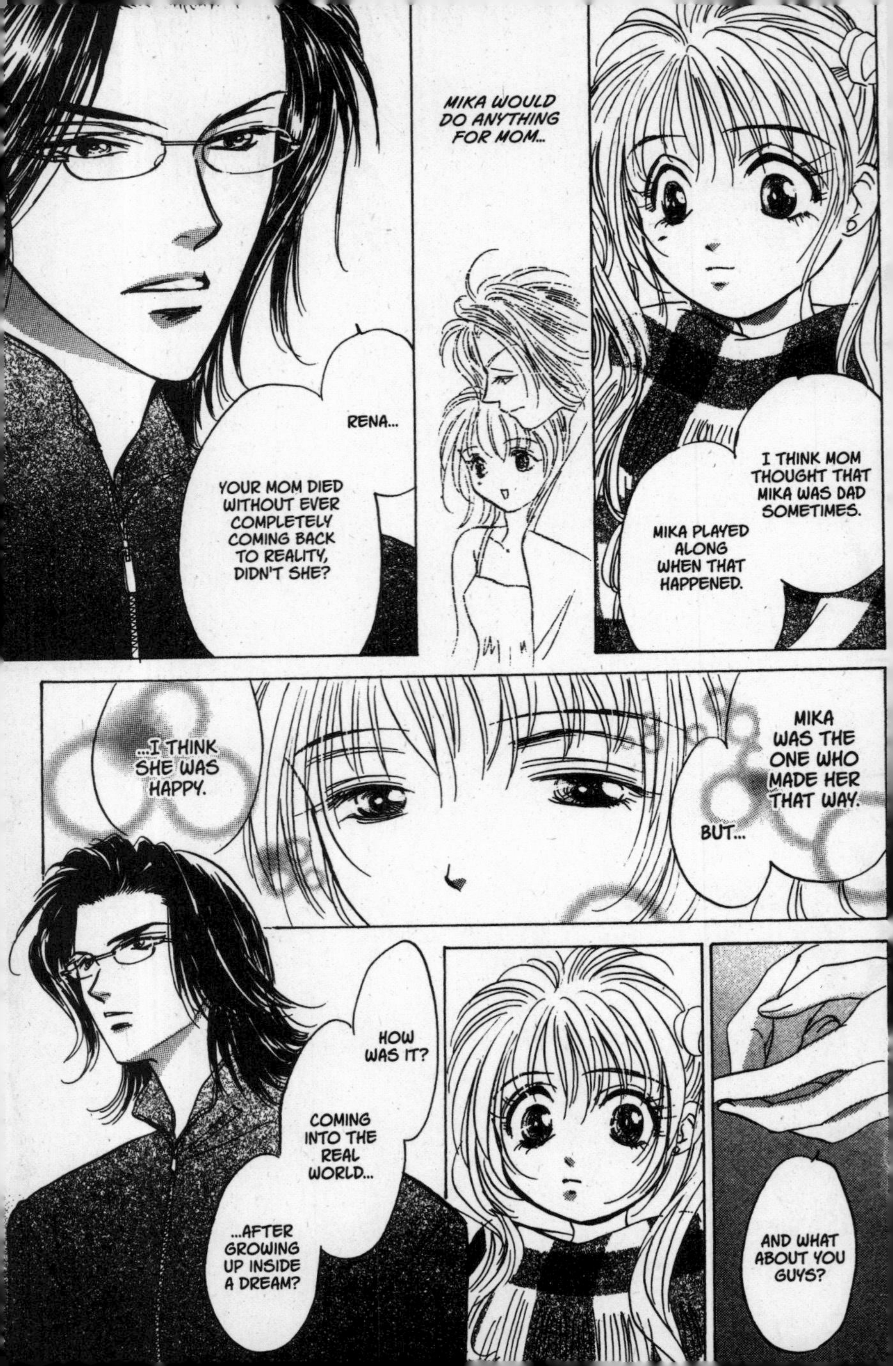
I THINK MOM THOUGHT THAT MIKA WAS DAD SOMETIMES.
MIKA PLAYED ALONG WHEN THAT HAPPENED.
MIKA WOULD DO ANYTHING FOR MOM...
RENA...
YOUR MOM DIED WITHOUT EVER COMPLETELY COMING BACK TO REALITY, DIDN'T SHE?
MIKA WAS THE ONE WHO MADE HER THAT WAY.
BUT...
...I THINK SHE WAS HAPPY.
AND WHAT ABOUT YOU GUYS?
HOW WAS IT?
COMING INTO THE REAL WORLD...
...AFTER GROWING UP INSIDE A DREAM?

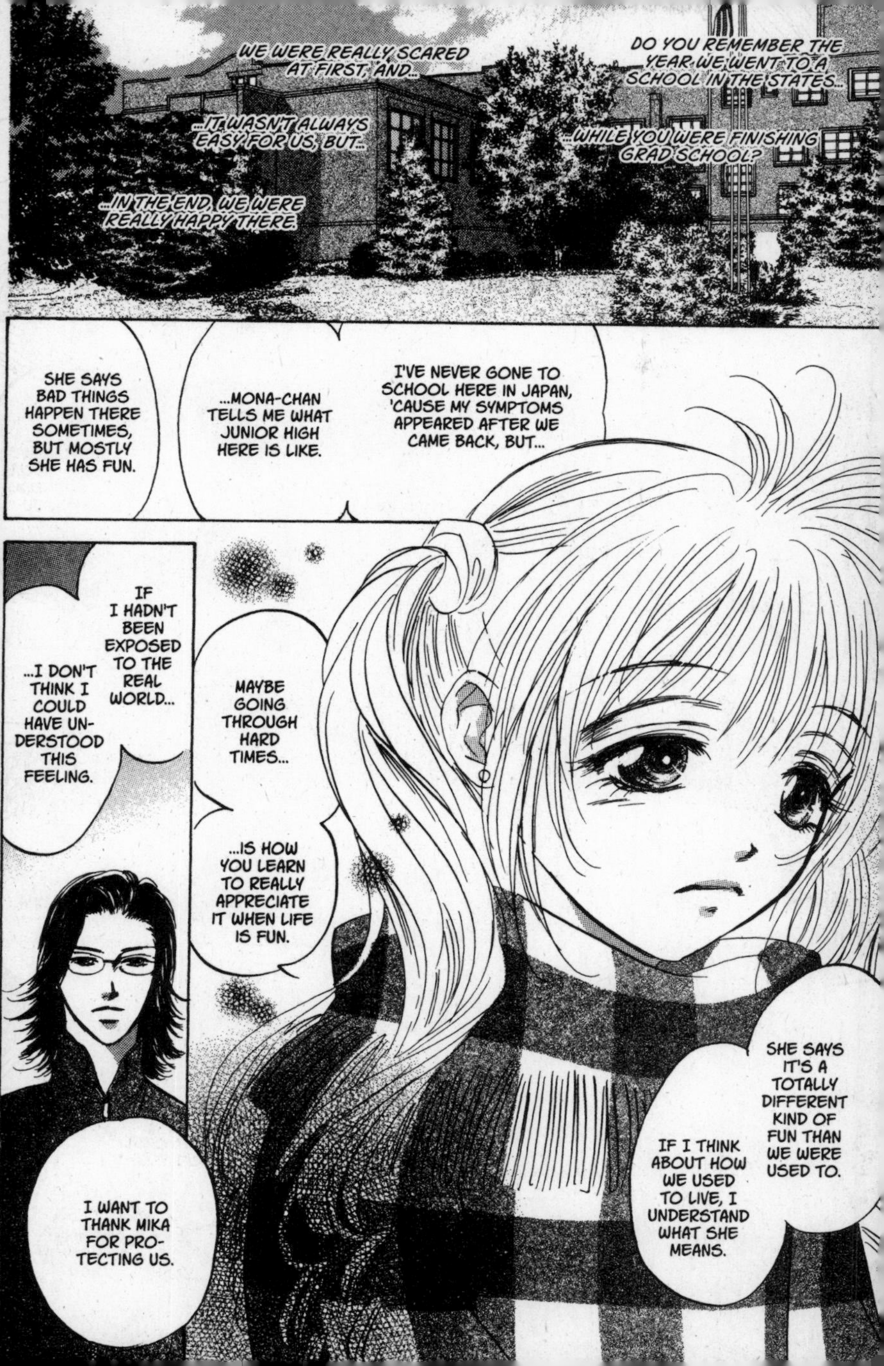
DO YOU REMEMBER THE YEAR WE WENT TO A SCHOOL IN THE STATES...
...WHILE YOU WERE FINISHING GRAD SCHOOL?
WE WERE REALLY SCARED AT FIRST, AND...
...IT WASN'T ALWAYS EASY FOR US, BUT...
...IN THE END, WE WERE REALLY HAPPY THERE.
I'VE NEVER GONE TO SCHOOL HERE IN JAPAN, 'CAUSE MY SYMPTOMS APPEARED AFTER WE CAME BACK, BUT...
...MONA-CHAN TELLS ME WHAT JUNIOR HIGH HERE IS LIKE.
SHE SAYS BAD THINGS HAPPEN THERE SOMETIMES, BUT MOSTLY SHE HAS FUN.
SHE SAYS IT'S A TOTALLY DIFFERENT KIND OF FUN THAN WE WERE USED TO.
IF I THINK ABOUT HOW WE USED TO LIVE, I UNDERSTAND WHAT SHE MEANS.
MAYBE GOING THROUGH HARD TIMES...
...IS HOW YOU LEARN TO REALLY APPRECIATE IT WHEN LIFE IS FUN.
IF I HADN'T BEEN EXPOSED TO THE REAL WORLD...
...I DON'T THINK I COULD HAVE UNDERSTOOD THIS FEELING.
I WANT TO THANK MIKA FOR PROTECTING US.

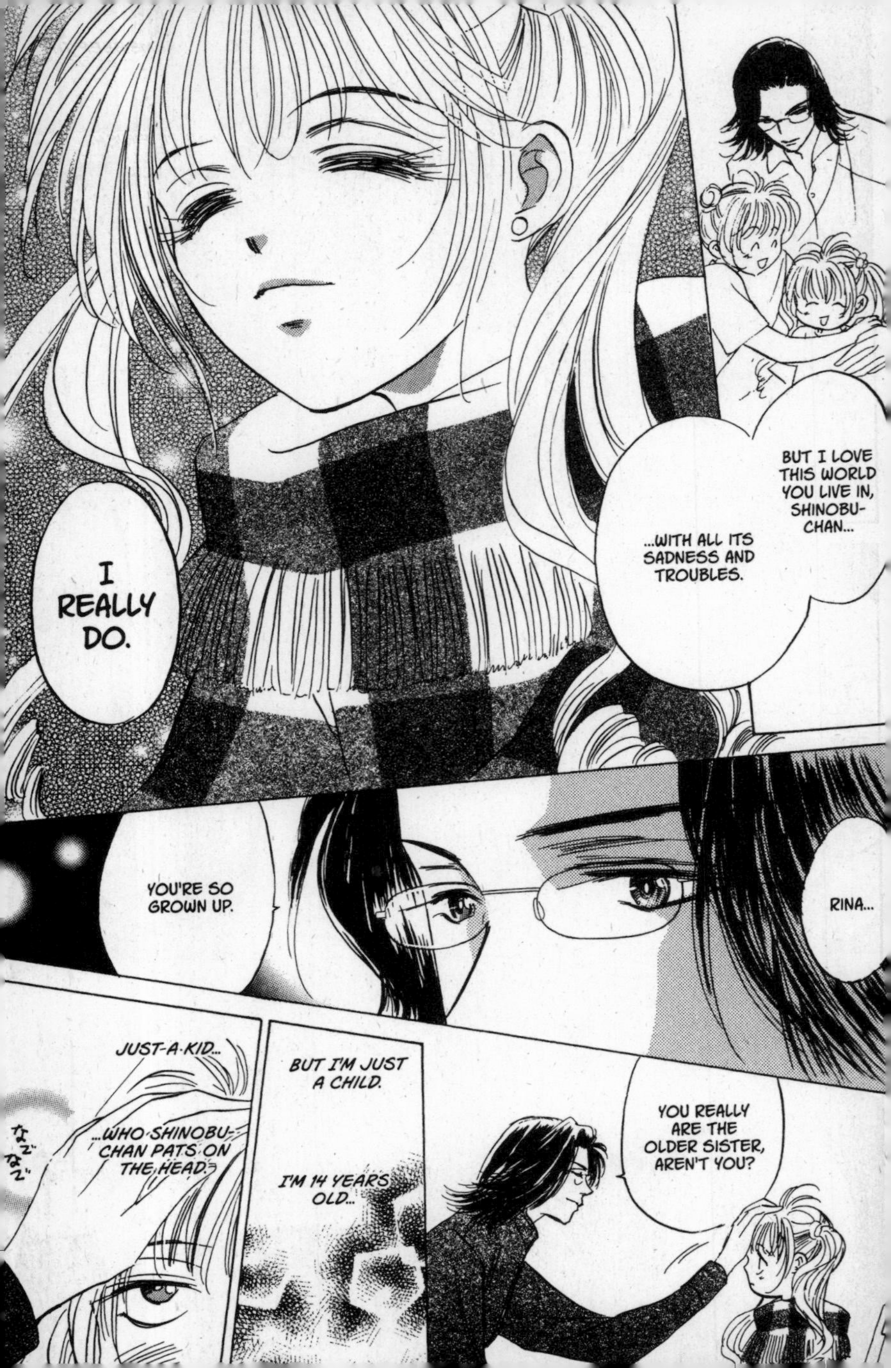
BUT I LOVE THIS WORLD YOU LIVE IN, SHINOBU-CHAN...
...WITH ALL ITS SADNESS AND TROUBLES.
I REALLY DO.
RINA...
YOU'RE SO GROWN UP.
YOU REALLY ARE THE OLDER SISTER, AREN'T YOU?
BUT I'M JUST A CHILD.
I'M 14 YEARS OLD...
JUST-A-KID...
...WHO SHINOBU-CHAN PATS ON THE HEAD.
なでなで

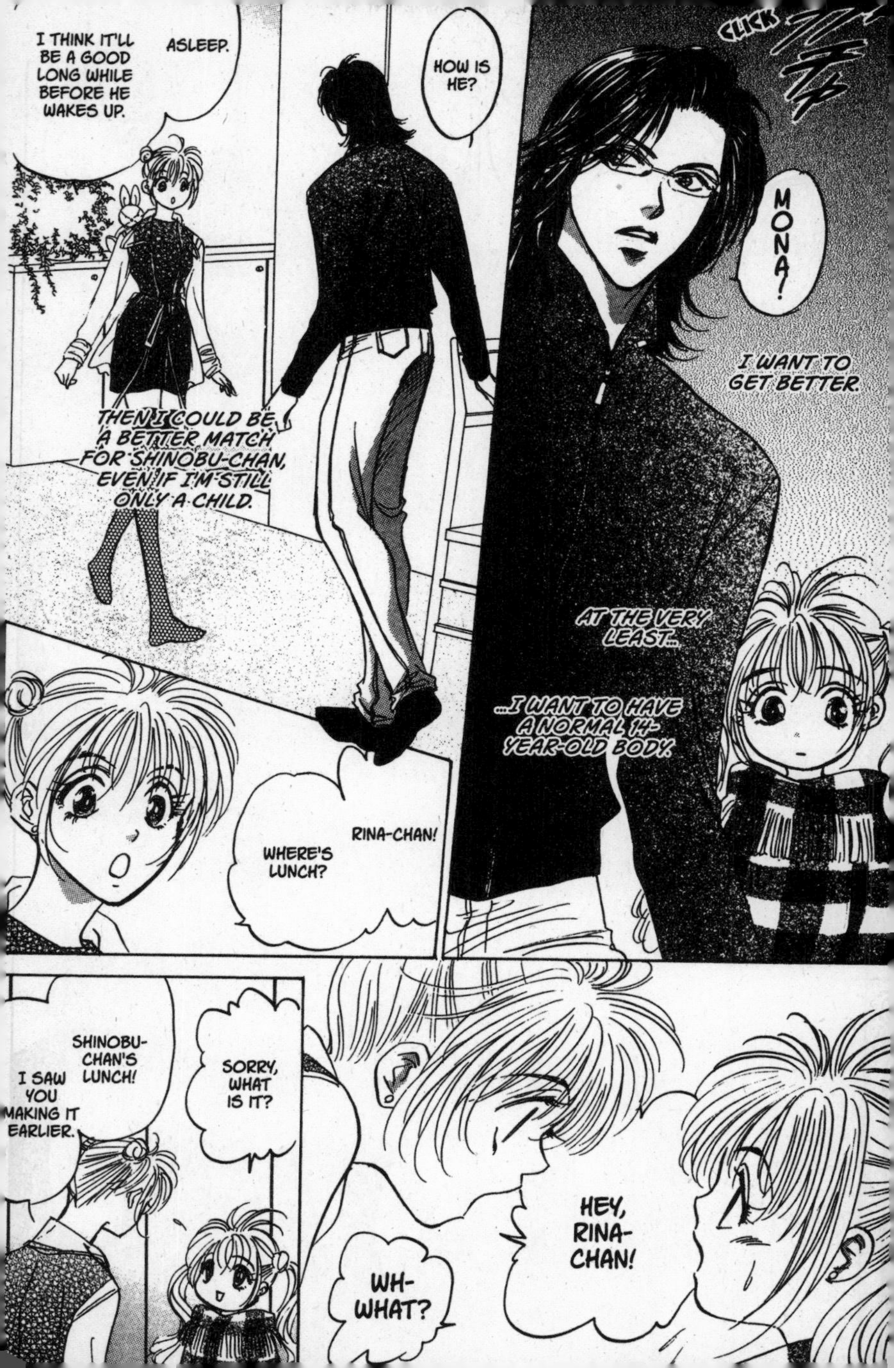
CLICK
MONA!
I WANT TO GET BETTER.
AT THE VERY LEAST...
...I WANT TO HAVE A NORMAL 14-YEAR-OLD BODY.
HOW IS HE?
ASLEEP.
I THINK IT'LL BE A GOOD LONG WHILE BEFORE HE WAKES UP.
THEN I COULD BE A BETTER MATCH FOR SHINOBU-CHAN, EVEN IF I'M STILL ONLY A CHILD.
RINA-CHAN!
WHERE'S LUNCH?
HEY, RINA-CHAN!
WH-WHAT?
SORRY, WHAT IS IT?
SHINOBU-CHAN'S LUNCH!
I SAW YOU MAKING IT EARLIER.

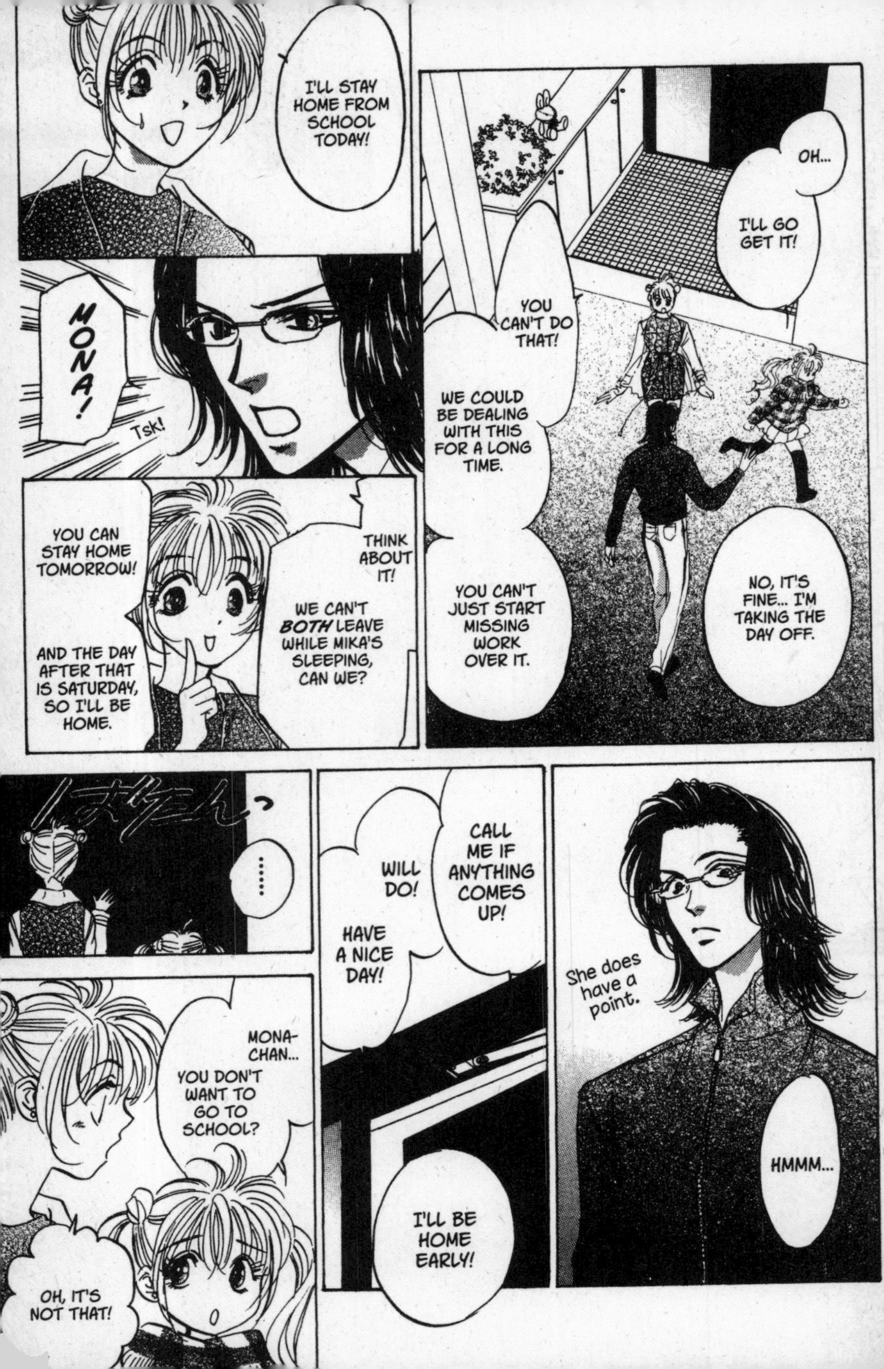

OH...
I'LL GO GET IT!
NO, IT'S FINE... I'M TAKING THE DAY OFF.
YOU CAN'T DO THAT!
WE COULD BE DEALING WITH THIS FOR A LONG TIME.
YOU CAN'T JUST START MISSING WORK OVER IT.
I'LL STAY HOME FROM SCHOOL TODAY!
MONA!
Tsk!
THINK ABOUT IT!
WE CAN'T *BOTH* LEAVE WHILE MIKA'S SLEEPING, CAN WE?
YOU CAN STAY HOME TOMORROW!
AND THE DAY AFTER THAT IS SATURDAY, SO I'LL BE HOME.
She does have a point.
HMMM...
CALL ME IF ANYTHING COMES UP!
WILL DO!
HAVE A NICE DAY!
I'LL BE HOME EARLY!
......
MONA-CHAN...
YOU DON'T WANT TO GO TO SCHOOL?
OH, IT'S NOT THAT!

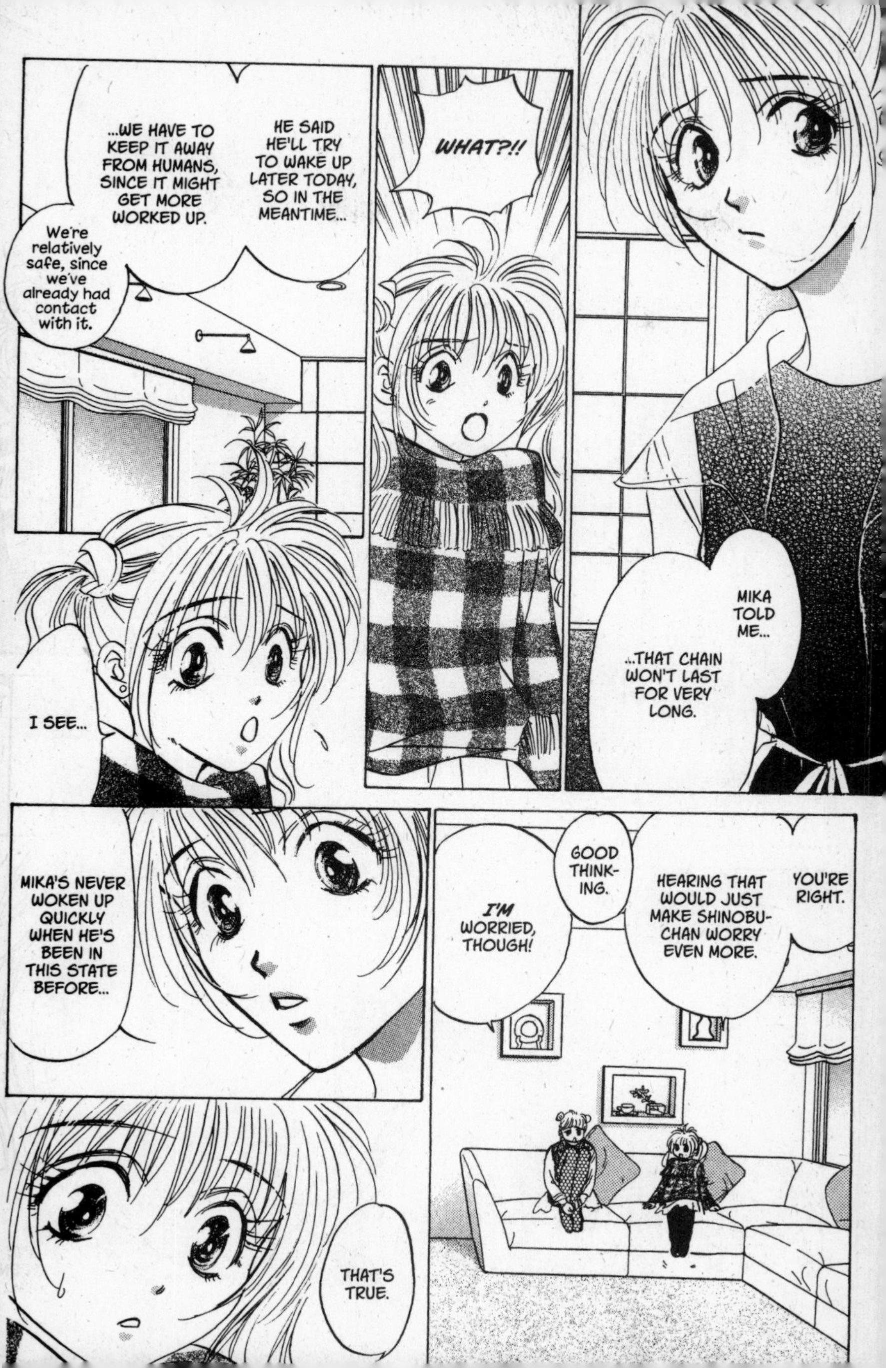
MIKA TOLD ME...
...THAT CHAIN WON'T LAST FOR VERY LONG.
WHAT?!!
HE SAID HE'LL TRY TO WAKE UP LATER TODAY, SO IN THE MEANTIME...
...WE HAVE TO KEEP IT AWAY FROM HUMANS, SINCE IT MIGHT GET MORE WORKED UP.
We're relatively safe, since we've already had contact with it.
I SEE...
YOU'RE RIGHT.
HEARING THAT WOULD JUST MAKE SHINOBU-CHAN WORRY EVEN MORE.
GOOD THINKING.
I'M WORRIED, THOUGH!
MIKA'S NEVER WOKEN UP QUICKLY WHEN HE'S BEEN IN THIS STATE BEFORE...
THAT'S TRUE.

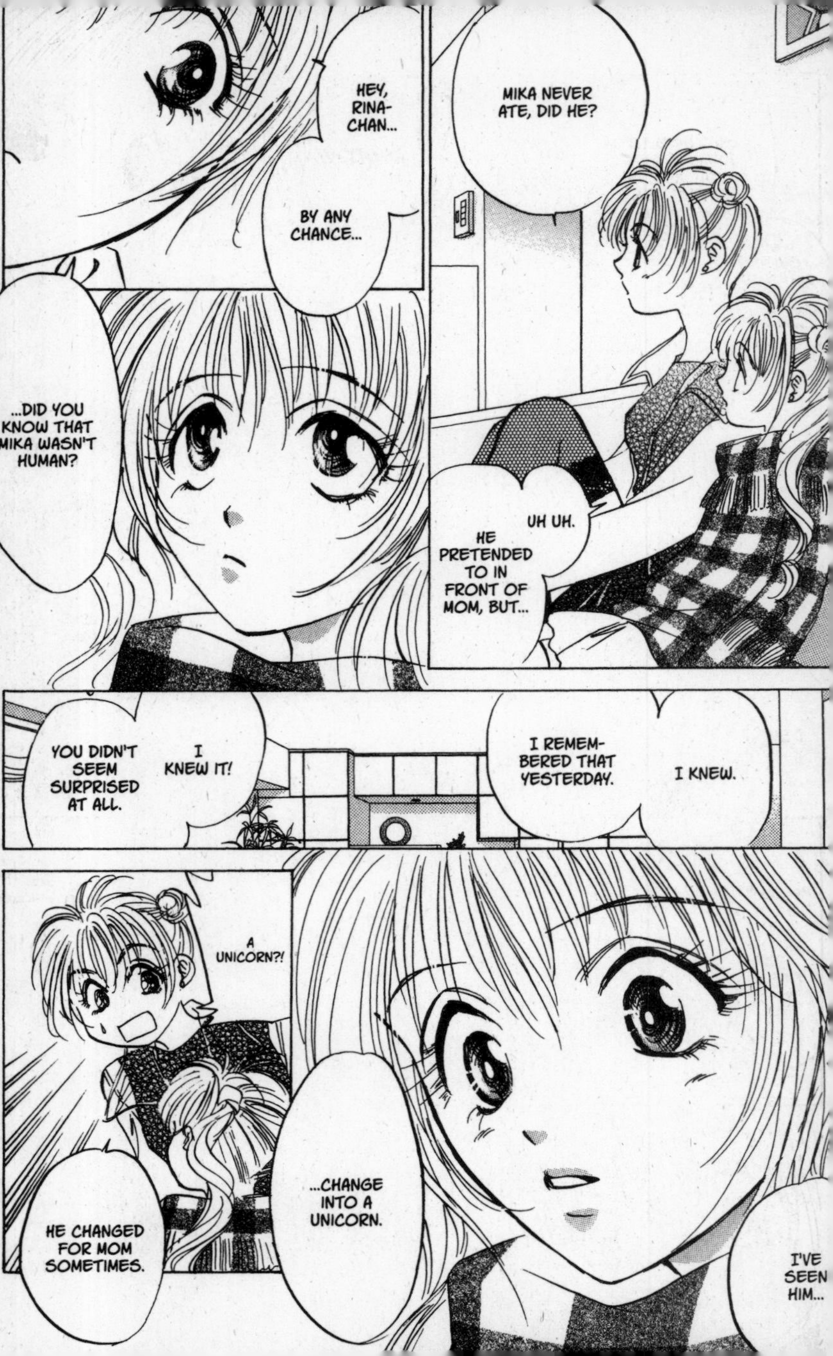
MIKA NEVER ATE, DID HE?
UH UH.
HE PRETENDED TO IN FRONT OF MOM, BUT...
HEY, RINA-CHAN...
BY ANY CHANCE...
...DID YOU KNOW THAT MIKA WASN'T HUMAN?
I KNEW.
I REMEMBERED THAT YESTERDAY.
I KNEW IT!
YOU DIDN'T SEEM SURPRISED AT ALL.
I'VE SEEN HIM...
...CHANGE INTO A UNICORN.
A UNICORN?!
HE CHANGED FOR MOM SOMETIMES.

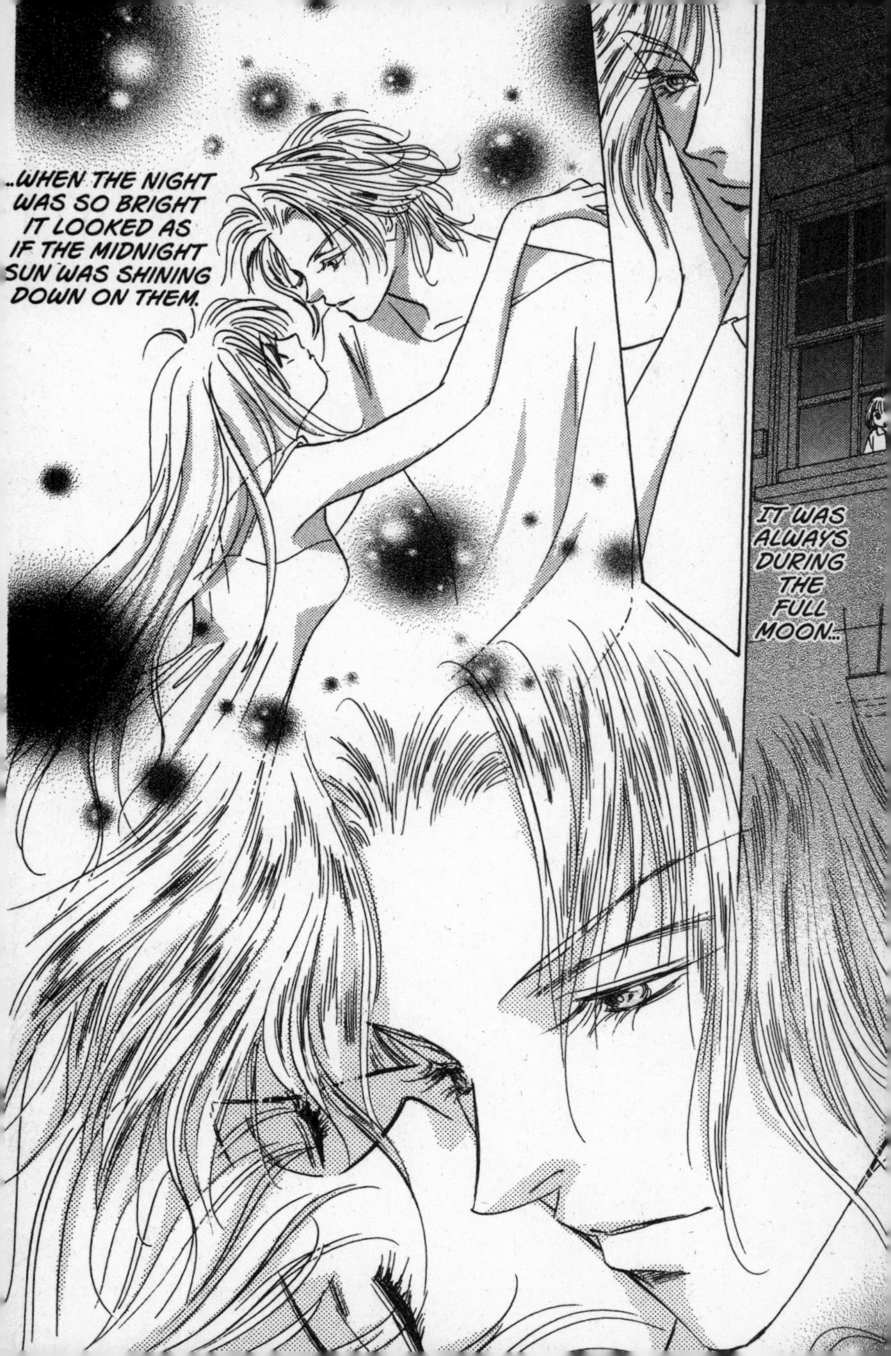
IT WAS ALWAYS DURING THE FULL MOON...
...WHEN THE NIGHT WAS SO BRIGHT IT LOOKED AS IF THE MIDNIGHT SUN WAS SHINING DOWN ON THEM.

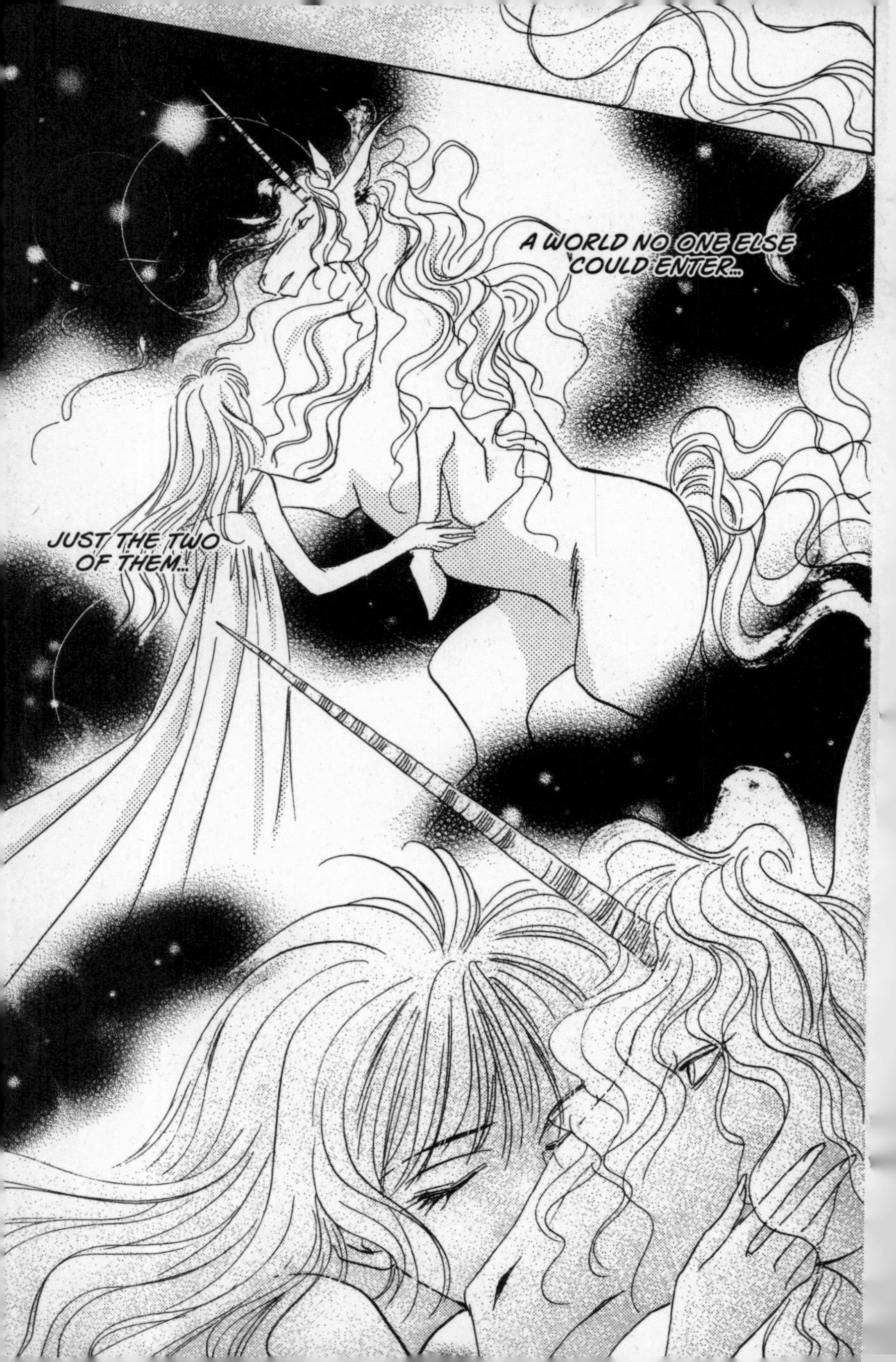
A WORLD NO ONE ELSE COULD ENTER...
JUST THE TWO OF THEM...

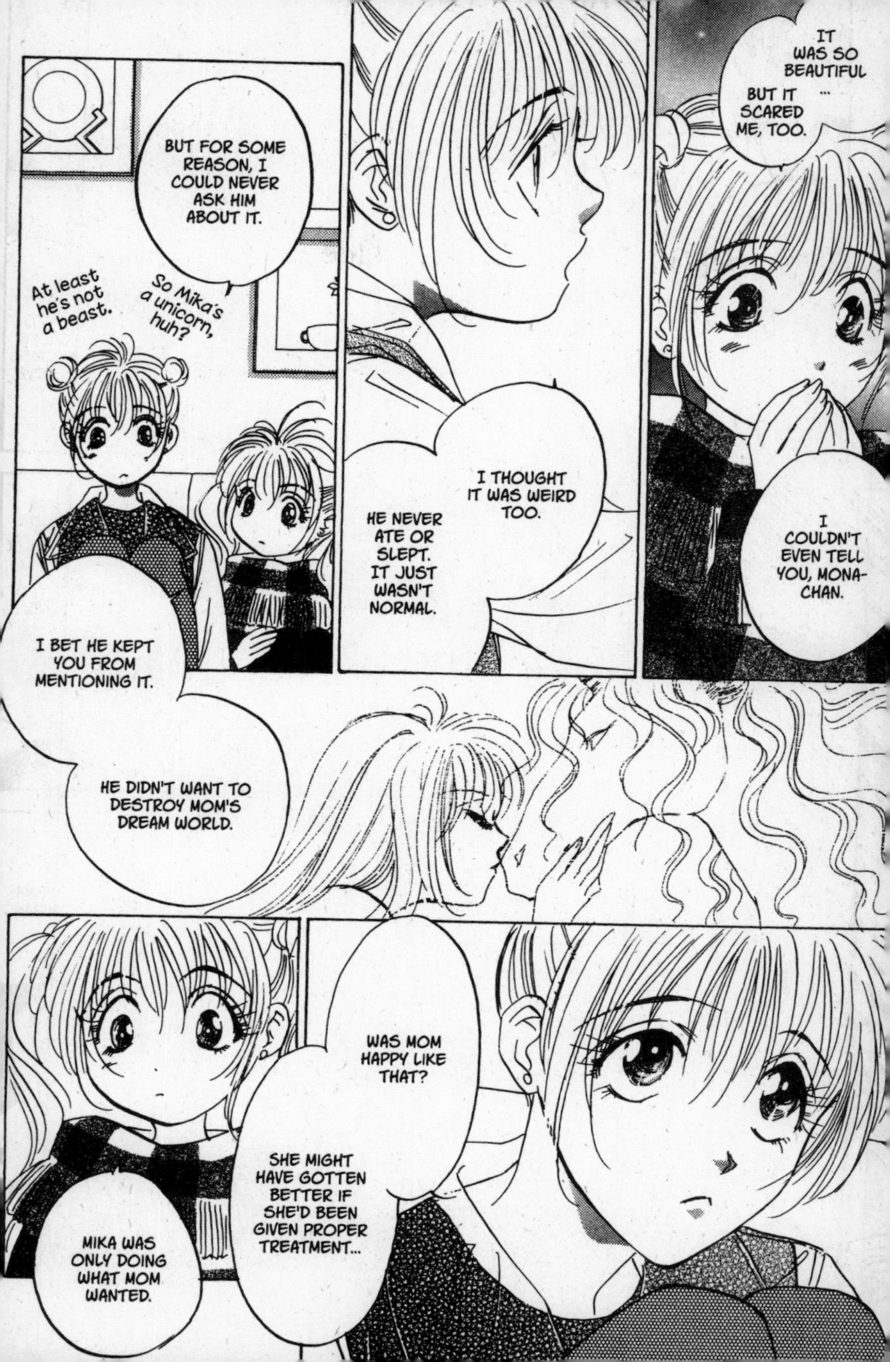

IT WAS SO BEAUTIFUL ... BUT IT SCARED ME, TOO.
I COULDN'T EVEN TELL YOU, MONA-CHAN.
I THOUGHT IT WAS WEIRD TOO.
HE NEVER ATE OR SLEPT. IT JUST WASN'T NORMAL.
BUT FOR SOME REASON, I COULD NEVER ASK HIM ABOUT IT.
So Mika's a unicorn, huh?
At least he's not a beast.
I BET HE KEPT YOU FROM MENTIONING IT.
HE DIDN'T WANT TO DESTROY MOM'S DREAM WORLD.
WAS MOM HAPPY LIKE THAT?
SHE MIGHT HAVE GOTTEN BETTER IF SHE'D BEEN GIVEN PROPER TREATMENT...
MIKA WAS ONLY DOING WHAT MOM WANTED.

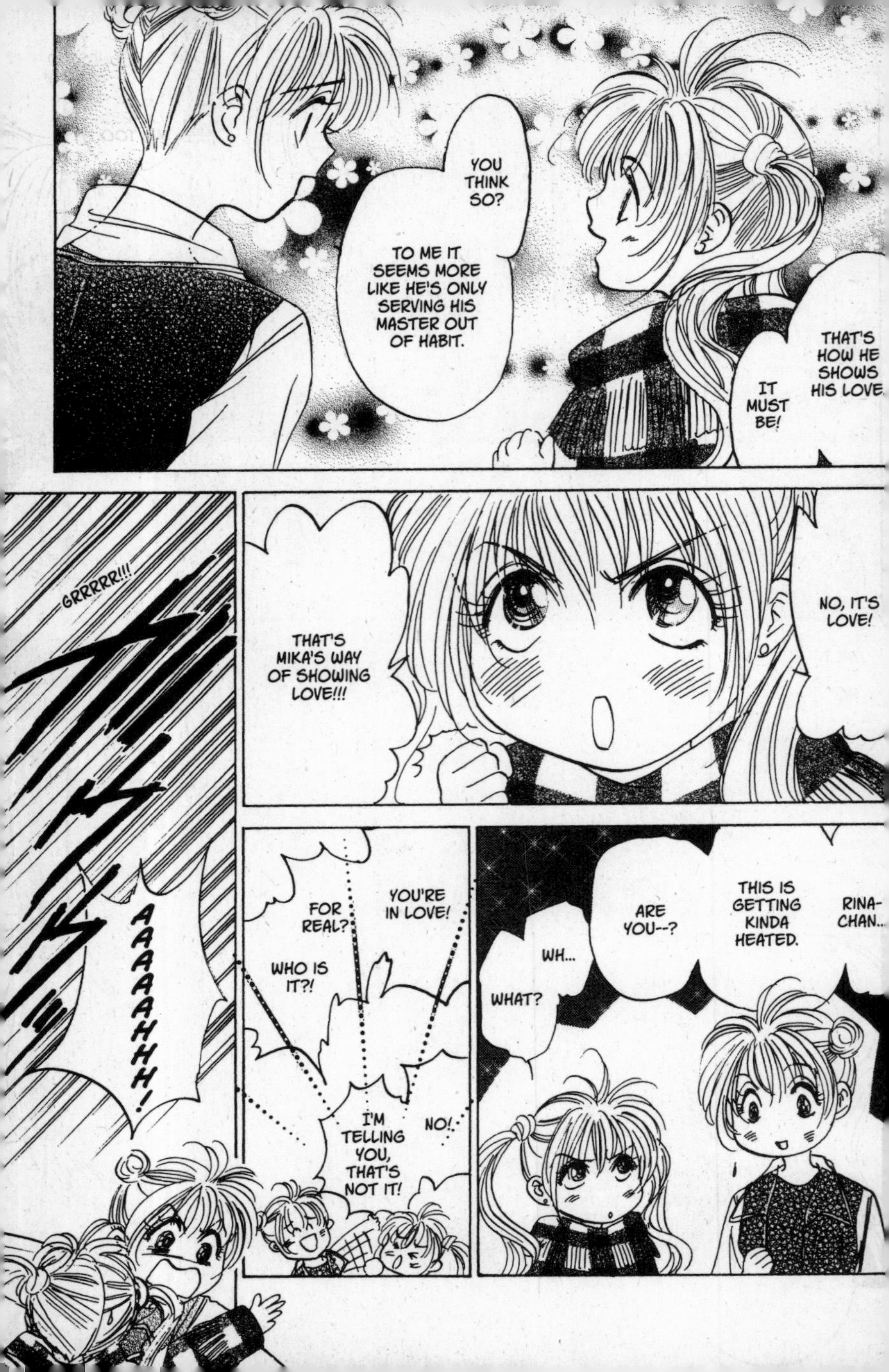
THAT'S HOW HE SHOWS HIS LOVE.
IT MUST BE!
YOU THINK SO?
TO ME IT SEEMS MORE LIKE HE'S ONLY SERVING HIS MASTER OUT OF HABIT.
NO, IT'S LOVE!
THAT'S MIKA'S WAY OF SHOWING LOVE!!!
RINA-CHAN...
THIS IS GETTING KINDA HEATED.
ARE YOU--?
WH...
WHAT?
YOU'RE IN LOVE!
FOR REAL?
WHO IS IT?!
NO!.
I'M TELLING YOU, THAT'S NOT IT!
GRRRRR!!!
AAAAAAHHH!

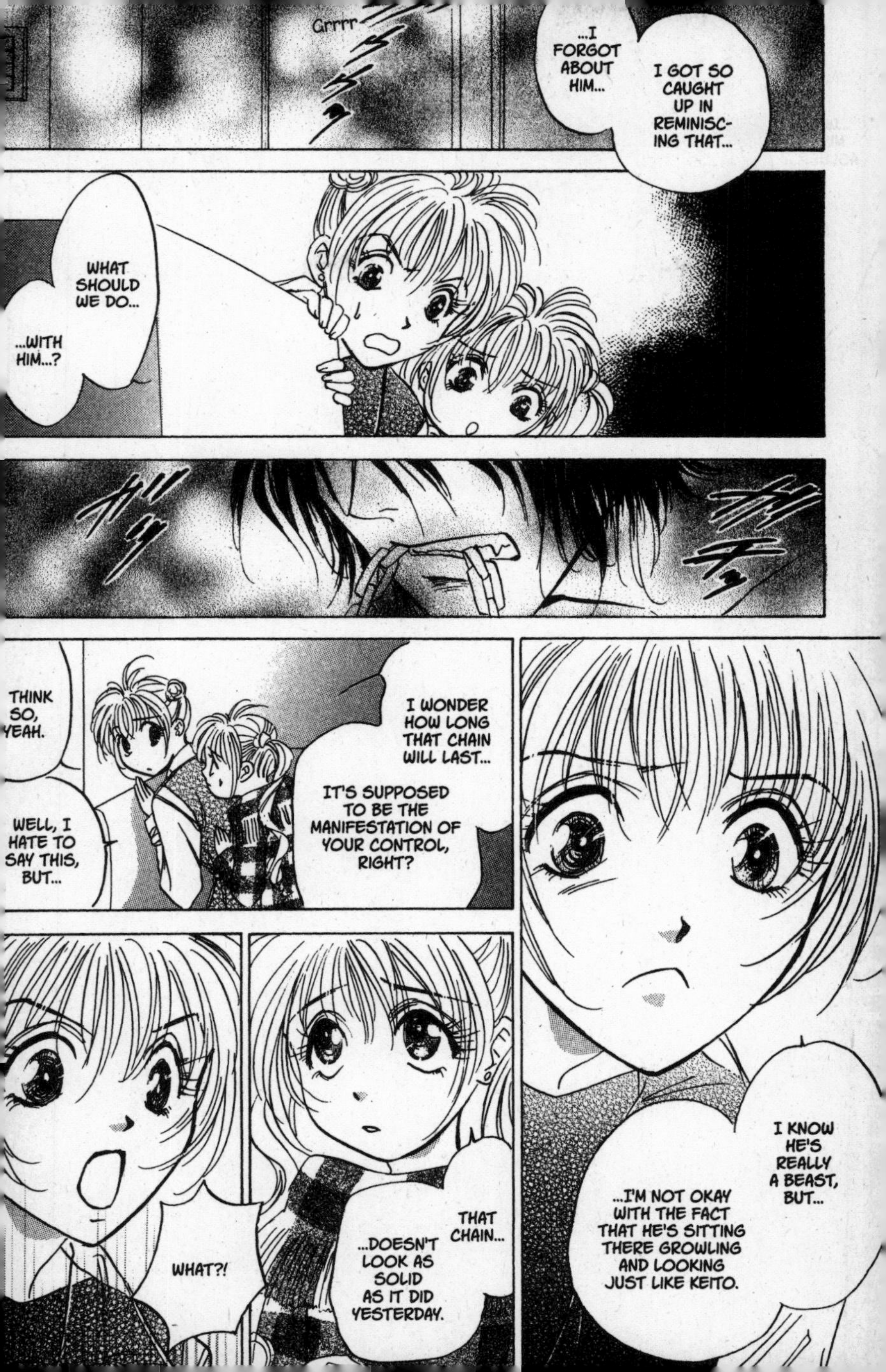
I GOT SO CAUGHT UP IN REMINISCING THAT...
...I FORGOT ABOUT HIM...
Grrrr
WHAT SHOULD WE DO...
...WITH HIM...?
I KNOW HE'S REALLY A BEAST, BUT...
...I'M NOT OKAY WITH THE FACT THAT HE'S SITTING THERE GROWLING AND LOOKING JUST LIKE KEITO.
I WONDER HOW LONG THAT CHAIN WILL LAST...
IT'S SUPPOSED TO BE THE MANIFESTATION OF YOUR CONTROL, RIGHT?
THINK SO, YEAH.
WELL, I HATE TO SAY THIS, BUT...
THAT CHAIN...
...DOESN'T LOOK AS SOLID AS IT DID YESTERDAY.
WHAT?!

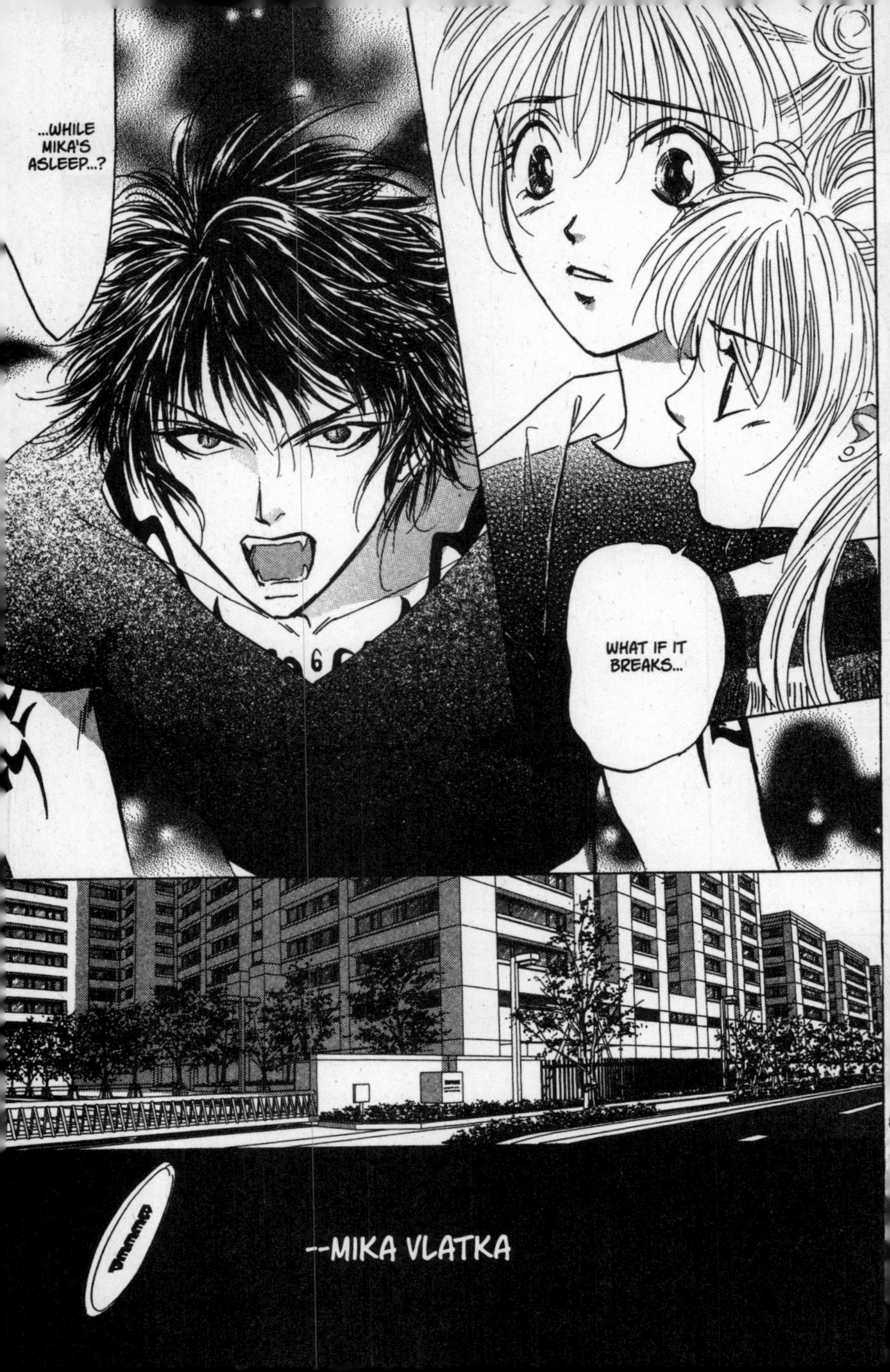
WHAT IF IT BREAKS...
...WHILE MIKA'S ASLEEP...?
--MIKA VLATKA

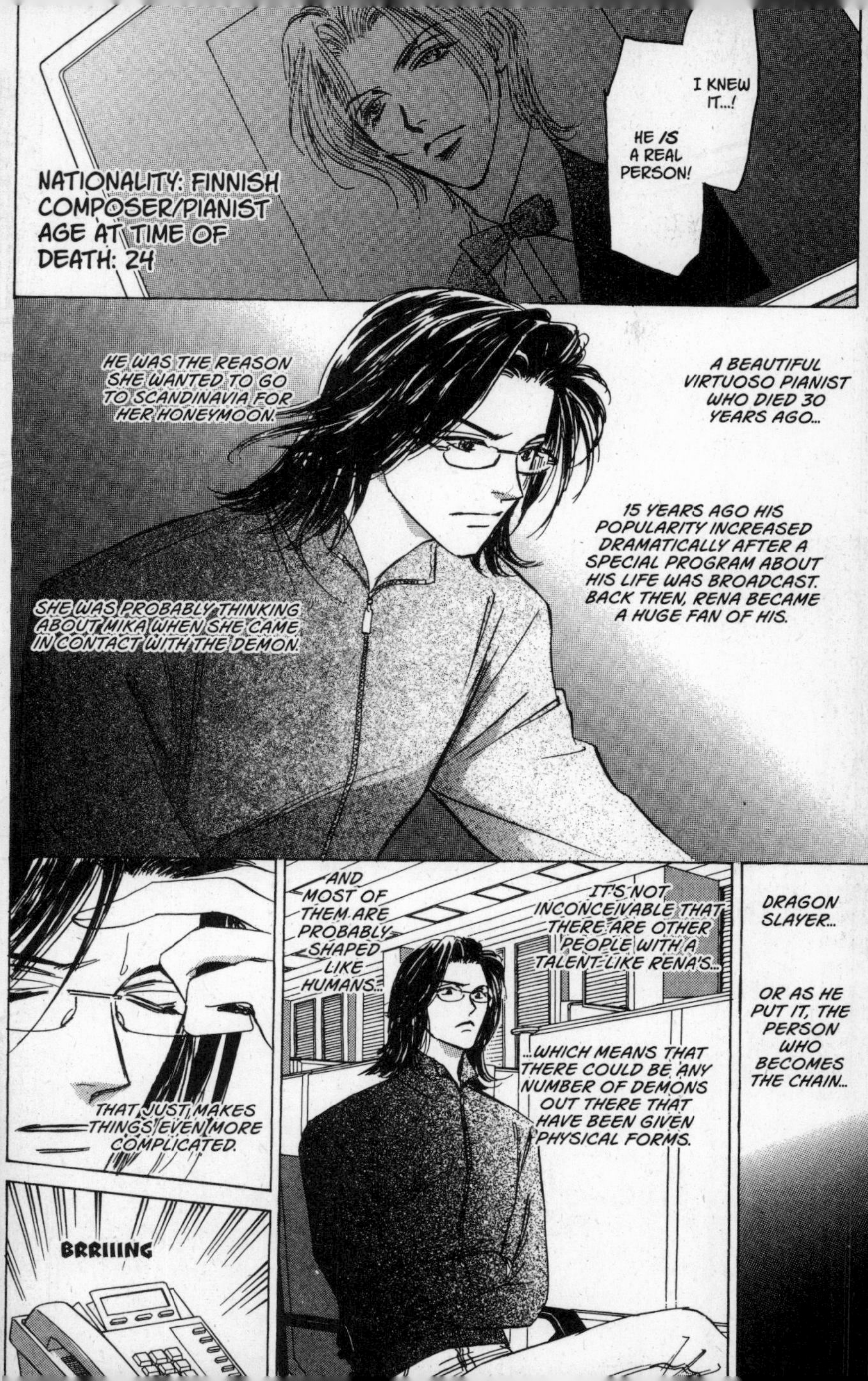
I KNEW IT...!
HE IS A REAL PERSON!
NATIONALITY: FINNISH
COMPOSER/PIANIST
AGE AT TIME OF DEATH: 24
A BEAUTIFUL VIRTUOSO PIANIST WHO DIED 30 YEARS AGO...
15 YEARS AGO HIS POPULARITY INCREASED DRAMATICALLY AFTER A SPECIAL PROGRAM ABOUT HIS LIFE WAS BROADCAST. BACK THEN, RENA BECAME A HUGE FAN OF HIS.
HE WAS THE REASON SHE WANTED TO GO TO SCANDINAVIA FOR HER HONEYMOON.
SHE WAS PROBABLY THINKING ABOUT MIKA WHEN SHE CAME IN CONTACT WITH THE DEMON.
DRAGON SLAYER...
OR AS HE PUT IT, THE PERSON WHO BECOMES THE CHAIN...
IT'S NOT INCONCEIVABLE THAT THERE ARE OTHER PEOPLE WITH A TALENT LIKE RENA'S...
...WHICH MEANS THAT THERE COULD BE ANY NUMBER OF DEMONS OUT THERE THAT HAVE BEEN GIVEN PHYSICAL FORMS.
AND MOST OF THEM ARE PROBABLY SHAPED LIKE HUMANS...
THAT JUST MAKES THINGS EVEN MORE COMPLICATED.
BRRIIING

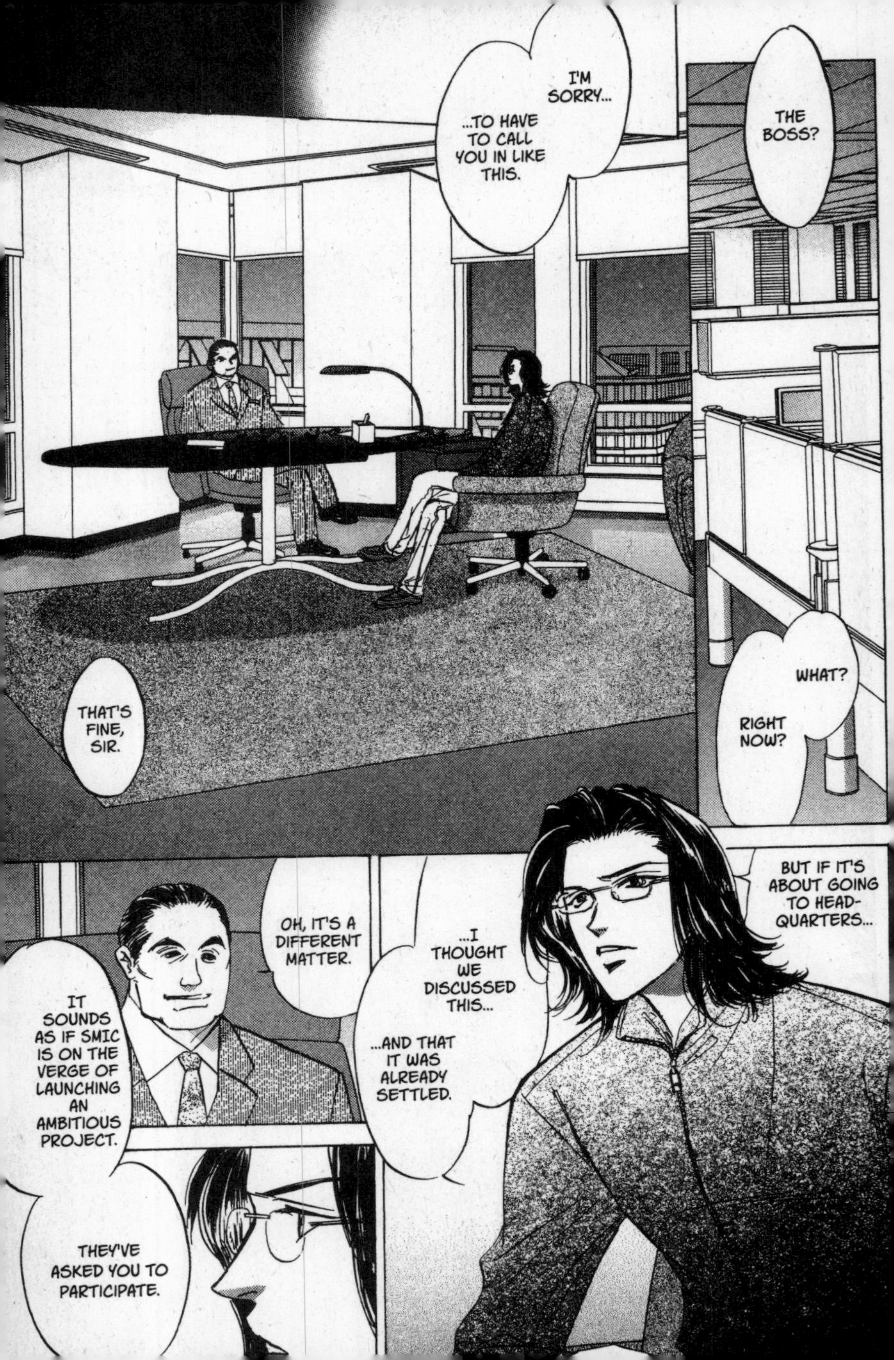
THE BOSS?
WHAT?
RIGHT NOW?
I'M SORRY...
...TO HAVE TO CALL YOU IN LIKE THIS.
THAT'S FINE, SIR.
BUT IF IT'S ABOUT GOING TO HEAD-QUARTERS...
...I THOUGHT WE DISCUSSED THIS...
...AND THAT IT WAS ALREADY SETTLED.
OH, IT'S A DIFFERENT MATTER.
IT SOUNDS AS IF SMIC IS ON THE VERGE OF LAUNCHING AN AMBITIOUS PROJECT.
THEY'VE ASKED YOU TO PARTICIPATE.

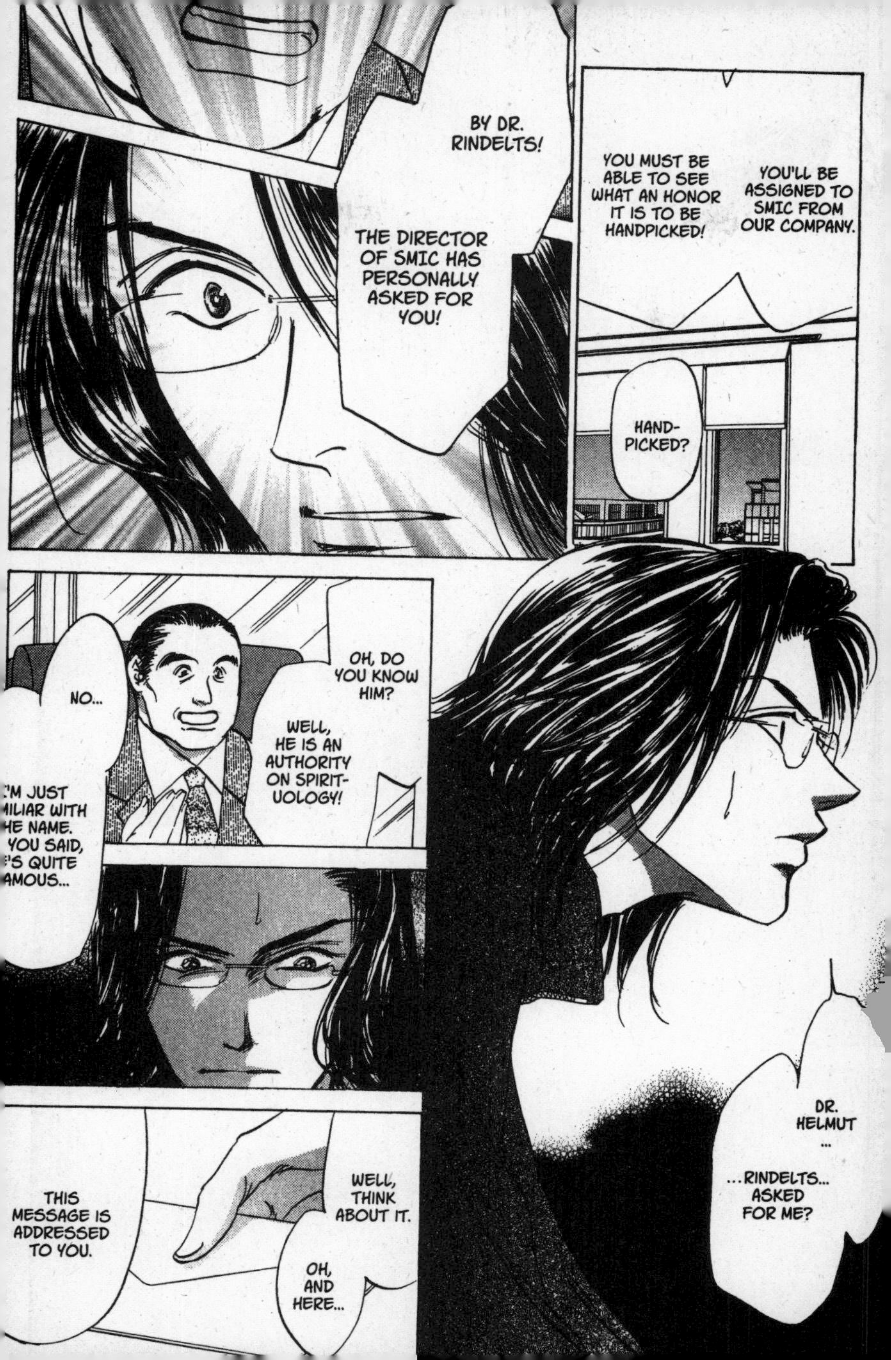
YOU'LL BE ASSIGNED TO SMIC FROM OUR COMPANY.
YOU MUST BE ABLE TO SEE WHAT AN HONOR IT IS TO BE HANDPICKED!
HAND-PICKED?
BY DR. RINDELTS!
THE DIRECTOR OF SMIC HAS PERSONALLY ASKED FOR YOU!
DR. HELMUT ...
...RINDELTS... ASKED FOR ME?
OH, DO YOU KNOW HIM?
WELL, HE IS AN AUTHORITY ON SPIRIT-UOLOGY!
NO...
'M JUST MILIAR WITH HE NAME. YOU SAID, E'S QUITE AMOUS...
WELL, THINK ABOUT IT.
OH, AND HERE...
THIS MESSAGE IS ADDRESSED TO YOU.

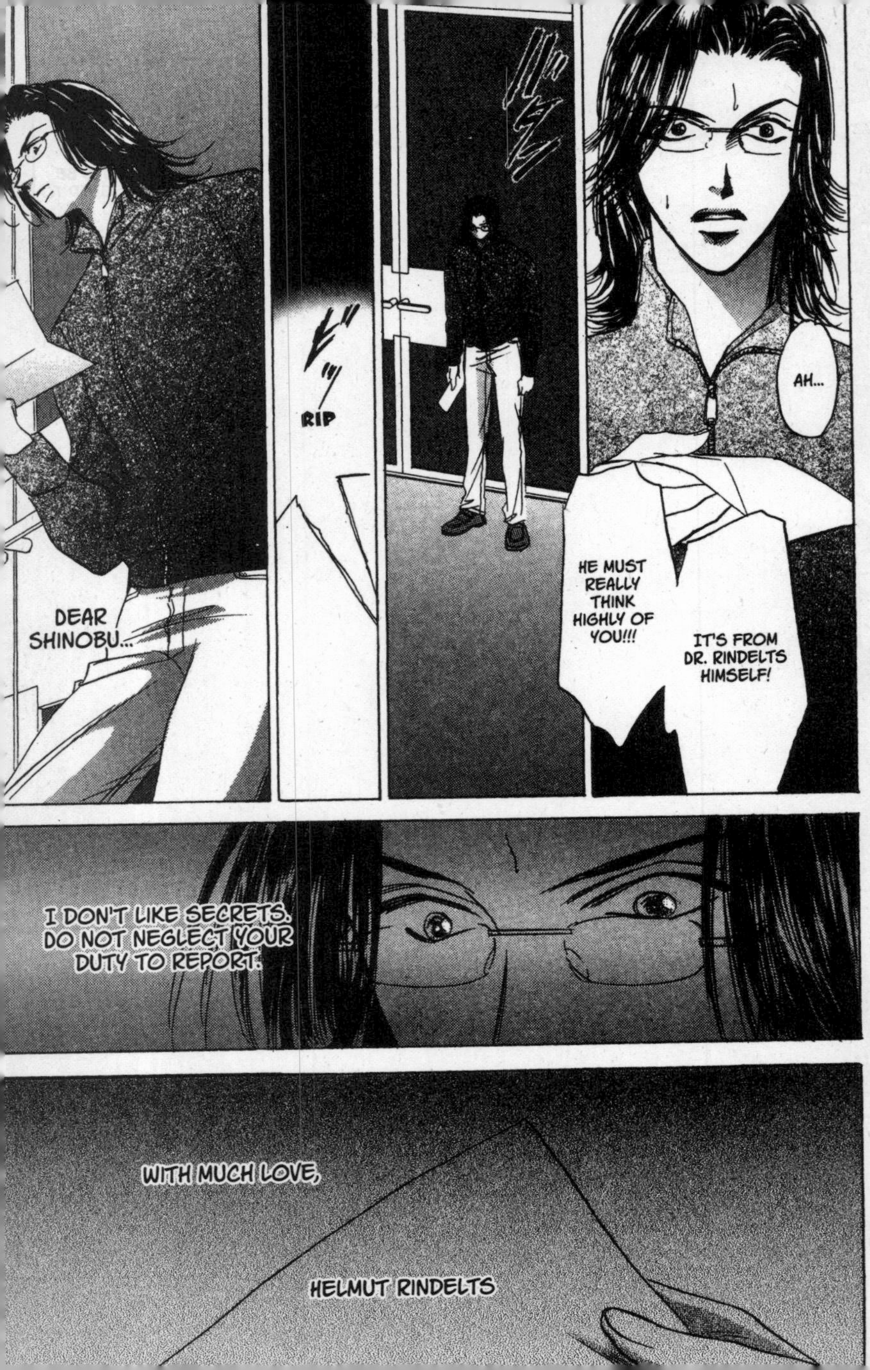
AH...
IT'S FROM DR. RINDELTS HIMSELF!
HE MUST REALLY THINK HIGHLY OF YOU!!!
RIP
DEAR SHINOBU...
I DON'T LIKE SECRETS. DO NOT NEGLECT YOUR DUTY TO REPORT.
WITH MUCH LOVE,
HELMUT RINDELTS

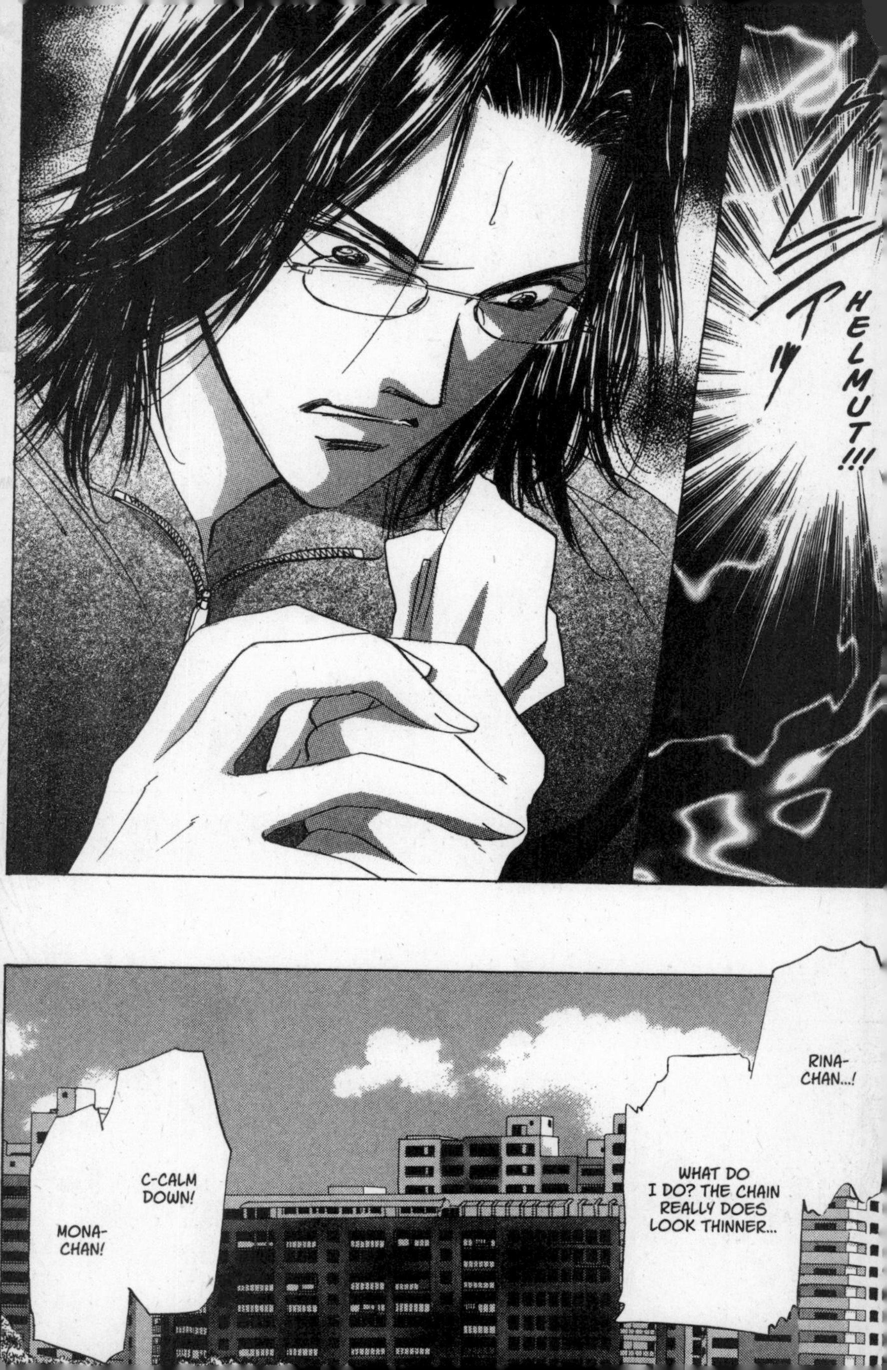
HELMUT!!!
RINA-CHAN...!
WHAT DO I DO? THE CHAIN REALLY DOES LOOK THINNER...
C-CALM DOWN!
MONA-CHAN!

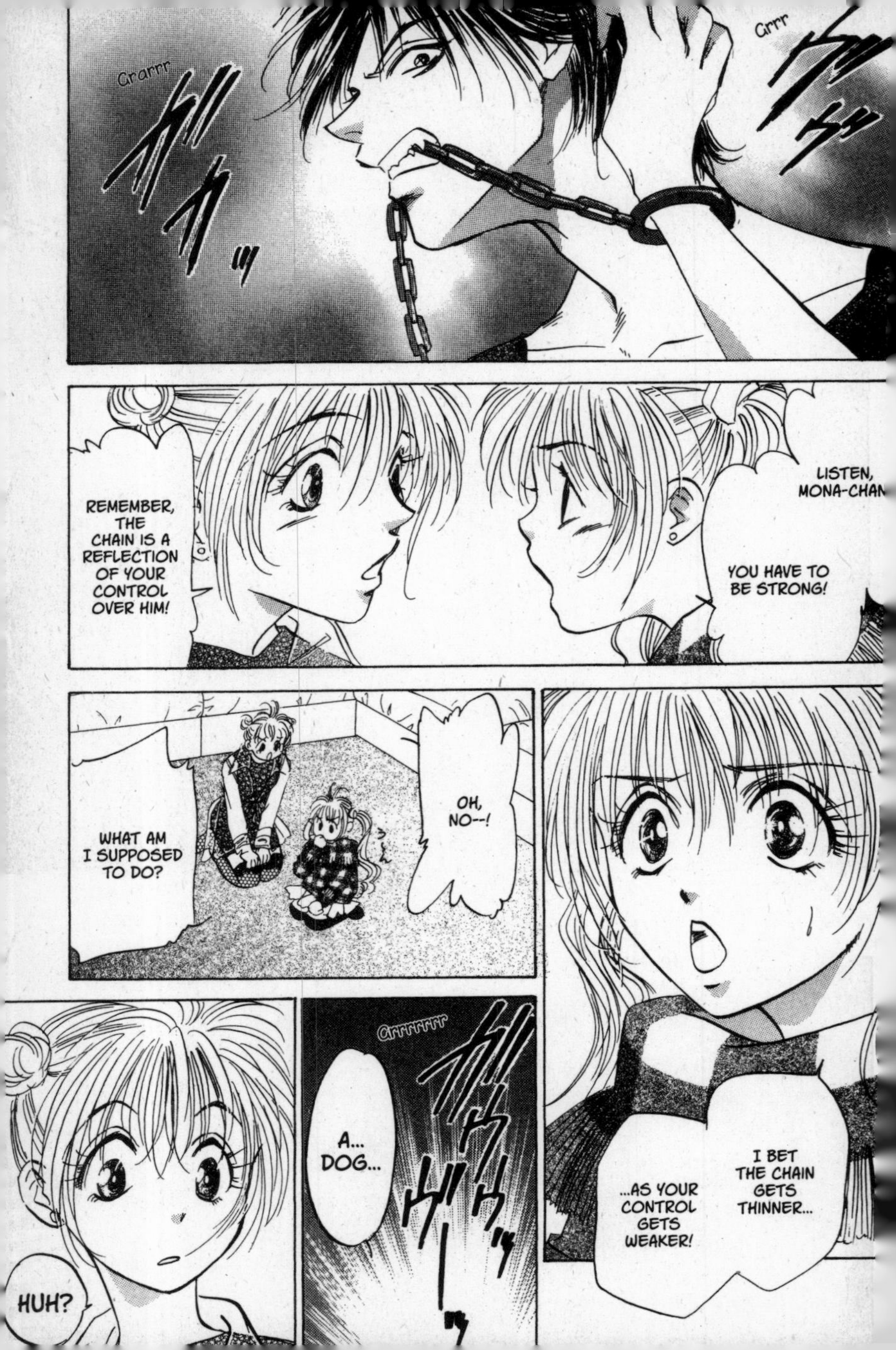
Grrr
Grarrr
LISTEN, MONA-CHAN
YOU HAVE TO BE STRONG!
REMEMBER, THE CHAIN IS A REFLECTION OF YOUR CONTROL OVER HIM!
I BET THE CHAIN GETS THINNER...
...AS YOUR CONTROL GETS WEAKER!
OH, NO--!
WHAT AM I SUPPOSED TO DO?
Grrrrrrrr
A... DOG...
HUH?

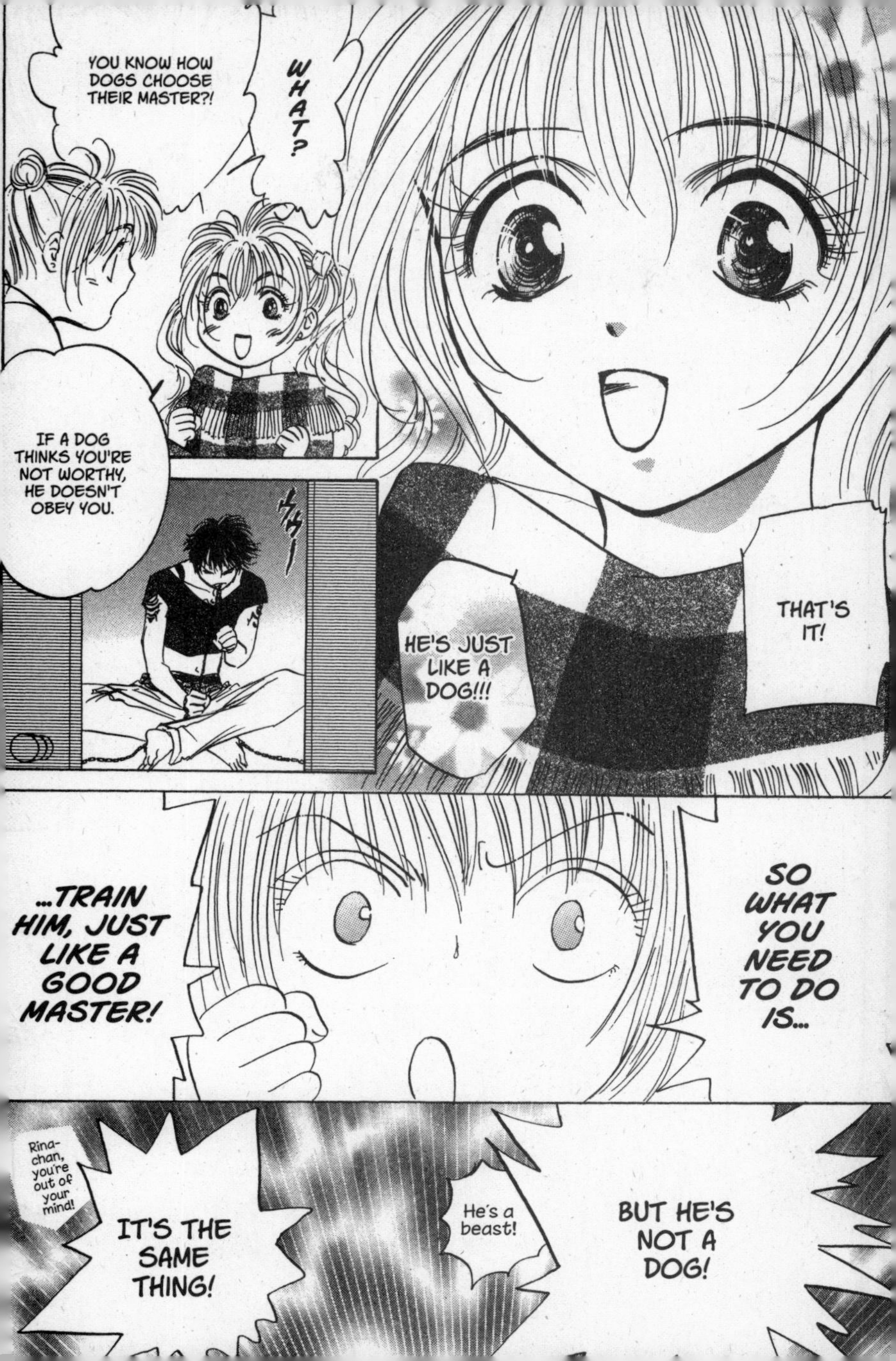
THAT'S IT!
HE'S JUST LIKE A DOG!!!
WHAT?
YOU KNOW HOW DOGS CHOOSE THEIR MASTER?!
IF A DOG THINKS YOU'RE NOT WORTHY, HE DOESN'T OBEY YOU.
SO WHAT YOU NEED TO DO IS...
...TRAIN HIM, JUST LIKE A GOOD MASTER!
BUT HE'S NOT A DOG!
He's a beast!
IT'S THE SAME THING!
Rina-chan, you're out of your mind!

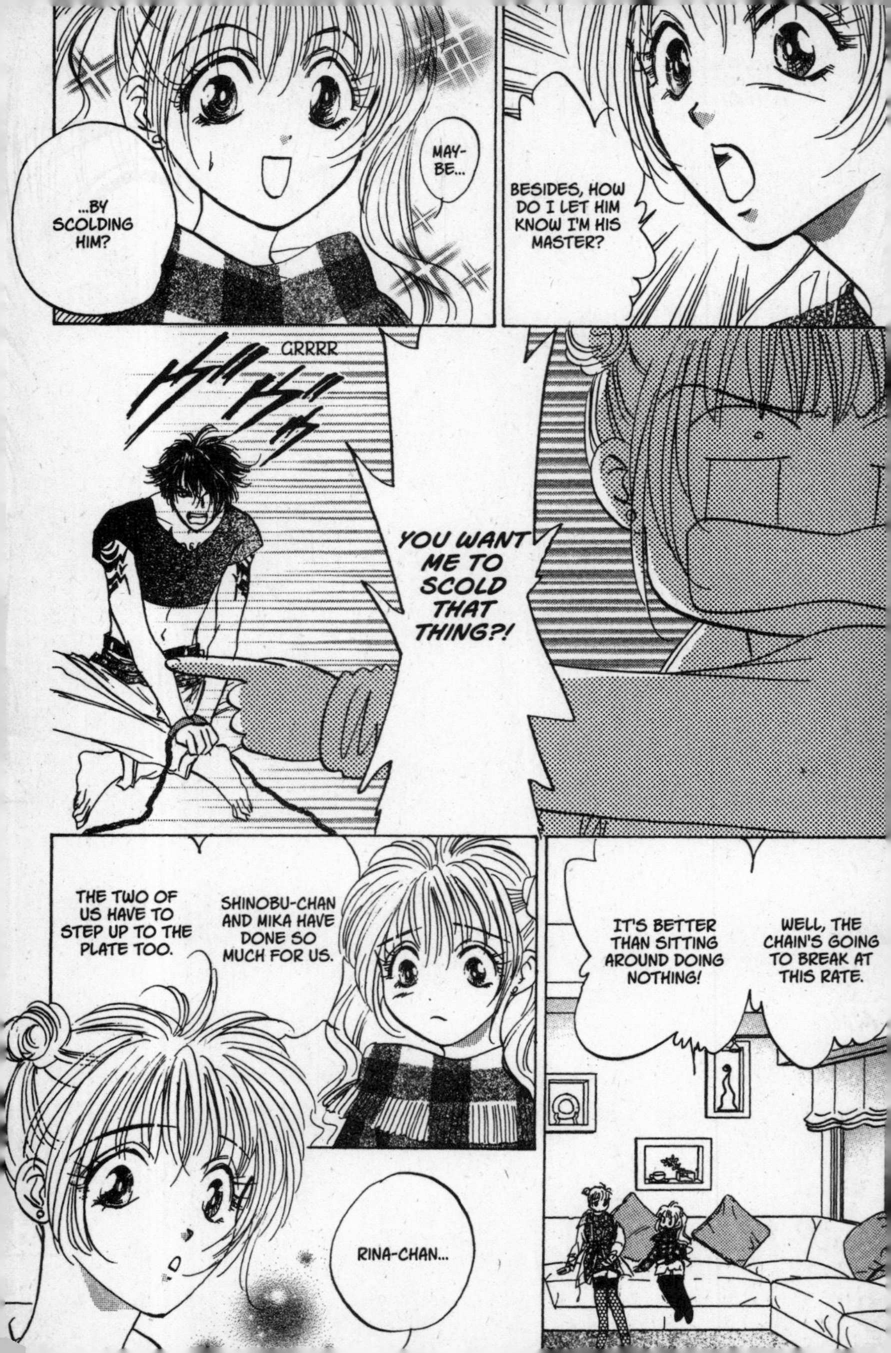
BESIDES, HOW DO I LET HIM KNOW I'M HIS MASTER?
MAY-BE...
...BY SCOLDING HIM?
YOU WANT ME TO SCOLD THAT THING?!
GRRRR
WELL, THE CHAIN'S GOING TO BREAK AT THIS RATE.
IT'S BETTER THAN SITTING AROUND DOING NOTHING!
SHINOBU-CHAN AND MIKA HAVE DONE SO MUCH FOR US.
THE TWO OF US HAVE TO STEP UP TO THE PLATE TOO.
RINA-CHAN...

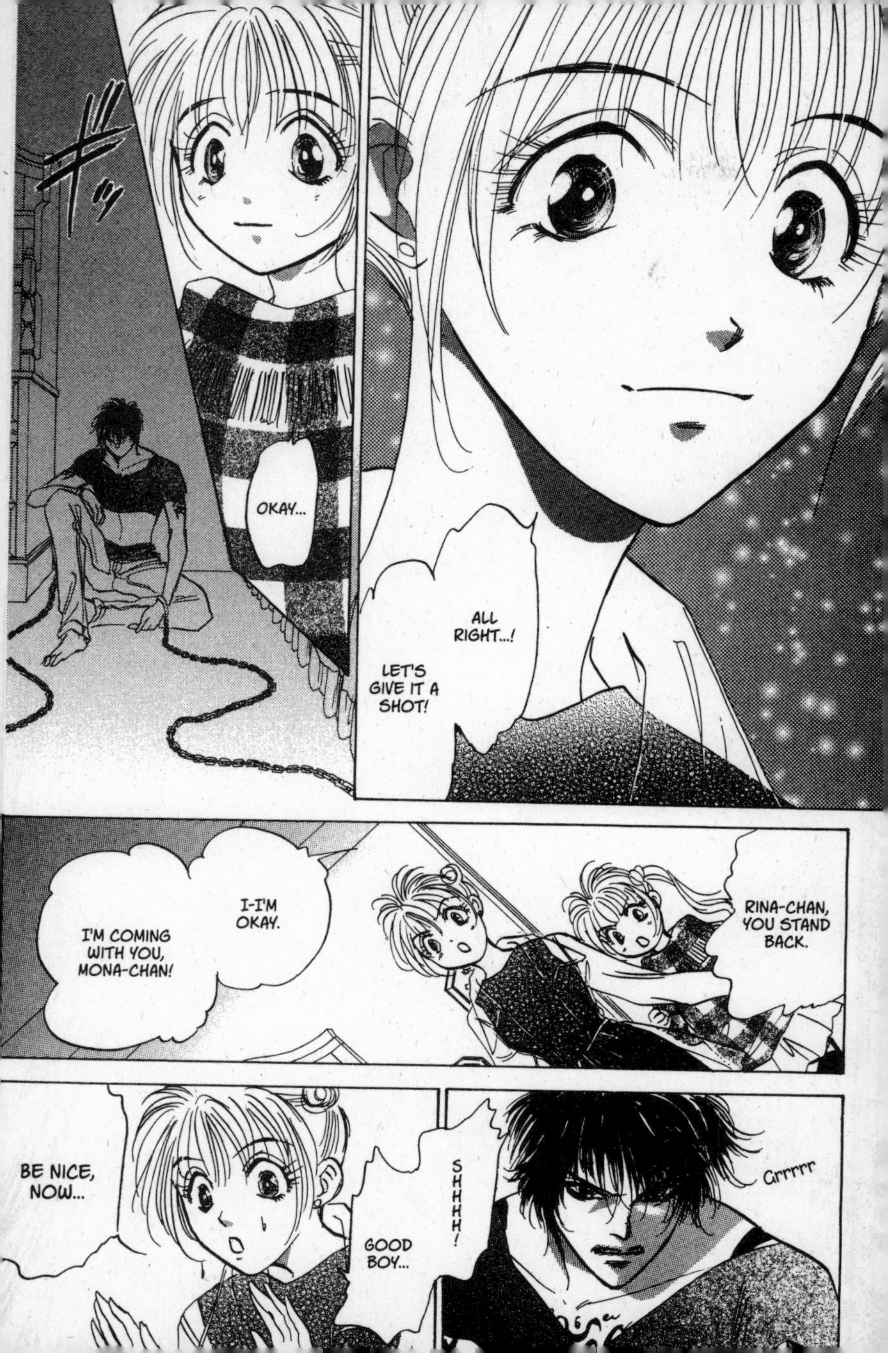
ALL RIGHT...!
LET'S GIVE IT A SHOT!
OKAY...
RINA-CHAN, YOU STAND BACK.
I-I'M OKAY.
I'M COMING WITH YOU, MONA-CHAN!
Grrrrr
SHHHH!
BE NICE, NOW...
GOOD BOY...

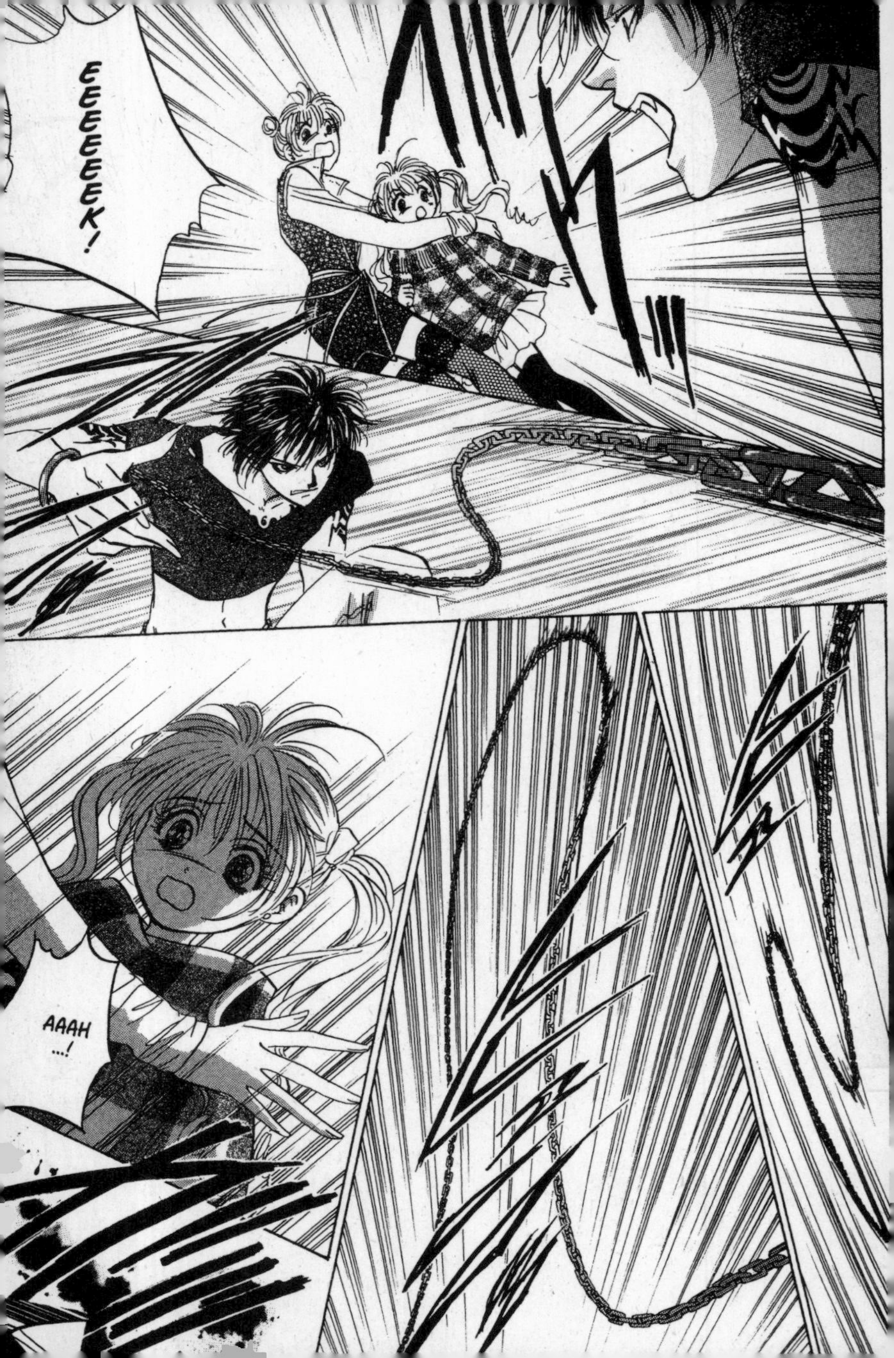
EEEEEEEK!
AAAH ...!

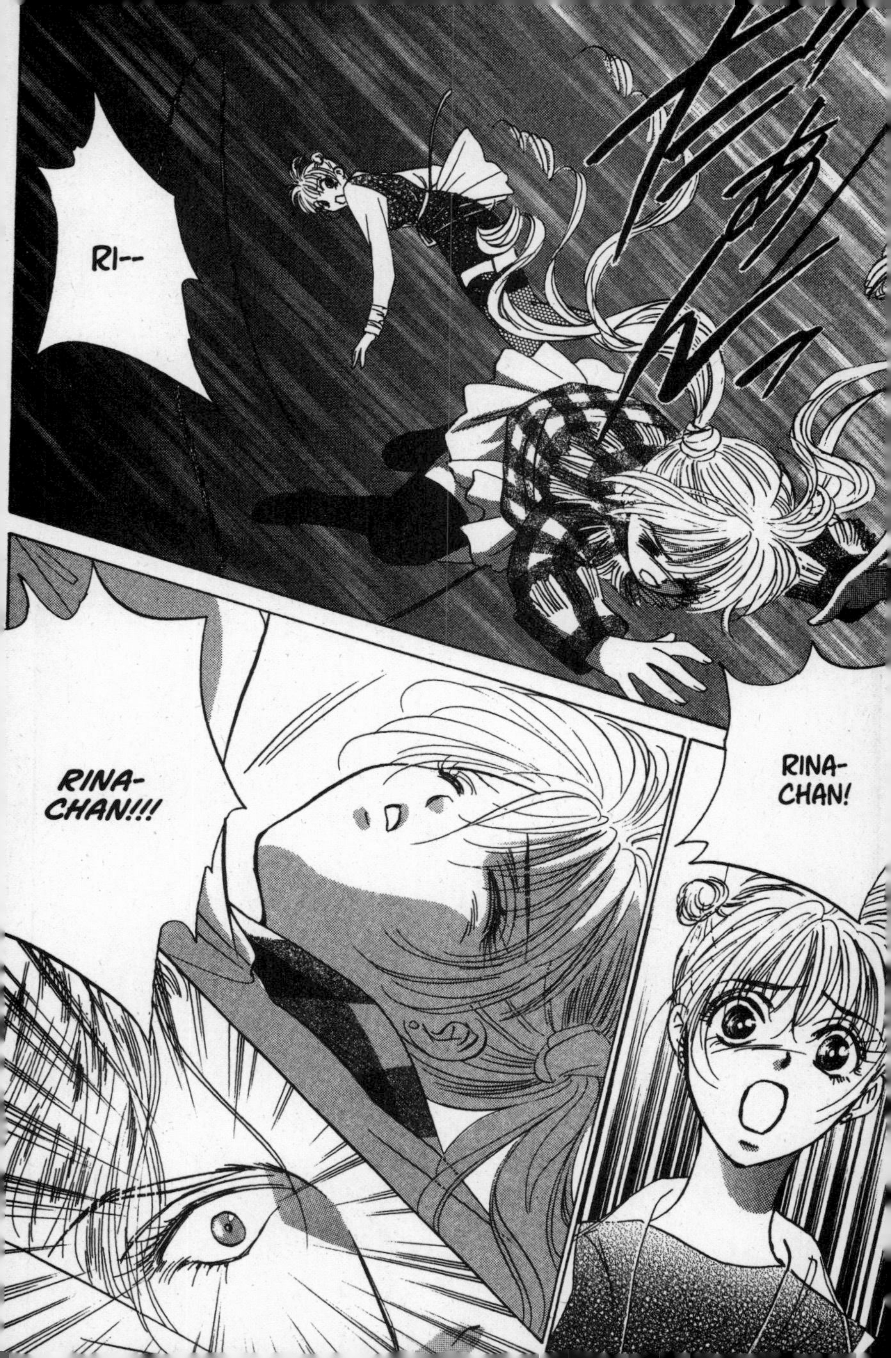
RI--
RINA-CHAN!
RINA-CHAN!!!

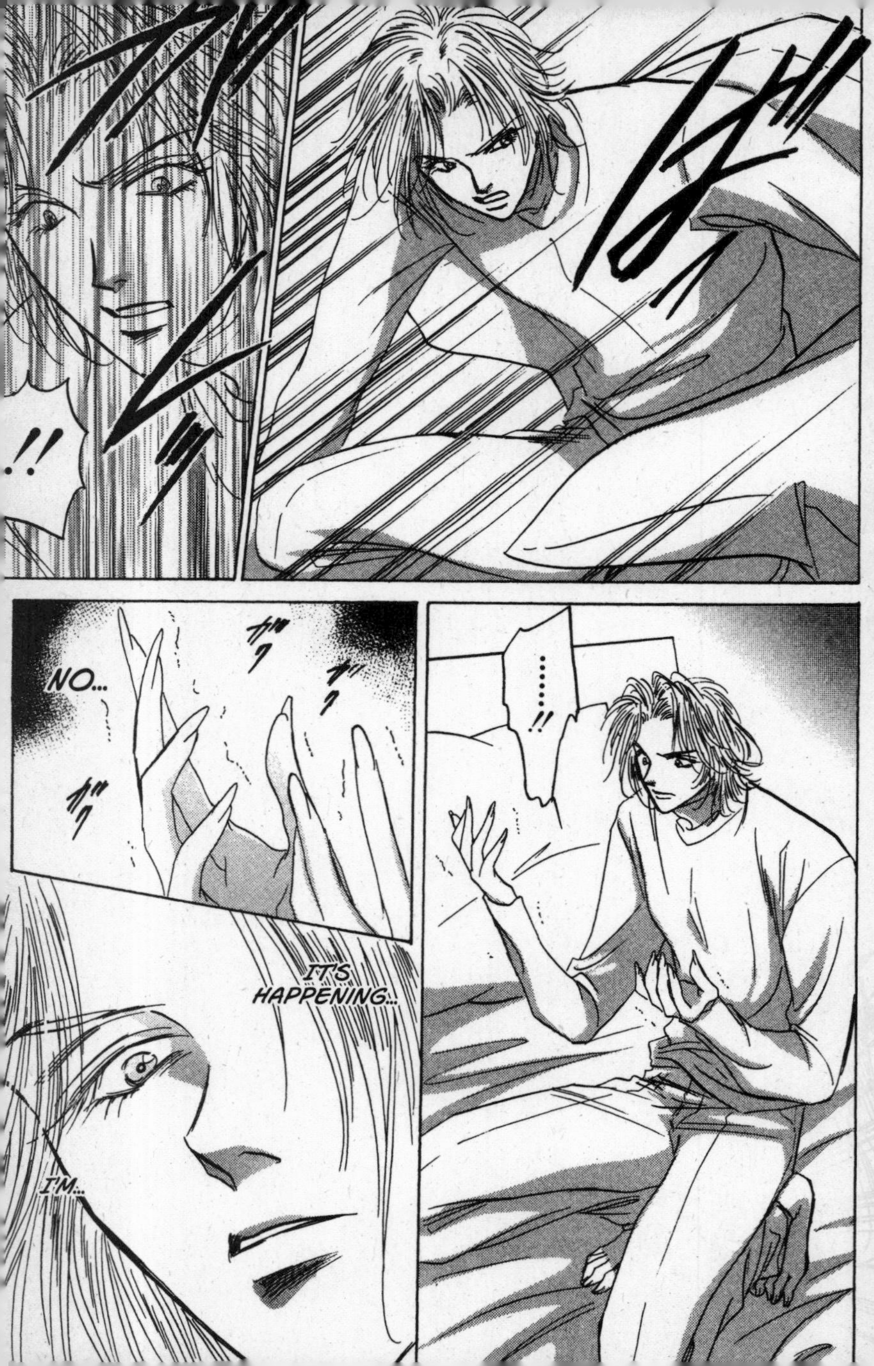
!!
......!!
NO...
IT'S HAPPENING...
I'M...

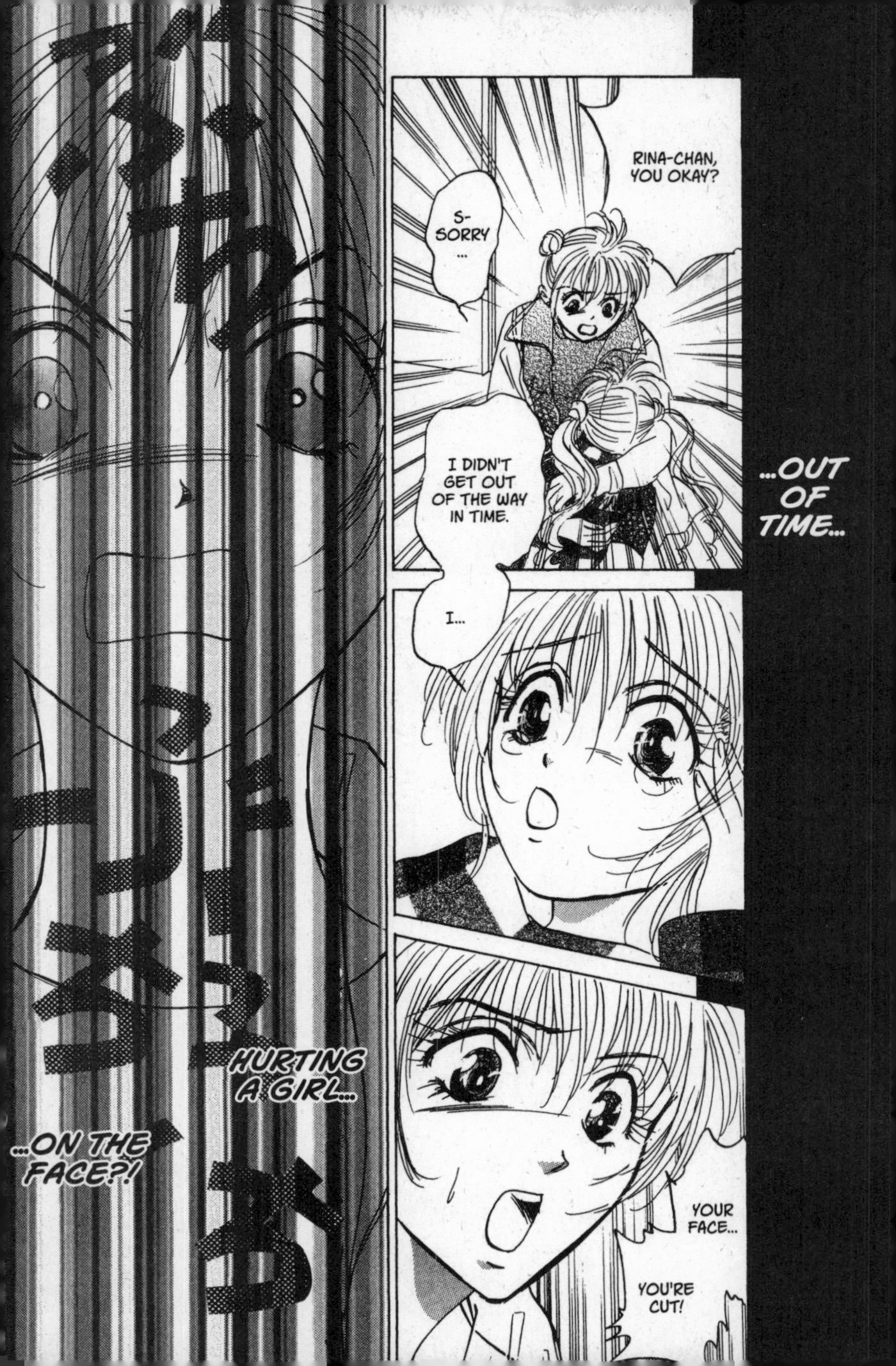
...OUT OF TIME...
RINA-CHAN, YOU OKAY?
S-SORRY...
I DIDN'T GET OUT OF THE WAY IN TIME.
I...
YOUR FACE...
YOU'RE CUT!
HURTING A GIRL...
...ON THE FACE?!

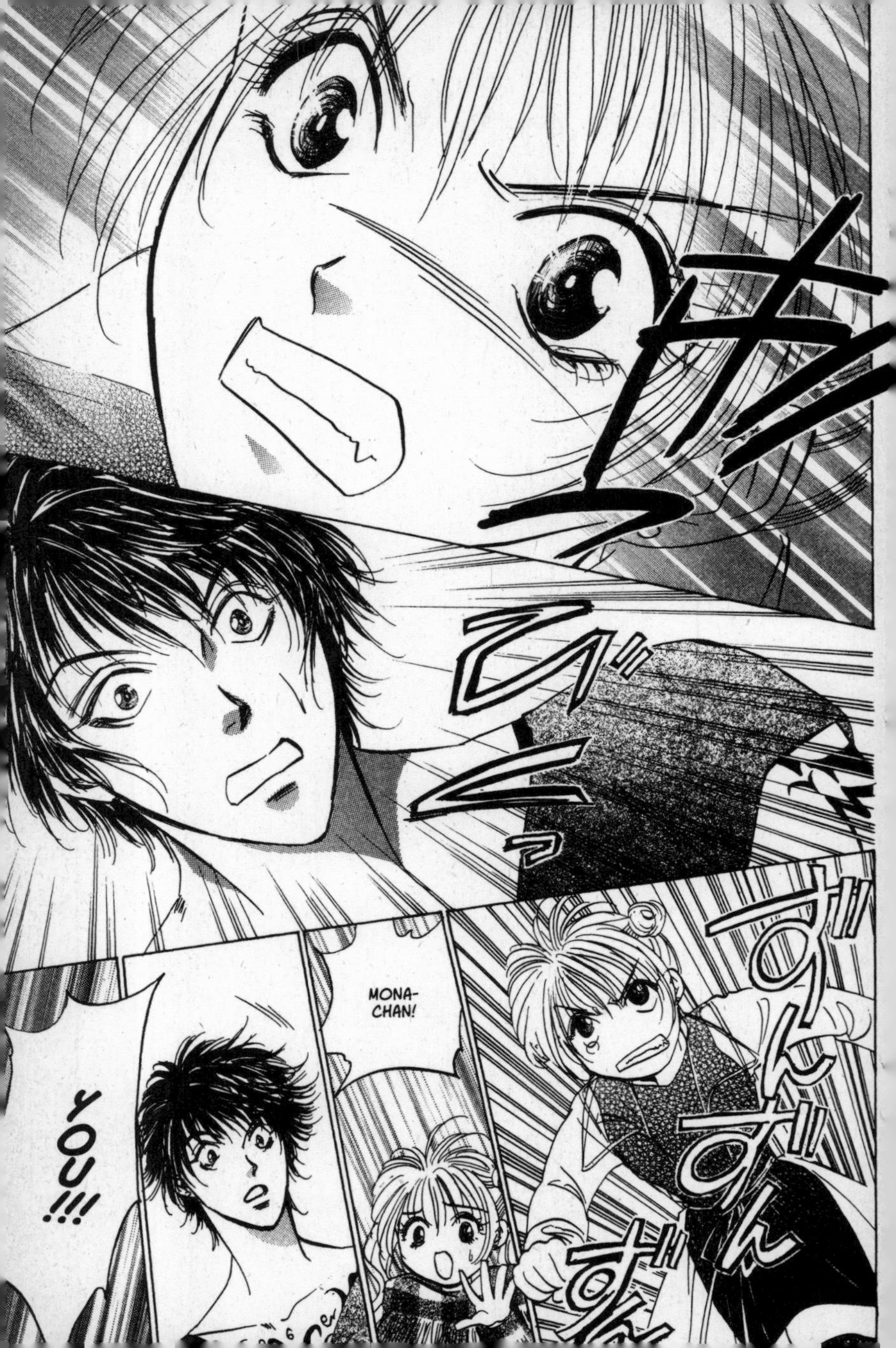

ぐいっ
ずんずんずん
MONA-CHAN!
YOU!!!

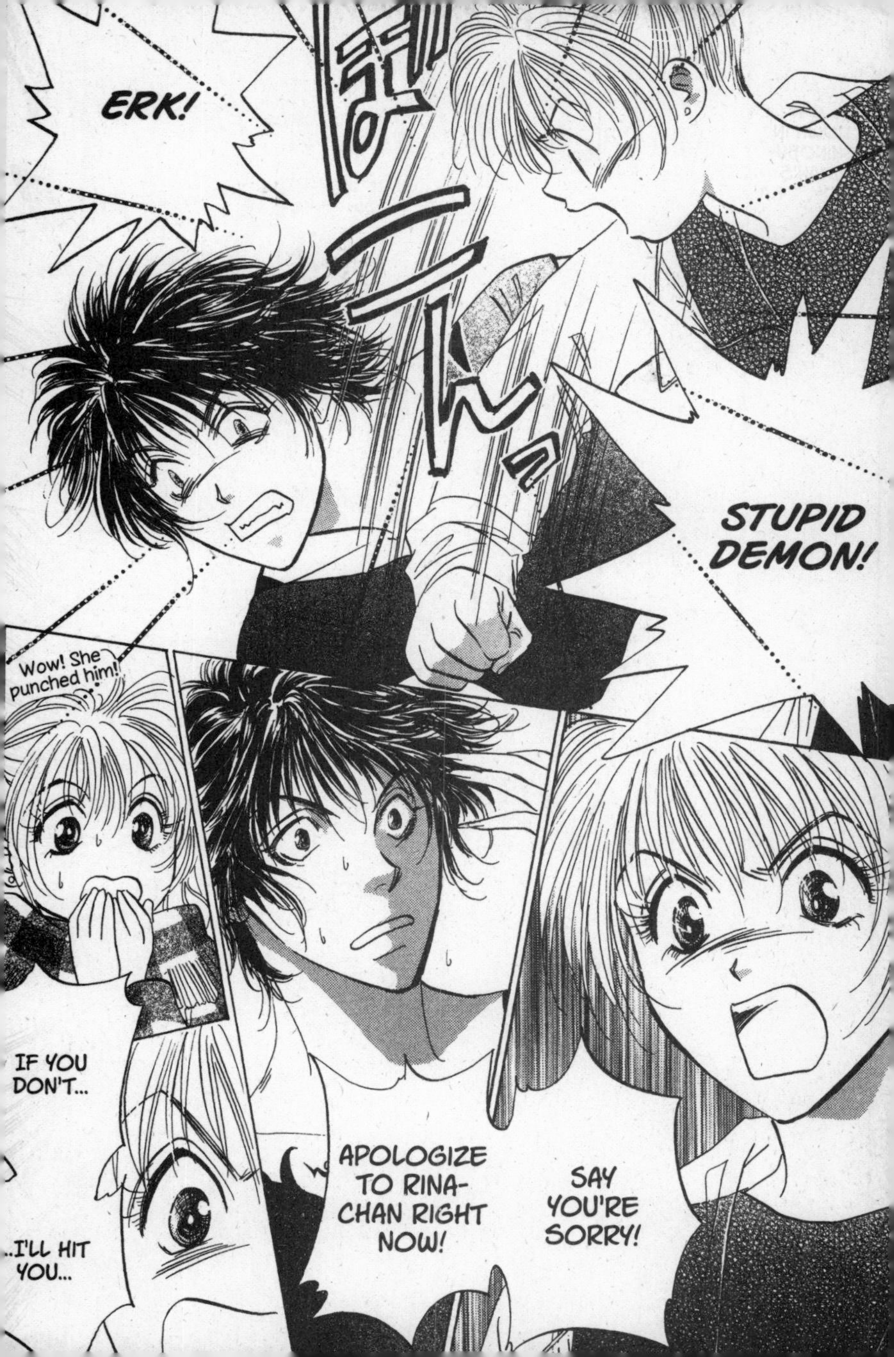
STUPID DEMON!
ERK!
SAY YOU'RE SORRY!
APOLOGIZE TO RINA-CHAN RIGHT NOW!
Wow! She punched him!
IF YOU DON'T...
...I'LL HIT YOU...

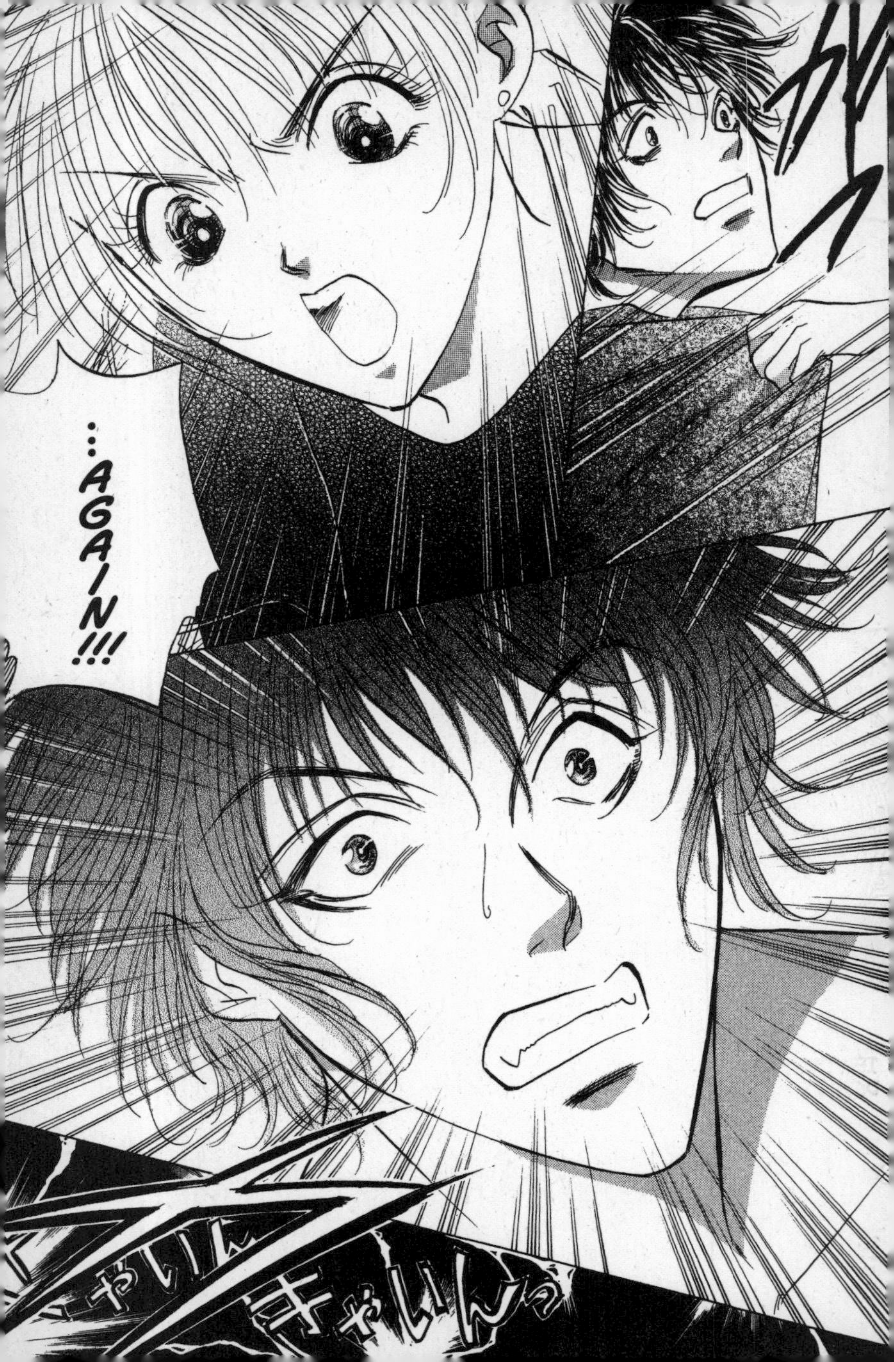
...AGAIN!!!

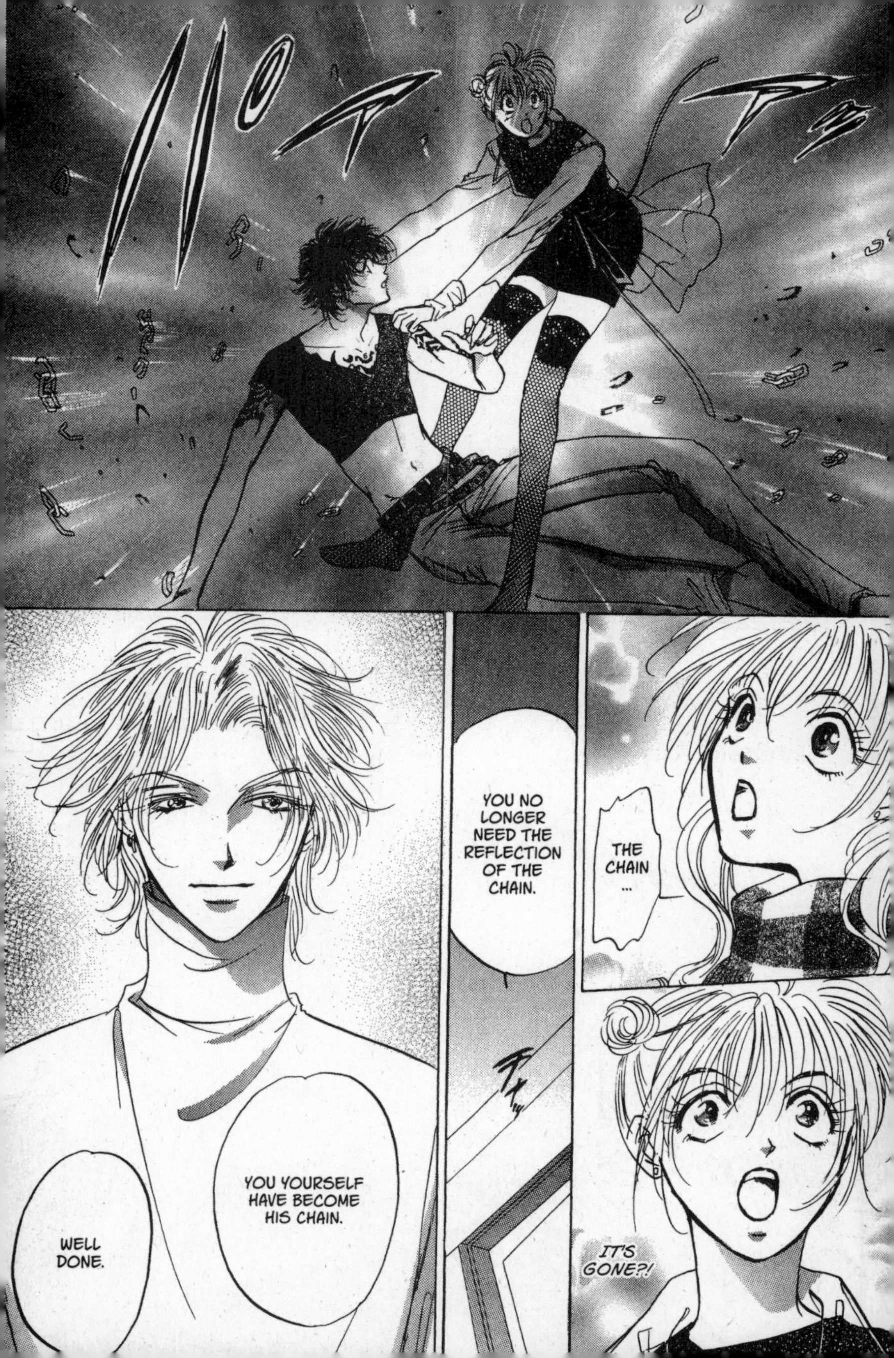
THE CHAIN ...
IT'S GONE?!
YOU NO LONGER NEED THE REFLECTION OF THE CHAIN.
YOU YOURSELF HAVE BECOME HIS CHAIN.
WELL DONE.

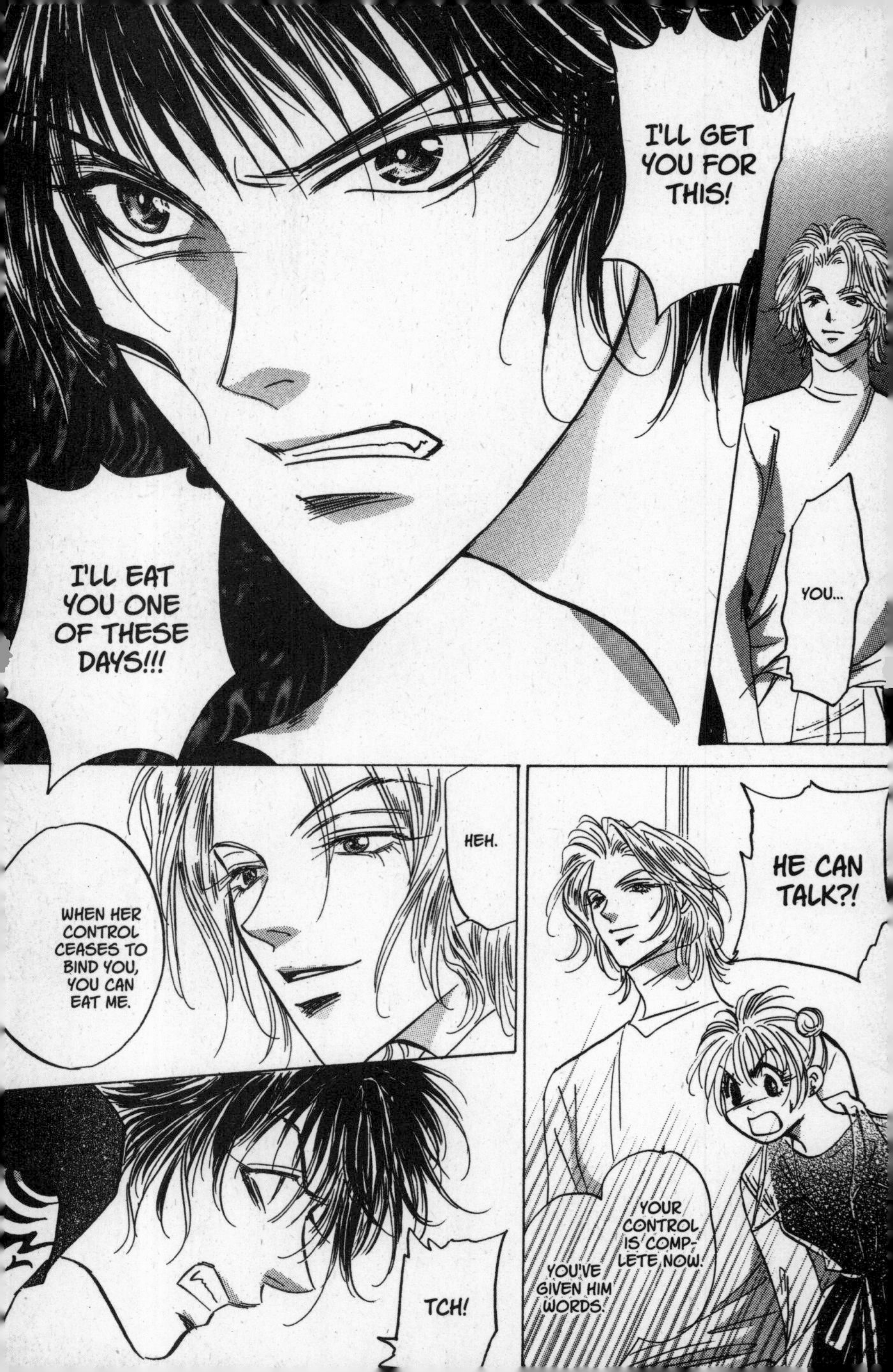
YOU...
I'LL GET YOU FOR THIS!
I'LL EAT YOU ONE OF THESE DAYS!!!
HE CAN TALK?!
YOUR CONTROL IS COMPLETE NOW.
YOU'VE GIVEN HIM WORDS.
HEH.
WHEN HER CONTROL CEASES TO BIND YOU, YOU CAN EAT ME.
TCH!

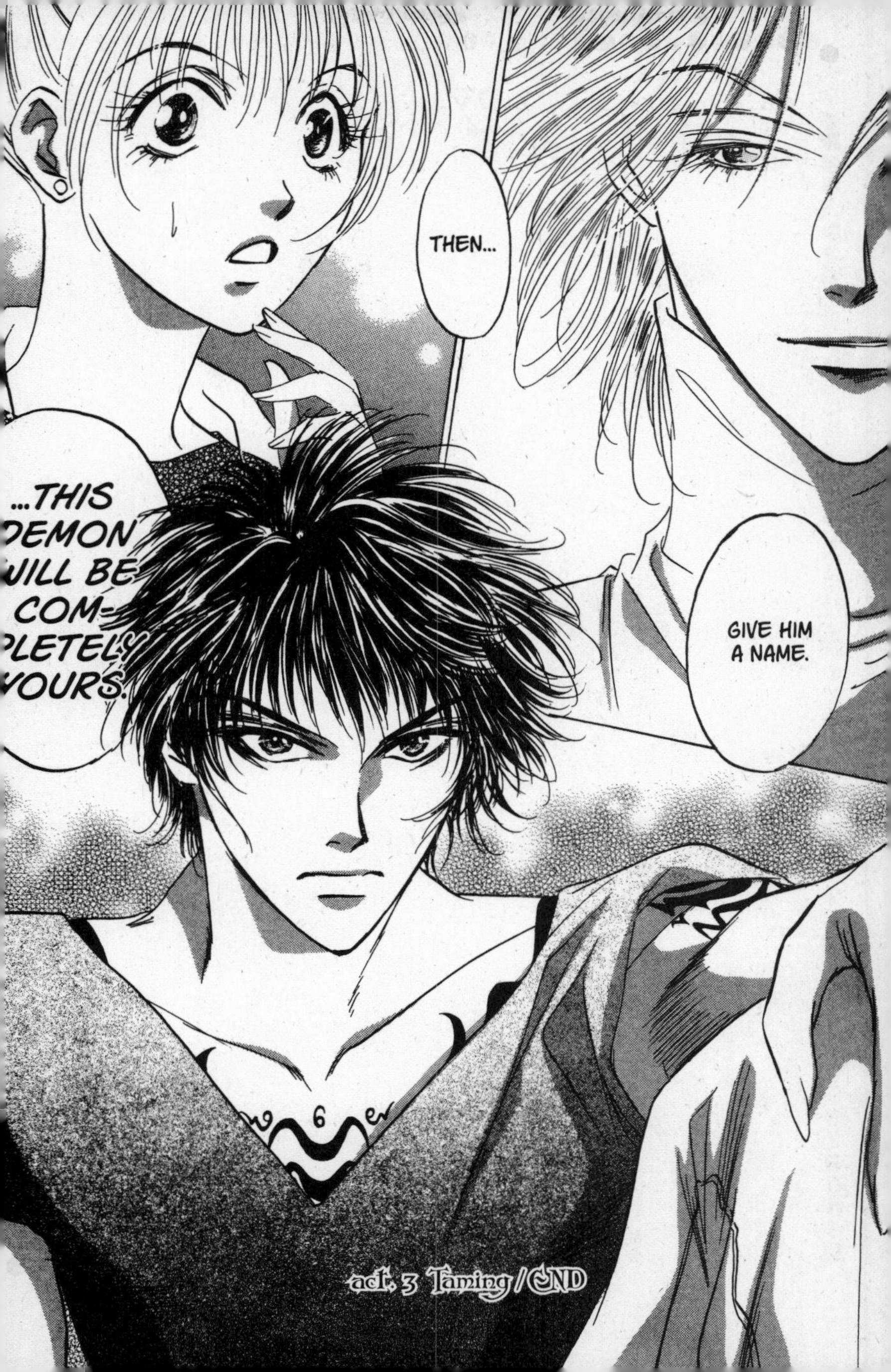
THEN...
GIVE HIM A NAME.
...THIS DEMON WILL BE COM-PLETELY YOURS.
act. 3 Taming / END

act. 4 Gluttony

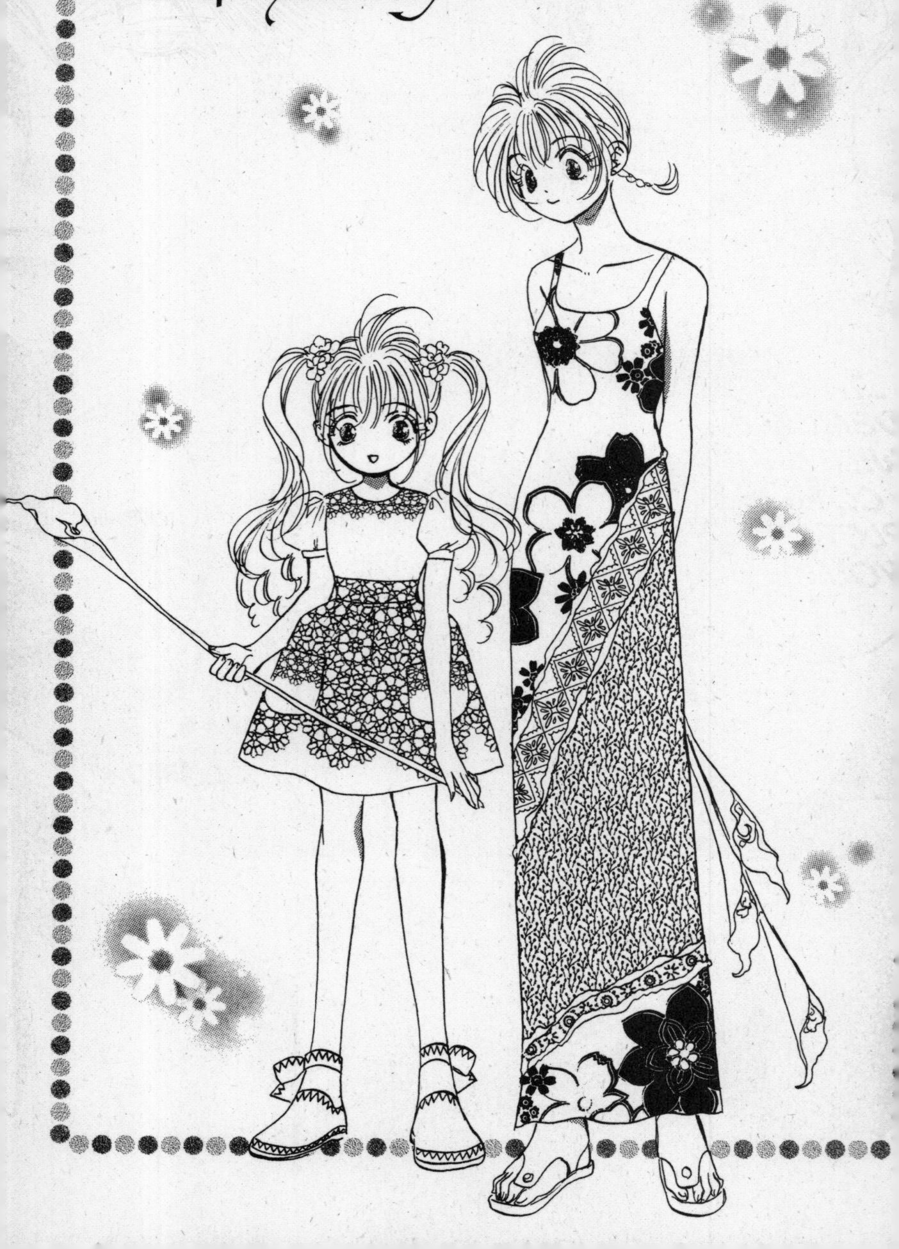

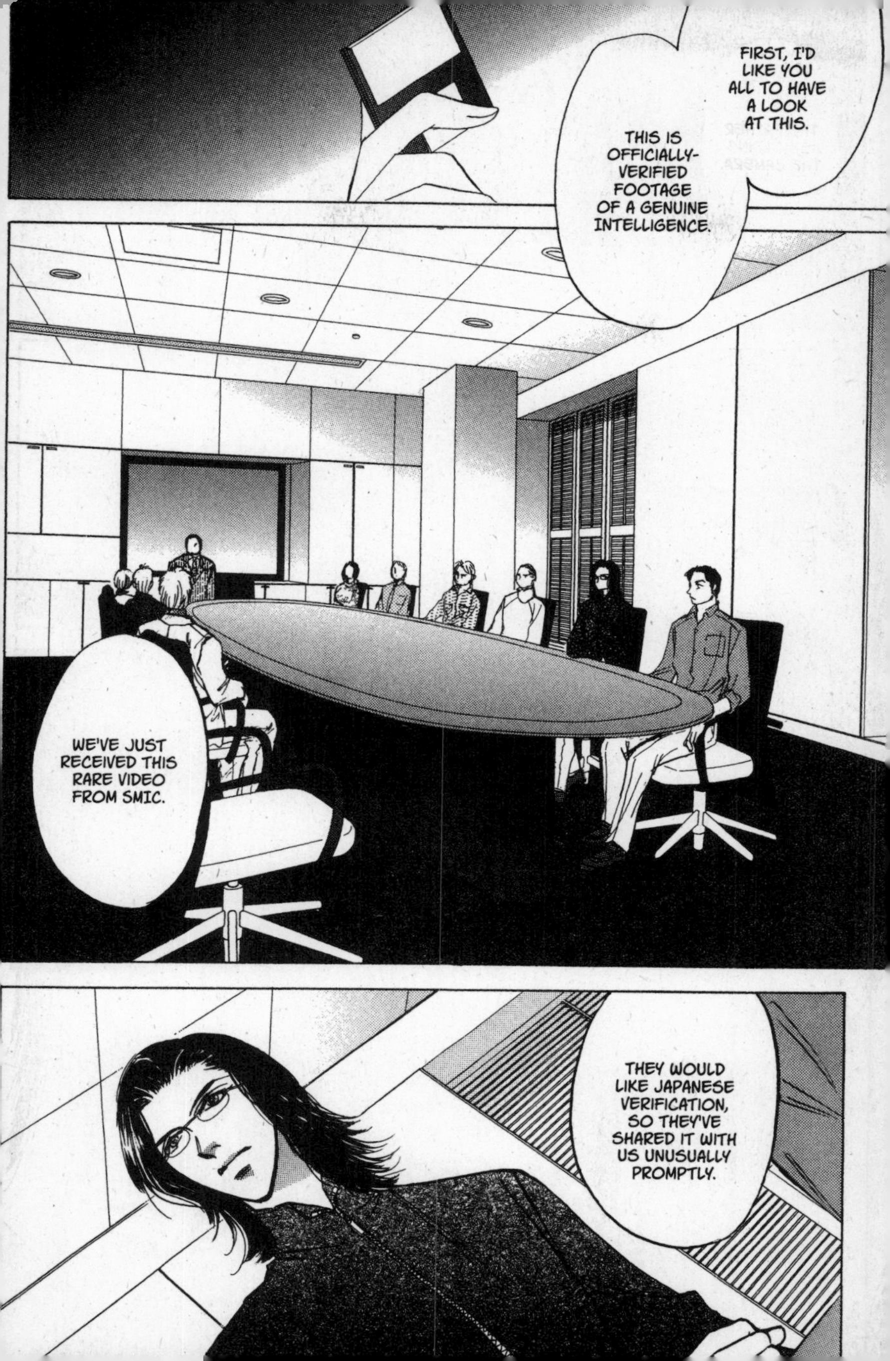
FIRST, I'D LIKE YOU ALL TO HAVE A LOOK AT THIS.
THIS IS OFFICIALLY-VERIFIED FOOTAGE OF A GENUINE INTELLIGENCE.
WE'VE JUST RECEIVED THIS RARE VIDEO FROM SMIC.
THEY WOULD LIKE JAPANESE VERIFICATION, SO THEY'VE SHARED IT WITH US UNUSUALLY PROMPTLY.

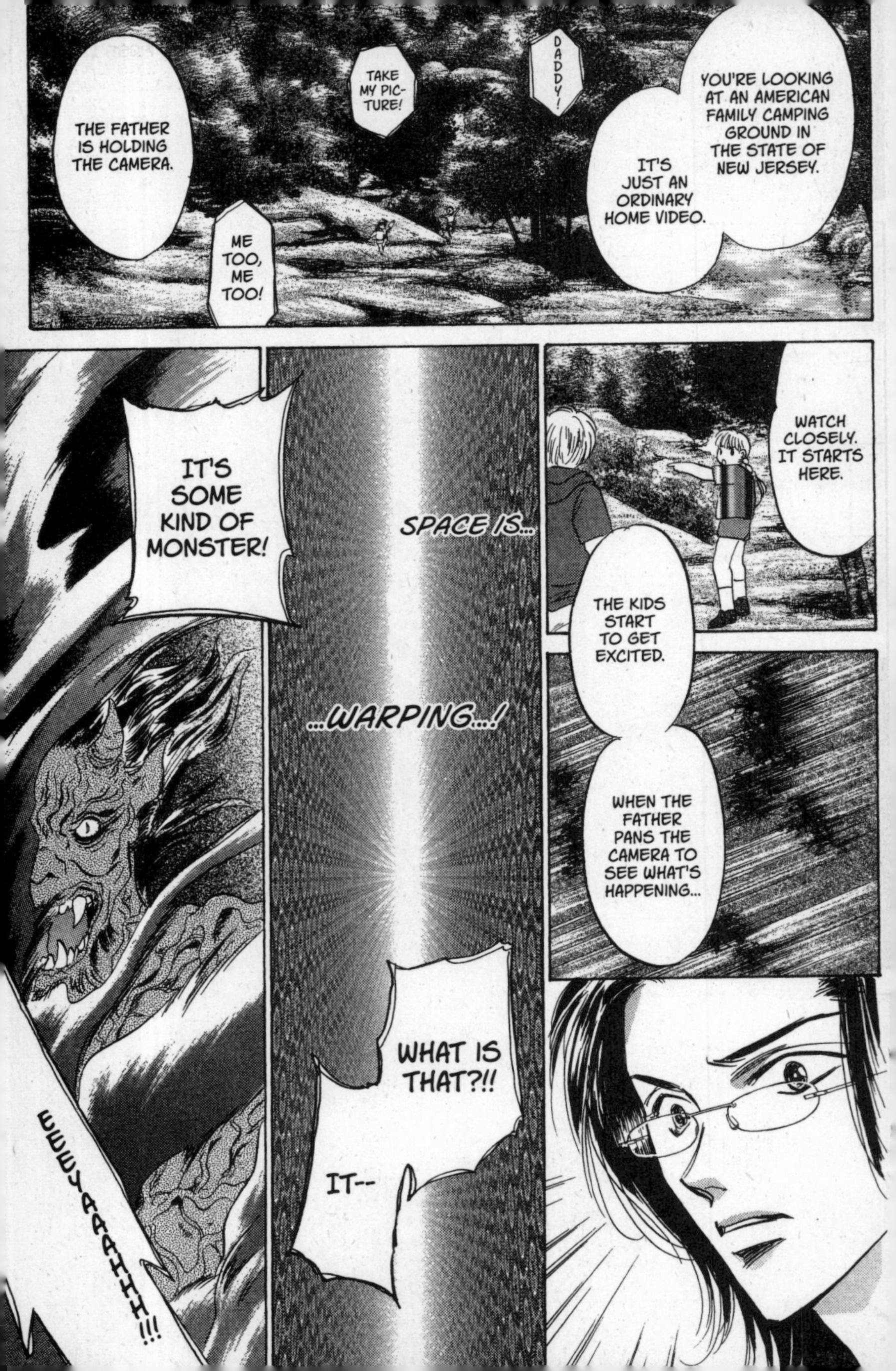
YOU'RE LOOKING AT AN AMERICAN FAMILY CAMPING GROUND IN THE STATE OF NEW JERSEY.
IT'S JUST AN ORDINARY HOME VIDEO.
DADDY!
TAKE MY PIC-TURE!
THE FATHER IS HOLDING THE CAMERA.
ME TOO, ME TOO!
WATCH CLOSELY. IT STARTS HERE.
THE KIDS START TO GET EXCITED.
WHEN THE FATHER PANS THE CAMERA TO SEE WHAT'S HAPPENING...
SPACE IS...
...WARPING...!
WHAT IS THAT?!!
IT--
IT'S SOME KIND OF MONSTER!
EEEYAAAHHH!!!

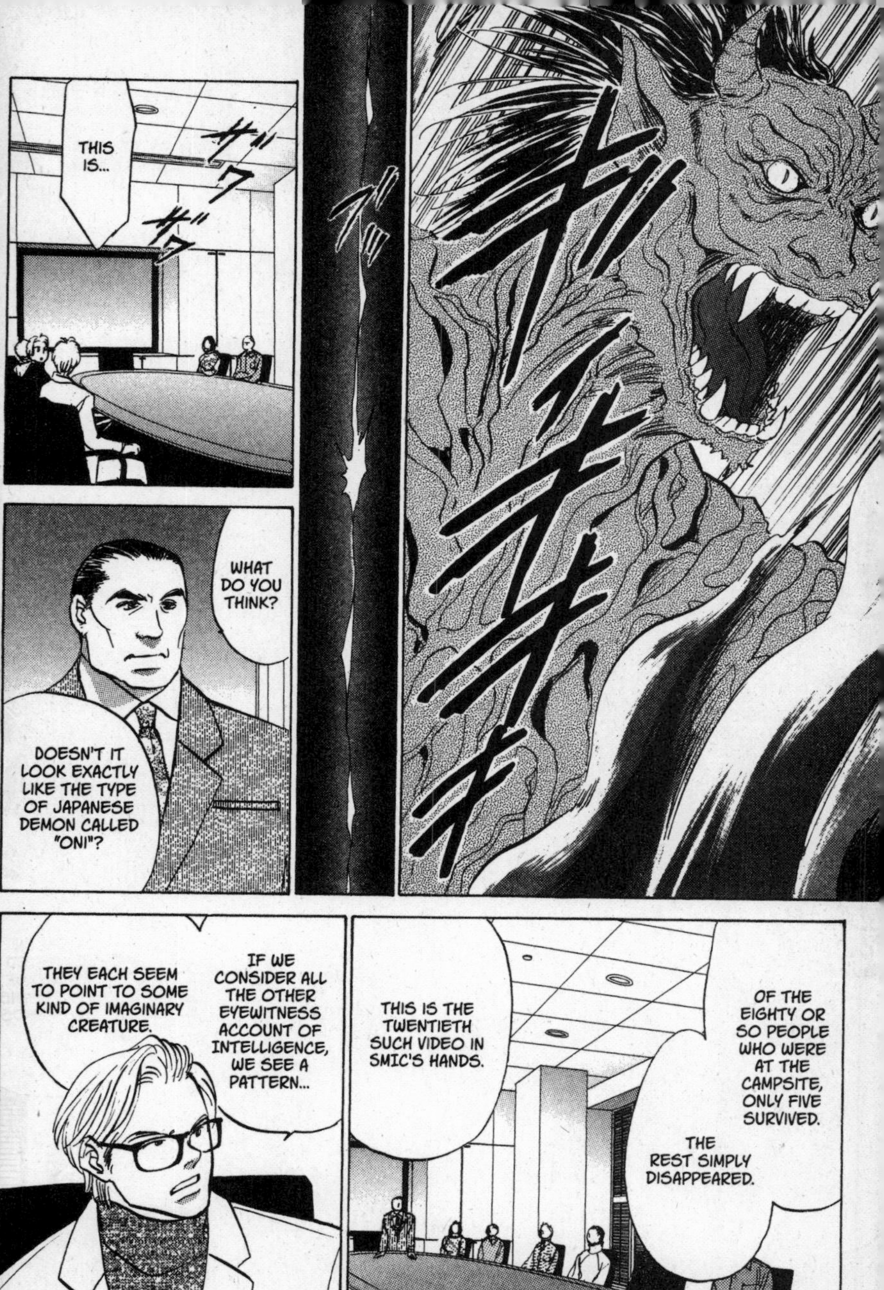

ザワ
ザワ
THIS IS...
WHAT DO YOU THINK?
DOESN'T IT LOOK EXACTLY LIKE THE TYPE OF JAPANESE DEMON CALLED "ONI"?
OF THE EIGHTY OR SO PEOPLE WHO WERE AT THE CAMPSITE, ONLY FIVE SURVIVED.
THE REST SIMPLY DISAPPEARED.
THIS IS THE TWENTIETH SUCH VIDEO IN SMIC'S HANDS.
IF WE CONSIDER ALL THE OTHER EYEWITNESS ACCOUNT OF INTELLIGENCE, WE SEE A PATTERN...
THEY EACH SEEM TO POINT TO SOME KIND OF IMAGINARY CREATURE.

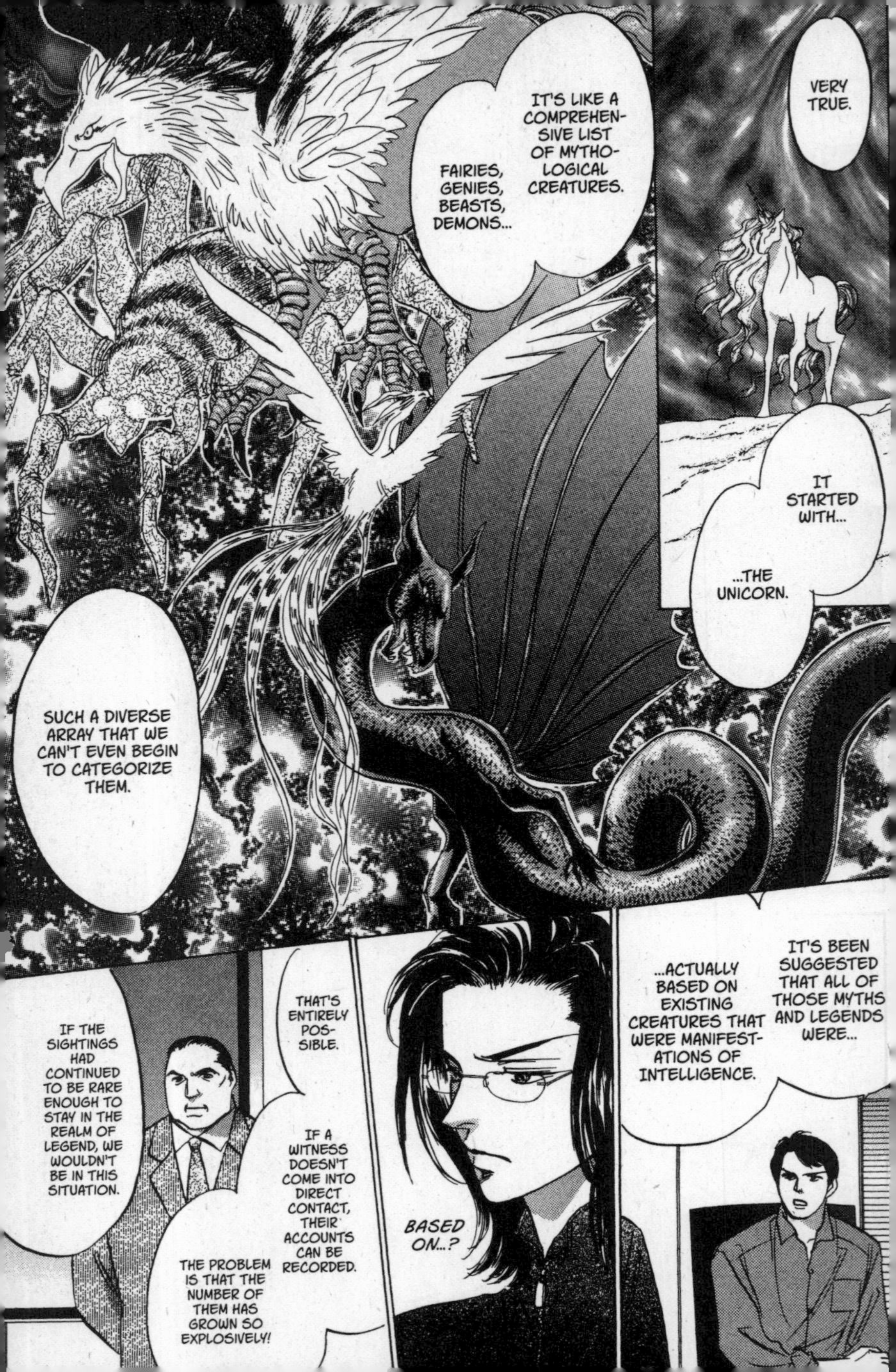
VERY TRUE.
IT STARTED WITH...
...THE UNICORN.
IT'S LIKE A COMPREHEN-SIVE LIST OF MYTHO-LOGICAL CREATURES.
FAIRIES, GENIES, BEASTS, DEMONS...
SUCH A DIVERSE ARRAY THAT WE CAN'T EVEN BEGIN TO CATEGORIZE THEM.
IT'S BEEN SUGGESTED THAT ALL OF THOSE MYTHS AND LEGENDS WERE...
...ACTUALLY BASED ON EXISTING CREATURES THAT WERE MANIFEST-ATIONS OF INTELLIGENCE.
BASED ON...?
THAT'S ENTIRELY POS-SIBLE.
IF A WITNESS DOESN'T COME INTO DIRECT CONTACT, THEIR ACCOUNTS CAN BE RECORDED.
THE PROBLEM IS THAT THE NUMBER OF THEM HAS GROWN SO EXPLOSIVELY!
IF THE SIGHTINGS HAD CONTINUED TO BE RARE ENOUGH TO STAY IN THE REALM OF LEGEND, WE WOULDN'T BE IN THIS SITUATION.

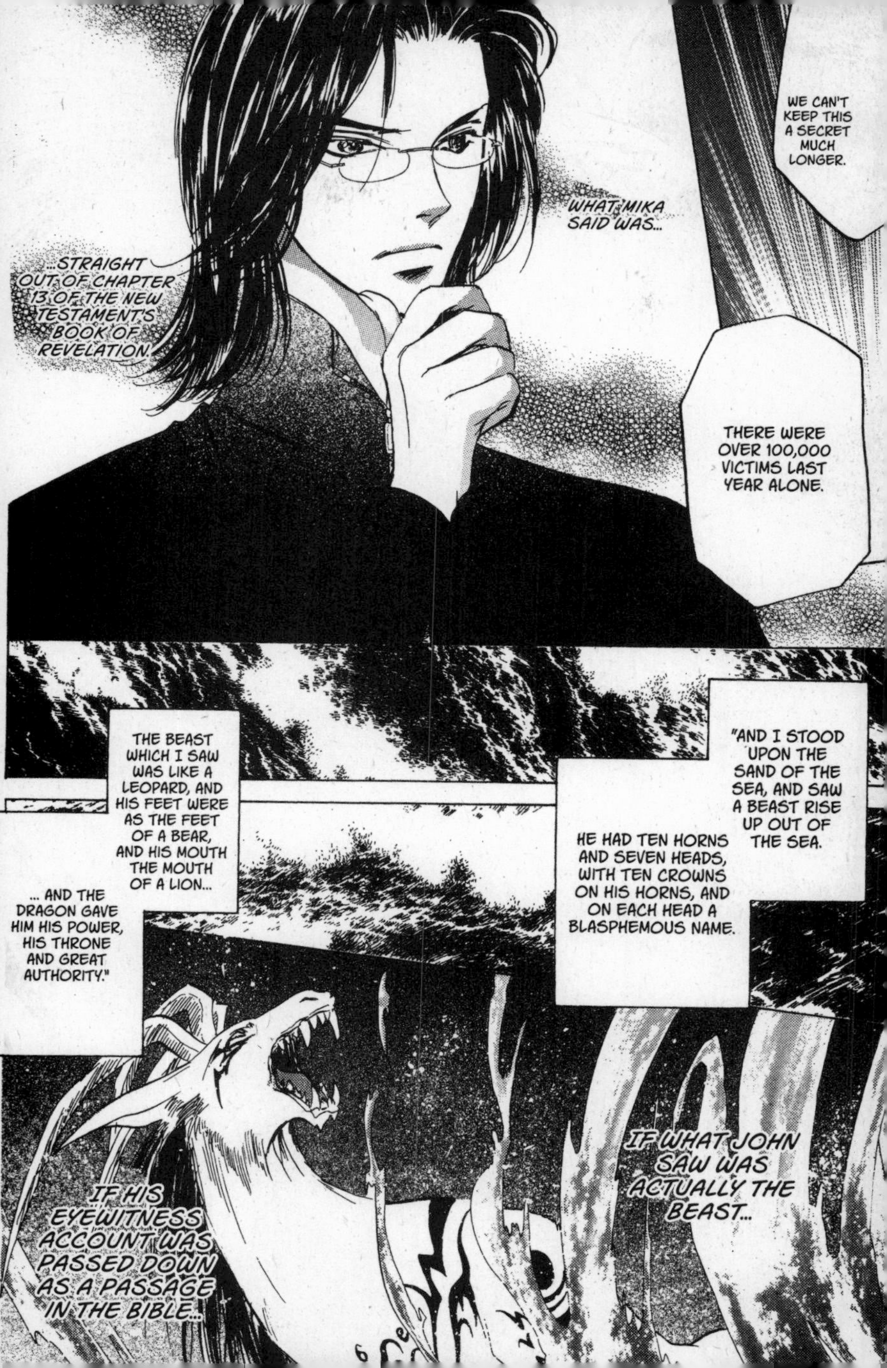
WE CAN'T KEEP THIS A SECRET MUCH LONGER.
THERE WERE OVER 100,000 VICTIMS LAST YEAR ALONE.
WHAT MIKA SAID WAS...
...STRAIGHT OUT OF CHAPTER 13 OF THE NEW TESTAMENT'S BOOK OF REVELATION.
"AND I STOOD UPON THE SAND OF THE SEA, AND SAW A BEAST RISE UP OUT OF THE SEA.
HE HAD TEN HORNS AND SEVEN HEADS, WITH TEN CROWNS ON HIS HORNS, AND ON EACH HEAD A BLASPHEMOUS NAME.
THE BEAST WHICH I SAW WAS LIKE A LEOPARD, AND HIS FEET WERE AS THE FEET OF A BEAR, AND HIS MOUTH THE MOUTH OF A LION...
... AND THE DRAGON GAVE HIM HIS POWER, HIS THRONE AND GREAT AUTHORITY."
IF WHAT JOHN SAW WAS ACTUALLY THE BEAST...
IF HIS EYEWITNESS ACCOUNT WAS PASSED DOWN AS A PASSAGE IN THE BIBLE...

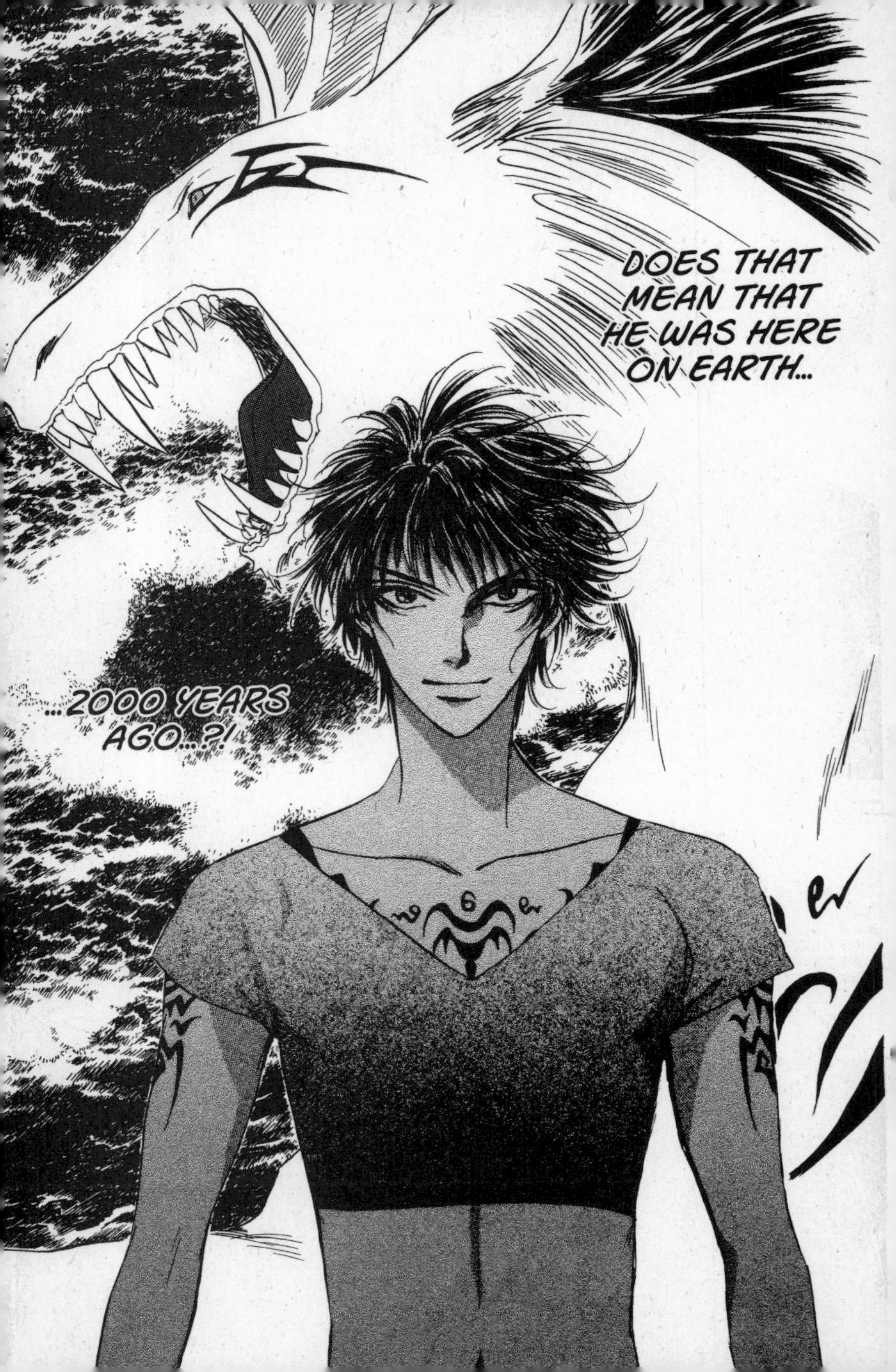
DOES THAT MEAN THAT HE WAS HERE ON EARTH...
...2000 YEARS AGO...?!

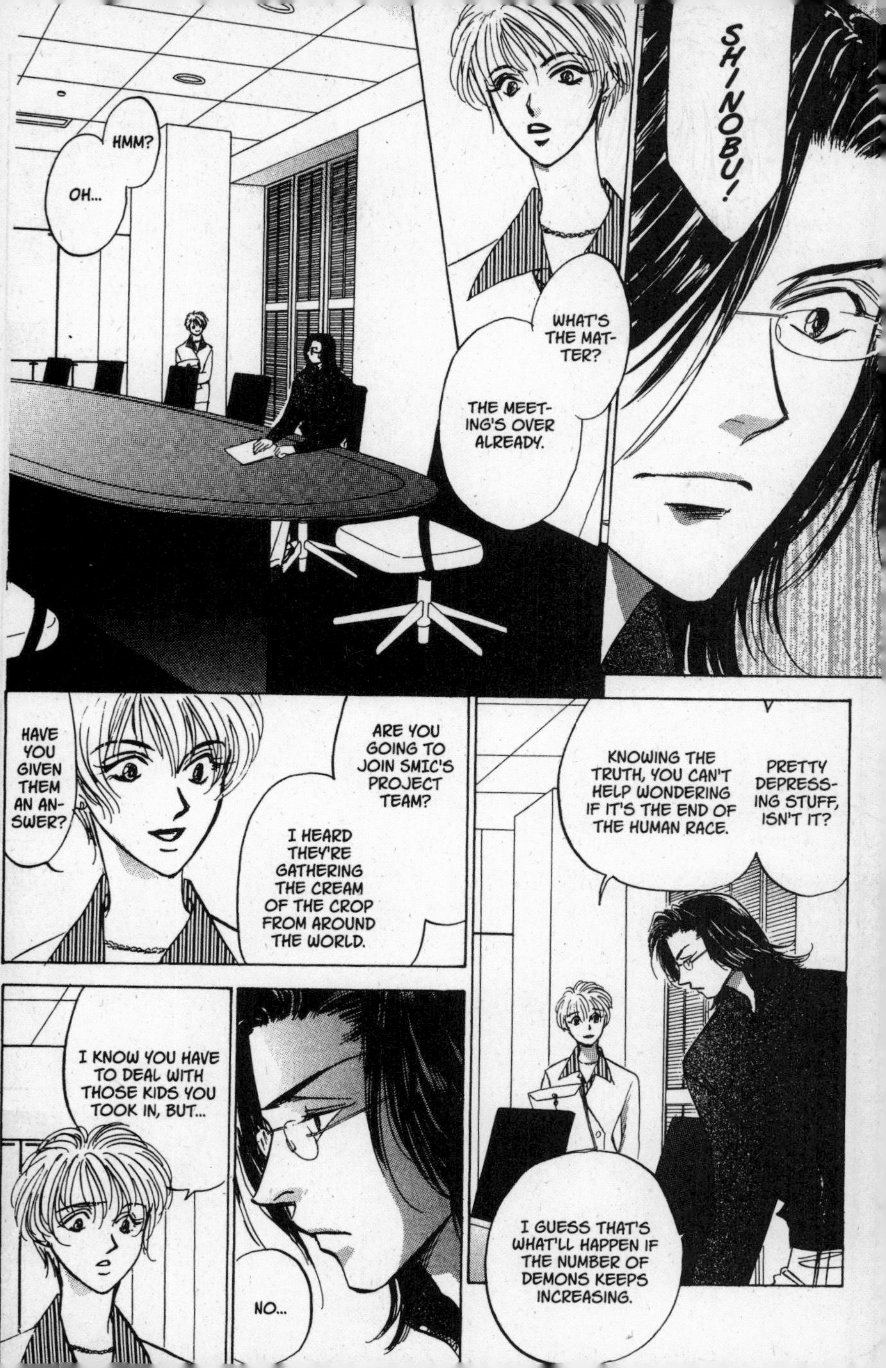
SHINOBU!
WHAT'S THE MATTER?
THE MEETING'S OVER ALREADY.
HMM?
OH...
PRETTY DEPRESSING STUFF, ISN'T IT?
KNOWING THE TRUTH, YOU CAN'T HELP WONDERING IF IT'S THE END OF THE HUMAN RACE.
I GUESS THAT'S WHAT'LL HAPPEN IF THE NUMBER OF DEMONS KEEPS INCREASING.
ARE YOU GOING TO JOIN SMIC'S PROJECT TEAM?
I HEARD THEY'RE GATHERING THE CREAM OF THE CROP FROM AROUND THE WORLD.
HAVE YOU GIVEN THEM AN ANSWER?
NO...
I KNOW YOU HAVE TO DEAL WITH THOSE KIDS YOU TOOK IN, BUT...

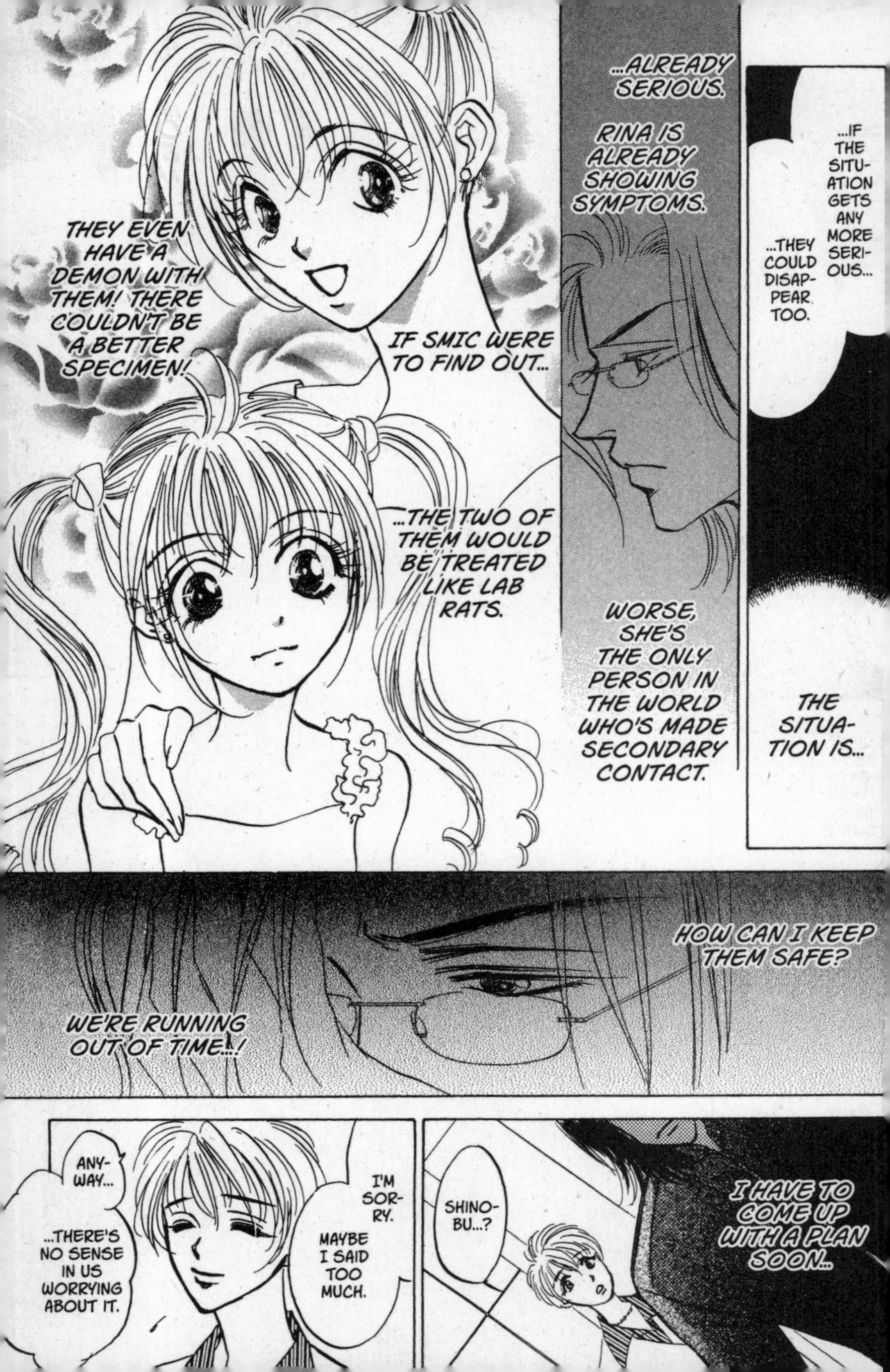
...IF THE SITUATION GETS ANY MORE SERIOUS...
...THEY COULD DISAPPEAR TOO.
THE SITUATION IS...
...ALREADY SERIOUS.
RINA IS ALREADY SHOWING SYMPTOMS.
WORSE, SHE'S THE ONLY PERSON IN THE WORLD WHO'S MADE SECONDARY CONTACT.
THEY EVEN HAVE A DEMON WITH THEM! THERE COULDN'T BE A BETTER SPECIMEN!
IF SMIC WERE TO FIND OUT...
...THE TWO OF THEM WOULD BE TREATED LIKE LAB RATS.
HOW CAN I KEEP THEM SAFE?
WE'RE RUNNING OUT OF TIME...!
I HAVE TO COME UP WITH A PLAN SOON...
SHINOBU...?
I'M SORRY.
MAYBE I SAID TOO MUCH.
ANYWAY...
...THERE'S NO SENSE IN US WORRYING ABOUT IT.

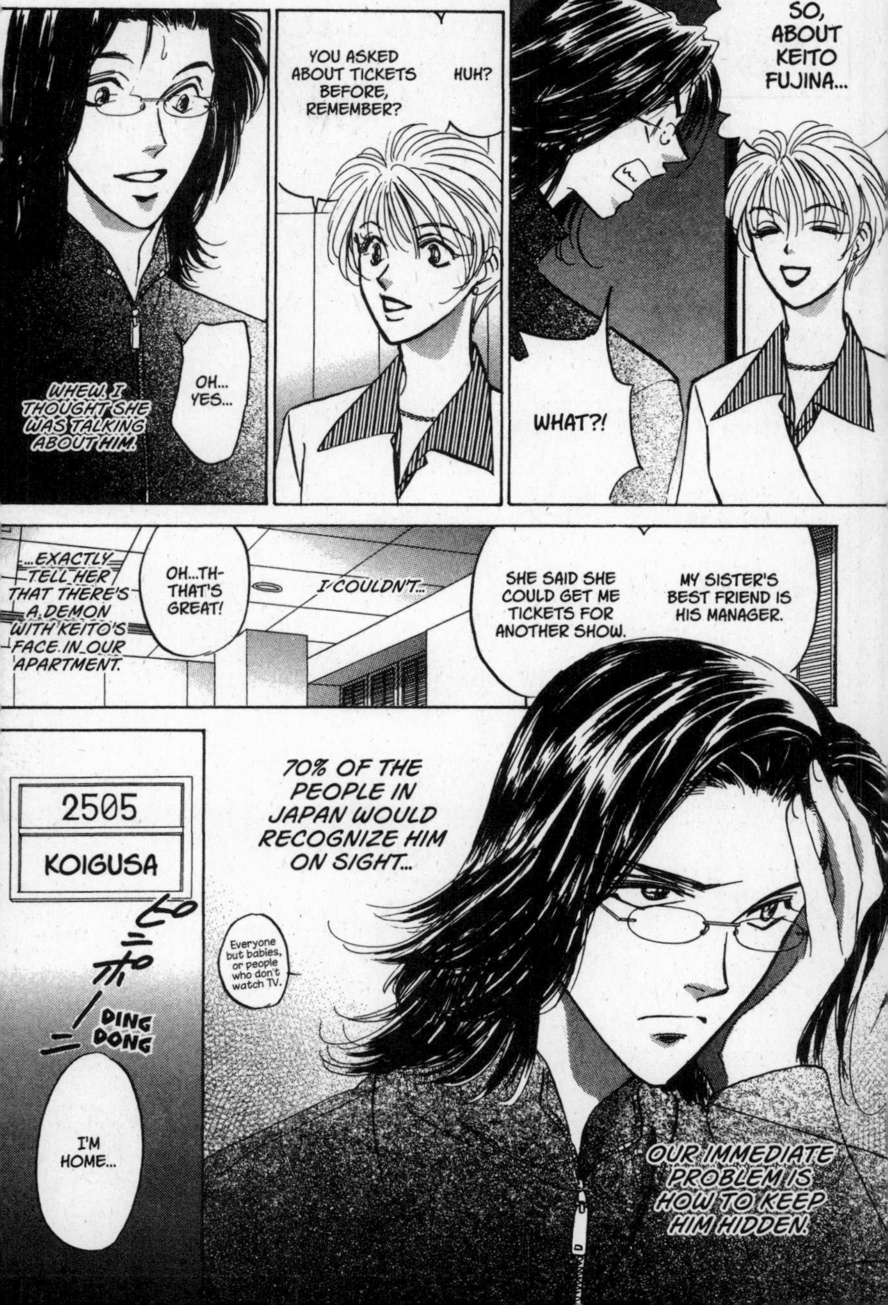
SO, ABOUT KEITO FUJINA...
WHAT?!
HUH?
YOU ASKED ABOUT TICKETS BEFORE, REMEMBER?
OH... YES...
WHEW. I THOUGHT SHE WAS TALKING ABOUT HIM.
MY SISTER'S BEST FRIEND IS HIS MANAGER.
SHE SAID SHE COULD GET ME TICKETS FOR ANOTHER SHOW.
I COULDN'T...
OH...TH-THAT'S GREAT!
...EXACTLY TELL HER THAT THERE'S A DEMON WITH KEITO'S FACE IN OUR APARTMENT.
70% OF THE PEOPLE IN JAPAN WOULD RECOGNIZE HIM ON SIGHT...
Everyone but babies, or people who don't watch TV.
OUR IMMEDIATE PROBLEM IS HOW TO KEEP HIM HIDDEN.
2505
KOIGUSA
DING DONG
I'M HOME...

FREE TALK
〈3〉

I'm so glad to be able to get Demon Sacred 1 out. This piece is a little different from my other work, with a slightly stronger touch of fantasy. It's been a lot of fun writing it. In volume 2 the relationships between the characters will become clearer, so stay tuned! The real Keito-kun will make an appearance, and so will the enigma, Helmut. I just love the sound of his name. I borrowed the name from Helmut Berger, a great actor from the past. He was a fixture in Visconti movies. See you next time!

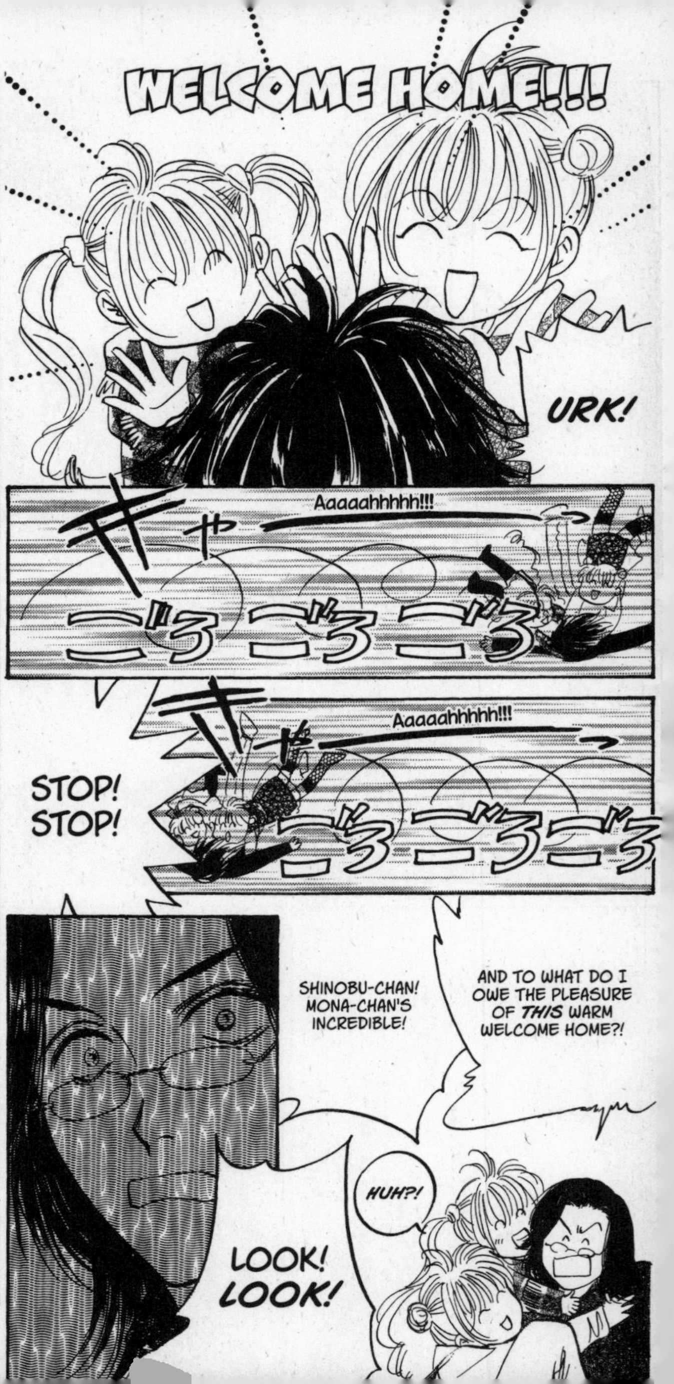

WELCOME HOME!!!
URK!
ギャー
Aaaaahhhhh!!!
ごろごろごろ
ギャー
Aaaaahhhhh!!!
STOP! STOP!
ごろごろごろ
AND TO WHAT DO I OWE THE PLEASURE OF THIS WARM WELCOME HOME?!
SHINOBU-CHAN! MONA-CHAN'S INCREDIBLE!
HUH?!
LOOK! LOOK!

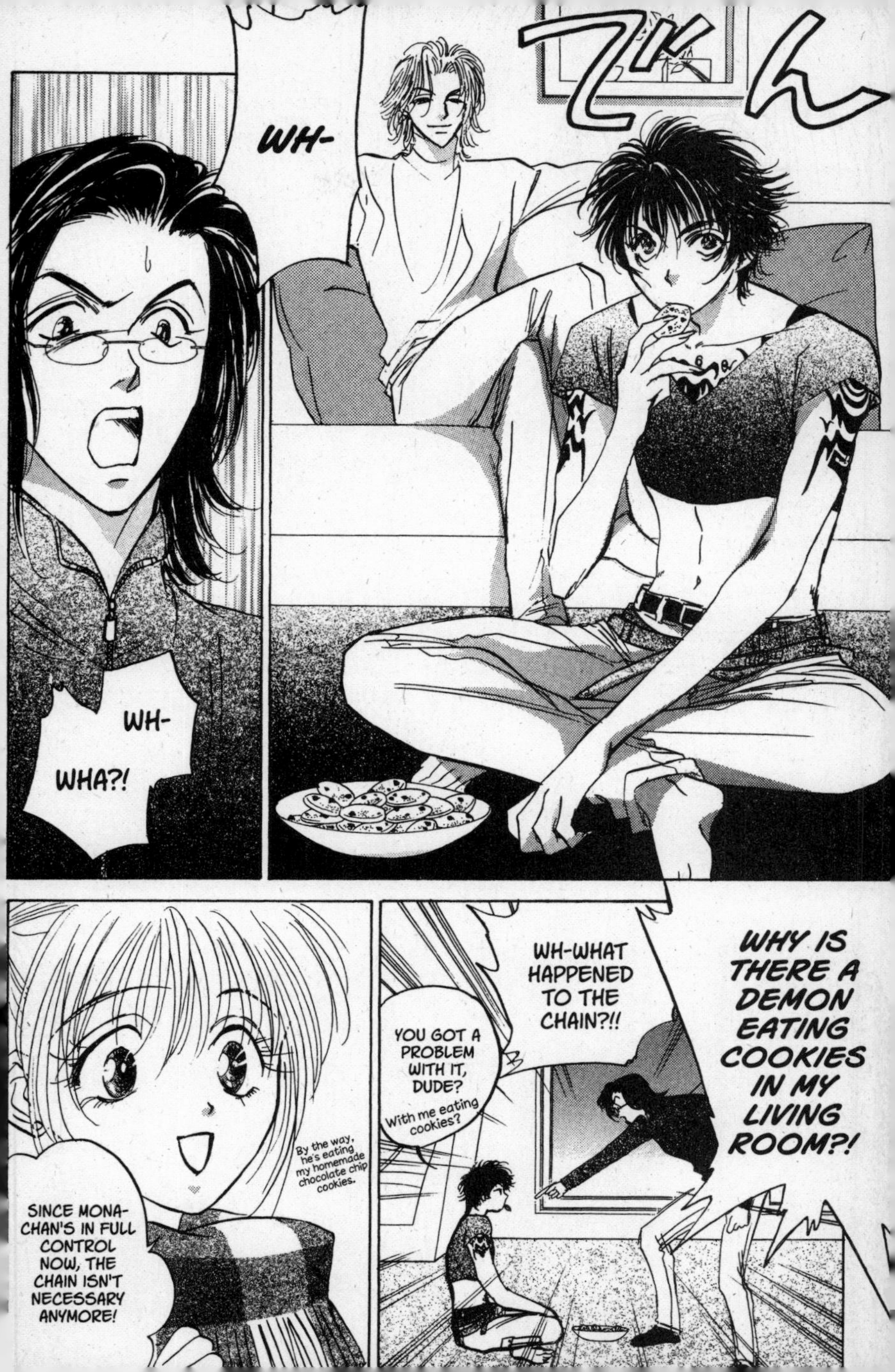
WH-
WH-
WHA?!
WHY IS THERE A DEMON EATING COOKIES IN MY LIVING ROOM?!
WH-WHAT HAPPENED TO THE CHAIN?!!
YOU GOT A PROBLEM WITH IT, DUDE?
With me eating cookies?
By the way, he's eating my homemade chocolate chip cookies.
SINCE MONA-CHAN'S IN FULL CONTROL NOW, THE CHAIN ISN'T NECESSARY ANYMORE!

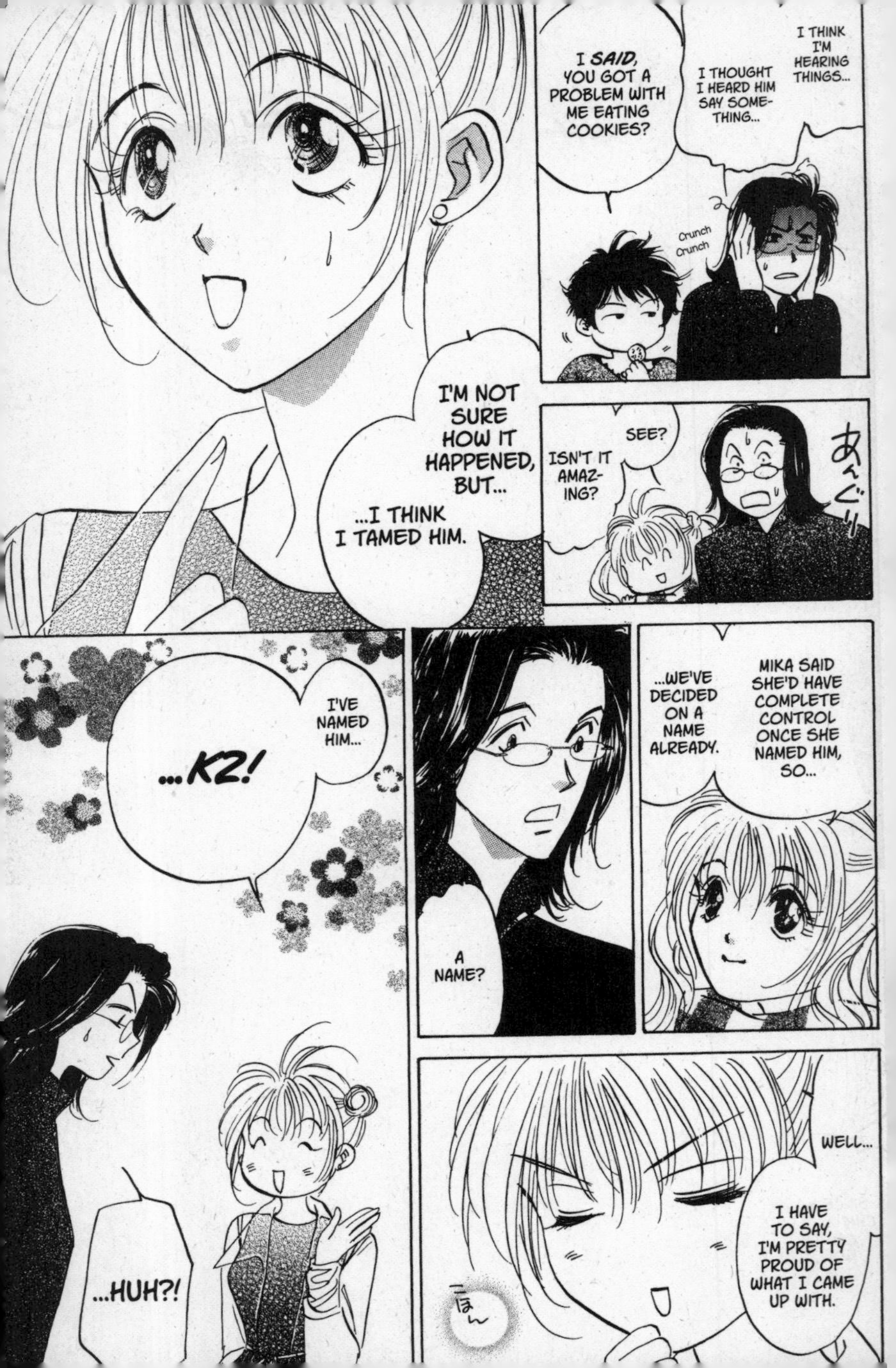
I THINK I'M HEARING THINGS...
I THOUGHT I HEARD HIM SAY SOME-THING...
I SAID, YOU GOT A PROBLEM WITH ME EATING COOKIES?
Crunch Crunch
あんぐり
SEE?
ISN'T IT AMAZ-ING?
I'M NOT SURE HOW IT HAPPENED, BUT...
...I THINK I TAMED HIM.
MIKA SAID SHE'D HAVE COMPLETE CONTROL ONCE SHE NAMED HIM, SO...
...WE'VE DECIDED ON A NAME ALREADY.
A NAME?
WELL...
I HAVE TO SAY, I'M PRETTY PROUD OF WHAT I CAME UP WITH.
ごほん
I'VE NAMED HIM...
...K2!
...HUH?!

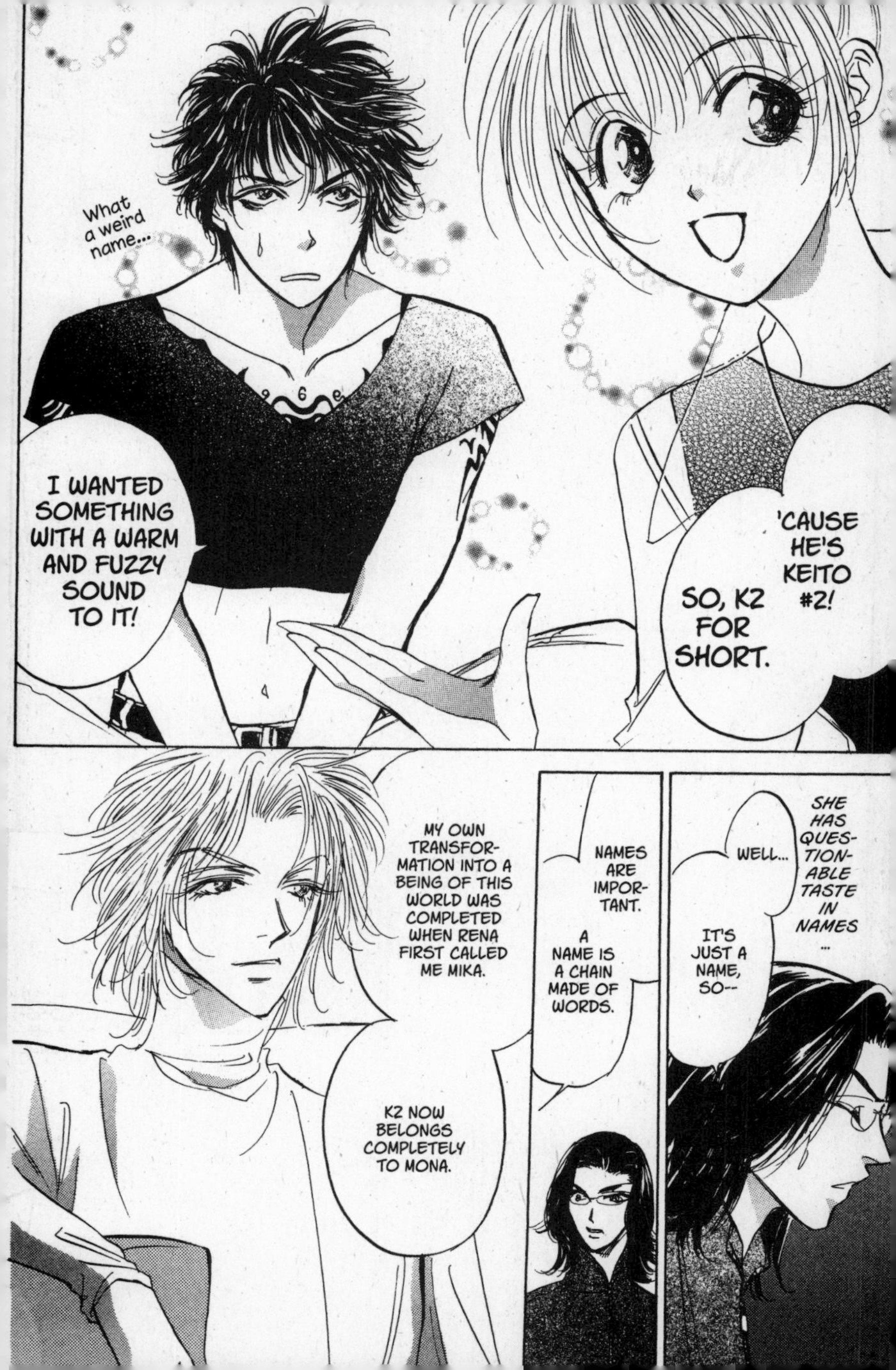
'CAUSE HE'S KEITO #2!
SO, K2 FOR SHORT.
What a weird name...
I WANTED SOMETHING WITH A WARM AND FUZZY SOUND TO IT!
SHE HAS QUESTIONABLE TASTE IN NAMES...
WELL...
IT'S JUST A NAME, SO--
NAMES ARE IMPORTANT.
A NAME IS A CHAIN MADE OF WORDS.
MY OWN TRANSFORMATION INTO A BEING OF THIS WORLD WAS COMPLETED WHEN RENA FIRST CALLED ME MIKA.
K2 NOW BELONGS COMPLETELY TO MONA.

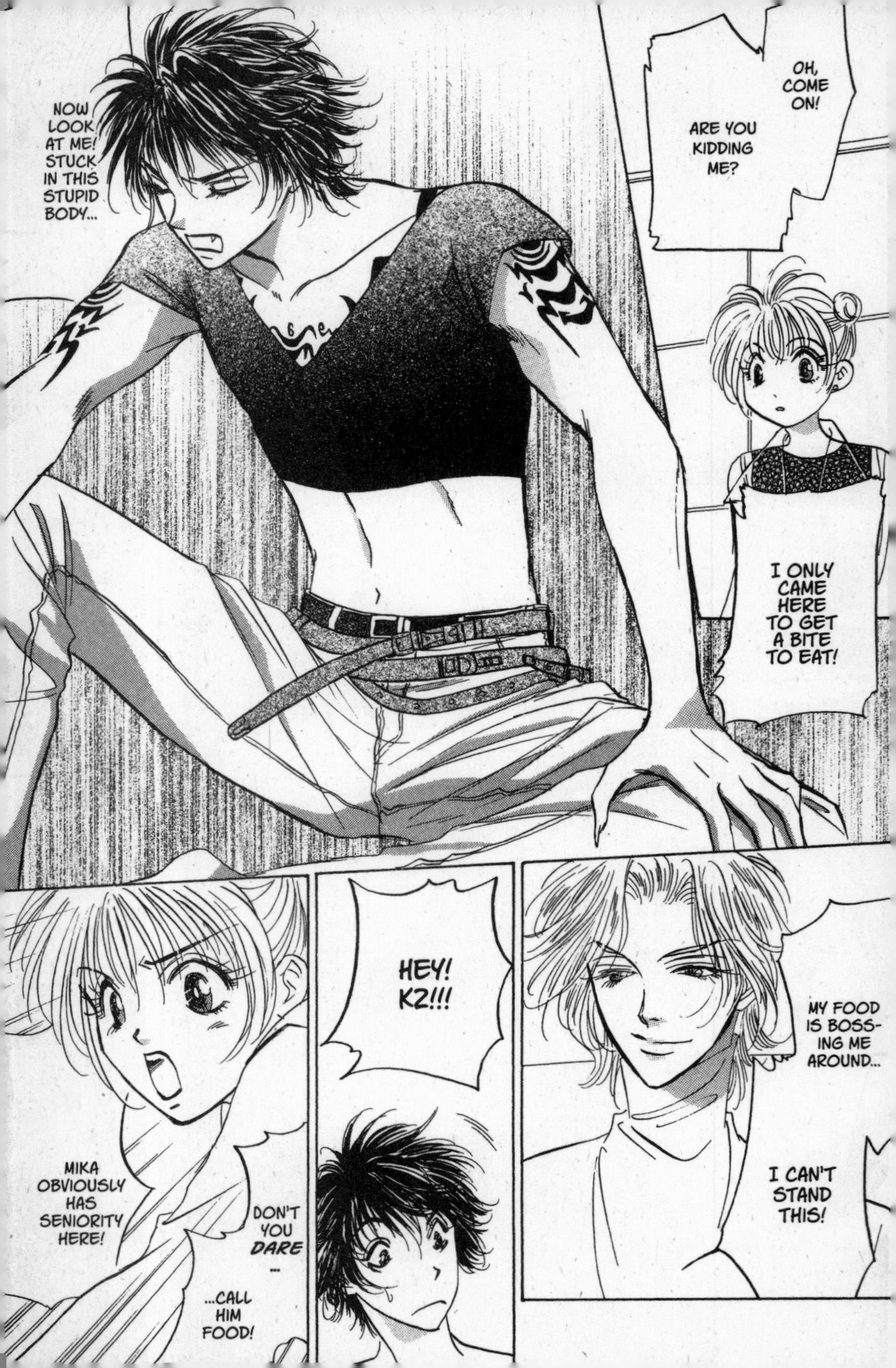
OH, COME ON!
ARE YOU KIDDING ME?
I ONLY CAME HERE TO GET A BITE TO EAT!
NOW LOOK AT ME! STUCK IN THIS STUPID BODY...
MY FOOD IS BOSSING ME AROUND...
I CAN'T STAND THIS!
HEY! K2!!!
MIKA OBVIOUSLY HAS SENIORITY HERE!
DON'T YOU *DARE* ...
...CALL HIM FOOD!

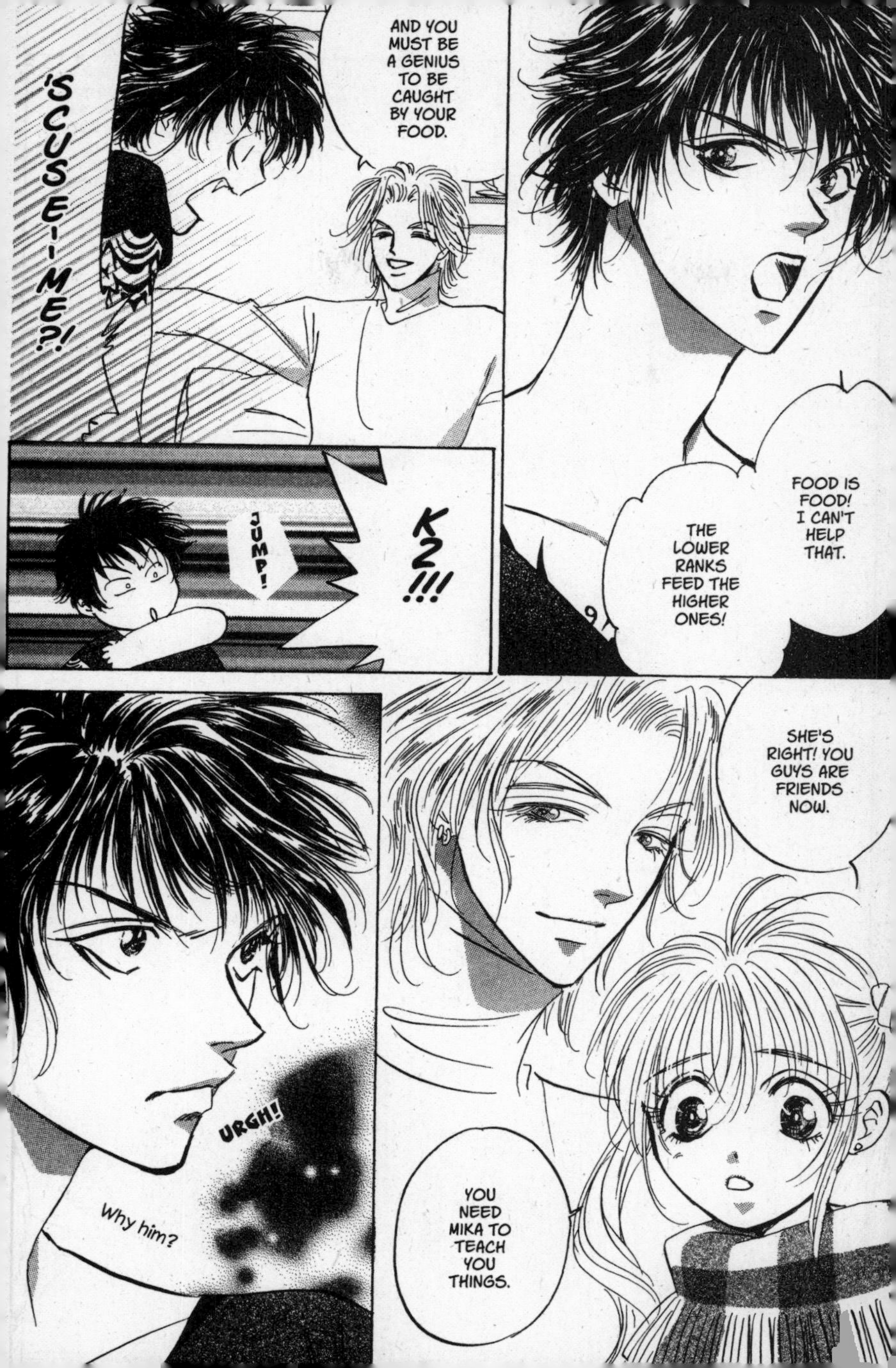
FOOD IS FOOD! I CAN'T HELP THAT.
THE LOWER RANKS FEED THE HIGHER ONES!
AND YOU MUST BE A GENIUS TO BE CAUGHT BY YOUR FOOD.
'SCUSE-ME?!
K2!!!
JUMP!
SHE'S RIGHT! YOU GUYS ARE FRIENDS NOW.
YOU NEED MIKA TO TEACH YOU THINGS.
URGH!
Why him?

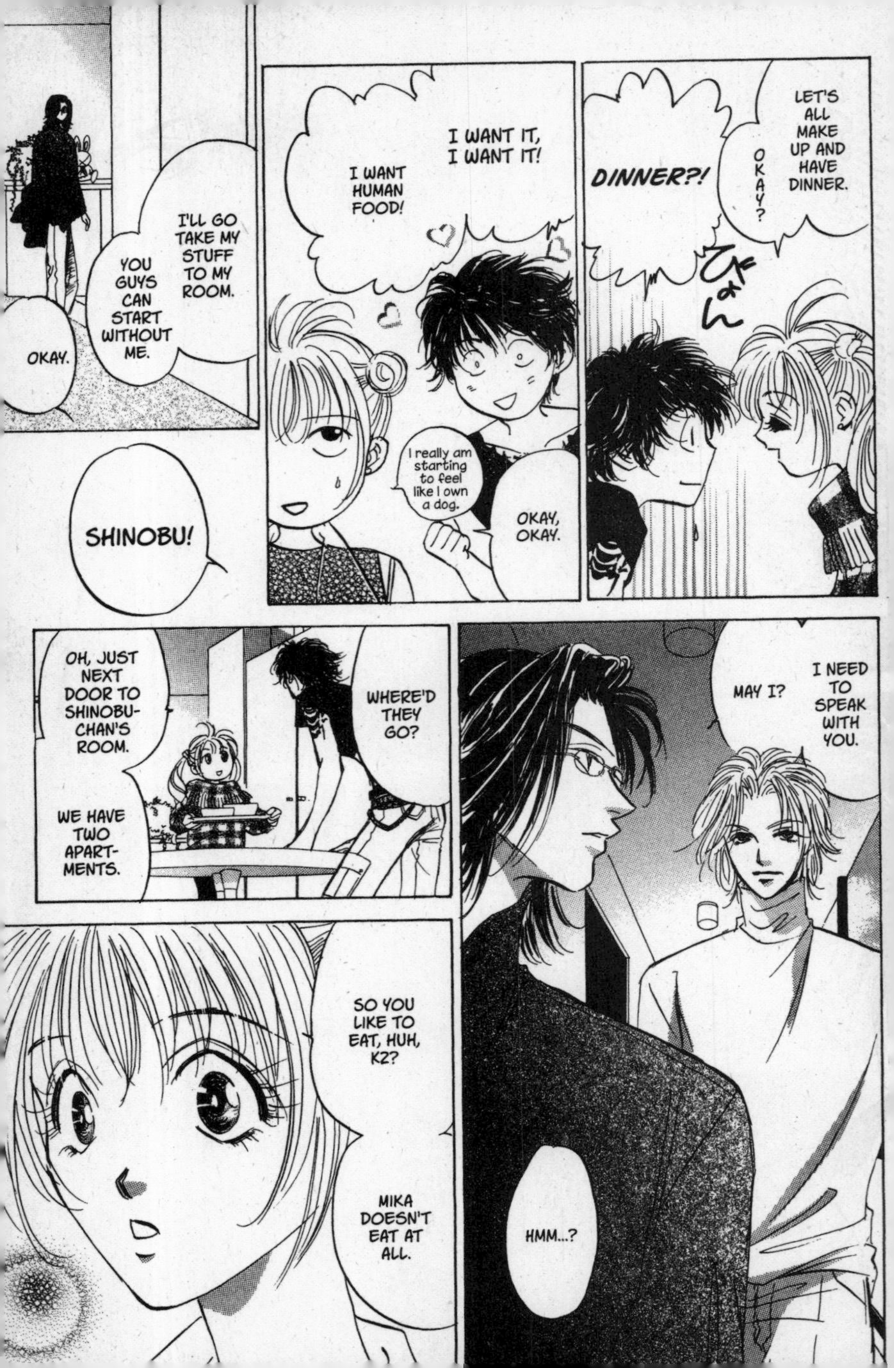
LET'S ALL MAKE UP AND HAVE DINNER.
OKAY?
DINNER?!
I WANT IT, I WANT IT!
I WANT HUMAN FOOD!
I really am starting to feel like I own a dog.
OKAY, OKAY.
I'LL GO TAKE MY STUFF TO MY ROOM.
YOU GUYS CAN START WITHOUT ME.
OKAY.
SHINOBU!
I NEED TO SPEAK WITH YOU.
MAY I?
HMM...?
WHERE'D THEY GO?
OH, JUST NEXT DOOR TO SHINOBU-CHAN'S ROOM.
WE HAVE TWO APARTMENTS.
SO YOU LIKE TO EAT, HUH, KZ?
MIKA DOESN'T EAT AT ALL.

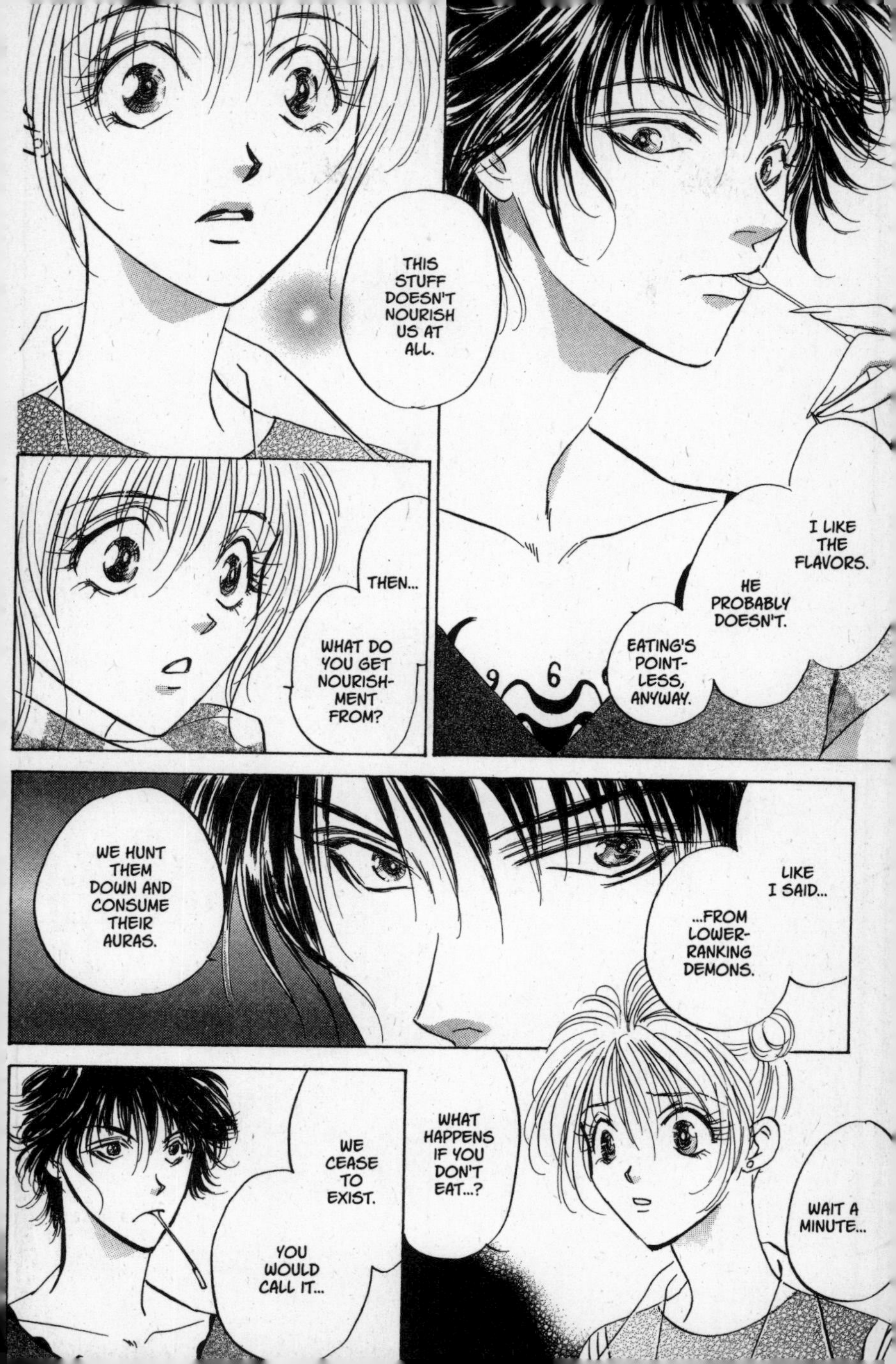
I LIKE THE FLAVORS.
HE PROBABLY DOESN'T.
EATING'S POINT-LESS, ANYWAY.
THIS STUFF DOESN'T NOURISH US AT ALL.
THEN...
WHAT DO YOU GET NOURISH-MENT FROM?
LIKE I SAID...
...FROM LOWER-RANKING DEMONS.
WE HUNT THEM DOWN AND CONSUME THEIR AURAS.
WAIT A MINUTE...
WHAT HAPPENS IF YOU DON'T EAT...?
WE CEASE TO EXIST.
YOU WOULD CALL IT...

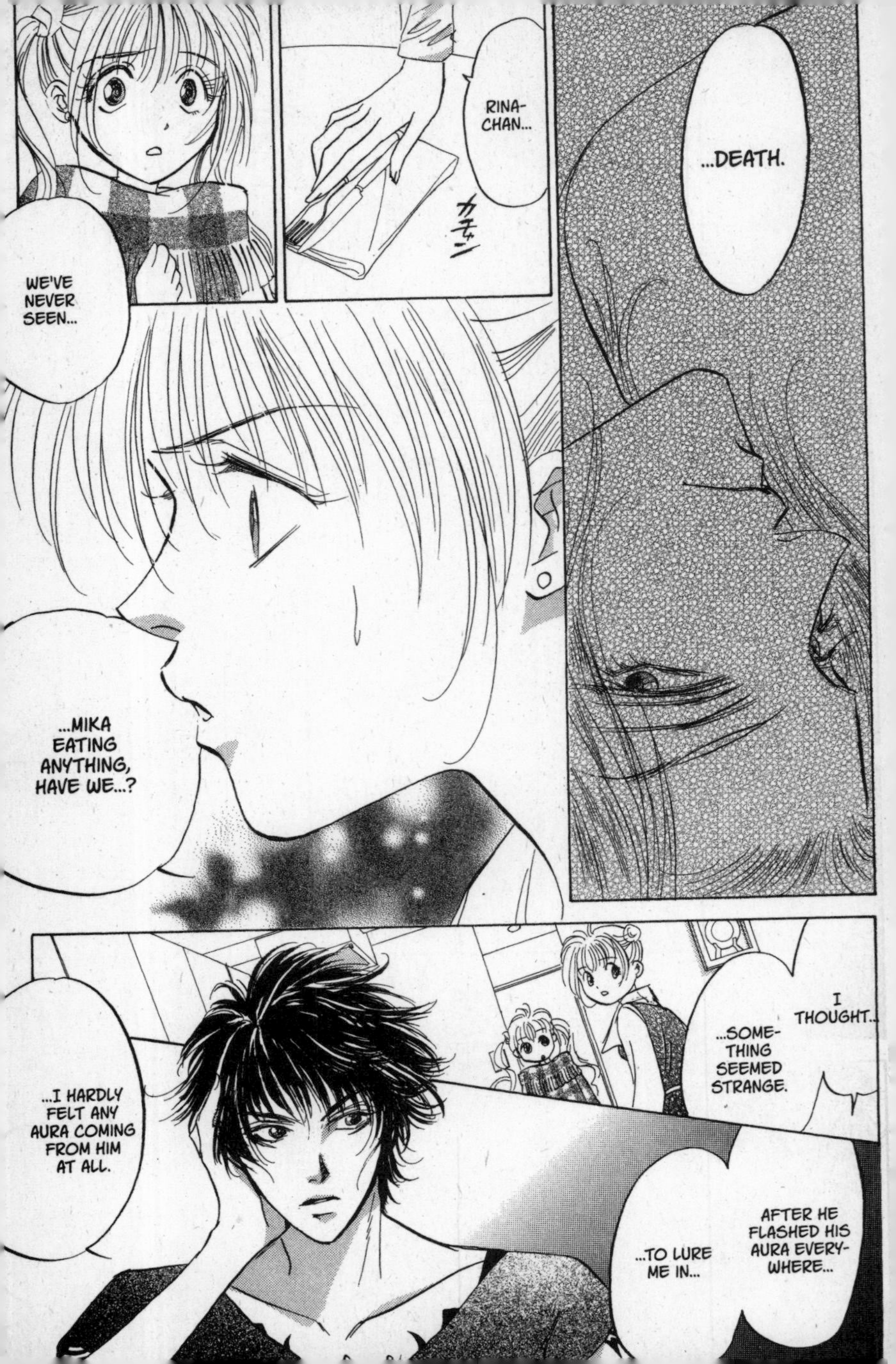
...DEATH.
RINA-CHAN...
カチャン
WE'VE NEVER SEEN...
...MIKA EATING ANYTHING, HAVE WE...?
I THOUGHT...
...SOME-THING SEEMED STRANGE.
AFTER HE FLASHED HIS AURA EVERY-WHERE...
...TO LURE ME IN...
...I HARDLY FELT ANY AURA COMING FROM HIM AT ALL.

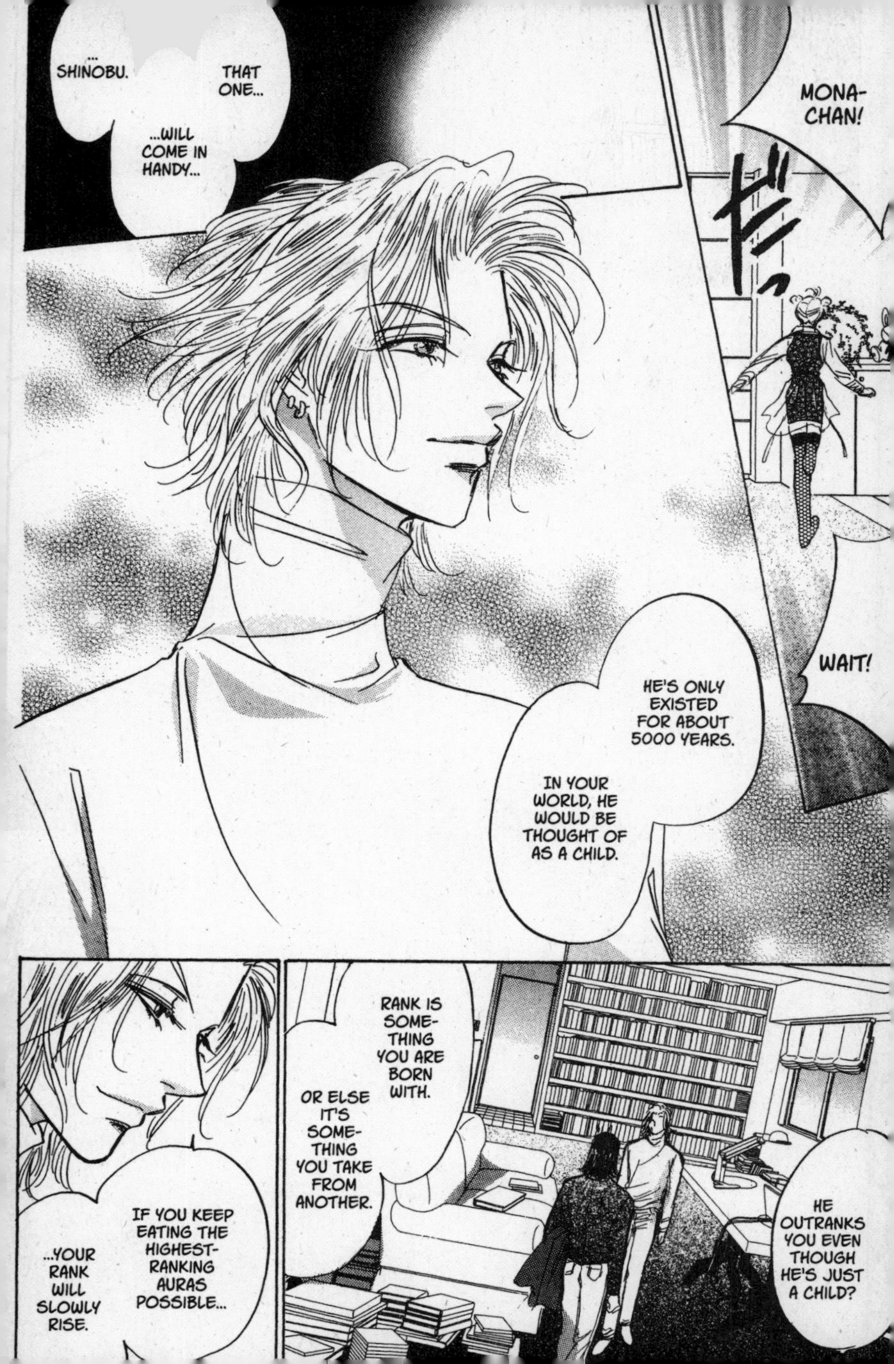
MONA-CHAN!
WAIT!
...SHINOBU.
THAT ONE...
...WILL COME IN HANDY...
HE'S ONLY EXISTED FOR ABOUT 5000 YEARS.
IN YOUR WORLD, HE WOULD BE THOUGHT OF AS A CHILD.
HE OUTRANKS YOU EVEN THOUGH HE'S JUST A CHILD?
RANK IS SOMETHING YOU ARE BORN WITH.
OR ELSE IT'S SOMETHING YOU TAKE FROM ANOTHER.
IF YOU KEEP EATING THE HIGHEST-RANKING AURAS POSSIBLE...
...YOUR RANK WILL SLOWLY RISE.

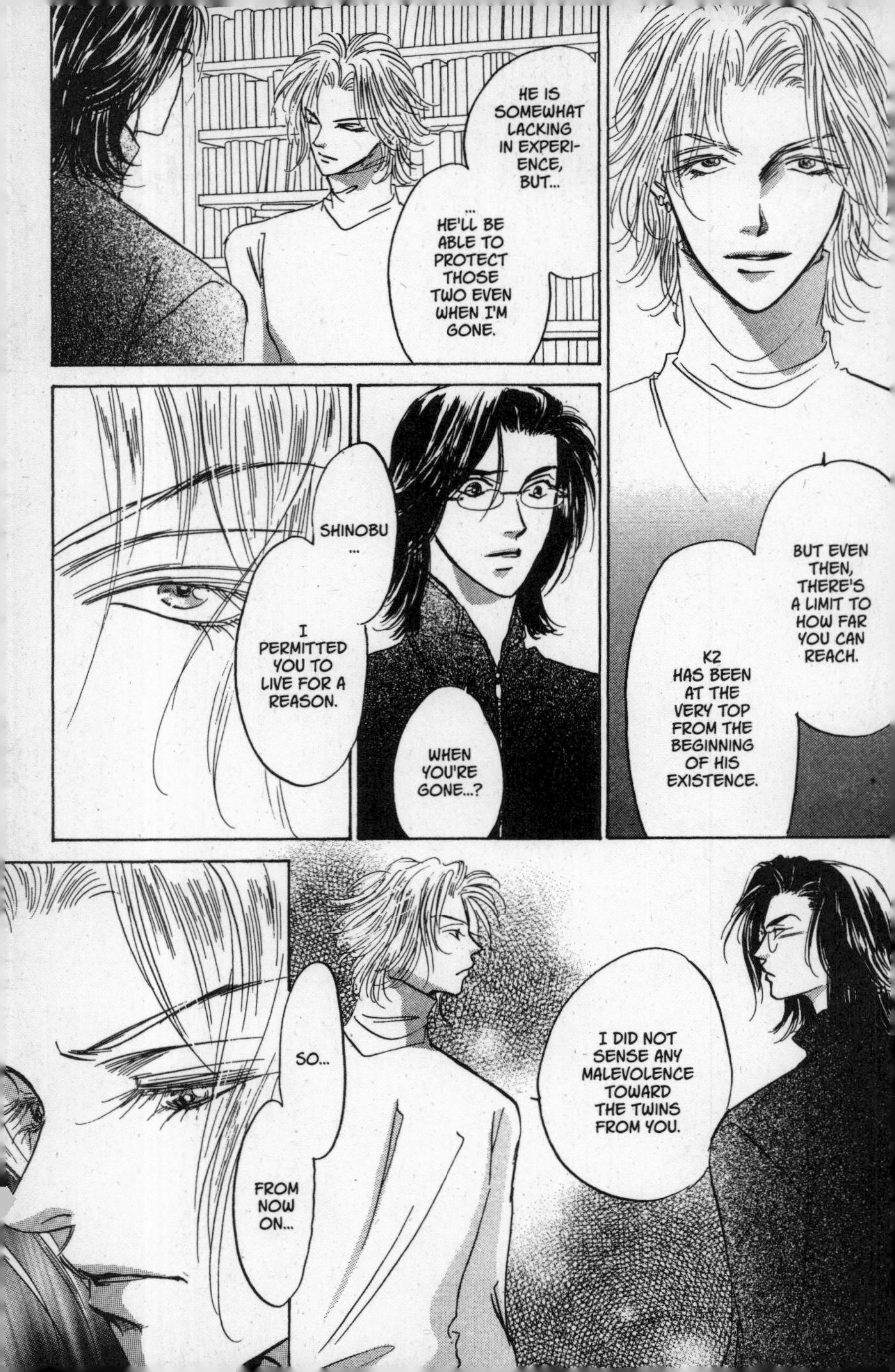
K2 HAS BEEN AT THE VERY TOP FROM THE BEGINNING OF HIS EXISTENCE.
BUT EVEN THEN, THERE'S A LIMIT TO HOW FAR YOU CAN REACH.
HE IS SOMEWHAT LACKING IN EXPERIENCE, BUT...
... HE'LL BE ABLE TO PROTECT THOSE TWO EVEN WHEN I'M GONE.
WHEN YOU'RE GONE...?
SHINOBU ...
I PERMITTED YOU TO LIVE FOR A REASON.
I DID NOT SENSE ANY MALEVOLENCE TOWARD THE TWINS FROM YOU.
SO...
FROM NOW ON...

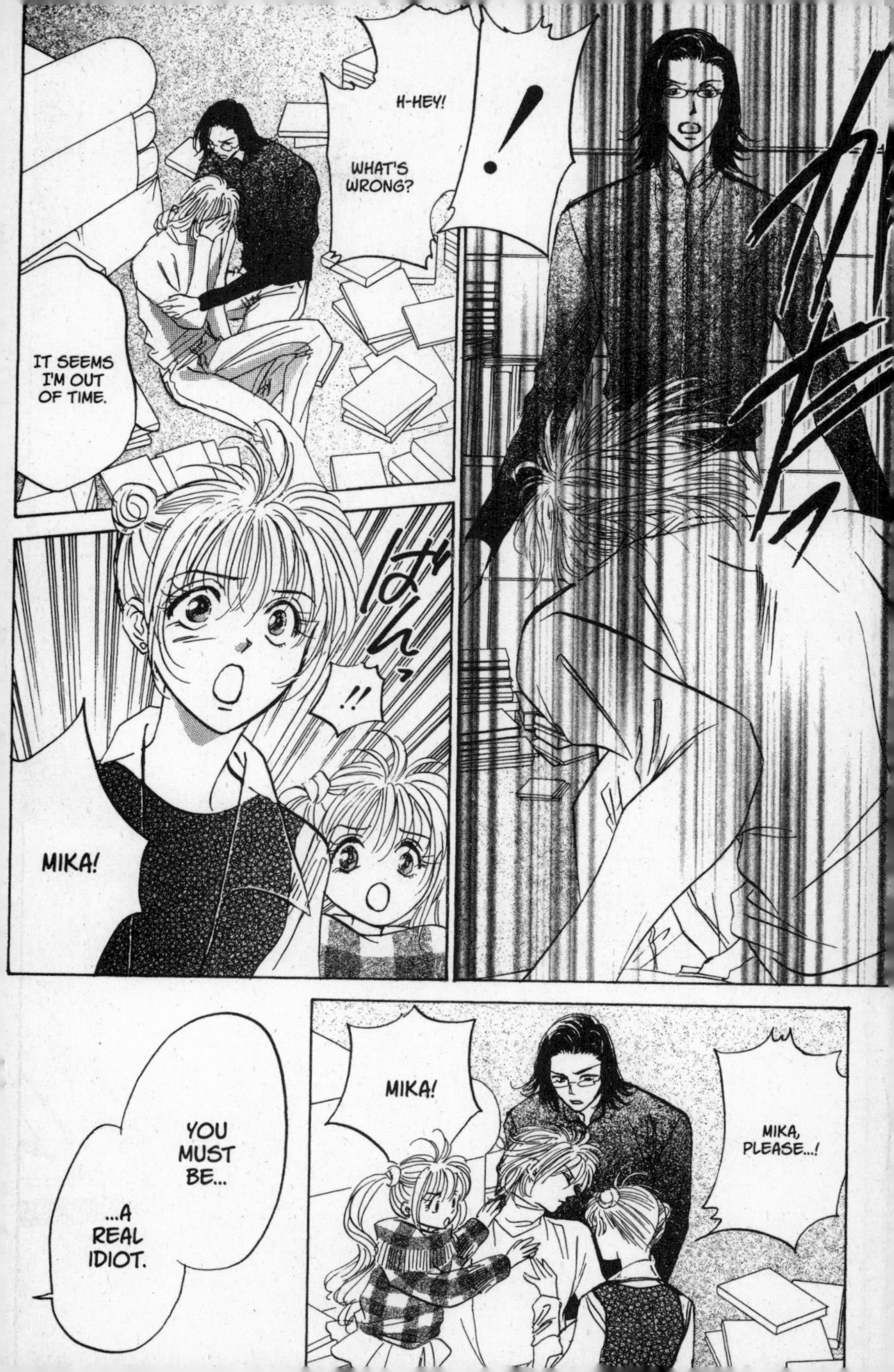
!
H-HEY!
WHAT'S WRONG?
IT SEEMS I'M OUT OF TIME.
ばんっ
!!
MIKA!
MIKA, PLEASE...!
MIKA!
YOU MUST BE...
...A REAL IDIOT.

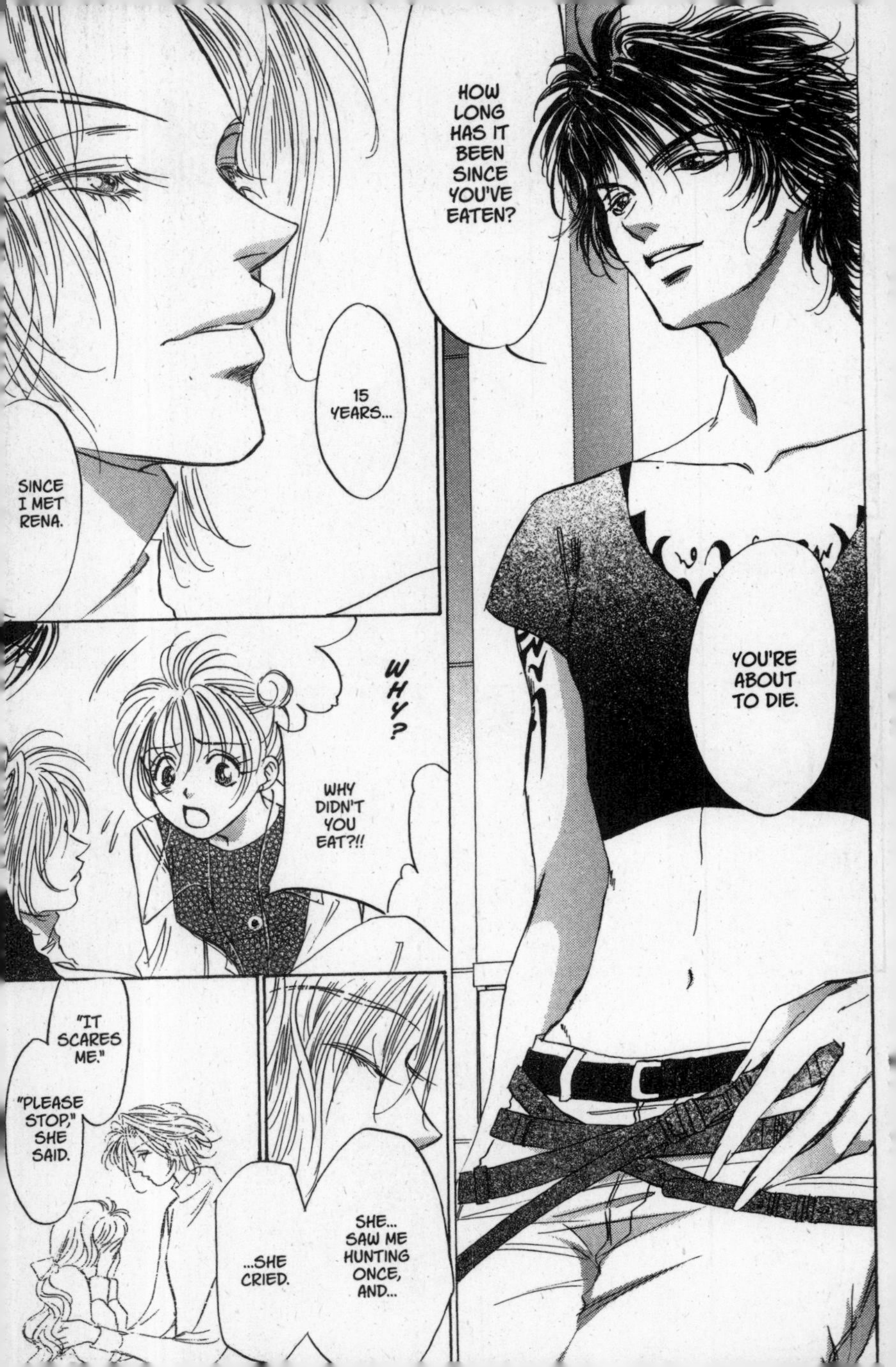
HOW LONG HAS IT BEEN SINCE YOU'VE EATEN?
YOU'RE ABOUT TO DIE.
15 YEARS...
SINCE I MET RENA.
WHY?
WHY DIDN'T YOU EAT?!!
SHE... SAW ME HUNTING ONCE, AND...
...SHE CRIED.
"IT SCARES ME."
"PLEASE STOP," SHE SAID.

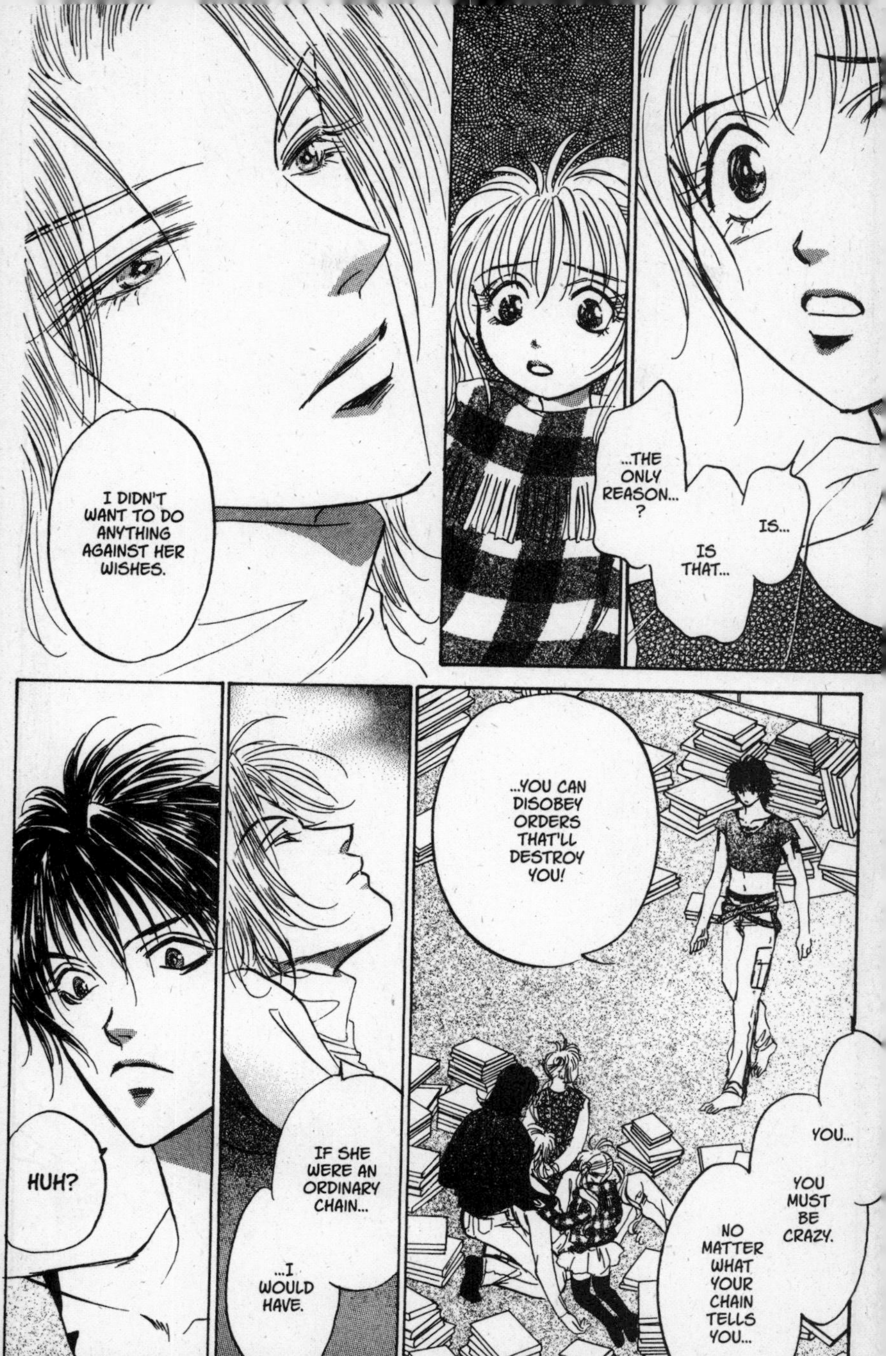
IS...
IS THAT...
...THE ONLY REASON...?
I DIDN'T WANT TO DO ANYTHING AGAINST HER WISHES.
YOU...
YOU MUST BE CRAZY.
NO MATTER WHAT YOUR CHAIN TELLS YOU...
...YOU CAN DISOBEY ORDERS THAT'LL DESTROY YOU!
IF SHE WERE AN ORDINARY CHAIN...
...I WOULD HAVE.
HUH?

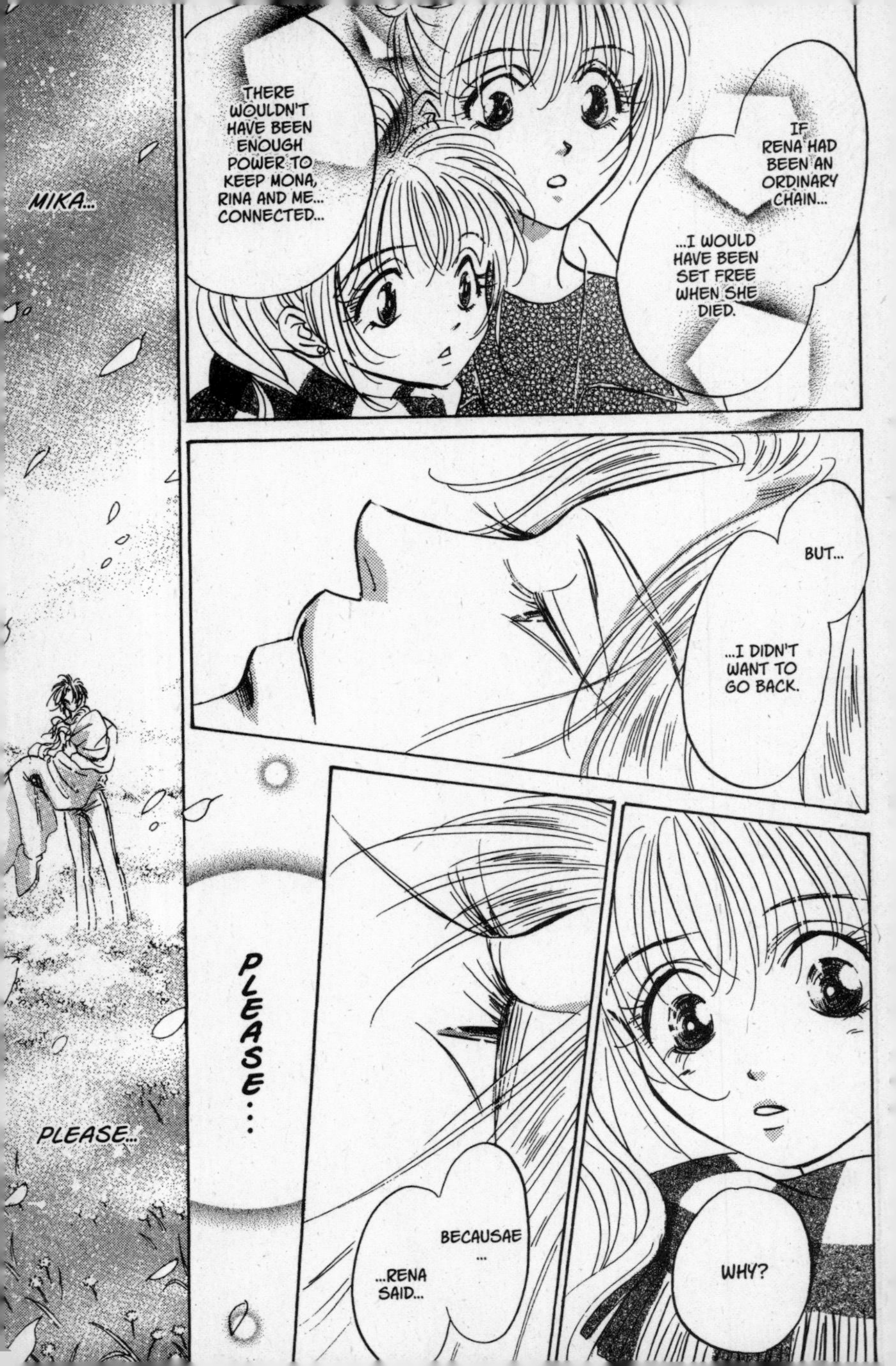
IF RENA HAD BEEN AN ORDINARY CHAIN...
...I WOULD HAVE BEEN SET FREE WHEN SHE DIED.
THERE WOULDN'T HAVE BEEN ENOUGH POWER TO KEEP MONA, RINA AND ME... CONNECTED...
BUT...
...I DIDN'T WANT TO GO BACK.
WHY?
BECAUSAE ...
...RENA SAID...
PLEASE...
MIKA...
PLEASE...

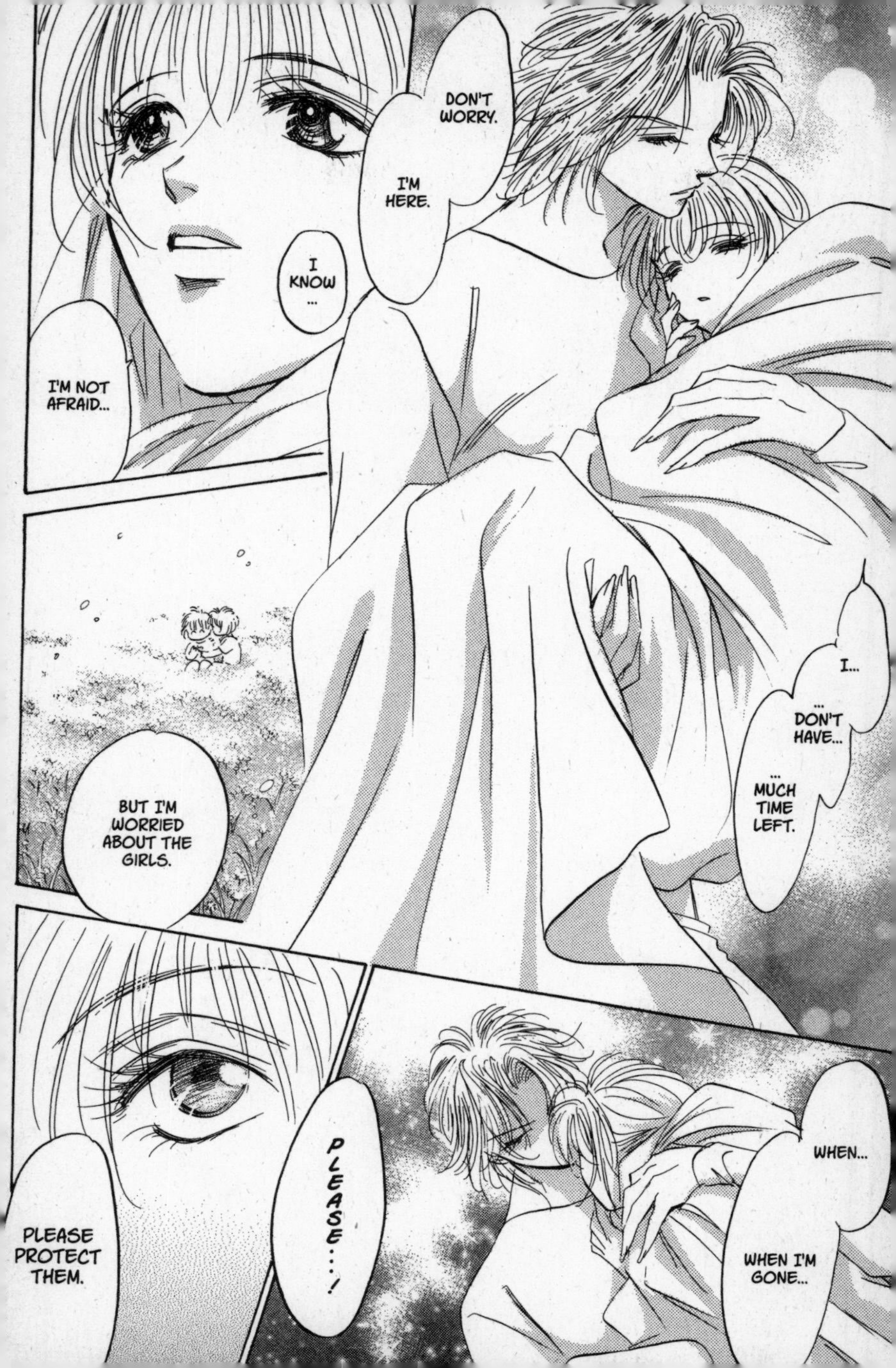
DON'T WORRY.
I'M HERE.
I...
... DON'T HAVE...
... MUCH TIME LEFT.
I KNOW ...
I'M NOT AFRAID...
BUT I'M WORRIED ABOUT THE GIRLS.
WHEN...
WHEN I'M GONE...
PLEASE...!
PLEASE PROTECT THEM.

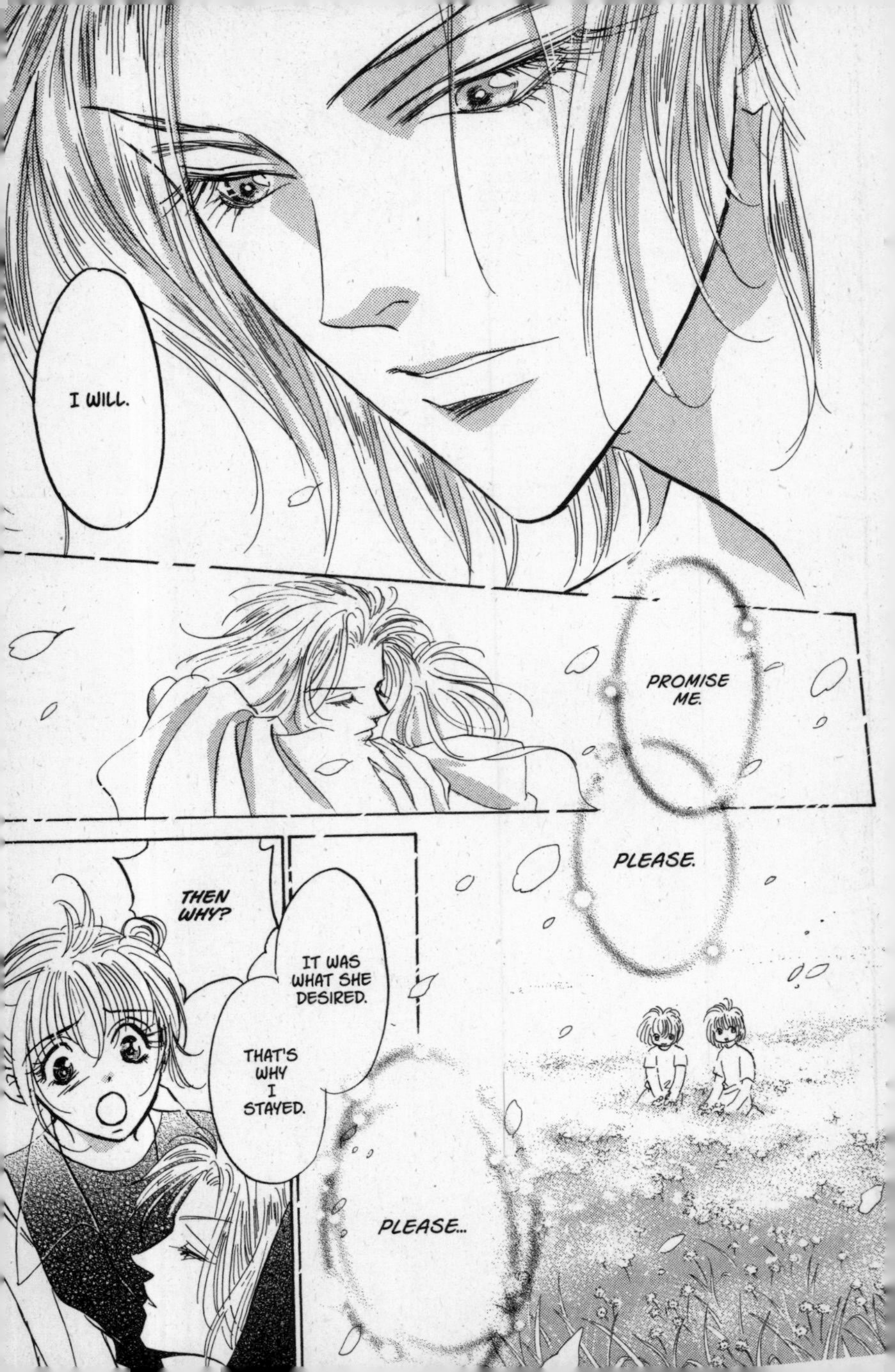
I WILL.
PROMISE ME.
PLEASE.
PLEASE...
IT WAS WHAT SHE DESIRED.
THAT'S WHY I STAYED.
THEN WHY?

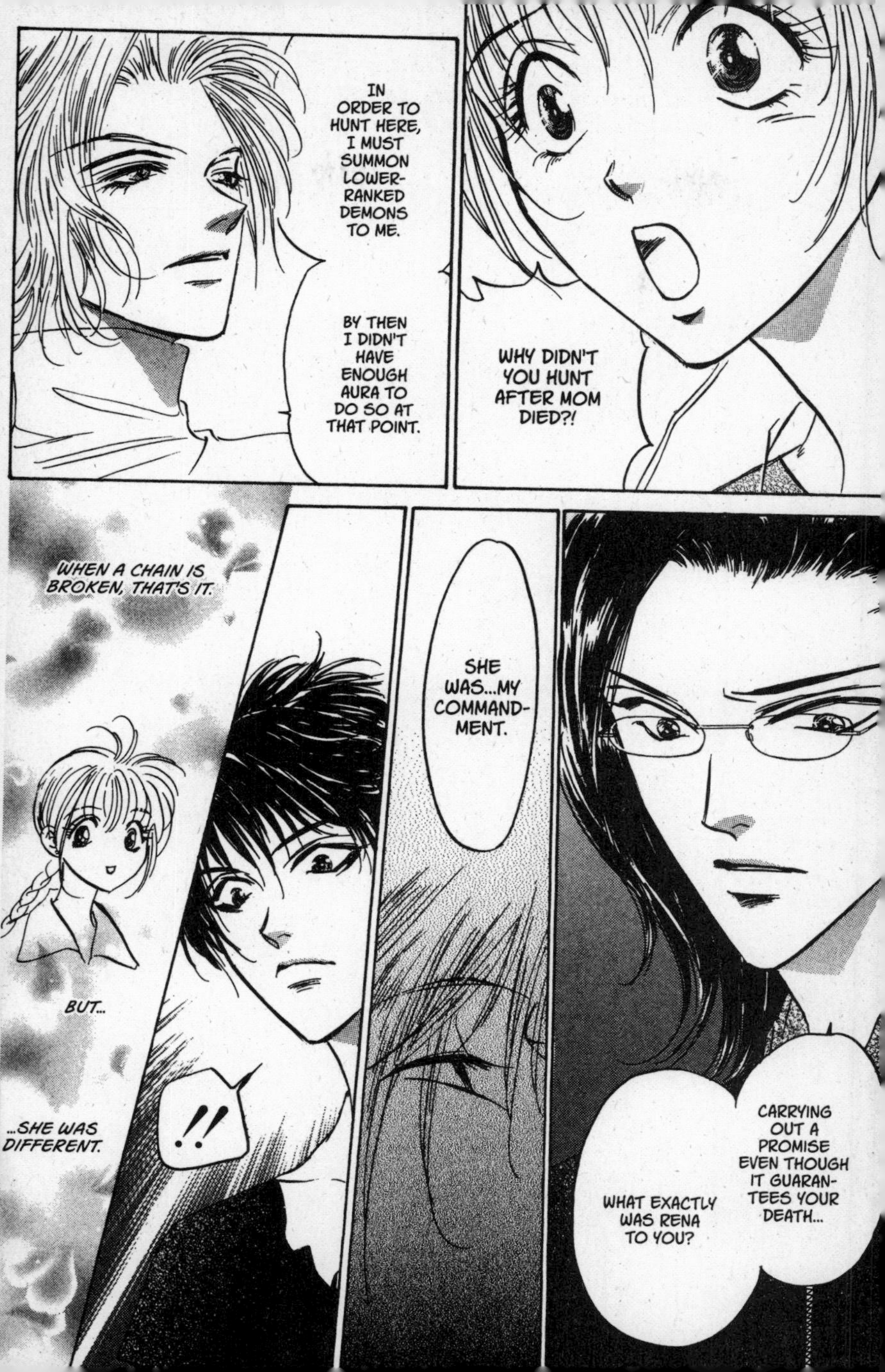
WHY DIDN'T YOU HUNT AFTER MOM DIED?!
IN ORDER TO HUNT HERE, I MUST SUMMON LOWER-RANKED DEMONS TO ME.
BY THEN I DIDN'T HAVE ENOUGH AURA TO DO SO AT THAT POINT.
CARRYING OUT A PROMISE EVEN THOUGH IT GUARANTEES YOUR DEATH...
WHAT EXACTLY WAS RENA TO YOU?
SHE WAS...MY COMMANDMENT.
!!
WHEN A CHAIN IS BROKEN, THAT'S IT.
BUT...
...SHE WAS DIFFERENT.

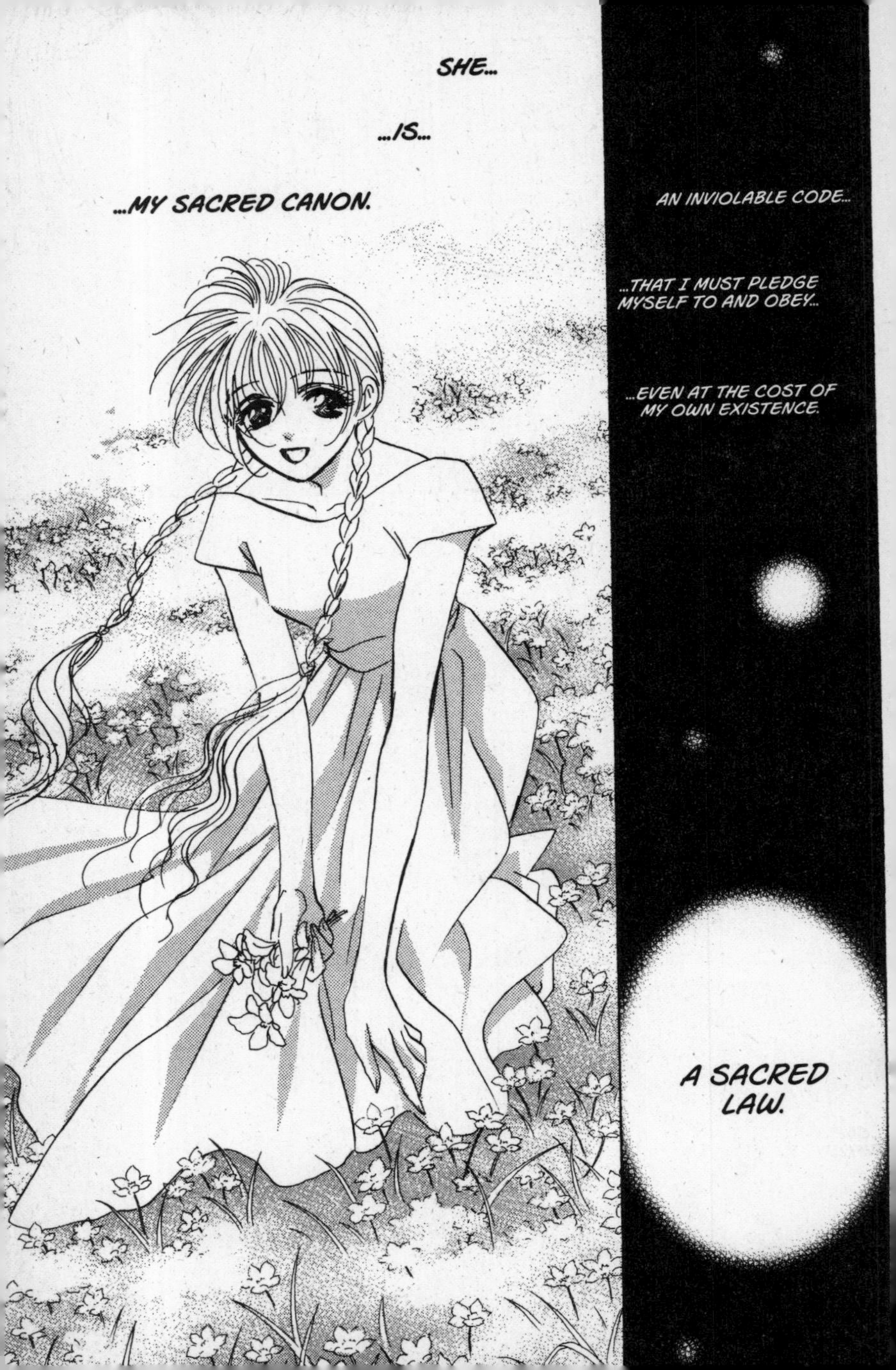
AN INVIOLABLE CODE...
...THAT I MUST PLEDGE MYSELF TO AND OBEY...
...EVEN AT THE COST OF MY OWN EXISTENCE.
A SACRED LAW.
SHE...
...IS...
...MY SACRED CANON.

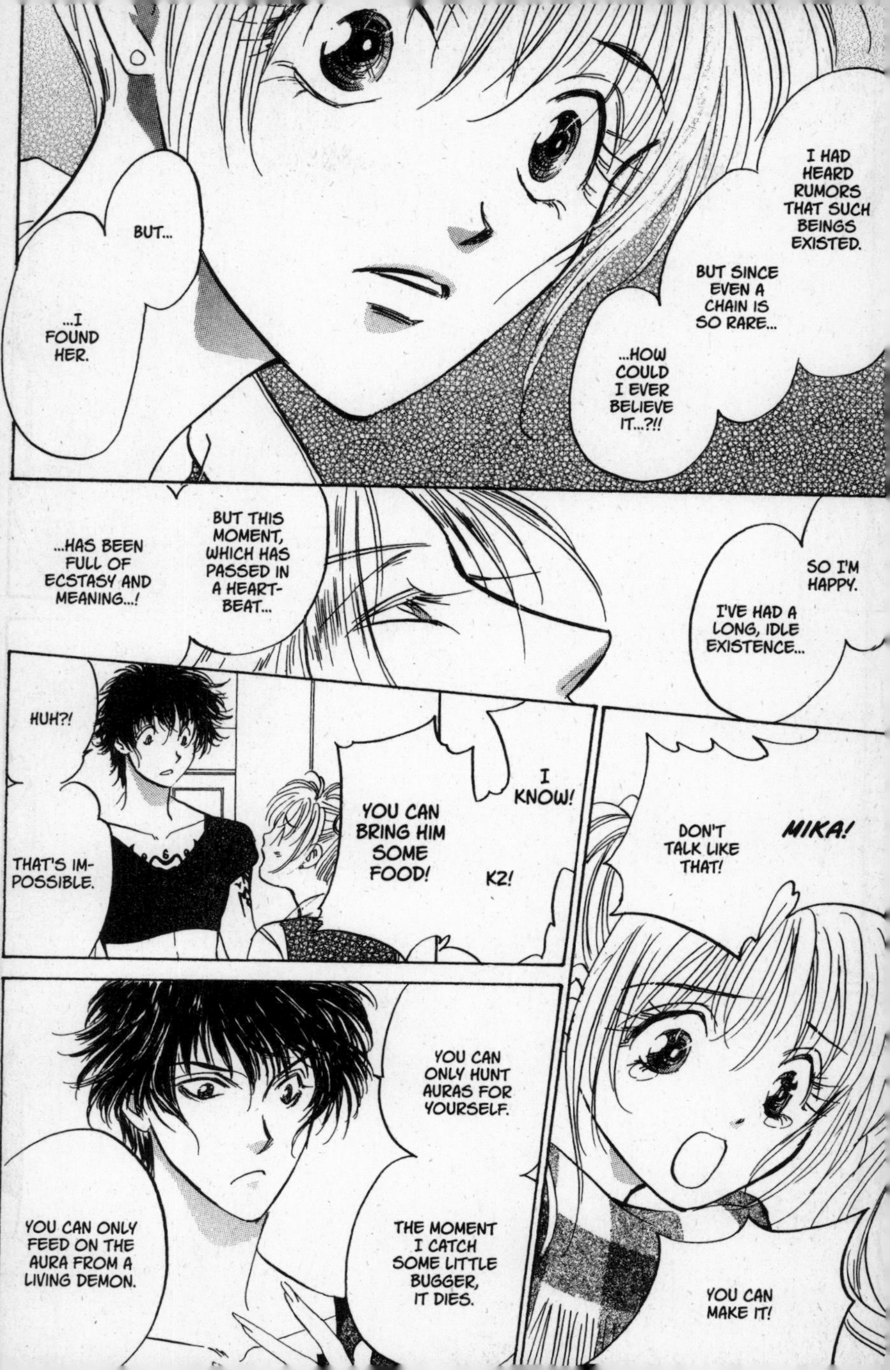
I HAD HEARD RUMORS THAT SUCH BEINGS EXISTED.
BUT SINCE EVEN A CHAIN IS SO RARE...
...HOW COULD I EVER BELIEVE IT...?!!
BUT...
...I FOUND HER.
SO I'M HAPPY.
I'VE HAD A LONG, IDLE EXISTENCE...
BUT THIS MOMENT, WHICH HAS PASSED IN A HEART-BEAT...
...HAS BEEN FULL OF ECSTASY AND MEANING...!
MIKA!
DON'T TALK LIKE THAT!
YOU CAN MAKE IT!
I KNOW!
KZ!
YOU CAN BRING HIM SOME FOOD!
HUH?!
THAT'S IM-POSSIBLE.
YOU CAN ONLY HUNT AURAS FOR YOURSELF.
THE MOMENT I CATCH SOME LITTLE BUGGER, IT DIES.
YOU CAN ONLY FEED ON THE AURA FROM A LIVING DEMON.

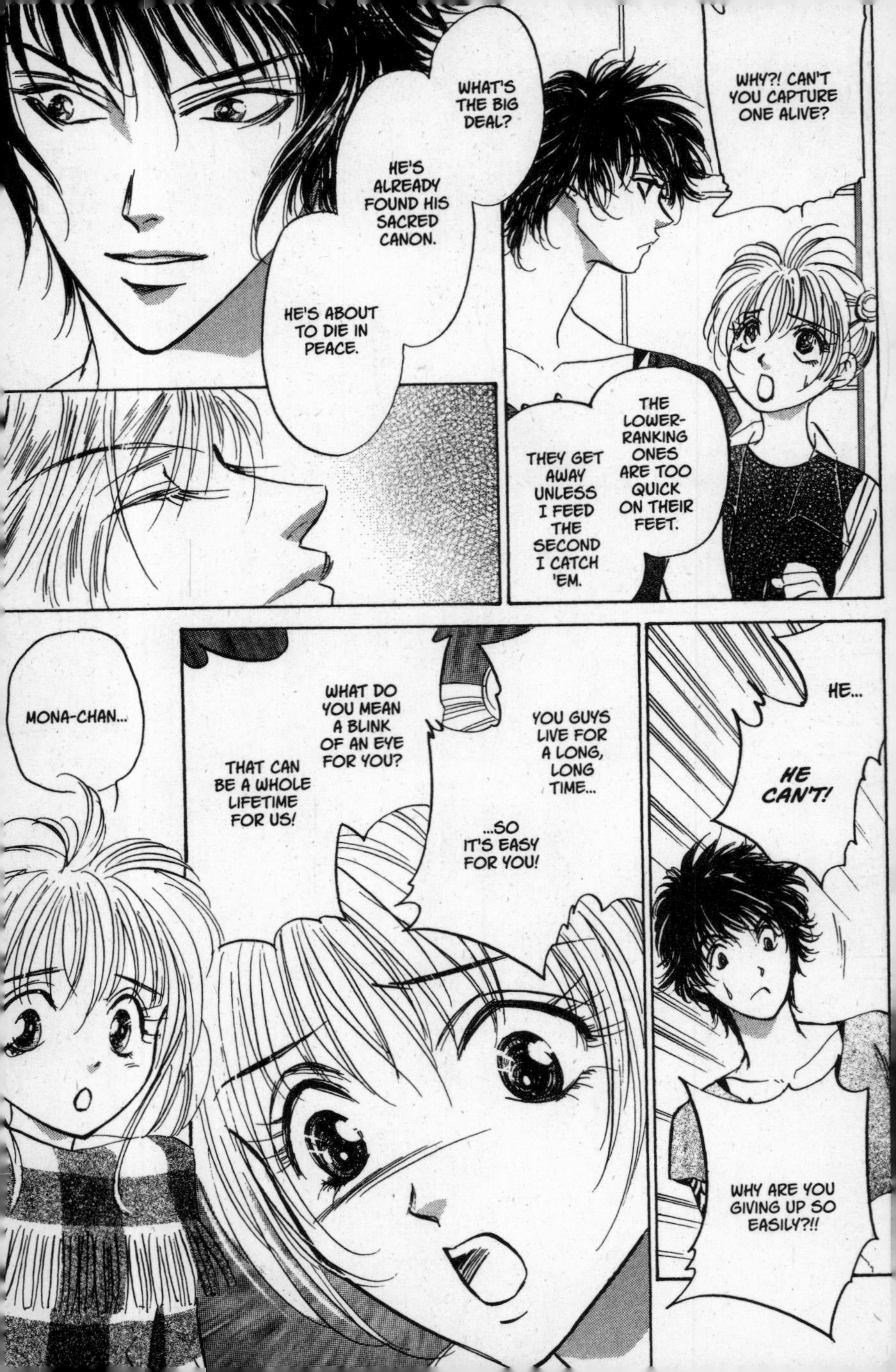
WHY?! CAN'T YOU CAPTURE ONE ALIVE?
THE LOWER-RANKING ONES ARE TOO QUICK ON THEIR FEET.
THEY GET AWAY UNLESS I FEED THE SECOND I CATCH 'EM.
WHAT'S THE BIG DEAL?
HE'S ALREADY FOUND HIS SACRED CANON.
HE'S ABOUT TO DIE IN PEACE.
HE...
HE CAN'T!
WHY ARE YOU GIVING UP SO EASILY?!!
YOU GUYS LIVE FOR A LONG, LONG TIME...
...SO IT'S EASY FOR YOU!
WHAT DO YOU MEAN A BLINK OF AN EYE FOR YOU?
THAT CAN BE A WHOLE LIFETIME FOR US!
MONA-CHAN...

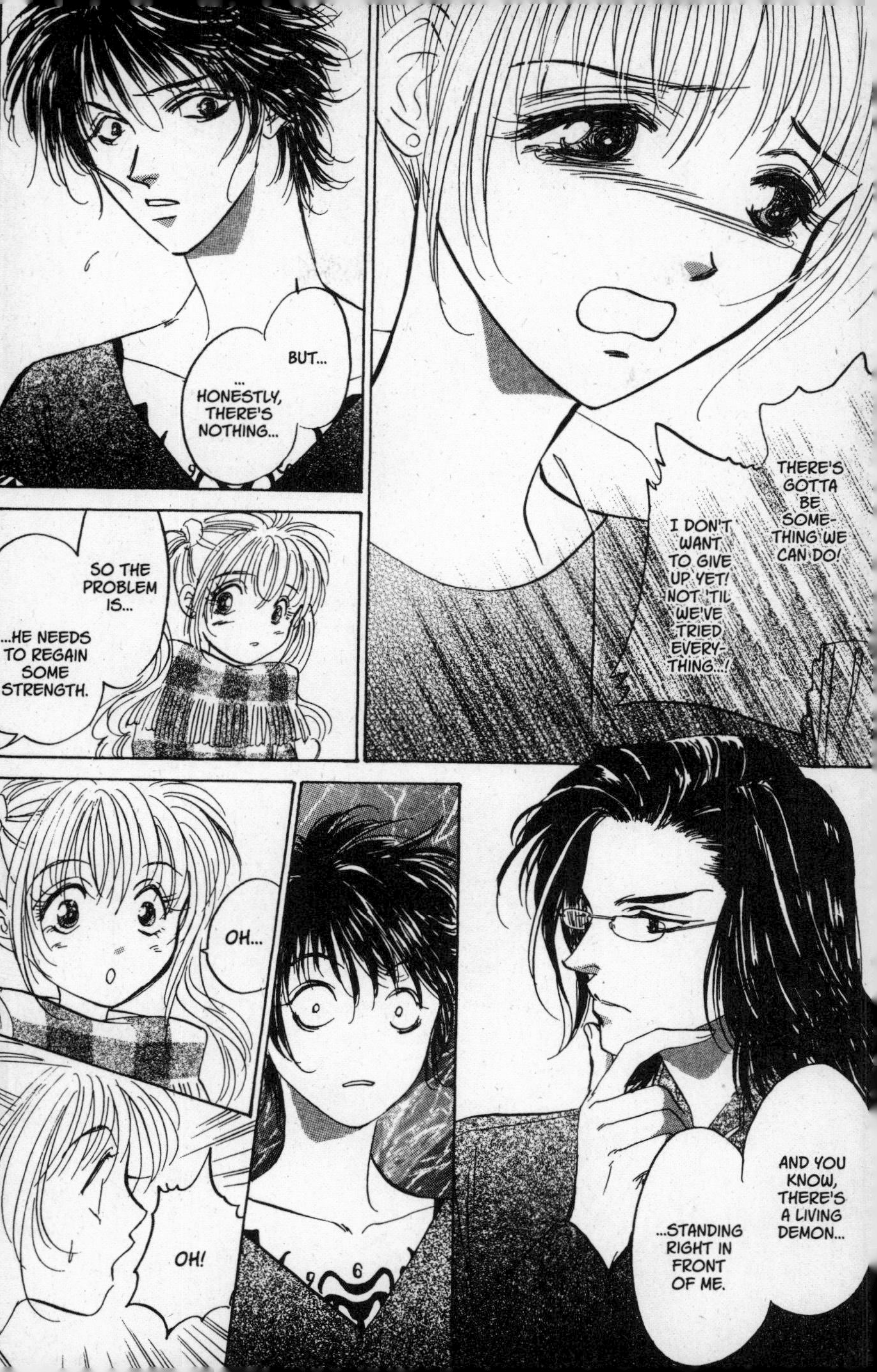
THERE'S GOTTA BE SOME-THING WE CAN DO!
I DON'T WANT TO GIVE UP YET! NOT 'TIL WE'VE TRIED EVERY-THING...!
BUT... ...HONESTLY, THERE'S NOTHING...
SO THE PROBLEM IS...
...HE NEEDS TO REGAIN SOME STRENGTH.
AND YOU KNOW, THERE'S A LIVING DEMON...
...STANDING RIGHT IN FRONT OF ME.
OH...
OH!

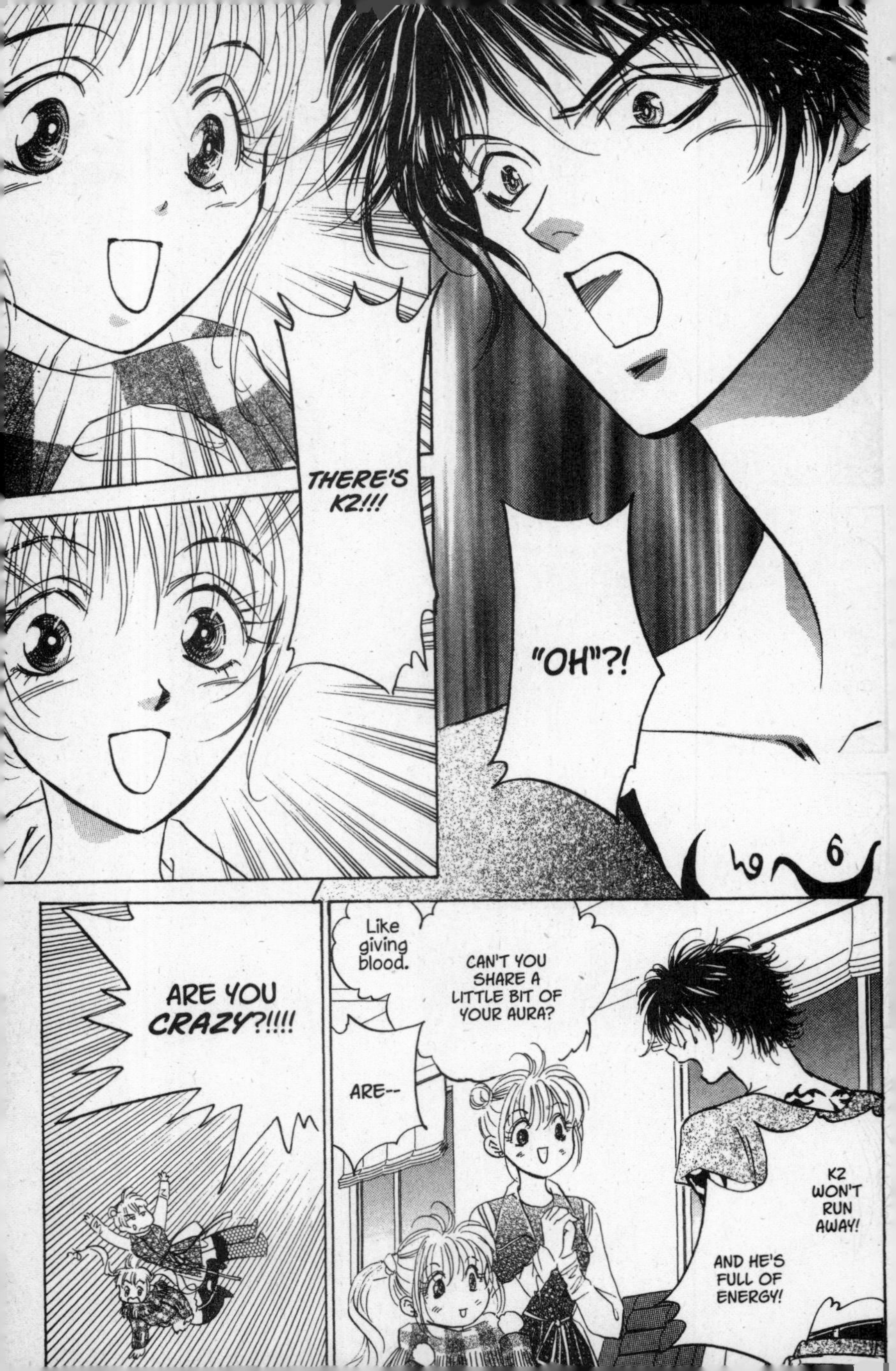
"OH"?!
THERE'S K2!!!
K2 WON'T RUN AWAY!
AND HE'S FULL OF ENERGY!
CAN'T YOU SHARE A LITTLE BIT OF YOUR AURA?
Like giving blood.
ARE--
ARE YOU CRAZY?!!!!!

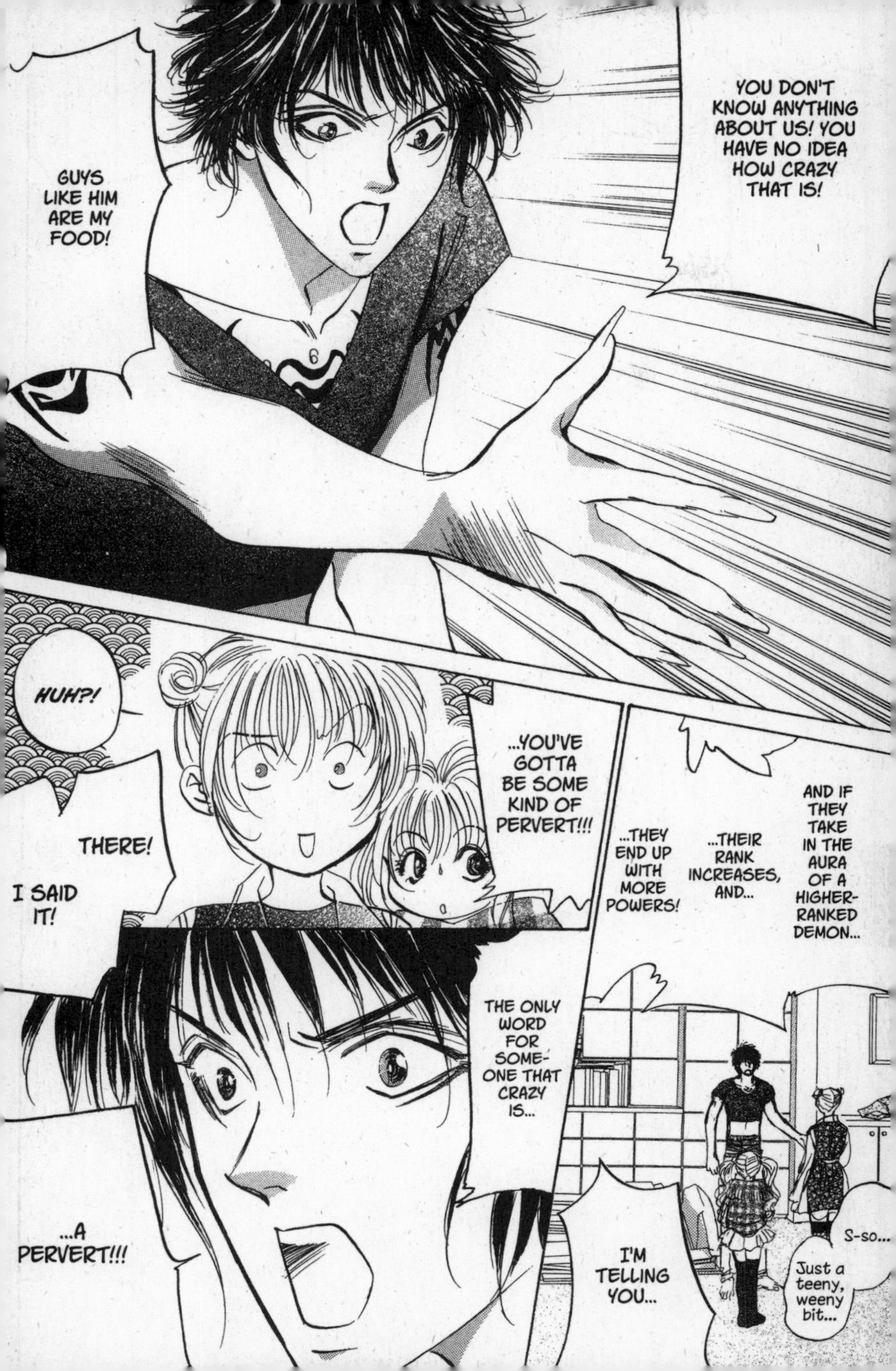

YOU DON'T KNOW ANYTHING ABOUT US! YOU HAVE NO IDEA HOW CRAZY THAT IS!
GUYS LIKE HIM ARE MY FOOD!
AND IF THEY TAKE IN THE AURA OF A HIGHER-RANKED DEMON...
...THEIR RANK INCREASES, AND...
...THEY END UP WITH MORE POWERS!
S-so...
Just a teeny, weeny bit...
I'M TELLING YOU...
...YOU'VE GOTTA BE SOME KIND OF PERVERT!!!
HUH?!
THERE!
I SAID IT!
THE ONLY WORD FOR SOME-ONE THAT CRAZY IS...
...A PERVERT!!!

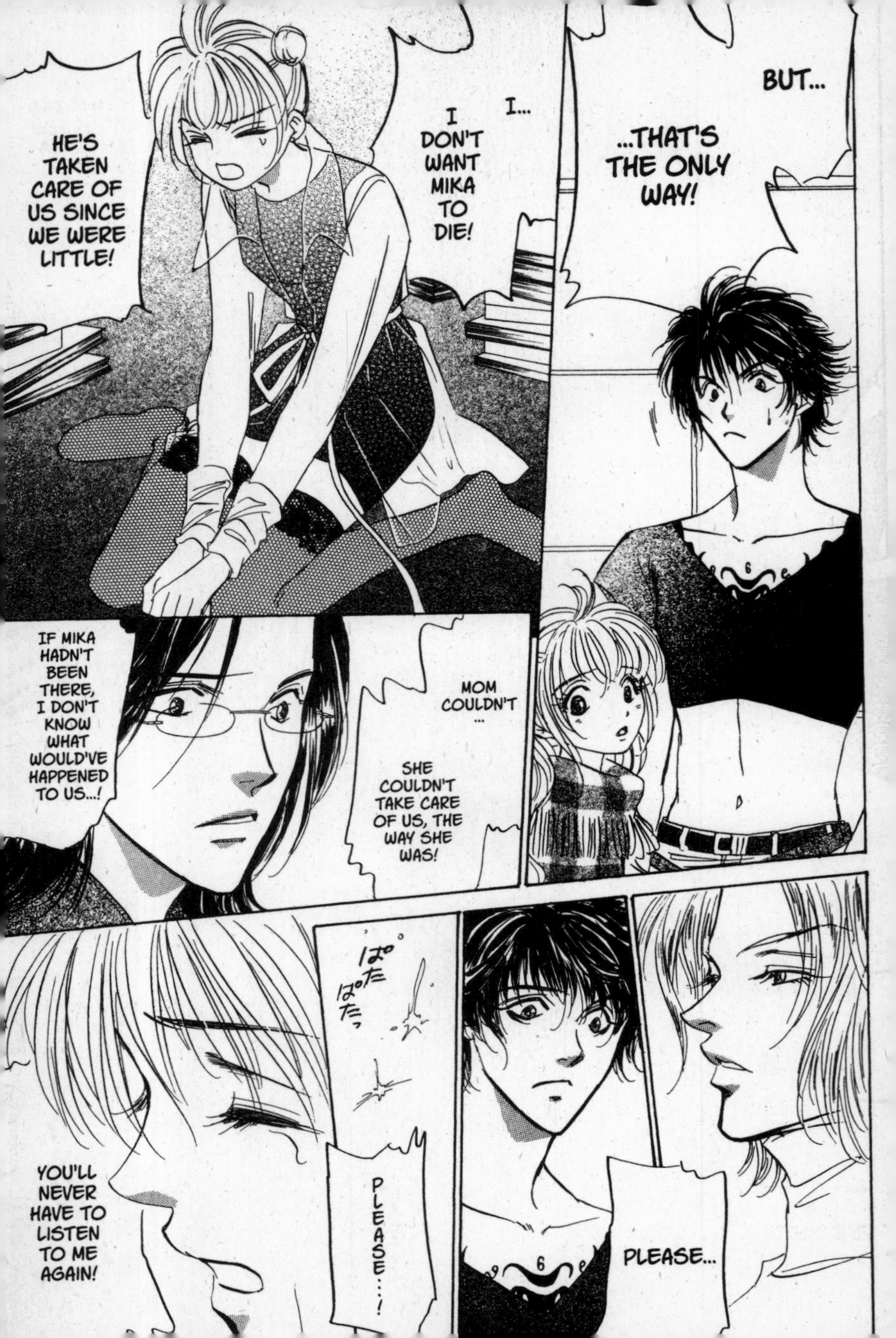
BUT...
...THAT'S THE ONLY WAY!
I...
I DON'T WANT MIKA TO DIE!
HE'S TAKEN CARE OF US SINCE WE WERE LITTLE!
MOM COULDN'T ...
SHE COULDN'T TAKE CARE OF US, THE WAY SHE WAS!
IF MIKA HADN'T BEEN THERE, I DON'T KNOW WHAT WOULD'VE HAPPENED TO US...!
PLEASE...
PLEASE...!
ぱたぱたっ
YOU'LL NEVER HAVE TO LISTEN TO ME AGAIN!

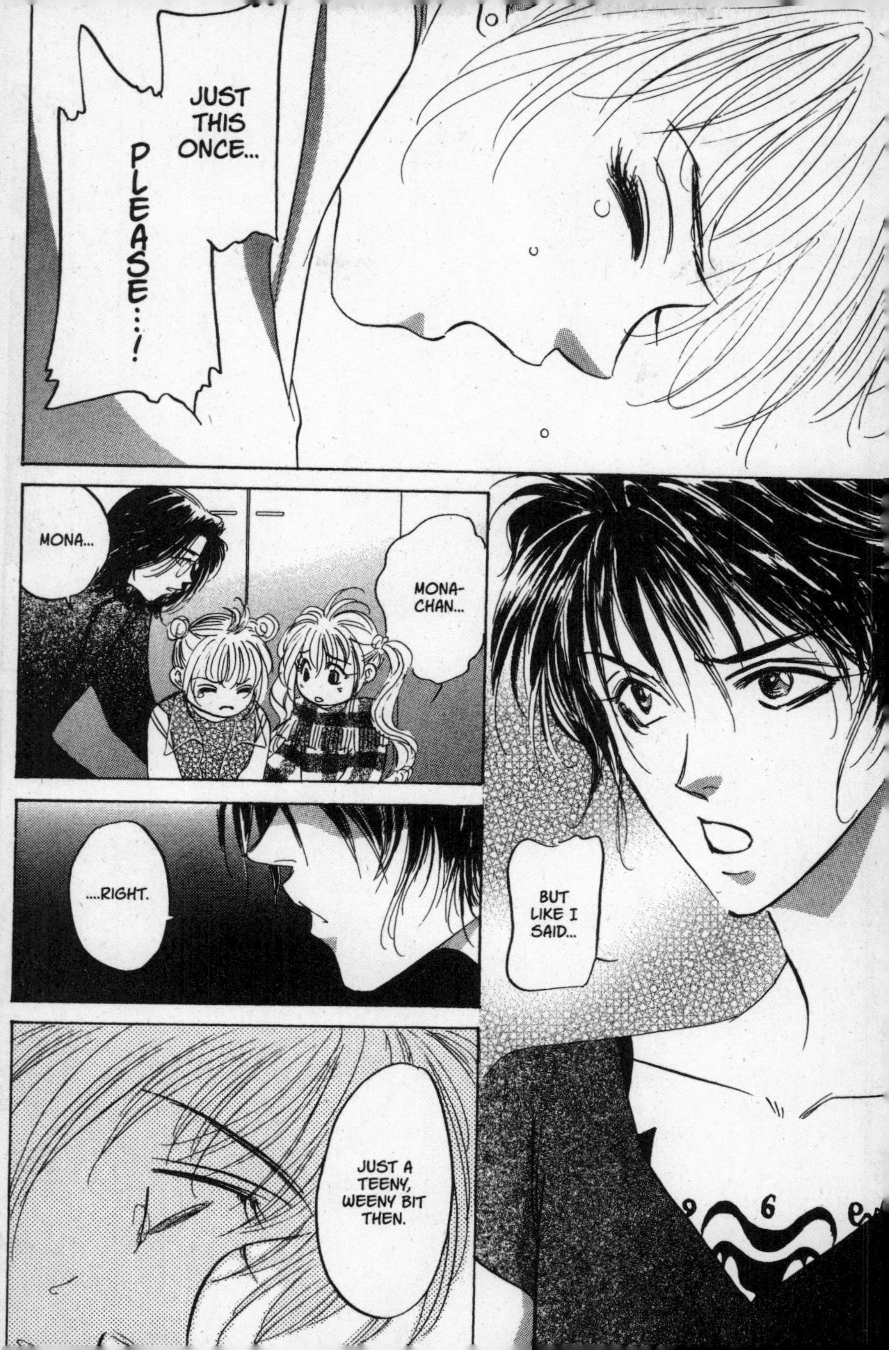
JUST THIS ONCE...
PLEASE...!
BUT LIKE I SAID...
MONA-CHAN...
MONA...
....RIGHT.
JUST A TEENY, WEENY BIT THEN.

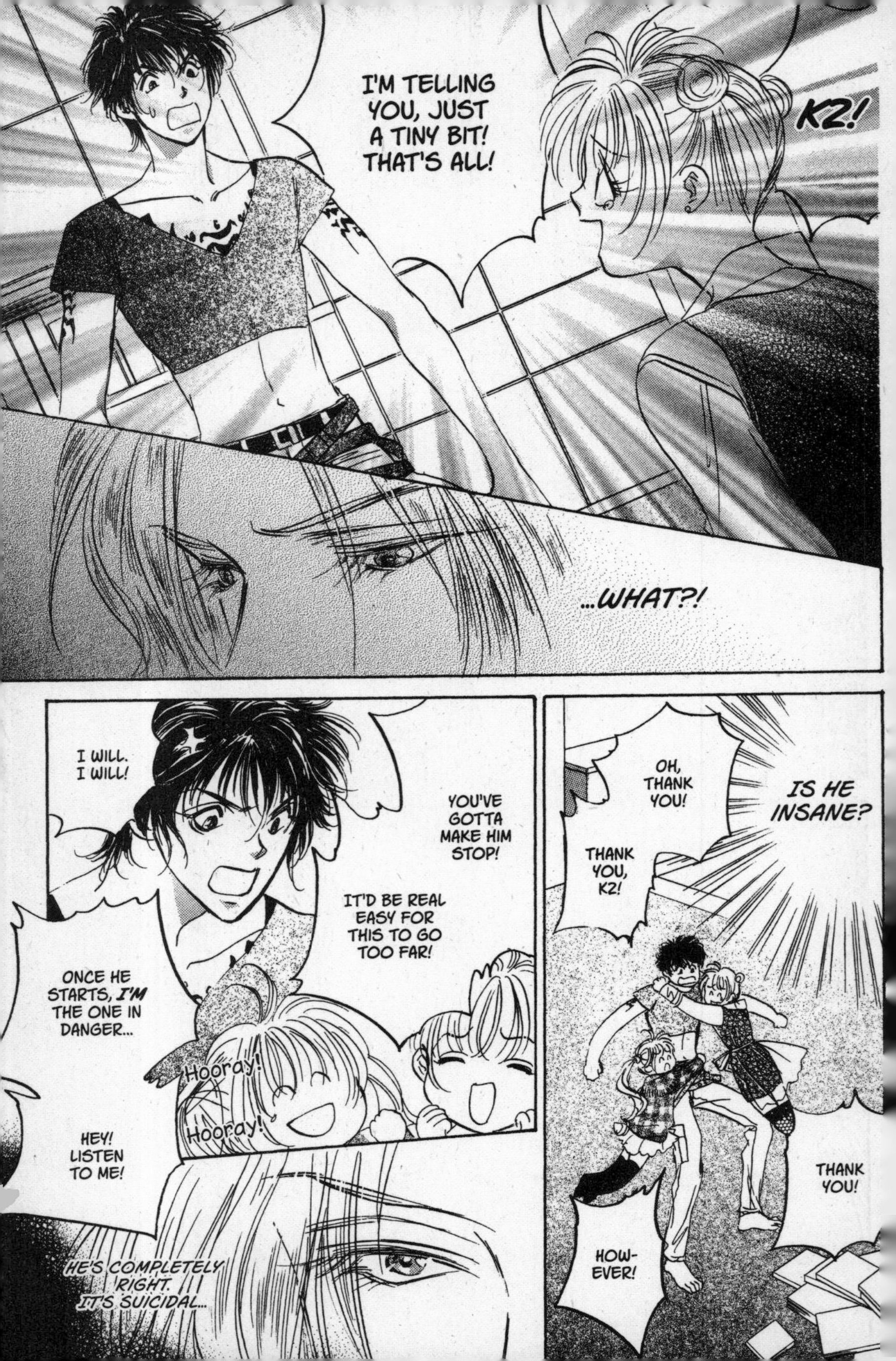
KZ!
I'M TELLING YOU, JUST A TINY BIT! THAT'S ALL!
...WHAT?!
IS HE INSANE?
OH, THANK YOU!
THANK YOU, KZ!
THANK YOU!
HOW-EVER!
YOU'VE GOTTA MAKE HIM STOP!
I WILL. I WILL!
IT'D BE REAL EASY FOR THIS TO GO TOO FAR!
ONCE HE STARTS, *I'M* THE ONE IN DANGER...
Hooray!
Hooray!
HEY! LISTEN TO ME!
HE'S COMPLETELY RIGHT. IT'S SUICIDAL...

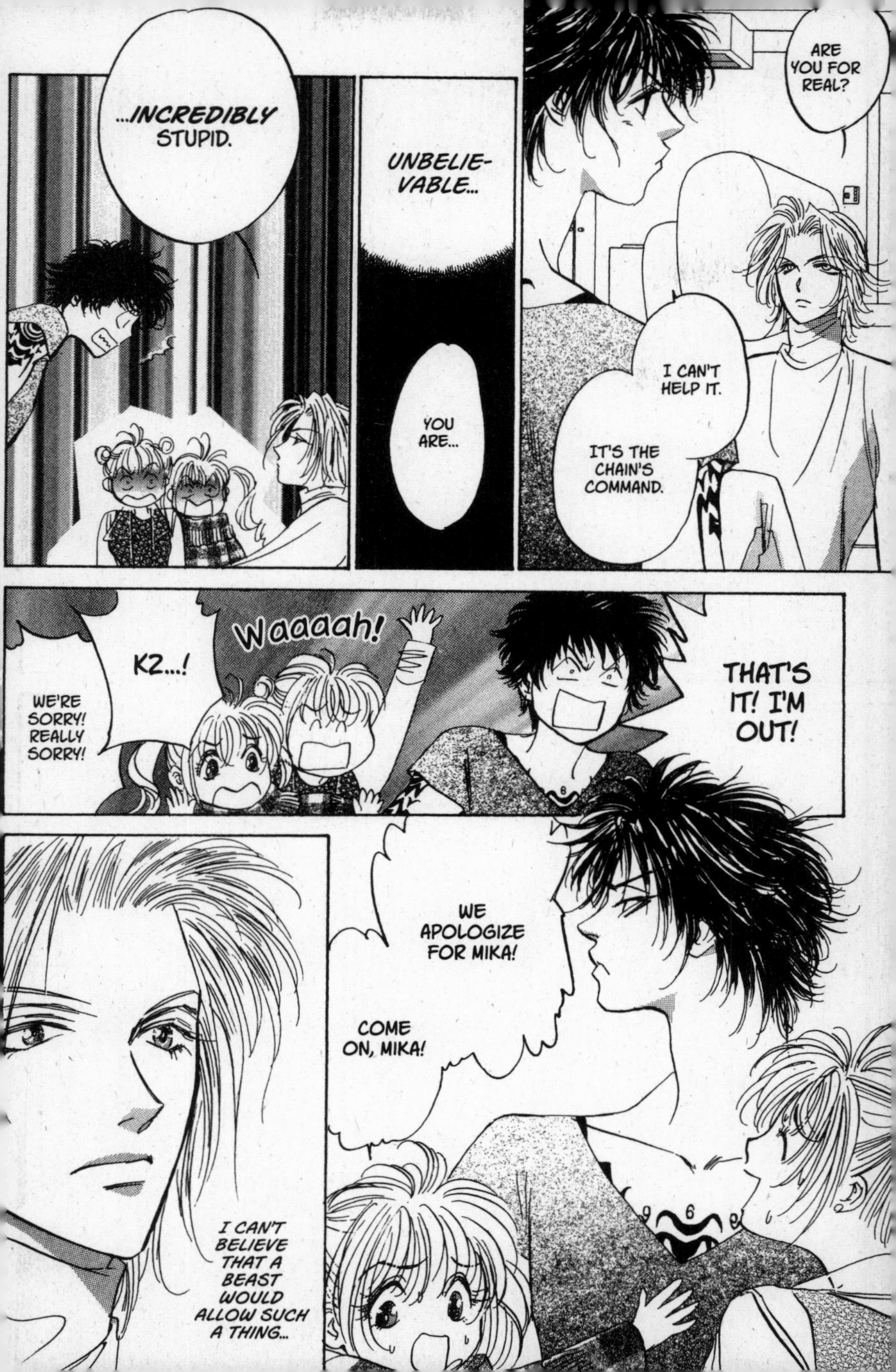
ARE YOU FOR REAL?
I CAN'T HELP IT.
IT'S THE CHAIN'S COMMAND.
UNBELIEVABLE...
YOU ARE...
...INCREDIBLY STUPID.
THAT'S IT! I'M OUT!
Waaaah!
K2...!
WE'RE SORRY! REALLY SORRY!
WE APOLOGIZE FOR MIKA!
COME ON, MIKA!
I CAN'T BELIEVE THAT A BEAST WOULD ALLOW SUCH A THING...

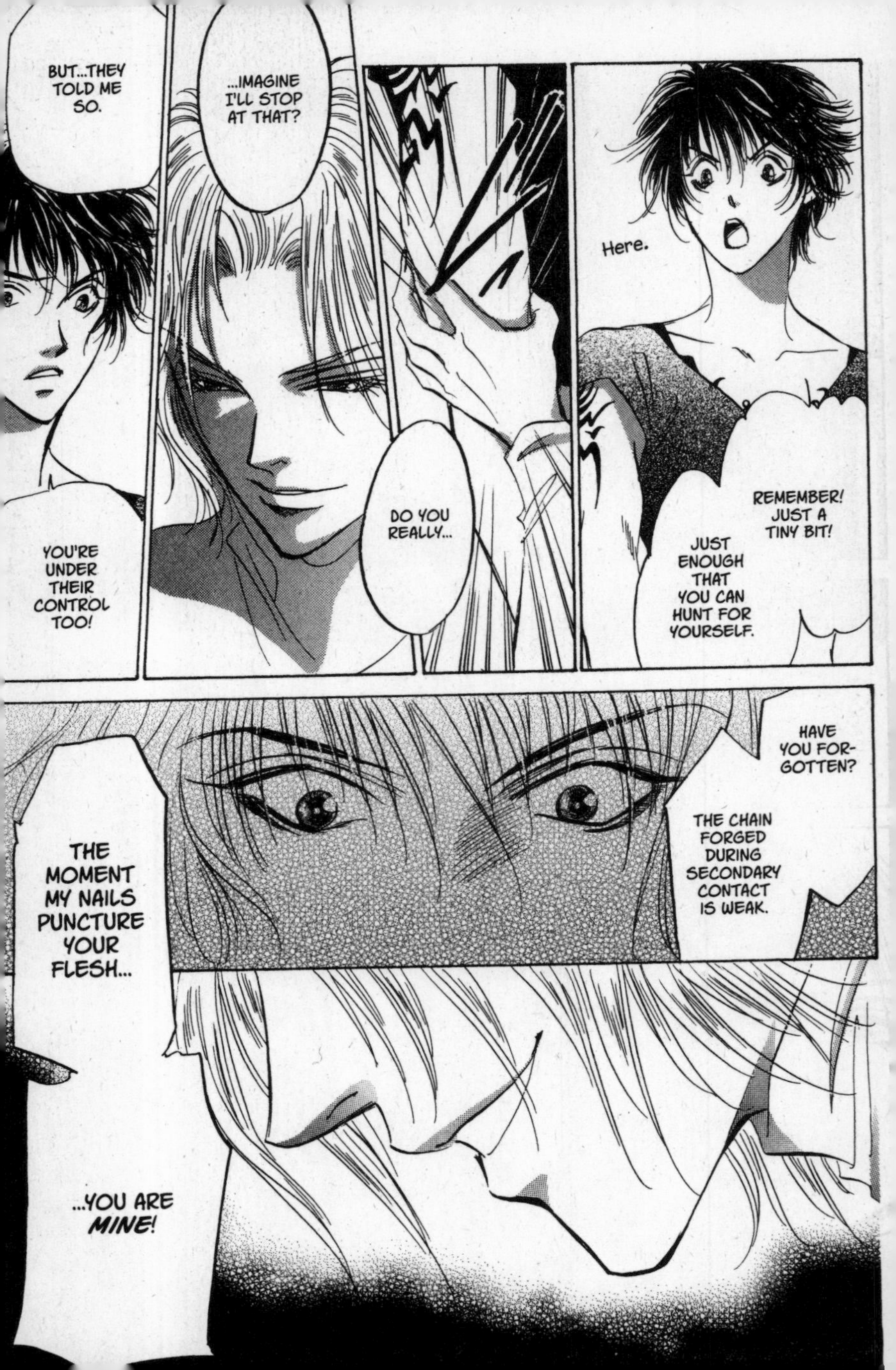

Here.
REMEMBER! JUST A TINY BIT!
JUST ENOUGH THAT YOU CAN HUNT FOR YOURSELF.
DO YOU REALLY...
...IMAGINE I'LL STOP AT THAT?
BUT...THEY TOLD ME SO.
YOU'RE UNDER THEIR CONTROL TOO!
HAVE YOU FOR-GOTTEN?
THE CHAIN FORGED DURING SECONDARY CONTACT IS WEAK.
THE MOMENT MY NAILS PUNCTURE YOUR FLESH...
...YOU ARE *MINE*!

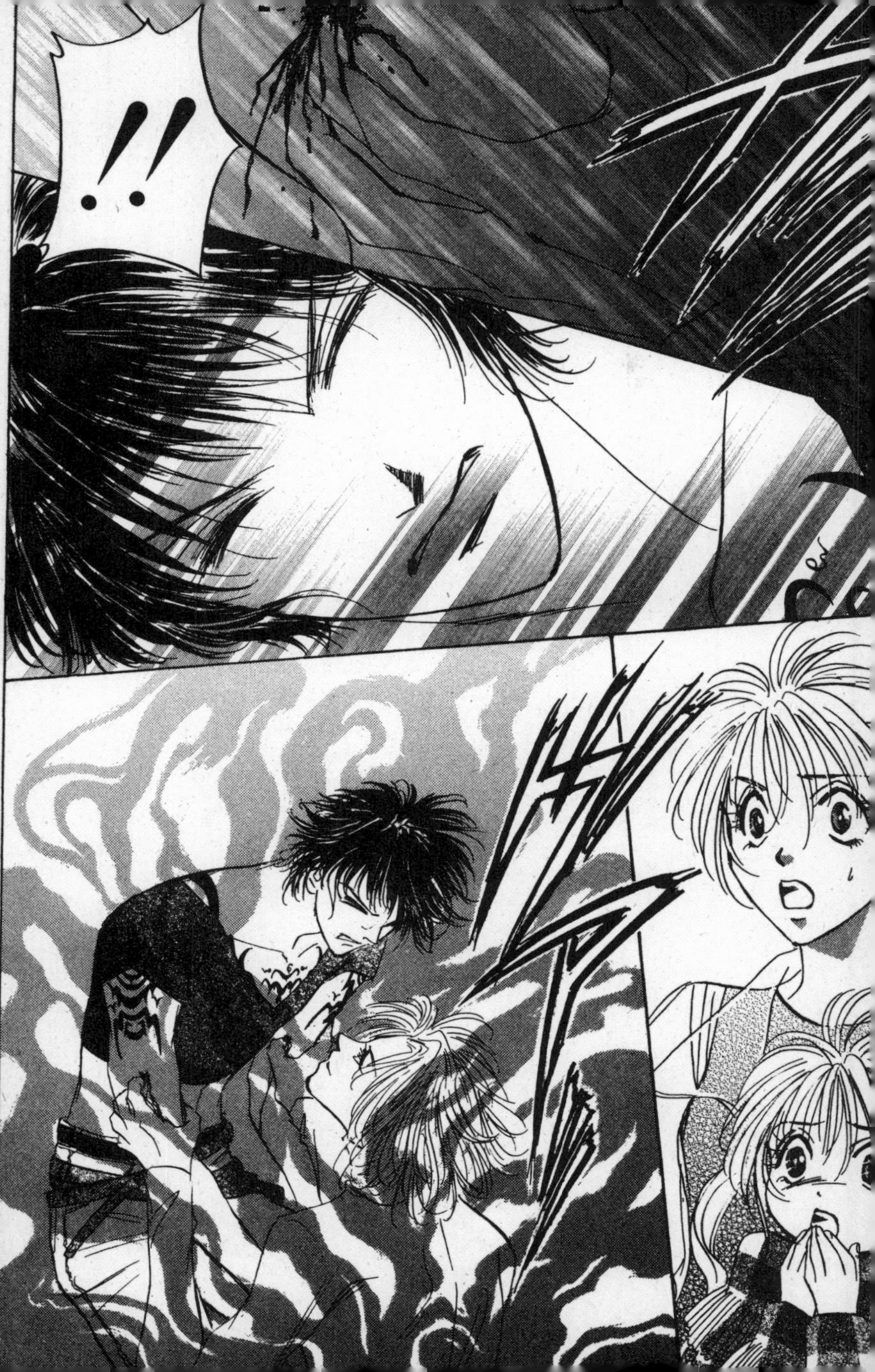
!!

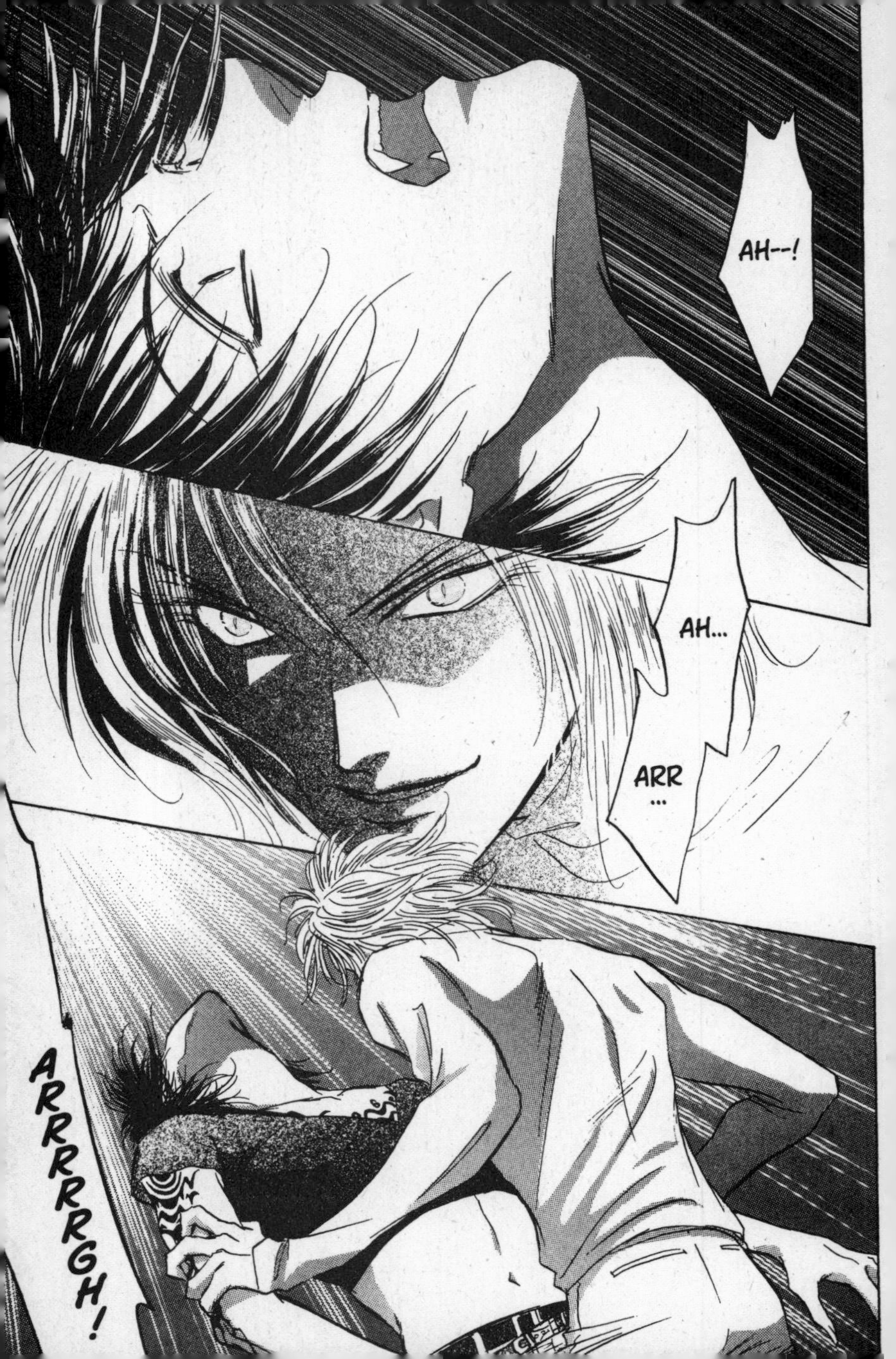
AH--!
AH...
ARR
...
ARRRRRGH!

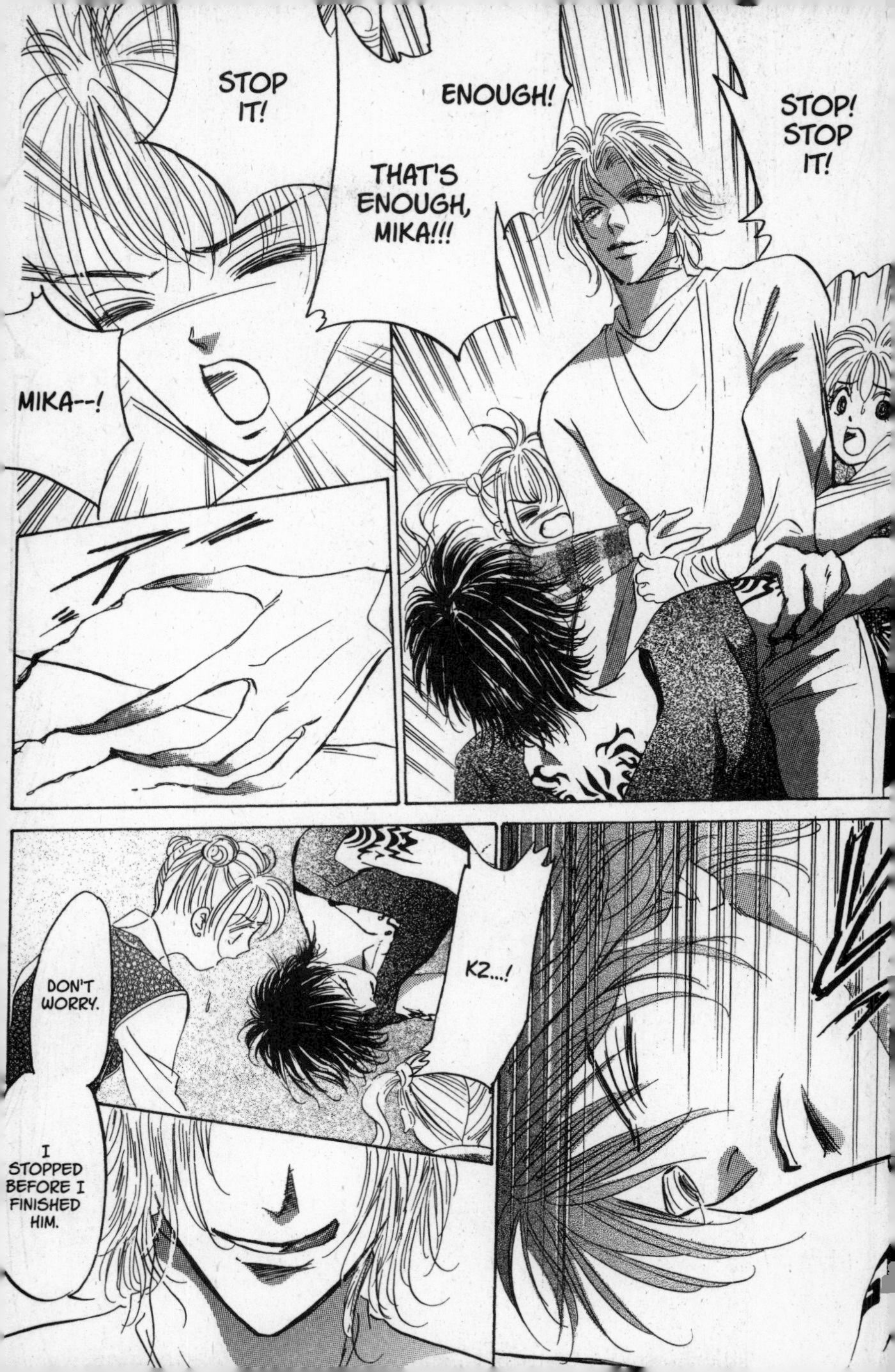
STOP! STOP IT!
ENOUGH!
THAT'S ENOUGH, MIKA!!!
STOP IT!
MIKA--!
KZ...!
DON'T WORRY.
I STOPPED BEFORE I FINISHED HIM.

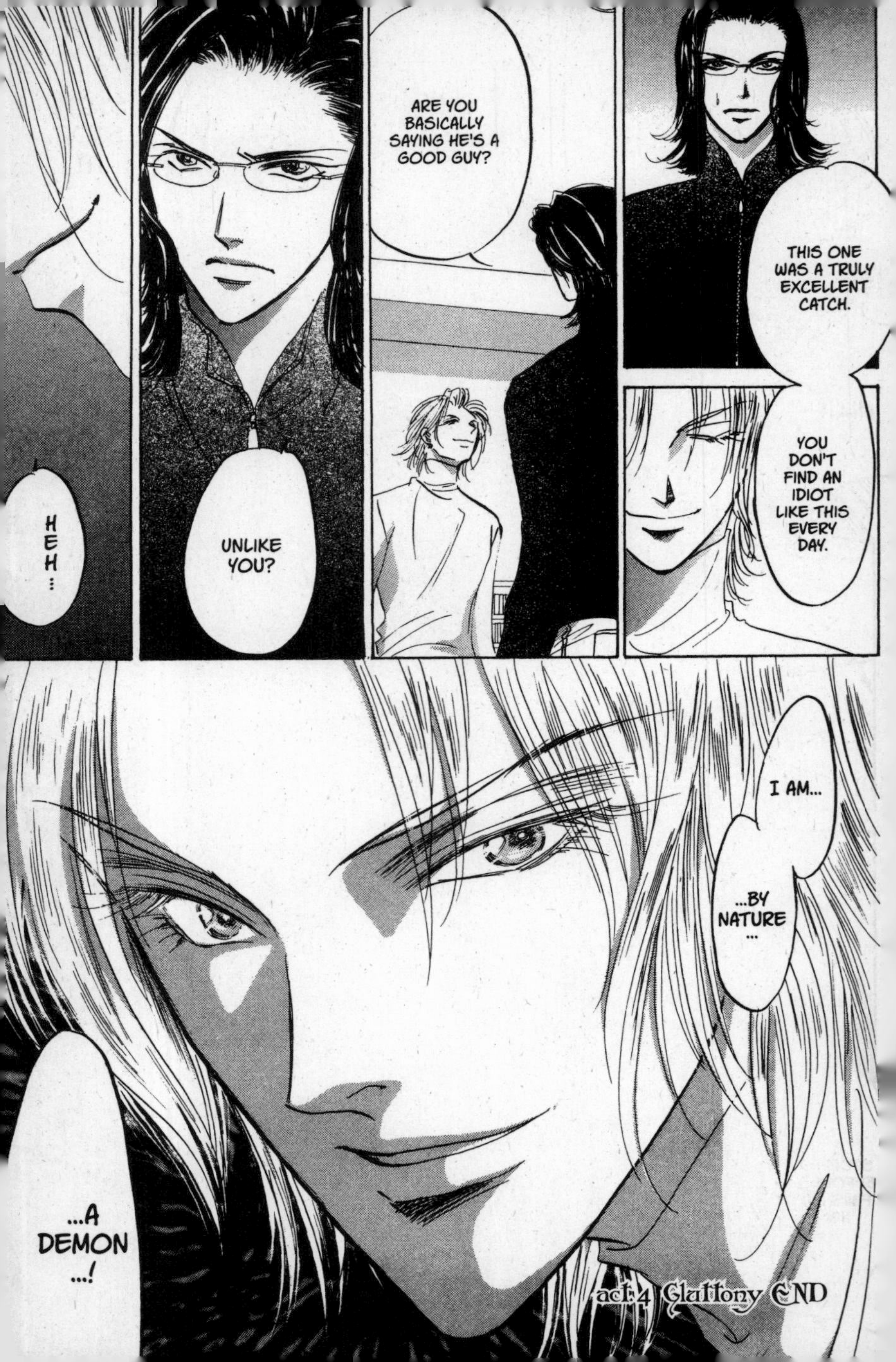
THIS ONE WAS A TRULY EXCELLENT CATCH.
YOU DON'T FIND AN IDIOT LIKE THIS EVERY DAY.
ARE YOU BASICALLY SAYING HE'S A GOOD GUY?
UNLIKE YOU?
HEH...
I AM...
...BY NATURE...
...A DEMON...!
act.4 Gluttony END

Story & Art
ITSUKI, Natsumi
Assistants
IZUTSU, Ai
OGAWA, Makiko
TAKADA, Chiyo
TANAKA, Sayoko
TANEDA, Tomoko
NOCHIOKA, Sumiko
HIROI, Michiko
YOKONO, Mariko
Consultant Manager
ASANUMA, Yuko
Editor
MASUI, Akihito(LaLa)
Editorial Agent
TAKEMURA, Toshiko(NAHT)

Natsumi Itsuki's Official Website - Natsumikan
http://ina-inc.jp/.

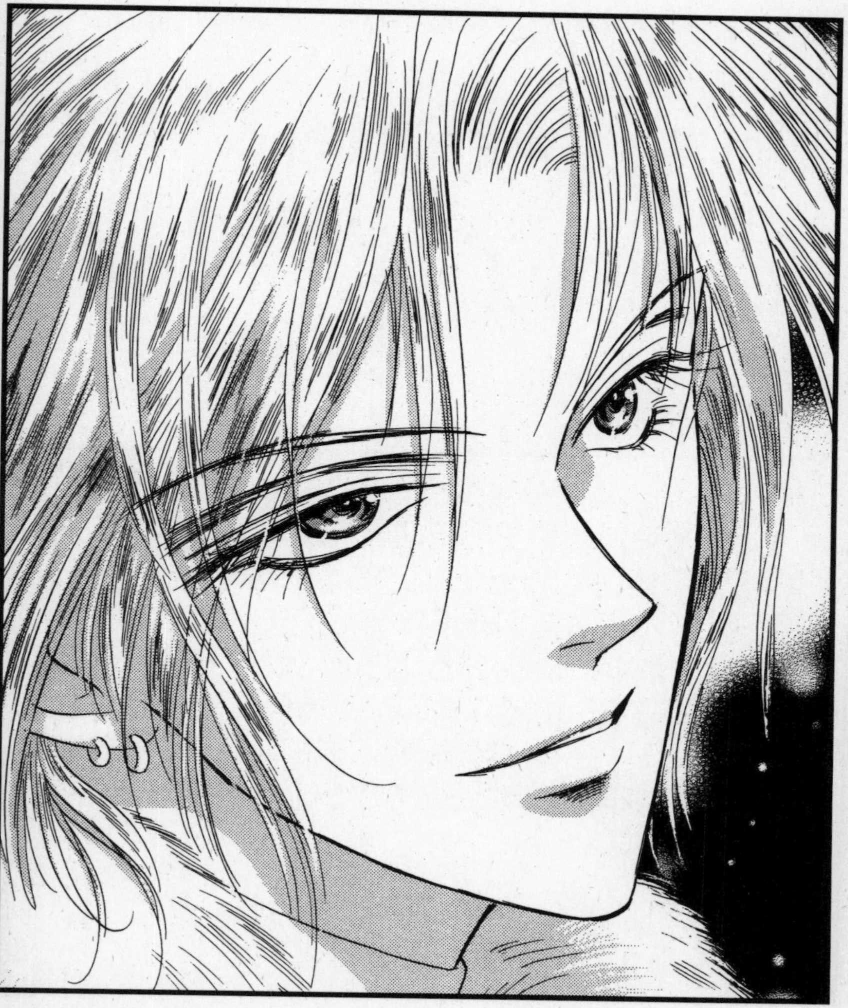

In the next volume of...

EMON
ACRED

WHEN MONA LEARNS THAT THE FATHER OF
ONE OF HER FRIENDS DIED OF RETURN
SYNDROME, SHE GOES TO VISIT HER,
BUT WHILE THERE SHE'S ATTACKED!
AND MIKA HAS HIS OWN PROBLEMS AS
HE MEETS ANOTHER POWERFUL DEMON
CALLED THE GRIFFIN. CAN MIKA ESCAPE
BEFORE BEING CONSUMED BY HIM?

RightStuf.com asks...

"What kind of OTAKU are you?"

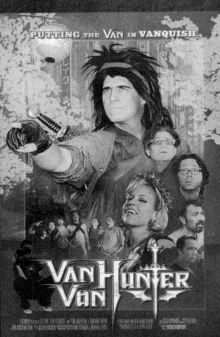

THE SMALLEST HERO!?

RATMAN
ラットマン

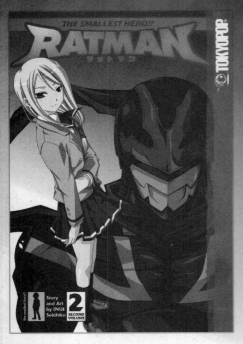

Not your typical good versus evil story

Even with a successful caper under his belt, Shuto Katsuragi is still not very comfortable with his role as the dark anti-hero "Ratman" for the evil secret organization "Jackal." Deciding to take advantage of Ratman's abilities, he tries his hand at some vigilante heroism on his off time from the organization. The first attempt goes well, as he even shows up in the papers as a "mysterious, unnamed hero." The second attempt does not go nearly as well, as he is mistaken for the criminal instead of the guy trying to stop the crime. The misunderstandings continue when he tries to break up a fight between members of a hero sentai team. He has to knock them out to do it, and a late-coming Ankaiser pounces on the excuse to pick a fight of his own!

the smallest hero?! Story and Art by INUI Sekihiko 2

ACTION

OT OLDER TEEN AGE 16+

© 2008 Sekihiko INUI / KADOKAWA SH

STOP!

This is the back of the book. You wouldn't want to spoil a great ending!

This book is printed "manga-style," in the authentic Japanese right-to-left format. Since none of the artwork has been flipped or altered, readers get to experience the story just as the creator intended. You've been asking for it, so TOKYOPOP® delivered: authentic, hot-off-the-press, and far more fun!

1
2
3
4
5
6
7
8
9
10

DIRECTIONS

If this is your first time reading manga-style, here's a quick guide to help you understand how it works.

It's easy... just start in the top right panel and follow the numbers. Have fun, and look for more 100% authentic manga from TOKYOPOP®!

THE MANGA REVOLUTION · LEADING THE MANGA REVOLUTION · LEADING

漫画革命